CULTURAL EXCHANGE IN
EARLY MODERN EUROPE

This volume explores the importance of correspondence and communication to cultural exchanges in early modern Europe. Leading historians examine the correspondence of scholars, scientists, spies, merchants, politicians, artists, collectors, noblemen, artisans and even illiterate peasants. Geographically the volume ranges across the whole of Europe, occasionally going beyond its confines to investigate exchanges between Europe and Asia or the New World. Above all, it studies the different networks of exchange in Europe and the various functions and meanings that correspondence had for members of different strata in European society during the early age of printing. This entails looking at different material supports, from manuscripts and printed letters to newsletters, and at different types of exchanges, from the familial, scientific and artistic to political and professional correspondence. This is a groundbreaking reassessment of the status of information in early modern Europe and a major contribution to the field of information and communication.

FRANCISCO BETHENCOURT is Charles Boxer Professor of History at King's College London. He was Director of the National Library of Portugal (1996–8) and Director of the Gulbenkian Cultural Centre in Paris (1999–2004).

FLORIKE EGMOND is a Researcher at the Scaliger Institute, University of Leiden. She has written, with Peter Mason, *The Mammoth and the Mouse: Microhistory and Morphology* (1997) and edited, with Rob Zwijnenberg, *Bodily Extremities: Preoccupations with the Human Body in Early Modern European Culture* (2003).

CULTURAL EXCHANGE IN EARLY MODERN EUROPE

General Editor: Robert Muchembled
Université de Paris XIII

Associate Editor: William Monter
Northwestern University, Illinois

At a time when the enlarged European Community asserts the humanist values
uniting its members, these volumes of essays by leading scholars from twelve
countries seek to uncover the deep but hidden unities shaping a common European past. These volumes examine the domains of religion, the city, communication and information, the conception of man and the use of material goods,
identifying the links which endured and were strengthened through ceaseless
cultural exchanges, even during this time of endless wars and religious disputes.
Volume I examines the role of religion as a vehicle for cultural exchange. Volume II surveys the reception of foreigners within the cities of early modern
Europe. Volume III explores the place of information and communication in
early modern Europe. Volume IV reveals how cultural exchange played a central
role in the fashioning of a first European identity.

Volumes in the series

I *Religion and Cultural Exchange in Europe, 1400–1700*
Edited by Heinz Schilling and István György Tóth†

II *Cities and Cultural Exchange in Europe, 1400–1700*
Edited by Donatella Calabi and Stephen Turk Christensen

III *Correspondence and Cultural Exchange in Europe, 1400–1700*
Edited by Francisco Bethencourt and Florike Egmond

IV *Forging European Identities, 1400–1700*
Edited by Herman Roodenburg

CULTURAL EXCHANGE IN
EARLY MODERN EUROPE

GENERAL EDITOR
ROBERT MUCHEMBLED

ASSOCIATE EDITOR
WILLIAM MONTER

CULTURAL EXCHANGE IN EARLY MODERN EUROPE

VOLUME III

Correspondence and Cultural Exchange in Europe,
1400–1700

EDITED BY

FRANCISCO BETHENCOURT
AND FLORIKE EGMOND

CAMBRIDGE UNIVERSITY PRESS

Cambridge, New York, Melbourne, Madrid, Cape Town, Singapore, São Paulo

Cambridge University Press
The Edinburgh Building, Cambridge CB2 8RU, UK

Published in the United States of America by Cambridge University Press, New York

www.cambridge.org
Information on this title: www.cambridge.org/9780521855532

First published 2007

Printed in the United Kingdom at the University Press, Cambridge

A catalogue record for this publication is available from the British Library

ISBN 978-0-521-84548-9 hardback

Only available as a four-volume set:
ISBN 978-0-521-85553-2

Contents

PART II: USES AND MEANINGS OF CORRESPONDENCE: ARTISTS, PATRONS, COLLECTORS

PART III: USES AND MEANINGS OF CORRESPONDENCE: NOBLEMEN, PEASANTS, SPIES

Illustrations

Notes on contributors

IRENE BALDRIGA works as an independent scholar. She collaborates with several Italian and international academic institutions, such as the Accademia dei Lincei. She has published extensively in Italian and English on Renaissance and Baroque art, the history of collecting and patronage, and the relation between art and science. She is the author of *L'occhio della Lince: i primi lincei tra arte, scienza e collezionismo, 1603–1630* (Rome, 2002).

ZSUZSA BARBARICS is an Assistant Lecturer of Medieval and Early Modern History at the University of Pécs, Hungary. She has published several articles on political propaganda, the role of media, and the situation of minorities in the Habsburg Empire.

FRANCISCO BETHENCOURT is Charles Boxer Professor at King's College London. He was director of the National Library of Portugal, director of the Calouste Gulbenkian Cultural Centre in Paris, and Professor at the Universidade Nova de Lisboa. His main publications include, as co-editor with Kirti Chaudhuri, *História da expansão portuguesa*, 5 vols. (Lisbon, 1998–9); *L'inquisition à l'époque moderne: Espagne, Portugal, Italie, XVe –XIXe siècles* (Paris, 1995), translated into Portuguese and Spanish, with a forthcoming English edition; *O imaginário da magia* (Lisbon, 1987; 2nd revised edn São Paulo, 2004). His current research is on racism in the Atlantic world, 1400–1800.

FERNANDO BOUZA is Professor of Early Modern History at Universidad Complutense, Madrid. He is the author of *El libro y el cetro: la biblioteca de Felipe IV en la Torre Alta del Alcázar de Madrid*

(Salamanca, 2005); *Communication, Knowledge, and Memory in Early Modern Spain* (Philadelphia, 2004); *Corre manuscrito: una historia cultural del Siglo de Oro* (Madrid, 2001); *Portugal no tempo dos Filipes: política, cultura, representações, 1580–1668* (Lisbon, 2000).

DEJANIRAH COUTO is Maître de conférences at the Ecole Pratique des Hautes Etudes, IVe section and Chargé de cours at the Université de Paris III. She has published extensively on the history of the Portuguese expansion and the Ottoman Empire. She is the author of *Histoire de Lisbonne* (Paris, 2000).

FLORIKE EGMOND is a post-doctoral researcher at the Scaliger Institute, University of Leiden, Netherlands, working on Clusius and the development of European botany. Her main publications include, as co-editor with Paul Hoftijzer and Robert Visser, *Carolus Clusius: Towards a Cultural History of a Renaissance Naturalist* (Amsterdam, 2006); as co-editor with Peter Mason, *The Whale Book. Whales and other Marine Animals as Described by Adriaen Coenen in 1585* (London, 2003); as co-editor with Robert Zwijnenberg, *Bodily Extremities: Preoccupations with the Human Body in Early Modern European Culture* (Aldershot, 2003); as co-author with Peter Mason, *The Mammoth and the Mouse: Microhistory and Morphology* (Baltimore, 1997)

MARIO INFELISE is Professor of Early Modern History at the Università Ca' Foscari, Venice. His publications include, as co-author with A. Stouraiti, *Venezia e la Guerra di Morea: guerra, politica e cultura alla fine del '600* (Milan, 2005); *Prima dei giornali: alle origini della pubblica informazione* (Rome and Bari, 2002); *I libri proibiti: da Gutenberg all'Encyclopédie* (Rome and Bari, 1999).

PETER MASON works as an independent scholar. He is Visiting Professor at the Casa de América, Madrid. He has been a consultant in Art and Anthropology for the Taller Experimental Cuerpos Pintados, Santiago de Chile. His main publications include, as co-author with Christian Báez, *En el jardín: fotografías de Fueguinos y mapuches en los zoológicos humanos europeos* (Santiago de Chile, 2006); *The*

Lives of Images (London, 2001); *Infelicities: Representations of the Exotic* (Baltimore and London, 1998).

RENATE PIEPER is Professor of Social and Economic History at Karl-Franzens-Universität Graz. Her main publications include, as co-editor with Peer Schmidt, *Latin America and the Atlantic World: Essays in Honour of Horst Pietschmann* (Cologne, Weimar and Vienna, 2005); *Die Vermittlung einer neuen Welt: Amerika im Kommunikationsnetz des habsburgischen Imperiums (1493–1598)* (Mainz, 2000); and two works which have also been translated into Spanish, *Die spanischen Kronfinanzen in der zweiten Hälfte des 18. Jahrhunderts (1753–1788): Ökonomische und soziale Auswirkungen* (Stuttgart, 1988) and *Die Preisrevolution in Spanien (1500–1640): Neuere Forschungsergebnisse* (Stuttgart, 1985).

ISTVÁN GYÖRGY TÓTH (1956–2005) was Professor of History at the Central European University and at the Institute of History of the Hungarian Academy of Sciences. His main publications include, as editor, *A Concise History of Hungary* (Budapest, 2005); *Religion et politique en Hongrie au XVIIe siècle* (Paris, 2004); as co-editor with Eszter Andor, *Frontiers of Faith: Religious Exchange and the Constitution of Religious Identities, 1400–1750* (Budapest, 2001); *Litteræ missionariorum de Hungaria et Transilvania* (Rome, 2002); *Literacy and Written Record in Early Modern Central Europe* (Budapest, 2000);

FRANCESCA TRIVELLATO is Assistant Professor of History at Yale University. She has been working extensively on craft guilds, women's work and merchant networks in early modern Italy and the Mediterranean. She is the author of *Fondamenta dei Vetrai: lavoro, tecnologia e mercato a Venezia tra Sei e Settecento* (Rome, 2000).

General editor's preface

The four volumes of this series represent the synthesis of works from 'Cultural Exchange in Europe, 1400–1700', a research programme sponsored by the European Science Foundation and financed by eighteen councils for research from seventeen countries. The adventure began in January 1997 when its originators decided to conduct an international investigation of the cultural roots of modern Europe. Research has increased considerably since this programme began and identifying the origins of the European identity has become a fundamental issue at the dawn of the twenty-first century.

Ultimately, our programme brought together over sixty regular members, plus a few dozen individuals who participated in one or more of our group meetings. It was a real linguistic Tower of Babel including specialists from various disciplines: history, art, architecture, theatre, literature, linguistics, folklore, clothing and dance. We have recruited well beyond the borders of the European Union, from St Petersburg to Chicago by way of Istanbul, although it was not always possible for every geographical location to be fully represented in each of our four groups.

This series is devoted to four major themes: religion; the city; communication and information; the conception of man and the use of material goods. The four volumes collectively include about a third of the papers presented throughout the programme.[1] Most have been discussed collectively, revised, and sometimes rewritten.

[1] Many other contributions prepared for this programme have appeared or will appear elsewhere: Eszter Andor and István György Tóth (eds.), *Frontiers of Faith: Religious Exchange and the Constitution of Religious Identities, 1400–1750* (Budapest: Central European University/ESF, 2001); José Pedro Paiva (ed.), *Religious Ceremonials and*

It was not always easy to conceptualise our theme collectively. The most difficult and time-consuming task was to get scholars to understand each other unambiguously when employing such apparently clear concepts as 'culture', which means different things in different languages and cultural traditions. Our first major task was simply to discover whether or not a European culture existed between 1400 and 1700, an intensely conflictual and profoundly tragic period which seemed to be characterised by ruptures rather than creation. From 1517, when Luther broke with Roman Catholicism, until the Peace of Westphalia in 1648, a series of terrible religious wars drowned the continent in blood, ending the medieval dream of a united Christendom. This age of intolerance was also one of fundamental inequality, particularly with respect to birth and sex, because any woman was considered fundamentally inferior to any man. Not only was the continent divided into at least five different cultural areas – the Atlantic, the Baltic, the Mediterranean, central Europe and eastern Europe – but also, and everywhere, those frontiers established in men's minds – both visible and invisible – conflicted with any residual hopes of unity, whether expressed in terms of imperial ideology, papal universalism, or Thomas More's humanistic Utopia, all of them swept away after 1520 by a wave of persecutions.[2]

And yet this very same Europe also bequeathed us powerful roots for the slow and difficult construction of a collective sensibility. Our research has unearthed traces of underlying unities, despite (or because of) formidable obstacles. This stubborn growth in some ways resembled an earlier process described by a prominent medievalist as the 'Europeanization of Europe'.[3] They have given substance and meaning to my working hypothesis: that European culture from 1400 to 1700 contained expressions of hidden cohesion against a background

Images: Power and Social Meaning (1400–1750) (Coimbra: Palimage, 2002). A volume on translations will be edited by Ronnie Po-Chia Hsia.

[2] Robert Muchembled, 'Frontières vives: la naissance du Sujet en Europe (xve–xviie siècle)', introduction to Eszter Andor and István György Tóth (eds.), *Frontiers of Faith*, pp. 1–8.

[3] Robert Bartlett, *The Making of Europe: Conquest, Colonization and Cultural Change 950–1350* (London, 1993).

of intense conflicts. If those conflicts were destabilising, they also created a dialectic which contributed to the overall advance of European civilisation.[4] Following Norbert Elias's argument, I believe that every human society is constantly seeking to attain a 'balance of power' through a mechanism of 'reciprocal dependency' which produces a clear evolutionary trend. Culture is a symbolic arena for both collective negotiations and the fashioning of the Self.[5] The enormous importance of the Self in today's Europe (and in the United States) is the result of a major cultural change which began during the Renaissance. In the face of the tragedy of real life, this new individualism provided a fresh means of expressing the continent's collective vitality and produced a growing conviction of its superiority and differences from all other places and people in the world.[6]

The 'culture' analysed in this series may be defined as that which simultaneously holds a society together and distinguishes it from other societies. If the Europe of 1400–1700 had little obvious regard for human rights, it did at least prefigure the time when they would be important. The humanistic lights which glimmered from time to time in the two dark and bloodstained centuries after 1520 were never to be completely extinguished. The Enlightenment revived them and honoured their Renaissance origins. But the tragic events that polluted its soil during the first half of the twentieth century proved that the Old Continent was not yet fully free from intolerance and persecution.

I should like to thank Wim Blockmans, who warmly supported the creation of this research programme; the European Science Foundation for its constant help; the eighteen institutions which provided generous funding over four years;[7] all the scholars who participated

---

[4] Robert Muchembled, 'Echanges, médiations, mythes unitaires, 1400–1700', plenary conference address, published in the programme's *Newsletter* no. 1 (2000), pp. 7–26.

[5] Norbert Elias, *The Society of Individuals*, trans. Edmund Jephcott (Oxford, 1991).

[6] Robert Muchembled, *A History of the Devil: From the Middle Ages to the Present* (Cambridge, 2003); *L'Orgasme et l'Occident: une histoire du plaisir du XVIe siècle à nos jours* (Paris, 2005, forthcoming in English translation).

[7] Austria: Österreichische Akademie der Wissenschaften; Fonds zur Förderung der wissenschaftlichen Forschung (FWF); Belgium: Fonds National de la Recherche Scientifique (FNRS) / Fonds voor Wetenschappelijk Onderzoek – Vlaanderen

in the experience, notably E. William Monter without whom this series would probably not have been published, and the late István György Tóth, codirector of volume I, who passed away unexpectedly on 14 July 2005; and last but not least Cambridge University Press for producing four superb books proving the great vitality of past and present European culture.

Robert Muchembled
Chair of the ESF programme
'Cultural Exchange in Europe, 1400–1700'

(FWO); Denmark: Statens Humanistiske Forskningsrad; Finland: Suomen Akatemia / Finlands Akademi; Germany: Deutsche Forschungsgemeinschaft (DFG); Greece: National Hellenic Research Foundation (NHRF); Hungary: Hungarian Academy of Sciences; Italy: Consiglio Nazionale delle Ricerche (CNR); Netherlands: Nederlandse Organisatie voor Wetenschappelijk Onderzoek (NWO); Norway: Norges Forskningsrad; Poland: Polska Akademia Nauk (PAN), Portugal: Instituto do Cooperação Científica e Tecnológica Internacional (ICCTI); Slovenia: The Slovenian Science Foundation; Spain: Consejo Superior de Investigaciones Cientificas (CSIC); Sweden: Humanistik Samhällsvetenskapliga Forskningsradet (HSFR) / Kungliga Vitterhets Historie och Antikvitets Akademien (KVHAA); Switzerland: Schweizerischer Nationalfonds zur Förderung der Wissenschaftlichen Forschung (SNF); United Kingdom: The British Academy.

Preface

This volume has been organised through a series of meetings in Strasbourg, Lisbon, Naples, Paris, Amsterdam and Leibnitz, Austria, in which historians from different countries defined the project and discussed their research. Our starting point was a shared interest in information and communication: we created a team dedicated to this issue inside the European Science Foundation project on Cultural Exchange in Europe, 1400–1700, launched by Robert Muchembled in 1999.

A collective book is always the result of a tension between aims and possibilities. We soon realised that the study of correspondence in its different dimensions on a European scale would be much more efficient than a loose and fragmented study on information and communication. The volume became coherent and we managed to integrate the theoretical discussions on the broader issue of communication, which helped to reshape our chapters.

The book also benefited from the general framework of the project on cultural exchange and from the different researchers who shared our discussions. The final volume does not include all the contributions collected over the years, because we decided to focus on the main aspects of correspondence, trying both to reinforce connections and to avoid repetitions. Thus, the chapters are a result of a long process of discussion and exchange between the authors.

We would like to thank the European Science Foundation for their support of the several meetings, which enabled us to organise this experimental project across European academic frontiers. We are especially grateful to William Monter, who was always available and played a major role in the final editing of the texts.

This volume is dedicated to the memory of István György Tóth, a brilliant researcher and friend, with whom we shared other initiatives, who was an outstanding example of a creative intellectual and productive academic. He left an unforgettable imprint as a cooperative, gentle and humorous person with whom it was a real pleasure to work.

Francisco Bethencourt and Florike Egmond

Introduction

Francisco Bethencourt and Florike Egmond

PEIRESC

When Nicolas-Claude Fabri de Peiresc (1580–1637) died, Pope Urban VIII pronounced a eulogy, the Roman academy of the humorists organised public mourning, while a *Monumentum* in his honour was published in Rome with epitaphs in forty languages. Sixty years later, Pierre Bayle (1647–1706) declared about Peiresc:

no man rendered more services to the republic of letters than this one. He was a kind of General Attorney of this republic: he encouraged authors, he provided lighting and materials, he used his revenues to buy or copy the most rare and useful monuments. His trade of letters embraced all parts of the world. Philosophical experiences, rarities of nature, productions of art, antiquities, history and languages were the object of his care and curiosity.[1]

Bayle also complained, however, that many French men of erudition of his own time had not even heard of Peiresc. He could not have foreseen that the name of Peiresc would be almost forgotten throughout the eighteenth century, to be only slowly rediscovered in the course of the nineteenth and twentieth centuries. The reason is obvious: Peiresc published almost nothing. How, then, could this man have come to be considered the 'General Attorney' of the republic of letters in his own time? The answer lies in the wide range and depth of his expertise, but equally so in his vast network and correspondence.

---

[1] Pierre Bayle, *Dictionnaire historique et critique*, 3rd edition, corrected by the author (Rotterdam: M. Böhm, 1720), vol. 3, pp. 2216–17 (our translation).

Peiresc left more than 10,000 letters.[2] He corresponded with more than 500 persons – from princes, popes, cardinals and bishops, to ambassadors, magistrates, scholars, librarians, secretaries, artists, writers, scientists, pharmacists, jewellers, merchants and clergymen. Although most of his correspondents lived in France (mainly Paris and Provence), the geographical range of his network was wide, comprising north and central Italy, the Low Countries, the Holy Roman Empire, England, Spain, the eastern Mediterranean, Middle East and even Asia (Goa). He could, moreover, use mediators to reach other parts of the world: the Portuguese jeweller Álvares, for instance, who was based in Paris, provided Peiresc with information about plants, precious stones and medals which he obtained from his own network of correspondents in Vijaiapur, Manila and Macao.[3] Peiresc crossed religious boundaries as well, corresponding regularly with Protestants and Jews.

Peiresc was interested in many scientific and cultural areas, such as physics, astronomy, optics, geology, mineralogy, botany, perfumery, zoology, medicine, anatomy, dissection, archaeology, weights and measures, numismatics, art, iconography, literature and music. Correspondents all over the world were crucial to some of the scientific experiments which he performed, such as the ones on longitude. He also calculated the width of the Mediterranean (correcting former data), advanced astronomic observations of the moon, started a project to create a cartography of the moon, and recalculated the distance between the earth and the moon, correcting information received from his correspondent Galileo. Despite his residence in a city of secondary importance – he lived in Aix en Provence as a counsellor of its parliament – he belonged to the most important academies in France and Italy and received several notables, such as Pope Urban VIII's

[2] Linda Van Norden, 'Peiresc and the English scholars', *The Huntington Library Quarterly* 12.4 (1949), 369–89; Paul Dibon, 'Les échanges épistolaires dans l'Europe savante du XVIIe siècle', *Revue de synthèse*, 3rd series, 81–2 (1976), 31–50; Robert Mandrou, *Histoire de la pensée européenne*, vol. 3: *Des humanistes aux hommes de science (XVIe et XVIIe siècle)* (Paris: Seuil, 1973), pp. 369–89; Agnès Bresson *Les correspondants de Peiresc*, electronic paper, website www.peiresc.org (1992).
[3] *Lettres inédites de M. de Peiresc*, ed. Faurius de Saint Vincent (Aix-en-Provence: Imprimerie d'Augustin Pontier, 1816).

nephew Cardinal Francesco Barberini.[4] Peiresc kept up a longstanding correspondence with the latter's secretary, Cassiano dal Pozzo, and exchanged gifts with him.[5]

Peiresc generally corresponded in French and Italian, even if he was considered a prince of the Latin republic of letters.[6] His refusal to become (and behave like) an author was related to the model of a man of letters he chose for himself. As a disciple of Gian Vincenzo Pinelli (1535–1601), he developed an ethos of detached and generously shared learning for the sake of learning. Part of this ethos was the promotion of knowledge as a process of cooperation in the literary and scientific community, which should be based on free exchange and far removed from the mean considerations of proprietorship that being an author entailed. This is the image Pierre Gassendi (1592–1655) presented in his biography of Peiresc.[7] Yet, the type of 'intellectual' (if we may use this anachronistic term) embodied by Peiresc was quite exceptional. First of all, he did not have to publish in order to find patrons and protectors. Second, his ethos presupposed a huge network of correspondents, who benefited from his generosity and recognised his merits. Finally, his detachment was less radical than it seemed. While using the available means of communication (correspondence) on a large scale to both increase his knowledge and disseminate it, he reinforced his own intellectual prestige. He knew that his letters were simultaneously private and public, confidential and open: they could be exchanged and read aloud in small groups, a common practice

---

[4] *Lettre de M. de Peiresc écrite d'Aix à son frère alors à Paris, dans laquelle il lui donne des détails sur une visite qu'il lui avait fait le cardinal Barberini, neveu du Pape Urbain VIII, légat en France, le 27 octobre 1625* (Aix-en-Provence: Imprimerie d'Augustin Pontier, 1816).

[5] Nicolas-Claude Fabri de Peiresc, *Lettres à Cassiano dal Pozzo (1627–1637)*, ed. and annotated by Jean-François Lhote and Danielle Joyal, preface by Jacques Guillerme (Clermont-Ferrand: Adosa, 1989).

[6] Marc Fumaroli, *Nicolas-Claude Fabri de Peiresc: Prince de la République des Lettres*, electronic paper, website www.peiresc.org (1992). See the global view proposed by Peter N. Miller, *Peiresc's Europe: Learning and Virtue in the Seventeenth Century* (New Haven: Yale University Press, 2000).

[7] Pierre Gassendi, *Vie de l'illustre Nicolas-Claude Fabri de Peiresc, conseiller au parlement d'Aix*, translation from the Latin by Roger Lassalle and preface by Jean Emelina (Paris: Belin, 1992).

in the republic of letters. 'Familiar' or 'friendly' correspondence had acquired the reputation of giving insight into the real thoughts of the author, which is why that type of correspondence circulated widely. But, as far as we know, Peiresc did not intend to publish his letters.

AIMS AND PERSPECTIVE

Although none of the essays in this volume discusses Peiresc as its main subject, he was in touch with some of the persons who figure in it. We have chosen him as icon of this volume, however, because of the geography of his correspondence, the European reach of his network, the wide social range of his correspondents, the issues raised by his systematic use of vernacular languages, the semi-public aspect of his letters, the way in which exchanges (of more than just information) played an important role in his correspondence, and his role in the republic of letters. In short, Peiresc's correspondence raises a number of issues that are discussed in this volume with respect to other early modern correspondents and correspondences.

Peiresc belonged to the social and political elite of early modern Europe. Correspondence was, however, by no means only relevant to members of his status group. In this volume we will explore a much wider range of correspondences and their relevance to cultural exchanges in early modern Europe. In social terms we will look at the correspondence of both scholars and scientists, spies, merchants, politicians, artists, collectors, noblemen, artisans, and even, perhaps unexpectedly, illiterate peasants. In terms of language we will pay far more attention to correspondence in the vernacular than to that in Latin. Above all, we are looking at different networks of exchange by means of correspondence in Europe and at various functions and meanings that handwritten correspondence had for members of different strata in European society during the early age of printing. Correspondence helped to create an ethos of social groups, to define new fields of research, satisfy administrative enquiries and articulate feelings. It was also an important means to collect and diffuse information, to express and create opinion, especially in the sixteenth and seventeenth centuries. What was the role of handwritten newsletters with respect to the spreading of information in Europe? How did information travel in manuscript newsletters across cultural barriers in Europe and between Europe and other parts of the world? Who were the agents of such exchanges? How did it relate to printed information?

Through the analysis of correspondence in its different manifestations we intend to reconsider the status of information and thus tackle a central issue in the field of information and communication. In doing so we focus on *cultural* issues rather than on economic or political ones, although the latter are clearly interwoven with the former. We do not discuss the enormously important infrastructure of exchanges by letter (such as postal services, and the various conditions on which safe and regular travel is predicated). And we do not regard the exchange of correspondence – or correspondence and exchange – as identical with the exchange of information. That would not only reduce letters (which are objects in their own right as well as carriers of information) purely to their contents, but moreover simplify the function of those contents to an unwarranted extent. As the example of Peiresc demonstrated and all contributions to this volume will make abundantly clear, there is much more to correspondence than just information exchange. In Peiresc's case, it served for instance, to create a scientific network and to spread a specific ethos. In most essays discussed in this volume, correspondence was an instrument of cultural exchange and transmission which could cross many boundaries and have unexpected and unintended effects. Besides the polite and learned letters that could be read aloud in almost any company, we will look therefore at the range of less polite, the more intimate, businesslike, emotional, or even secret correspondence. Although we will by no means neglect the correspondence of erudite and generally upper-class men – such as humanists, scholars, princes, patron-collectors and scientists – a large part of this volume is purposely devoted to correspondence by members of other social categories, since we believe that the relevant criterion for selecting correspondence to be studied should not necessarily be a similarity of social background, literary style, or scholarly influence, but first and foremost the phenomenon of letter writing and reading itself.

Evidently, 'exchange' is a complex concept, which has triggered a great deal of discussion by historians and social scientists, besides playing a central role in the ESF project of which this volume is one of the results. This is hardly the place to repeat that discussion, but it should be stressed that, following Georg Simmel, we are looking for the two-sided, reciprocal effects of exchange in human interaction. For Simmel, exchange represented a new and creative process of transformation and not merely the addition of two processes of giving and receiving.[8] Exchange is never pure and symmetrical; moreover, it is usually fashioned by relations of power and expresses different presuppositions (and positions) of the persons or groups involved. Considering cultural exchange at a European level, we should take into account both Braudel's assumption of cultural resistance to innovation and Shils's notion of centres and peripheries of cultural production.[9] The latter seems more flexible and efficient, because it can help us identify geographical and social asymmetries, inclusions and exclusions, in the process of cultural exchange.

EARLY MODERN CORRESPONDENCE AS A LITERARY GENRE

For a long time the historiography of early modern correspondence has focused on the letters written by important humanists or scientists, and on the status and form of correspondence as a literary genre. Those aspects are relevant to the discussion in the present volume as well, because the literary conventions that were newly developed or adapted during this age continued to leave their mark on letters written not only by those who were aware of these models, but even by men and women who were less familiar with them. Cultural models travel across geographical borders as well as social boundaries, and letters are a special example, since they embodied certain cultural models on the one hand, and formed a means of travel across such boundaries on

[8] Georg Simmel, 'Exchange', in *On Individuality and Social Forms*, ed. with an introduction by Donald N. Levine (Chicago: University of Chicago Press, 1971), pp. 43–69.
[9] Fernand Braudel, *Civilisation matérielle, économie et capitalisme*, vol. 2: *Les jeux de l'échange* (Paris: Armand Colin, 1979); Edward Shils, *Center and Periphery: Essays in Macrosociology* (Chicago: University of Chicago Press, 1975).

the other hand. Even the illiterate should therefore not be regarded as beyond the reach of literary or epistolary models.

Literary traditions concerning correspondence went back a long way. Roman antiquity had already set the model for writing in the epistolary mode – the famous examples of the *Epistulæ* of Cicero, followed by Seneca, Pliny the Younger and others – but it was the second generation of Italian humanists who were to (re)define correspondence as a new, formalised literary genre. Poggio Bracciolini (1380–1459) – notary, secretary of seven popes, and chancellor of Florence – compiled three different series of correspondence in 1436, 1438 (enlarged in 1444) and 1455 that were shown to interested men of letters.[10] He created the style of the 'familiar' letter addressed to public figures, scholars and friends. In these he reflected on philological, theological, artistic, literary and political issues, addressed matters of daily life (friendship, marriage, education of children, everyday conflicts), and reinforced the ethos of the humanist community, which for the first time had been defined as a republic of letters by his correspondent Francesco Barbaro in a letter written in 1417.

By editing and printing his own letters, Erasmus (1469–1536) set a decisive step in the process of turning correspondence into a literary genre. His first 'official' compilation of 617 Latin letters in 1521, *Epistolæ ad diversos*, was followed by a second edition in 1529, *Opus epistolarum*, which added another 400 letters.[11] It is interesting to see how the geographical network of Erasmus's correspondents was much wider than that of Poggio, with many more letters going to England,

[10] After his death, his friends added another set of his letters from 1455 to 1459. Poggio Bracciolini, *Lettere*, ed. Helène Harth, 3 vols. (Florence: Leo Olschki, 1984–7). See also *Two Renaissance Book Hunters: The Letters of Poggius Bracciolini to Nicolaus de Niccolis*, translated from the Latin and annotated by Phyllis Walter Goodhart Gordan (New York: Columbia University Press, 1974).

[11] The definitive modern edition of Erasmus's letters by Percy Stafford Allen comprises 3,162 Latin letters, including over 1,600 written by Erasmus to hundreds of correspondents in Europe, princes, popes, dignitaries of the church, reformers, politicians, humanists, scholars, bankers or merchants. Erasmus, *Opus epistolarum*, ed. P. S. Allen et al., 12 vols. (Oxford: Clarendon Press, 1906–58, reprint 1992); *The Correspondence of Erasmus*, Allen's edition translated into English by R. A. B. Mynors and D. F. S. Thomson, annotated by Wallace K. Ferguson, 12 vols. to date (Toronto: University of Toronto Press, 1974–2003).

France, Italy, Flanders, the Holy Roman Empire and Iberia. The themes discussed by Erasmus were also extremely varied, from high-level interventions in theological, philological and political debates, to minor details concerning his personal and financial problems.

The first correspondence printed in the vernacular appeared in 1538: a selection of 320 of Pietro Aretino's (1492–1556) Italian letters; he wrote many more.[12] Precisely through the process of selection, organisation and editing for publication, this printed edition testifies to the changing status of those letters. Aretino united the roles of courtier, journalist, poet and writer of satires in one person, and enjoyed an enormously high reputation among popes, the emperor, kings (in particular François I), princes, scholars and humanists. All of them desired the 'privilege' of having access to Aretino's letters, which contained information, analyses and prognoses concerning the European political situation. The geographic range of Aretino's correspondence was wide, on account of his political connections, even if most of his correspondents were Italians. Aretino generally preferred the 'familiar' type of letter, but his publication project caused a dramatic change in his style. His letters became much more thematic (on friendship, fortune, truth and lies, time and memory), and were designed to be read by a larger public. From 1535 he devoted himself almost exclusively to the writing of letters, which confirmed the status of correspondence as a literary genre. Aretino's project to publish his correspondence was almost contemporary with the project carried out by Pietro Bembo, and it preceded other similar compilations of letters by Guidiccione, Caro, Ruscelli, Domenichi, Tasso or Tolomei.[13]

Within the domain of the art of rhetoric there was no classical tradition concerning the writing of letters.[14] Throughout the Middle Ages, however, the art of the sermon and the art of letter writing were regarded as the two major prose genres.[15] Innovation came especially

[12] The critical edition reveals a total of 3,290 letters written by Aretino. See Pietro Aretino, *Lettere*, ed. Paolo Procaccioli, 6 vols. (Rome: Salerno Editrice, 1997–2002).

[13] Jeanine Basso, *Le genre épistolaire en langue italienne (1538–1662): répertoire chronologique et analytique*, 2 vols. (Nancy: Presses Universitaires de Nancy, 1990).

[14] Marc Fumaroli, 'A l'origine d'un art français: la correspondance familière', in *La diplomacie de l'esprit: de Montaigne à La Fontaine* (Paris: Hermann, 1998), pp. 163–81.

[15] James J. Murphy, *Rhetorics in the Middle Ages: A History of Rhetoric Theory from St Augustine to the Renaissance* (Berkeley: University of California Press, 1974).

with Erasmus and Justus Lipsius, who both wrote decisive books on the subject, the former stressing the idea of exchange between absent friends, the latter the concept of a cooperative community.[16] Both of these innovations were therefore invented and developed as a format during the period on which this volume focuses, and reflected contemporary practices and mentalities. But they had long-term effects as well. Their expansion of the art of rhetoric influenced a series of correspondence manuals which were published throughout the sixteenth and the seventeenth centuries and integrated in the French *Bibliothèque Bleue* and similar popular series in other European countries. Such manuals disseminated general formats for letter writing, types of 'familiar' letters, indications for merchants' letters, and the use of courtly or popular language.[17] Not everyone approved of such formats at the time. As Roger Chartier has pointed out, Montaigne reacted against them. He was in favour of the expression of spontaneous feelings in correspondence and contrasted the etiquette of ceremonial letters with the freedom and sincerity of less formal writing.[18] This perspective would much later be developed in a literary form. While the publication of letters as a literary genre was established in the sixteenth century, novels and essays in an epistolary form emerged only in the seventeenth and especially the eighteenth century.[19]

---

[16] Erasmus, *De conscribendarum epistolarum ratio* (Lyon: S. Gryphium, 1531). Justus Lipsius, *Principles of Letter-Writing: A Bilingual Text of Justi Lipsii Epistolica institutio*, ed. and trans. R. V. Young and M. Thomas Hester (Carbondale: Southern Illinois University Press, 1996). See also Marc Fumaroli, 'La conversation savante', in Hans Bots and Françoise Waquet (eds.), *Commercium litterarium, 1600–1750* (Amsterdam and Manrosen: Ape/Holland University Press, 1994), pp. 67–80.

[17] For instance Francesco Sansovino, *Del secretario* (Venice, 1564); Battista Guarini, *Il segretario* (Venice, 1594); Gabriel Chappuys, *Le secrétaire* (Lyon, 1588); Angel Day, *The English Secretary* (1st edn 1586), ed. with an introduction by Robert O. Evans (Gainsville, FL: Scholar's Facsimiles & Reprints, 1967); Henry Care, *The Female Secretary* (London, 1671).

[18] Roger Chartier, 'Des "secrétaires" pour le peuple?', in Chartier (ed.), *La correspondance: les usages de la lettre au XIXe siècle* (Paris: Fayard, 1991), pp. 159–87. The references concerning Montaigne were quoted from essay XL on Cicero. For the previous period see Alain Boureau, 'La norme épistolaire, une invention médiévale', in Chartier (ed.), *La correspondance*, pp. 127–57.

[19] That topic lies beyond both the temporal and thematic boundaries of this volume. See, however, Dena Goodman, *The Republic of Letters: A Cultural History of the French Enlightenment* (Ithaca and London: Cornell University Press, 1994).

SHIFTING GEOGRAPHY AND NETWORKS OF ERUDITE
CORRESPONDENCE

As several of the contributions to the present volume demonstrate, wide-ranging networks (in terms of either geography or number of correspondents) and vast amounts of correspondence were by no means limited to the small circle of famous humanists. They were unusual, however, even among the erudite elite of Europe. So much is clear if we compare the geographical distribution of Erasmus's correspondents with the much smaller network of Pedro Mártir de Anglería (*c*.1456–1526), an Italian humanist based in Spain. He was a chaplain, historian, ambassador and counsellor of the Spanish monarchs, from Isabel of Castile to Charles V and wrote the early history of the European discovery of the Americas. Pedro Mártir de Anglería left a compilation of 813 Latin letters, which was published in 1530.[20] The great majority of his correspondents were Spaniards, though there were a few Italians and Portuguese. Through his prolific production of chronicles he played an extremely important role in the dissemination in Europe of the discovery and exploration of America, but he had only a limited network of correspondents.

His contemporary Erasmus occupied a central position in the early sixteenth-century European republic of letters and none of the other humanists ever equalled his influence, which comprised both northern and southern Europe. Yet, the large-scale production of the Italian humanists undeniably turned Italy into the intellectual centre of Europe and made the Italian language a point of reference for the men of letters in the course of the sixteenth century. This situation changed in the seventeenth century. The centre of the republic of letters shifted to France. This change was marked (and stimulated) by the emergence of Parisian academies, such as the one established in 1635 by Marin Mersenne (1588–1648) and the new organisational culture proposed by the brothers Pierre (1582–1651) and Jacques Dupuy (1591–1656).

---

[20] Pedro Mártir de Anglería, *Opus epistolarum* (Alcalá de Henares: Compluti, 1530; 2nd edn Amsterdam: Danielum Elzevirium, 1670). There is a Spanish translation, *Epistolario*, ed. José López de Toro, 4 vols. (Madrid: Imprenta Gongora, 1953–7).

Their cabinet (1617–56) was a place for intellectual debate and the reception and diffusion of news. It produced and attracted dozens of thousands of letters. A large number of these can be classified as newsletters containing literary and scientific information, which were addressed to an increasingly large public.[21]

Concurrently – even while Italy's prominence as an intellectual centre was undisputed – another centre of production of erudite letters could be found much further north: in the southern and northern Netherlands, as the massive correspondence left by Justus Lipsius (1547–1606),[22] Hugo Grotius (1583–1645)[23] and Constantijn Huygens (1596–1687)[24] (followed by his three sons) demonstrates. Thus, in terms of cultural geography and chronology, the first centre of gravity of learned correspondence was located in Italy during most of the sixteenth century, while a second centre developed – and was certainly influenced by the example of Erasmus – in the Low Countries throughout the second half of the sixteenth and most of the seventeenth century. The shift of the centre of gravity in the republic of letters to France in the seventeenth century thus coincided with the continued flourishing of learned correspondence in the Low Countries, while this tradition certainly did not die in Italy in the seventeenth century. For instance, Antonio Magliabechi (1633–1714), librarian of Duke Cosimo III, developed an extraordinary network of correspondents all over Europe without leaving Florence.[25] The enormous

[21] Simone Mazauriac, 'La diffusion du savoir en dehors des circuits savants: le bureau d'adresse de Théophraste Renaudot', in Bots and Waquet (eds.), *Commercium litterarium, 1600–1750*, pp. 151–72; *Correspondance de Jacques Dupuy et Nicolas Heinsius (1646–1656)*, ed. Hans Bots (The Hague: Martinus Nijhoff, 1971).

[22] Justus Lipsius, *Epistolæ* (under publication), ed. A. Gerlo et al., 13 vols. (Brussels: Koninklijke Academie voor wetenschappen, letteren en schone kunsten van België, 1978–87); *Epistolario de Justo Lipsio y los españoles (1577–1606)*, ed. Alejandro Ramirez (Madrid: Castalia, 1966).

[23] Hugo Grotius, *Briefwisseling*, 17 vols. (The Hague: Martinus Nijhoff / Instituut voor Nederlandse Geschiedenis, 1928–2001).

[24] Constantijn Huygens, *De briefwisseling*, ed. J. A. Worp, 6 vols. (The Hague: Martinus Nijhoff, 1911–17). See also A. G. H. Bachrach, *Sir Constantine Huygens and Britain, 1596–1687: A Pattern of Cultural Exchange* (Leiden: Leiden University Press, 1962).

[25] *Lettere e carte Magliabechi: regesto*, ed. Manuela Doni Garfagnini, 2 vols. (Rome: Istituto Italiano per l'età moderna e contemporanea, 1981). Magliabechi also created

correspondence created by individual scholars in Germany testifies to the gradual extension of the republic of letters to central and part of eastern Europe in the course of the seventeenth century. Gottfried Leibniz (1646–1716) is an extraordinary example of a polymath, who was involved in the creation of new academies in Berlin, Dresden and St Petersburg. His correspondence comprises 15,000 letters which were sent to more than 600 correspondents. It is significant, however, that 60 per cent of Leibniz's correspondents outside Germany were residents of only five cities: Paris, London, Rome, The Hague and Amsterdam.[26]

LETTER WRITING IN A HISTORICAL CONTEXT

We have already been turning slightly away from the literary and rhetorical aspects of correspondence and towards the topics that are the core interest in the present volume: the as yet less explored aspects of the various functions and meanings of correspondence in early modern Europe and the way in which diverse networks of correspondence operated at the time in terms of cultural exchange and exchange of information.

Speaking of the functions of correspondence, we should briefly look here at the wider context of early modern society in which new demands on many sides stimulated (and often required) an increasing amount of correspondence. A major factor consisted of the new and rapidly growing administrative needs of state building and development of the church. The reorganisation of the Holy Roman Empire in the thirteenth century imposed new administrative standards that spread in western and central Europe. Over the next centuries, the

a remarkable collection of books (30,000 printed and manuscripts), which is kept at the National Library of Florence. See Françoise Waquet, 'L'espace de la république des lettres', in Bots and Waquet (eds.), *Commercium litterarium, 1600–1750*, pp. 175–89.

[26] Hans Bots and Françoise Waquet, *La république des lettres* (Paris: Belin, 1997). Christiane Berkvens-Stevelinck, Hans Bots and Jens Häseler (eds.), *Les grands intermédiaires culturels de la République des Lettres: études de réseaux de correspondence du XVIe au XVIIIe siècles* (Paris: Honoré Champion, forthcoming) had been announced at the time this volume was being finished but we have not been able to consult it.

Mediterranean expansion of the republics of Genoa and Venice created a new political organisation which had an impact on the future Hispanic models. The success of the Iberian kingdoms was reflected not only in the political intervention of Aragon in southern Italy and the western Mediterranean, but also in the overseas expansion of Portugal and Castile. The same period witnessed the growing strength of France and England, and the emergence of a new political culture, ensuing from an increasingly complex bureaucracy which was structured on the basis of different levels of competence and required regular communication between centres and peripheries. Noblemen, clergymen, architects, musicians, writers, jewellers, craftsmen and painters were attracted to princely courts, which defined a regular network of social and cultural exchange all over Europe. This court society was stimulated by the organisation of weddings, rituals and feasts, the building of palaces and urban planning. The circulation of aristocrats and artists through the main courts increased the exchange of information and reproduction of cultural models.[27] International political conflicts, which accompanied the consolidation and expansion of states in different regions of Europe, required the creation of a system of consultation and information gathering. Regular exchanges of ambassadors were established in the course of the fifteenth century. But these developments also provided new opportunities and challenges to spies and others with an interest in secrecy for gathering and conveying information. All of this boosted letter writing, the exchange of information on paper, and the transmission of directives.

The organisation of mendicant orders in the thirteenth century triggered an impressive process of convent building and the diffusion of libraries during the next few centuries. The creation of new dioceses, the growth of ecclesiastical justice, and the development of central institutions dependent on the pope (chancellery, treasury,

---

[27] Norbert Elias, *The Court Society*, translated from German by Edmund Jephcott (Oxford: Blackwell, 1983). For path-breaking publications on correspondence in Spanish court and aristocratic society, see Fernando Bouza, *Comunicación, conocimiento y memoria en la España de los siglos XVI y XVIII* (Salamanca: Seminario de Estudios Medievales e Renacentistas, 1999); *Corre manuscrito: una historia cultural del Siglo de Oro* (Madrid: Marcial Pons, 2001).

financial accounting) are the other main features of administrative development of the Roman Church. The Iberian expansion entailed an increase in the activity of missionaries, first especially by the mendicant orders and after the 1540s by the Company of Jesus. The culture of the Jesuits was based on constant exchange of information – both between the missionaries themselves and between the missionaries and their superiors at various levels. It forms an extreme case of religious culture based on correspondence, because the annual letters sent by the different missions were edited and published in different cities all over Europe, as a means of spreading information, education and propaganda.[28]

The disruption of Christianity as a religious community created new demands for communication. The intense theological dispute of the period was conducted to a large extent via books, pamphlets and pictures – but letter writing too was reinforced as an essential means of exchange, debate and mobilisation. Martin Luther left 3,500 letters.[29] The expansion of the reformed church and the politics of evangelical union are expressed in the thousands of letters written by Zwingli during the 1520s, even if the geographic area covered by his correspondence was limited.[30] Calvin's range of influence was much larger, as is shown by his vast correspondence written between 1542 and 1563. At first he mainly covered Switzerland, but his letters increasingly reached France and Germany, and to a lesser extent the north of Italy, Scandinavia, Poland, England and Scotland.[31] Bullinger may have been the Protestant reformer with the most intensive correspondence:

[28] *Epistolae S. Francisci Xaverii aliaque eius scripta (1535–1552)*, ed. Georgius Schurhammer and Josephus Wicki, 2 vols. (Rome: Monumenta Historica Societatis Iesu, 1944–5); Adriano Prosperi, 'L'Europa cristiana e il mondo: alle origine dell'idea di missione', in *America e Apocalisse e altri saggi* (Pisa and Rome: Istituti Editoriali e Poligrafici Internazionali, 1999), pp. 89–112.

[29] Horst Wenzel, 'Luthers Briefe im Medienwechsel von der Manuskriptkultur zum Buchdruck', in Thomas A. Brady (ed.), *Die deutsche Reformation zwischen Spätmittelalter und Früher Neuzeit* (Munich: R. Oldenbourg Verlag, 2001), pp. 203–29.

[30] To southern and eastern Switzerland and the Holy Roman Empire south of the line running from Strasbourg to Augsburg through Ulm. See Philip Benedict, *Christ's Churches Purely Reformed: A Social History of Calvinism* (New Haven: Yale University Press, 2002), pp. 36–7.

[31] *Ibid.*, pp. 109–14.

he left some 15,000 letters (written by and to him). Most of his correspondents lived in Switzerland, but he maintained epistolary relations with England, Poland, Hungary, France and Italy as well.[32]

Naturally, political or religious administrative needs were not the only stimulus for the expansion of correspondence. The foundation of universities from the thirteenth century onwards stimulated letter writing among the communities of scholars in order to exchange information and points of view. Nor should we forget the increase in the number of schools and the activities of teachers at the lower level of a loose educational system, which created a widely dispersed group of letter writers who could serve the daily needs of the illiterate population. European economic growth between the thirteenth and sixteenth century, which fuelled political and administrative changes, also had an autonomous role. In conjunction with the growing role of the judiciary it created new needs, such as writing contracts, registering property, making inventories of assets and wills. Private and public conflicts were increasingly dealt with by tribunals – which entailed the corresponding augmentation of requirements, petitions, declarations and the accompanying written communication about them. The professionals involved, such as notaries, lawyers, judges – along with the politicians, governors, ambassadors, secretaries, scholars and clergymen – expanded the practice of letter writing enormously in the period covered by our volume, 1400–1700.

MARKETS OF INFORMATION

Two specific domains of early modern correspondence should be mentioned here at greater length, because of the special attention they have received from historians and the fact that they play an important part in this volume as well: merchants' letters and newsletters. Both have been the subject of special analysis, the former in particular by economic historians looking for information that could throw light on economic practices and developments; the latter because they are a crucial source in a relatively new field of historiography, the history

---

[32] *Ibid.*, pp. 63–4.

of information and communication. In both domains, historians have focused mainly on these letters as the carriers of information. Merchants' letters circulated and were kept as legal documents from the fourteenth century. They were used by rulers, diplomats and missionaries as an important source of information and, thanks to their special value, tens of thousands of them still survive today.

Focusing on letters as a means of transmitting information, Pierre Sardella studied the impact of manuscript merchants' letters and newsletters in the Venetian world from 1496 to 1534: how they defined the framework and expansion of this world economy, involving the Middle East, Italy, northern Africa, Iberia, France, Germany, England and Flanders. These newsletters concerned not only prices and products in different regions (scarcity or abundance would have an immediate impact on prices), but also political and military events (war had a direct impact on maritime insurance). He also studied the postal system, its main itineraries and costs, calculated the intensity and geography of communications, and drew attention to the 'marginal uses' of letter writing.[33] Sardella's findings concerning the frequency and reach of communications with Venice are particularly suggestive with respect to the geography of communication in early modern Europe: there was daily correspondence from Rome, Florence and Milan; weekly correspondence from Genoa, Naples and Innsbruck; fortnightly from Paris, Augsburg and Budapest; and monthly from Palermo, Madrid, Valladolid, London, Constantinople and Alexandria.

Federigo Melis analysed the intensity of commercial communication between twenty European, Mediterranean and Atlantic cities by the end of the fifteenth century (London, Bruges, Paris, Lyon, Lisbon, Funchal, Palma de Mallorca, Barcelona, Avignon, Milan, Venice, Genoa, Pisa, Florence, Rome, Naples, Palermo, Ragusa, Constantinople and Alexandria). Collecting a massive amount of information from correspondence addressed to 443 localities, his findings confirmed the

---

[33] Pierre Sardella, *Nouvelles et spéculation à Venise au début du XVIe siècle* (Paris: Armand Colin, 1948).

central position of Venice and of the axis northern Italy–France–Western Germany–Flanders–England.[34]

The geographical area with a high level of *commercial* communication at the end of the fifteenth century is therefore roughly the same as the one in which concentrated *intellectual* exchange took place by means of correspondence throughout the sixteenth and seventeenth centuries – even if the central position of Italy eroded in favour of France, and the northern Netherlands only became relevant from the late sixteenth century onwards. What followed in the course of the seventeenth century, mainly due to the Thirty Years' War and the Civil Wars in England,[35] was an intensification of the exchange of newsletters, the further diffusion of newspapers, and the enlargement of correspondence networks. The expanded geographical area covered by regular cultural exchanges came to include western France, the Holy Roman Empire, central Europe, the parts of Scandinavia that were connected with the Baltic, and parts of the Iberian peninsula, in particular Barcelona and Madrid. Until the eighteenth century, eastern Europe, large parts of Scandinavia and most of the Iberian peninsula did not participate in any major way in the principal network of cultural exchanges.

Stéphane Haffemayer studied the geography of information in the *Gazette* of Théophraste Renaudot from 1647 to 1663: 56 per cent of the items studied concerned continental urban Europe (within the abovementioned axis area, including northern Italy), 25 per cent the Mediterranean, 15 per cent the Atlantic, and 4 per cent the Baltic. Spain did not produce its own information until 1659, which, even after this date, was transmitted via Genoa, Milan or Brussels. 'National' and political items naturally occupied an important place in the contents

---

[34] Federigo Melis, 'L'intensità e regolarità nella diffusione dell'informazione economica generale nel Mediterraneo e in Occidente alla fine del Medioevo', in *Mélanges en l'honneur de Fernand Braudel*, vol. 1: *Histoire économique du monde méditerranéen, 1450–1650* (Paris: Privat, 1973), pp. 389–424.

[35] Brenden Dooley and Sabrina Baron (eds.), *Politics of Information in Early Modern Europe* (London: Routledge, 2001). The early diffusion of newspapers in the Holy Roman Empire and in England is clearly connected with the wars.

of most newsletters and newspapers, but the geography of the news in the *Gazette* was surprisingly dominated by Italy (at least 25 per cent of the total information, more than France). In spite of the decline of Italian influence in France this phenomenon persisted until 1775. It can only be explained by the traditional vitality of communications in Italy, which had the densest urban network in the world, an efficient postal service, and many offices of manuscript newsletters, especially in Venice and Rome.[36]

Both Sardella and Melis stressed the importance of the creation of an information market – for political, commercial and communicational reasons. But they mainly used diplomatic and commercial correspondence, *avvisi* (or newsletters), or diaries based on such material, for their research about information and its economic impact. Michel Morineau further widened the scope. He studied Dutch gazettes, correspondence of the Venetian ambassadors, *Fuggerzeitungen*, *relaciones* of Cabrera de Cordoba, newsletters of the Frankfurt fairs, Italian *avvisi*, correspondence of Spanish and Portuguese merchants and Jesuits, *Relations véritables* printed in Brussels, the *Gaceta de Madrid* and the *Correo Mercantil* from the sixteenth to the eighteenth century. His purpose was still a strictly economic historical one, however.[37]

The structuring of a market of information has only fairly recently become a subject of research in its own right. Mario Infelise has pointed out that an efficiently organised network of information was established in Italy during the second half of the sixteenth century. It produced an enormous quantity and variety of documents, especially *avvisi* and reports – mostly in the form of manuscripts. These were distributed by the weekly rhythm of the post. In terms

---

[36] Stéphane Haffemayer, 'La géographie de l'information dans la Gazette de Renaudot de 1647 à 1663', in Henri Duranton and Pierre Rétat (eds.), *Gazettes et information politique sous l'Ancien Régime* (Saint-Etienne: Publications de l'Université de Saint-Etienne, 1999), pp. 21–31.

[37] His findings triggered an important theoretical debate in economic history about the actual importance of American precious metals, and the anachronism of the projection into the past of the theory of cycles and the relation between precious metals and prices. Michel Morineau, *Incroyables gazettes et fabuleux métaux: les retours des trésors américains d'après les gazettes hollandaises (XVIe–XVIIIe siècles)* (Paris: Maison des Sciences de l'Homme, 1985).

of contents they focused mainly on political and military events. Non-printed, manuscript information remained crucially important in Europe throughout the sixteenth, seventeenth and even the eighteenth centuries. It escaped censorship, speeded up the diffusion of news and avoided costs of printing. Newsletters were printed only on exceptional occasions, usually in connection with major events. While printed information was of more direct importance to the creation of public opinion, the effects of the regular and intense dissemination of manuscript newsletters should not be underestimated. They might be sent to only a few dozen subscribers, but were often read aloud and provided the type of news that would later (from the first half of the seventeenth century) be offered by the printed gazettes. Infelise has also drawn attention to the cultural importance of the offices which produced and copied newsletters, even if they employed very few professionals. Such offices functioned as real agencies of information with correspondents in different cities and abroad, distributing manuscript newsletters to subscribers.[38] Peter Burke regards the central place occupied by Venice in the early market of information as a result of the strong subcultures in the city (e.g. Greek, Jewish, Slavonian) and the distinctive structure of the state, with its *Maggior Concilio* of some two thousand members.[39]

[38] Mario Infelise, 'Le marché d'information à Venise au XVIIe siècle', in Duranton and Rétat (eds.), *Gazettes et information politique*, pp. 117–28. He regards the absence of a corporation of copyists in Venice as a major reason for the number of newsletter offices. See also V. Castronovo, G. Ricuperati and C. Capra, *La stampa italiana dal Cinquecento all'Ottocento* (Bari: Laterza, 1976); Giorgio Doria, 'Conoscenza del mercato e sistema informativo: il know-how dei mercanti-finanzieri genovesi nei secoli XVI e XVII', in Aldo de Maddalena and Hermann Kellenbenz (eds.), *La repubblica internazionale del denaro tra XV e XVII secolo* (Bologna: Il Mulino, 1986), pp. 57–121; François Moreau, *De bonne main: la communication manuscrite au XVIIIe siècle* (Paris: Universitas, 1993).

[39] Peter Burke, 'Early modern Venice as a center of information and communication', in John Martin and Dennis Romano (eds.), *Venice Reconsidered: The History and Civilisation of an Italian City-State, 1297–1997* (Baltimore: Johns Hopkins University Press, 2000), pp. 389–419. See also Peter Burke, 'Rome as a center of information and communication for the Catholic world, 1550–1650', in Pamela M. Jones and Thomas Worcester (eds.), *From Rome to Eternity: Catholicism and the Arts in Italy, ca. 1550–1650* (Leiden: Brill, 2002), pp. 253–69.

The status of the documents which provided the information circulating in this market cannot be easily defined, since the *avvisi* drew on commercial letters and diplomatic reports as well as 'familiar' correspondence. The same range of documents could also form the basis for diaries. Although the *avvisi* generally limited their news to political and military events, they also included *faits divers* taken from irregular or incidental pamphlets, such as the French *canards*. These had led an autonomous life since the end of the fifteenth century. *Canards* specialised in violent deaths, adulterous scandals, monstrous animals, wonders, signs and battles in the sky, miracles and acts of sacrilege, manifestations of the devil, or natural catastrophes. This type of 'events' created its own market of information, and it is not surprising that the first periodical publications, such as the *Mercure Français* (which was launched in 1605), introduced *faits divers* in their set of news.⁴⁰ Religious and political printed tracts (in France *libelles*) were often based on correspondence and had an enormous reach. Even if they mainly served propagandistic purposes they can still be compared with the *avvisi*.⁴¹ The publication of regular periodicals like the gazettes presupposed a network of correspondents. Similar networks would later become indispensable for the intellectual and scientific exchanges carried on in journals like the *Journal des Savants* (Paris 1665–), the *Philosophical Transactions* (London 1665–), the *Giornale de' Letterati* (Rome 1668–), *Acta eruditorum* (Leipzig 1682–), *Les nouvelles de la république des lettres* (Rotterdam 1684–), *Bibliothèque universelle et historique* (Amsterdam 1686–), *Athenian Mercury* (Cambridge, Massachusetts, 1691–) and *Gentleman's Journal* (London 1692–).⁴²

IMPACT OF CORRESPONDENCE

Behind the double status of correspondence in early modern Europe – as means of communication and literary genre – a multitude of

---

⁴⁰ Jean Pierre Seguin, *L'information en France de Louis XII à Henri II* (Geneva: Droz, 1961); *L'information en France avant le périodique: 517 canards imprimés entre 1529 et 1631* (Paris: Maisonneuve et Larose, 1964).

⁴¹ Christian Jouhaud, *Mazarinades: la Fronde des mots* (Paris: Aubier, 1985).

⁴² Norman Fiering, 'The transatlantic republic of letters: a note on the circulation of learned periodicals to early eighteenth century America', *The William and Mary Quarterly*, 3rd series, 33.4 (1976), 642–60.

functions and effects are hidden, not all of which may have been equally evident to the correspondents themselves. To name some of its indirect but crucial effects: correspondence helped to create a community of learned persons inside and outside universities, who were interested in the advance of knowledge. It reinforced the ethos of the republic of letters, with its sense of identity, pride, taste, values, rules of behaviour, like the exchange of gifts, ideas and results of research.[43] It spread the ideal of the scholar who was relatively indifferent to affiliations and systems of beliefs, which facilitated networks and exchanges across religious and political frontiers. It revealed the public and private sides of those who corresponded, in terms of both thought and emotions, and thereby helped to spread the cultural notion of private and public sides to personalities. It facilitated transfers from the culture of the notary or the secretary to the culture of the philologist, the literary writer, or the first 'journalists', who made a living from newsletters. Through the varying intensity of exchanges it helped to create centres and peripheries of intellectual life in Europe, defining which regions were more involved in cultural exchange and intellectual debate, and how this geography changed over time.

The organisational culture of erudite correspondence, in which concepts like relative equality of status, dignity of men, intellectual merit, and free exchange played a decisive role, had a political impact in the long run. It eroded the constitutional framework of the *ancien régime*. But we also have to consider how correspondence was used in everyday life by members of virtually all social strata, most of them illiterate, who had letters written or read aloud on a regular basis for personal and professional reasons. Letter writing had a major effect on the expression and diffusion of ideas and emotions, linking the individual with the society in which he or she was acting. The correspondence of women, for instance, had a major impact on the promotion of their status in different European countries, asserting new values and raising gender issues. It is not by chance that women participated actively in the emergence of the novel as a new literary genre, and that Madame de Lafayette used the letter in *La Princesse de Clèves* (1678) as a device

---

[43] Bots and Waquet (eds.), *Commercium litterarium, 1600–1750*.

to develop the narrative.[44] Migration stimulated the spread of letter writing all over Europe, and this holds true not only for inter-regional and international migrations within Europe, but also for the emigration overseas,[45] which was extremely important throughout the sixteenth and seventeenth centuries (in Spain and Portugal alone this phenomenon involved more than 1 million people). In this context, letters helped to maintain family ties and to establish competing, plural identities, reinforcing imagined communities and diffusing visions of social success in the New World.

ORGANISATION OF THE VOLUME

The structure of this volume was determined by two main areas of research and analysis: networks and markets of information; functions and meanings of correspondence. Since the latter area of research, in this volume, comprehended different fields with a specific culture, we have divided the part on uses and meanings into two segments, one concerning the field of the arts, the other concerning political space.

The first part of this volume concentrates on markets of information, newsletters and agents, intercontinental exchanges of information by merchants and commercial correspondence, and on early scientific networks in Europe.

Mario Infelise emphasises the late medieval origin of a market of information based on merchant and diplomatic correspondence. The

---

[44] Madame de Lafayette, *La Princesse de Clèves*, ed. Jean Mesnard (Paris: Imprimerie Nationale, 1980; reprinted by Flammarion, 1996). Here, we have not tackled the huge variety of letter writing by women. Some of the fascinating issues it raises are explored in the following publications: *Letters of Medieval Women*, ed. Anne Crawford (Stroud: Sutton, 2002); Anne R. Larsen and Colette H. Winn (eds.), *Renaissance Women Writers: French Texts / American Context* (Detroit: Wayne State University, 1994); Kim Walker, *Women Writers of the English Renaissance* (New York: Twayne Publishers, 1996); Katherine M. Wilson and Frank J. Warnke (eds.), *Women Writers of the Seventeenth Century* (Athens and London: University of Georgia Press, 1989); B. G. MacCarthy, *The Female Pen: Women Writers and Novelists, 1621–1818* (Cork: Cork University Press, 1994); and Sharon M. Harris (ed.), *American Women Writers to 1800* (Oxford: Oxford University Press, 1996).
[45] Enrique Otte, *Letters and People of the Spanish Indies: The Sixteenth Century* (Cambridge: Cambridge University Press, 1976).

Venetian diaries of Girolamo Priuli and Marino Sanudo reveal the enormous quantity of letters and *avvisi* which were already in circulation by the end of the fifteenth century. The creation of a postal network which covered large parts of Europe in the first half of the sixteenth century was crucial to the spreading of news. The fact that the name of the author was increasingly often omitted in the *avvisi* in the course of the sixteenth century is interpreted by Infelise as an indication of the creation of a field of information which was less dependent on personal trust and addressed to a larger public. He also analyses the change from letters to *avvisi* by the late fifteenth century. Extracting news from various personal letters implied the creation of a new text which should be of general interest: a newssheet, with a specific layout, headlines, references to sources, summaries of the news included, and lists of places where the news had been compiled. The art of compiling news and its professional network of agents were recognised in papal documents of the 1560s and 1570s.

Zsuzsa Barbarics and Renate Pieper focus on both manuscript and printed newsletters, stressing how important manuscript newsletters remained especially in the sixteenth and seventeenth centuries, but even up to the French Revolution. Their analysis shows how the biggest collections of manuscript newsletters were brought together during the second half of the sixteenth century in southern Germany (Fugger, Count of Pfalz-Neuburg, Duke of Bavaria), central Europe (Imperial Chancery, Estates of Inner Austria, Count of Bethlenfalva), Switzerland (*Wickiana* and *Bullinger Zeitungen*), and Italy (Duke of Urbino, Duke of Florence, Holy See). Their contribution discusses how these newsletters were organised in archives – separately or together with personal letters and reports – which functions they had, which languages were used (vernacular, with the predominance of Italian in the sixteenth century), and how the needs of the recipient shaped the contents of newssheets. A comparison of letters sent by merchants, ambassadors, friends or relatives on the one hand, and newsletters created and diffused by professional agents, predecessors of journalists and editors on the other hand, shows overlaps and a shared use of news. Barbarics and Pieper also identify professional agents and their circles of contributors, clients and patrons. Their case study of the manuscript and printed news about the battle of Lepanto demonstrates that the latest news was distributed by fast and short handwritten reports (most of them produced in Venice), while the larger printed newsletters followed more slowly and were mostly based on the information in the handwritten ones. Their investigation of the full range of newsletters in the Fuggers' collection between 1571 and 1573 confirms the central position of Venice in the market of information, followed by Rome, and then by Antwerp, which shows the emergence of north-western Europe in the network of newsletters.

Francesca Trivellato challenges Habermas's opposition of medieval business correspondence and the public dissemination of economic news, which began in the late seventeenth century. His evolutionist thesis was based on the contrast between 'private' and 'public', and illuminates neither commercial practices nor markets of information. In practice, the topics of the news spread by merchants, diplomats, missionaries and travellers overlapped. Partly because of its legal use in court, 'private' correspondence continued to play a funda- mental role, moreover, also *after* the emergence of printed economic periodicals. Trivellato provides an overview of the major archives of commercial letters, merchants' manuals, and the effective role of busi- ness newspapers. She stresses that 'private' merchant correspondence fulfilled yet another essential role besides providing economic and political information: by bringing together and spreading informa- tion about the merchants and agents themselves, which was essential for a business based on trust. While historians have studied cultural and social dimensions of trade, she argues that most recent studies have only considered homogeneous ethnic and communitarian net- works. In contrast, Trivellato presents a case study of correspondence among merchants involved in intercontinental trade, cutting across religious and cultural boundaries. It is based on almost 14,000 letters written between 1704 and 1746 by the Ergas and Silvera, a partner- ship of Sephardic Jews from Livorno (Tuscany), with coreligionists and non-Jews all over the Mediterranean, western and north-western Europe, and Goa. Trivellato singles out 246 letters (written in Italian) to Christian (mostly Italian) merchants in Lisbon and 86 (written in Portuguese) to Hindu merchants in Goa, concerning the exchange of Mediterranean coral for Indian diamonds. Trust in this interethnic (and durable) environment was built through the intensity and widespread circulation of business letters.

Florike Egmond's essay focuses on correspondence in the circle of the botanist Carolus Clusius (1526–1609), who played a major role in creating natural history as a new field of expertise during the second half of the sixteenth century. He left 1,500 letters, the majority of which were sent to him (some 1,150) and the rest written by him (some 350). This correspondence shows the specificity of the new field of expertise, partly because natural history had no academic tradition or clear status. Participants in this field came from a wide variety of social backgrounds – aristocrats, merchants, apothecaries, perfumers, druggists, farmers, folk healers. Several women of aristocratic and bourgeois background were among Clusius's correspondents and informants. The novelty of natural history (botany in particular) and its relatively neutral status in religious and scientific debates contributed to this social openness, which is also attested by the languages used in this correspondence. Although the majority of his 300 correspondents knew Latin, about half of the letters were written in vernacular languages (French, Italian, German, Spanish or Dutch). Clusius was a polyglot, who could read and write all of these languages (plus Latin and Greek and possibly Portuguese), and his interest in local knowledge and the folk nomenclature of plants may well have contributed to his linguistic proficiency. Correspondence in this case helped to both create a new European community of experts and define a field of expertise with its own customs of exchange.

In the second part in this volume the focus is on the uses and meanings of correspondence in the artistic field. We concentrate here on the transmission of the ethos of collectors, aristocratic patrons and painters, as well as the models and purposes of collecting.

Fernando Bouza mentions many examples of the exchange of portraits in Spain, England and the Holy Roman Empire arranged via the correspondence of courtiers. These exchanges contributed to the formation of collections and galleries, such as the one organised during the last decades of the sixteenth century by Archduke Ferdinand of Tyrol consisting of weapons and portraits. The correspondence from

1542 to 1581 between Cardinal Antoine Perrenot de Granvelle and the
Duke of Villahermosa, Don Martín de Aragón, forms the focus of this
chapter. Granvelle acted as agent of the duke all over Europe, and not
only sent a large number of gifts to both the duke and the first duchess
(some of which Granvelle had made himself, since he was a virtuoso
jeweller), but also constantly provided them with information about
the life and work of artists he patronised. Granvelle even found time
to write in his own hand to the duke, as a sign of deference. Looking
at various cases, Fernando Bouza sketches the code of ethics of aristocratic patrons of art, with its intricate values of patronage, obligation
and service. He stresses the importance of courtly correspondence
as exchange of information, ideas and values, but also as a means to
exchange gifts and as a gift in itself. Autograph letters are the most
valuable examples of gifts, since they express a use of time which was
a valuable item in courtly life.

Peter Mason's contribution focuses on writing in both the correspondence and the paintings of the French artist Nicolas Poussin. In
studies of correspondence, little attention has been paid on the whole
to the physical dimension: the tangible and visible form of the written
word on paper or some other support. This omission is all the more
crucial when the writer happens to be an artist. The article draws
on a number of Poussin's letters, down to the artist's final year of
1665, though it reproduces and concentrates on the famous letter to
Paul Fréart de Chantelou of April 1639 connected with the painting
Israelites Gathering the Manna. Such concentration on a single letter
is shown to be in accordance with Poussin's own recommendations
on how to read his paintings. Poussin's famous injunction to 'read the
story and the painting' is interpreted as showing how the temporality
of letter writing and exchange in many ways resembles the temporal
structure of a painting and the time it takes a viewer to comprehend
it. At the same time, this letter is situated within the context of the rest
of the correspondence, of Poussin's fraught relations with the French
court, and of the situation of other artists of the period, in particular
Peter Paul Rubens. In this way a network involving artists, patrons and
politicians is sketched whose nodes intersect in the letter to Chantelou.

Irene Baldriga tackles the issue of art collecting and correspondence,
showing how the creation of galleries and museums of *naturalia* and

artificialia in the sixteenth and seventeenth centuries depended on correspondence. Discussing the Gonzagas' celestial gallery, Marquis Vincenzo Giustiniano's collection, Thomas Howard, Earl of Arundel's collection, and Athanasius Kircher's museum, Baldriga shows how correspondence was an instrument of transmission of the patterns or styles of collecting and creating art galleries on a European scale. These sets of correspondence evince a constant exchange between southern and northern Europe. In 1629 the publication of *Marmora Arundeliana* promoted the principal pieces in the Earl of Arundel's collection in the form of a 'paper museum' made of engravings. Seven years later, in 1636, his friend Vincenzo Giustiniano followed his example, publishing (in the *Galleria Giustiniana*) a set of engravings which represented the statues, busts and bas-reliefs of his collection. The purpose of these first illustrated catalogues may have been to prolong the lives of these collections beyond the lives of what they contained. Letters were also a common object to be depicted as one of the items in a collector's portrait: a phenomenon that Baldriga interprets as a status symbol and a means to stress the wide-ranging contacts on which the creation of a collection was predicated. Her analysis of the emergence of '*cabinets d'amateurs*', as a genre of Flemish painting in the seventeenth century, shows a 'vulgarisation' of the practice of collecting, which runs parallel with the creation of a market of copies after famous works of art. This new trend of 'ready-made' museums explains to a certain extent the decline of the role of correspondence in this domain. The recognition of the importance of correspondence, which was connected with the subtle and sophisticated connections that were essential for the formation of unique museums in the preceding period, explains the new status of letters. They themselves were transformed into a collectable object that could be included in a museum.

The third part of the volume is devoted to the field of political action. It discusses political influence through letter writing, the encoded transmission of political information about enemy states, and the conveyance by letter of feelings, political notions and administrative documents by illiterate peasants.

Francisco Bethencourt compares the letters of the two main Iberian *conquistadores*, Albuquerque and Cortés, written to their respective kings in Portugal and Spain. The struggle of Albuquerque to maintain political support is contrasted with that of Cortés to obtain political legitimacy. These military commanders not only instigated political events which changed the position of the Iberian kingdoms in Europe, but also reflected on the political issues that were raised by their actions. Through their letters they intervened at the highest level in order to influence political decisions and assert their positions. The different destinies of these *conquistadores* were portrayed by the main chroniclers and biographers of the sixteenth century; even during the Enlightenment their fate still inspired reflection on the fairness of the kings. The creation of *jus gentium* as an area of theoretical develop-ment of international law was a result of the intense debate in Spain that followed the consequences of conquest and political dominion over people who had their own right to property and a political sys-tem. The Portuguese claim to impose the doctrine of *mare clausum* was contradicted by developments in international law, and within a century had become obsolete because of changes in the international balance of naval power.

Dejanirah Couto reconstructs a hidden facet of sixteenth-century political international life: spying in order to collect secret state infor-mation. This important issue of how to access classified information – a common practice in Europe already in those days – is rarely tackled in studies of communication. Couto provides a major synthesis of the systems of codification in use, the different logics of cryptic infor-mation, the struggle to access the main keys, and the development of those keys. In this area too there were centres and peripheries, each of which had its own dynamics of innovation, reproduction, or delay in adopting the most recent trends, aiming to break the enemy's key or to avoid being exposed. Couto focuses mainly on spying in the Ottoman Empire. She explores the different procedures of Christian spies who collected secret information for their masters, most of them Venetians, Romans, Spaniards or Portuguese.

Istvan György Tóth addresses the issue of correspondence among illiterate people, the large majority of the population in early mod-ern Europe, through the analysis of correspondence among illiterate peasants in Hungary. Only 2–3 per cent of the Hungarian peasants could sign documents in the eighteenth century, while there were very few who could read and write during the preceding period. Even local judges and the officials of landlords (such as bailiffs) could hardly read or write. Yet they had to write and answer letters to present petitions to landlords, respond to administrative enquiries, exchange information or feelings between lovers or distant relatives, such as soldiers who had been recruited in the countryside. They did so almost invariably thanks to the help of a third party: schoolmasters, parish priests or pastors, students or merchants. Although illiterate, peasants could forge documents for financial reasons or to cover bigamy, send 'scandalous' love letters, and address political messages to other villages in the context of revolts. As shown by Tóth's extensive examples, delegated writing (and reading) was a major means of communication in daily life, while oral messages were generally used to reinforce or detail written messages.

In terms of a geography of exchange and correspondence these contributions show how various fields of correspondence intensified throughout the fifteenth and sixteenth centuries in western Europe, mainly through the axis Italy–England, which formed the main connection of exchange between southern and northern Europe. This central area of communication expanded throughout the seventeenth and eighteenth centuries encompassing central Europe and the Iberian peninsula.

The different texts in this volume thus present a more complicated geography of the market of information, while confirming that Venice, Rome, Antwerp and Amsterdam were the main centres of production. The geographical extent and expansion of this market and the professional structure of the agents involved have become much more clear. With respect to the input of information, we see how gathering news was a major interest which connected several networks of correspondents, using newsletters from many different origins. The market of information was centred in western Europe and structured by the axis Italy–France–Flanders–England. Yet, it is striking that centres of production (and collecting) of information in Germany, Austria, Switzerland and Iberia became quite important, just like the provincial cities of France and Flanders. In short, the output of information reveals an increasing density of networks in the traditional axis, a slow transfer of centrality from Italy to France and northern Europe, and the widening of professional networks to include central Europe, Spain and Portugal. The contributions in this volume definitely question the differences in status and possibilities of diffusion of manuscript and printed newsletters. They demonstrate the importance (and long life) of manuscript newsletters in the market of information, where they did not only act as sources for the printed sheets but directly shaped public opinion, and had a much more important reception than might have been thought.

Correspondence shows also how European expansion played a crucial role in the self-perception of Europe, because letter writing from, in and to other continents imposed a completely new geography and cartography, helping to reshape nautical science and contributing to the creation of natural history.

However diverse the subjects of these chapters, they demonstrate the importance of correspondence in *all* spheres of social life, including that of the illiterate majority in early modern Europe. Topics that are given new emphasis here are the role of letters in the creation of new scientific and academic fields of knowledge; the importance of manuscript newsletters in the foundation and development of the market of information; the precocious use of vernacular languages in the correspondence of many scholars and scientists; the role of women in some new fields of research, like natural history; the role of letters in the definition of status groups, such as courtiers; the early practice of writing political letters to influence opinion at court and in society; the importance of letters to the diffusion of social models of collectors; and the role of merchants' letters in the creation of cross-cultural and interethnic networks. By drawing new attention to these topics, we hope to make clear that a limitation of the study of correspondence to either the letters of scholarly elites, correspondence as a literary genre, or correspondence purely as a container of information is unwarranted. Writing letters is a cultural and social phenomenon of specifically European dimensions with wide implications for the formation of a plural, competing European cultural identity.

PART I

Networks and markets of information

From merchants' letters to handwritten political avvisi: notes on the origins of public information

Mario Infelise

In the spring of 1497 a Venetian merchant, Girolamo Priuli, noted in his diary that a letter from Damascus, dated 8 March, and one from Alexandria bearing the date of 10 April, had arrived. They bore the news of bloody revolts in both Syria and in Cairo. Priuli further remarked that 'everyone in Venice was thrown into confusion by this news'. There were fears for the safety of the many Venetians living in the area where the revolts had taken place and, more prosaically, there was also concern that the flow of spices would be interrupted.[1] Priuli often mentioned in his diary the merchants, the news and the anxiety that such news could arouse. In this instance, he also noted a significant detail: the means by which this news had travelled.

In the late Middle Ages, information was above all a mercantile asset. A principal means of its circulation was merchants' letters. Growing numbers of couriers and the establishment of commercial colonies at key transit points both in the Mediterranean and in Europe served to speed up the flow of news which was now arriving in a fairly constant stream, if not yet at regular intervals. The network of Italian merchants and traders, usually based either in Genoa or in Venice, ensured that information about matters with potential economic repercussions was always available on a more or less regular basis until the seventeenth century. Many scholars have highlighted the commercial, political and psychological impact of the arrival of news

[1] Girolamo Priuli, *I diarii*, 4 vols. (Città di Castello and Bologna: Lapi and Zanichelli, 1912–39), vol. 1, p. 68.

from the Levant on the Rialto marketplace.[2] In this study I propose
to examine the means by which news travelled and explore the birth
of modern public information.

In a letter from Alexandria, where he had arrived in August 1499,
Girolamo Priuli noted some news brought to Cairo by travellers
arriving from India. They reported that three caravelles, commanded
by Christopher Columbus and sailing under the colours of the King
of Portugal, had arrived in Calicut. Priuli commented: 'this news and
its impact seems to me to be very important, if it is true. However,
I do find it hard to believe.' The route around the Cape of Good
Hope had already been discovered the year before but, as the news
travelled westwards, it had been changed to the point that Vasco
da Gama became Christopher Columbus. However, despite Priuli's
scepticism, there is no doubt that this type of news could very quickly
have profound effects. Two years later, when the news was confirmed
beyond any doubt, it caused far greater consternation in the city than
any military defeat would have done; 'everyone was stupefied . . . and
this news was considered by informed people to be the worst ever
received by the Venetian Republic other than losing its freedom'.[3]

In the final decades of the 1400s, the growing need of diplomatic
envoys for information enhanced newsgathering and contributed to

---

[2] On the repercussions on the market of the arrival of news see, P. Sardella, *Nouvelles
et spéculations à Venise au début du XVIe siècle* (Paris: Colin, 1949). On the circulation
of information from the dawn of time until the early modern era, F. Melis, 'Intensità
e regolarità nella diffusione dell'informazione economica generale nel Mediterraneo
e in Occidente alla fine del Medioevo', in *Mélanges en l'honneur de Fernand Braudel*,
vol. 1: *Histoire économique du monde méditerranéen 1450–1650* (Toulouse: Privat, 1973),
pp. 389–424; H. Kissling, 'Venezia come centro di informazione sui Turchi', in *Venezia
centro di mediazione tra Oriente e Occidente (secoli XV–XVI): aspetti e problemi* (Florence:
Olschki, 1977), pp. 97–109; G. Doria, 'Conoscenza del mercato e sistema informativo:
il know-how dei mercanti-finanzieri genovesi nei secoli XVI e XVII', in A. De Maddalena
and H. Kellenbenz (eds.), *La repubblica internazionale del denaro tra XV e XVII secolo*
(Bologna: Il Mulino, 1986), pp. 57–115; A. Caracciolo Aricò (ed.), *L'impatto della
scoperta dell'America nella cultura veneziana* (Rome: Bulzoni, 1990); P. Burke, 'Early
modern Venice as a centre of information and communication', in J. Martin and D.
Romano (eds.), *Venice Reconsidered: The History and Civilization of an Italian City–
State 1297–1797* (Baltimore and London: The Johns Hopkins University Press, 2000),
pp. 389–419.

[3] Priuli, *I diarii*, vol. 1, p. 153; vol. 2, p. 156. G. Lucchetta, 'L'Oriente mediterraneo
nella cultura di Venezia tra Quattro e Cinquecento', in *Storia della cultura veneta*,
6 vols. (Vicenza: Neri Pozza, 1976–86), vol. 3, pp. 411–12.

speeding up the flow of news. In those years a stable network of ambassadors worked at various courts in both Italy and transalpine Europe, increasing demand for a regular supply of information useful to them. Until then, it had always been merchants who had sought and circulated news; now, with permanent diplomatic relations established between states, both the type and scale of news sought changed. As the 'eyes and ears' of princes, ambassadors tended to report only what they had observed directly – indeed the earliest diplomatic dispatches mainly contain first-person accounts of meetings and negotiations. But their range of observation soon broadened. In his dispatches to the Venetian senate, sent from the court of King Ferrante of Aragon, Zaccaria Barbaro, the Venetian ambassador to Naples from 1471 to 1473, recounted what he personally saw and heard. Yet, from time to time he also referred to, or enclosed, other material, even though he clearly considered it to be less reliable. In fact he extracted news (or better, *nove*) from letters arriving in Naples from abroad, sending it almost from a sense of duty to report everything, while at the same time exhorting the Venetian authorities to verify this news through more reliable sources before believing it or acting upon it. His news usually came from 'merchants' letters' (*lettere de merchadanti*), often Genoese, dealing mostly with such matters as movements of Turkish galleys in the Aegean Sea, dangerous epidemics in Constantinople, or pirate activities at Zara and Segna. Sometimes he enclosed extracts from these letters, and sent copies to the Venetian ambassador in Rome to check the veracity of his news there too.[4] In a situation of increasing interest in any event with potential political or economic significance, it is hardly surprising that merchants, many with long experience and an established network of contacts, were quick to exploit their advantage in areas outside trade by using their abilities to gather reliable information and analyse the way events were evolving. The great Florentine traveller Benedetto Dei was known as the 'trumpet of truth' and proved a subtle, yet reliable, informant and consultant to both princes and cardinals.[5]

---

[4] Zaccaria Barbaro, *Dispacci: 1 novembre 1471–7 settembre 1473*, ed. G. Corazzol (Rome: Istituto Poligrafico dello Stato, 1994).

[5] R. Balducci, 'Dei, Benedetto', in *Dizionario Biografico degli Italiani* (Rome: Istituto dell'Enciclopedia Italiana, 1961–), vol. 36 (1988), pp. 252–3.

The merchants' *avvisi*, which formed the basis of the unusual diary kept by the merchant Girolamo Priuli, also appear in the even more remarkable diary kept by another Venetian patrician, Marino Sanudo, an astute daily observer of the republic's political life.[6] Each day the contents of private letters, sent by a great number of men involved in commercial activities throughout the Mediterranean, were mixed with the news contained in official dispatches sent to the organs of Venetian government or Venetian magistrates by an equally large network of ambassadors, envoys, residents, consuls and secretaries, and by *provveditori* of the Venetian fleet which was stationed in the most important ports and towns. One has only to leaf through the pages of Sanudo's diary in order to feel the palpable urgency in the seething turmoil of news flooding into Venice from all over Europe and the Mediterranean in the late fifteenth and early sixteenth centuries. Indeed, in this period, Venice was the main European centre for news, which flowed into the lagoon city from both East and West. Politicians were even more careful than merchants both in checking the reliability of their sources and in keeping their news up to date. They checked each item of information; they meticulously recorded, with almost manic precision, its origin, as well as the dates of sending and receiving news, in the belief that these were crucial elements for assessing both the quality and the reliability of their information:

9 August 1499, 2 o'clock [noted the Venetian patrician Marino Sanudo in the item] By letter of the magnificent Signor Domenego Malipiero superintendent of the armed forces of Lepanto, on the fifth of this month, who has discovered from a letter sent by the brother of a citizen of Lepanto who was in Adrianopoli by 25 June and states that the Turks left there on the 24th and arrived in Frisopuli on the 27th and there had the ambassador of the King of Naples imprisoned and ordered the release of all Christians detained for debt, and that the Turkish army was to leave on the 24th from Gallipoli and to sail towards Negroponte and that it planned to go to Apulia.[7]

---

[6] Marin Sanudo, *I diarii*, 58 vols. (Venice: Visentini, 1879–1903).

[7] 'Per lettere dil magnifico misier Domenego Malipiero provedador di l'armata da Lepanto de dì 5 dil presente, per le qual se intese: come per una lettera de uno fratello de uno citadin da Lepanto che se atrovava in Andrianopoli fata di 25 zugno, aferma come il Turcho partì a dì 24 ditto, et arivò a Frisopuli a dì 27 lontan dal ditto et lì fe

Sanudo's diary spans forty years of history, but any entry, chosen at random, reveals the speed at which news and information travelled. On 2 November 1519, letters arrived from the ambassadors at Rome and Naples and from Francesco Corner in Barcelona, from the captain of galleys anchored in Trapani and from the *provveditori* of the army of Corfu. Furthermore, the letters from Trapani referred, in turn, to messages from Palermo and Messina. Private letters from Francesco Corner to his brothers came on the same day. The next day, letters from ambassadors in France, Spain and Milan arrived. On 4 November letters came from the *bailo* in Constantinople: these dispatches were immediately read aloud in the senate. On 7 November, letters arrived from various rectors in Dalmatia and, on the next day from Verona as well. Also that same day, messages came in from Istria containing news of the Levant, while further news arrived from Milan, France and Verona. On 10 November, dispatches were delivered from Hungary, France and Milan and two days afterwards, from Dalmatia, Rome and Verona. Further letters arrived from Rome on 15 November, along with correspondence from Aleppo via Rome.[8]

It is worthwhile to consider the manner in which the contents of official dispatches intertwined with facts recounted in private letters. Even when they dealt with the same events, the two types of missive often did not give the same information. Thus private accounts could add further details and offer different perspectives from people who could testify about some event, but who did not have to report on it formally. Furthermore, cross-reference was common. Each letter or dispatch invariably mentioned other letters or dispatches. The captain of the fleet in Trapani referred to a letter he had received from 'Barbary', while messages from Constantinople referred, in turn, to other messages that had come from Syria and Aleppo.

Naturally, Venice also re-exported news which was considered reliable at an international level. The first account of the battle of Pavia

---

poner lo ambasador del re di Napoli in prexon, et de quelli castelli faceva trar fuora tutti li cristiani per dubito et che l'armata dovea partir a dì ditto 24 da Gallipoli et andar verso Negroponte, et che aferma voer andar in Puja.' Sanudo, *Diarii*, vol. 2, col. 1056.

[8] Sanudo, *Diarii*, vol. 28, coll. 47–70.

(25 February 1525), during which King Francis I of France had been captured by Emperor Charles V, already reached Constantinople on 26 March. But the *bassà*, not trusting the source, did not pass the news on to the sultan. However, three days later confirmation came in a ducal letter addressed to the *bailo* Bragadin and the sultan was immediately informed because, as the *bailo* wrote, 'the *bassà* believes news from Venice but not from elsewhere'.

Despite the meticulous care with which Sanudo noted the sources of each item of news, at times he remained ambiguous. He mentioned generic *avvisi* or *reporti* and sometimes added that they had come from unknown authors. The omission, whether intentional or not, of the name of the original author or source marks an important moment in the development of a more modern news and information network. It indicates the transformation of the private letter into an anonymous *avviso*, written deliberately for a general, anonymous, public. Naturally this process was gradual. In the sixteenth century, a number of newssheets were in circulation: replicas of private letters, signed *avvisi* (newssheets bearing the author's name) and anonymous *avvisi*. Over time, the author's name was increasingly omitted, especially when the *avviso* underwent multiple copies. The authors themselves, who were gradually becoming professionals in the field of information, also stopped signing what they had written – partly out of caution.

This transformation played an important role in the development of the handwritten political *avviso* as a means used specifically to communicate political and military information. As we have seen, in their private letters, travellers and diplomats tended to mix personal news with information of interest to a wider audience. Some authors then began to extract news worthy of wider interest from private or merchants' letters and write it separately. Zaccaria Barbaro told the senate about news that he had taken from merchants' letters and had enclosed with his dispatches both to Venice and to the ambassador in Rome. The process of selecting interesting passages and copying them onto other sheets of paper forms the basis of the development of the *avviso*, which remained the primary vehicle of news communication until the end of the eighteenth century. The origins of the *avviso* can, however, be traced back to the late fifteenth century. Particularly informative parts of letters were increasingly excerpted and incorporated into the *avviso* with other excerpts of the same nature. Occasionally, an entire letter would be copied, including the name of the sender. The result was a text made up of short informative chapters, giving news that was considered of general interest but which was not destined for any particular person or group. Between 1470 and 1480, Benedetto Dei, who maintained a complex network of epistolary relations with many diplomats and courtiers, also sent short informative notes to his correspondents, quite similar in style and form to those later used in *avvisi*. For example, in 1478, Dei wrote, in his characteristic Tuscan vernacular prose which was as elementary as it was effective:[9]

I have news from Pistoia from 15 December until 9 January 1478

I have news from Genoa that the Doge has knighted Batistino and sent away the [families of] Adorni and Raonesi

I have news from Lyon, the trade fair has been very very good; a lot of textiles have been sold and a good deal of money gained too

I have news from France that nine ambassadors are coming to Italy with 200 horses to make peace for everyone.

These four news items, selected at random from the almost fifty mentioned in Dei's manuscript, offer information from the main Italian cities as well as news from beyond the Alps, in this case, France. Dei already realised the importance of the role he was playing, and boasted to his correspondents about his ability to send regularly, every Saturday, 'the news from Asia and from Africa and from Europe always'. Those who received his news repaid him with their own news as well as reports about the utility of his notes even outside the close circle of his own correspondents. In 1490, Pandolfo della Stufa wrote to Dei

---

[9] 'Ho nuove aute in Pistoia da 15 di dicenbre 1478 insino a dì 9 di giennaio 1478/Ho nuove di Gienova el dogie fatto messer Batistino e chaciato via di certto gl adornj e raonesi el signor Ruberto/Ho nuove da Lyone la fiera d ora è stata buonissima averassi ispaciato assai drappi e presi assay di denari/Ho nuove di Francia chome venggono 9 anbasciadori in Italia chon 200 chavaglj per mettere pacie per tutto.' C. Marzi, 'Degli antecessori dei giornali', *Rivista delle biblioteche e degli archivi* 24 (1913), 181–5; P. Orvieto, 'Un esperto orientalista del '400: Benedetto Dei', *Rinascimento* 20 (1969), 205–75.

from Cortona to tell him that as soon as his letters arrived, they were immediately reproduced in numerous copies.

Over the next few decades the layout of the *avvisi* was gradually being perfected. Sometimes the news was introduced by headlines, which would also state the origins of each item: for example, 'copy of letters', 'excerpted passages from letters', 'summary of an *avviso*' or simply 'summary of news'. Indeed, *avvisi* were beginning to take on an entirely different aspect from that of a real letter. By the early sixteenth century, headlines such as 'News from the field, 15 March 1514' or 'News from Venice, 30 March 1514' or even 'In a letter of 13 April 1546 from Constantinople' could be found.[10] The news itself began to be presented in a form that would be adopted for several decades: one or more sheets with news organised according to the place where it had been collected rather than where the event reported had in fact taken place. For example, under the dateline Rome, the reader would find all the news coming from Rome, even when it referred to events that had taken place in other, often distant places such as Poland or Bosnia. Thus readers could follow news gathered in Milan, France or Constantinople. This way of cataloguing, of organising, news reporting would not change for centuries. It bears witness to the fact that the material gathered was rarely revised before being recopied, and that, furthermore, there was a need to offer some indication about whether an item of news sent from a place like Constantinople had arrived directly or through intermediary channels.

The places where news was gathered were key points, hubs, of Europe's fledgling postal system. Obviously, there were close connections between the activities of ordinary couriers and the spread of information, which can be clearly seen in the headlines of many daily newssheets. During the first half of the sixteenth century, the postal network improved radically and, despite being very expensive, the postal service began to be seen as a public service which could be used by anyone. A network of postal routes that covered the whole of continental Europe was established, regular collection and delivery

---

[10] The examples given here are all from the series of *avvisi* held in the Archivio di Stato di Modena, *Cancelleria ducale, avvisi e notizie dall'estero*, bb. 1–3, which has one series from 1393, and others dated back to the early fifteenth century.

times began to be fixed, and the time for a letter to travel from one place to another became relatively constant. Usually, a letter sent from Rome reached Venice in four or five days, Milan in eight, Vienna in twelve to fifteen days, while Paris required as much as twenty days. The main postal routes began to offer regular weekly or twice-weekly services, which followed a fixed, published timetable and which ultimately dictated the rhythm and speed of communication.[11] *Avvisi* began to be copied or written in conjunction with the schedule of postal service collections and deliveries; consequently, they began to be produced on a more regular basis. Partly for this reason, news began to lose the casual, occasional nature it had when it was merely a by-product of a normal correspondence carried on for other reasons.

Such developments suggest that a true 'market' for news had developed during the mid sixteenth century, which, in turn, led to the creation of a specific professional figure, able to meet the growing demand for information. A bull issued by Pius V in 1568 defined compiling newssheets as a 'new art', leaving one to suppose that a new profession was emerging. Three years later, in Venice, one of the first documents attempting to regulate newsgathering and publishing activities offered a brief description of this new occupation. A decree published on 8 February 1572 began by asserting that 'there are many people in this city who have made writing news their profession, they are paid by various people who have scribal desks, houses and writers for this purpose'.[12] A number of Germans and Flemings were engaged in compiling *avvisi*, which were then sent all over Europe. Among these early professionals, one Flemish writer, Nicolas de Stoop (Stopio/Stopius), who was active between 1558 and 1563, stands out. De Stoop was a man of letters, particularly interested in geography,

---

[11] For mid-sixteenth-century postal service regulations see J. Delumeau, *Vie économique et sociale de Rome dans la seconde moitié du* XVIe *siècle* (Paris: De Boccard, 1957), pp. 37–53; C. Fedele and M. Gallenga, *'Per servizio di nostro signore': strade, corrieri e poste dei papi dal medioevo al 1870* (Prato: Istituto di Storia Postale, 1988); B. Caizzi, *Dalla posta del re alla posta di tutti: territorio e comunicazioni in Italia dal* XVI *secolo all'Unità* (Milan: Angeli, 1993).

[12] Archivio di Stato di Venezia, *Consiglio dei X, parti comuni*, reg. 30, f. 86v, published in S. Romanin, *Storia documentata di Venezia*, 10 vols. (Venice: Filippi, 1972–5, 3rd edition), vol. 6, pp. 94–5.

who collaborated with Venetian printers. He usually sent detailed newssheets containing information either gathered from sources in Rome or written by himself on the basis of information supplied by people with access to the Venetian chancellery and who attended the public readings of dispatches sent from abroad.[13] Such 'professional' newsgatherers were called *menanti* in Rome, *reportisti* in Venice and *novellari* in Genoa. Later, they came to be called *gazzettieri*. While many *gazzettieri* limited themselves to passively copying newssheets compiled by others, the better-organised and more enterprising among them set up authentic news agencies in the modern sense of the word. They received correspondence and other *avvisi* from abroad through the postal service and added in local news, which had been gathered more or less legally – often by frequenting circles of powerful people or by eavesdropping on any gossip that was circulating. They would edit this material to produce a regular newssheet in addition to other writings, which were then sent off to their customers. In fact, these gazzettieri were able to offer their customers a variety of different services, subject to different rates and charges. For example, they offered Italian and foreign newssheets, public *avvisi* with accounts of well-known events, or secret *avvisi* with reserved information. Many of these writers also had a repertory of political or satirical tracts, already prepared or which could be produced to order, and some of them even produced a catalogue of available works with current prices.[14]

---

[13] *Avvisi* signed by Niccolò Stopio are in the Biblioteca Apostolica Vaticana, *Urb. Lat.* 1038–9. Copies of others can also be found in the same Biblioteca Apostolica Vaticana, V*at. Lat.* 8223. A biographical note can be found under item 'N. De Stoop' by J. Roulez in *Biographie nationale publiée par l'Académie Royale des sciences, des lettres et des beaux-arts de Belgique* (Brussels: 1866–1986), vol. 5 (1876), p. 810.

[14] On the profession of *gazzettiere*, especially in the seventeenth century, see my publications: *Prima dei giornali: alle origini della pubblica informazione (secoli XVI–XVII)* (Bari and Rome: Laterza, 2002); 'Le marché des informations à Venise au XVIIe siècle', in H. Duranton and P. Rétat (eds.), *Gazettes et information politique sous l'Ancien Régime* (Saint-Etienne: Université de Saint-Etienne, 1999), pp. 117–28; 'The war, the news and the curious: military gazettes in Italy', in B. Dooley and S. Baron (eds.), *The Politics of Information in Early Modern Europe* (London and New York: Routledge, 2001), pp. 216–36; 'Roman *avvisi*: information and politics

The main clients of the *gazzettieri* were princes and ambassadors. As we have mentioned, by the late fifteenth century, the establishment of a stable diplomatic network of embassies in various courts both in Italy and northern Europe did much to encourage the production of written, informative accounts of events and other news: courts and embassies were also strategic places where news was both made and gathered. Diplomats and their entourages became the stars of the news market, either because they had access to state secrets or because they were ardent gatherers and purveyors of any item of information they judged might interest their rulers. They found the newssheets produced by the *menanti* extremely useful for their information-gathering activities and many allusions to different ways in which the diverse chancelleries used such sheets can be found in their preserved official correspondence from this period. One of the main duties of accredited ambassadors was to compile and edit a periodical dispatch. Increasingly, these ambassadors began to complement their comments and information with news gleaned from other sources, even though they always remained careful to distinguish between news they had personally gathered and checked from that which they had not verified in person. Thus many of them began to rely on *avvisi* when drawing up their dispatches, despite the care they exercised when relaying news from such sources. Ambassadors usually enclosed the *avvisi* sheets, to which they were referring, with the dispatch they had written themselves. They obviously felt it was important to keep the two types of communication separate; as the Spanish diplomat Juan Antonio de Vera advised in a well-known tract, it was indispensable that an official dispatch not be considered in the same terms as 'a gazette from Rome or Germany'.[15] However, not all diplomats thought this way. Venetian diplomats tended to mix together all their information from whatever source in their regular diplomatic correspondence, so as to offer a single version of events, yet one that resulted from a critical selection

---

in the seventeenth century', in G. Signorotto and M. A. Visceglia (eds.), *Court and Politics in Papal Rome 1492–1700* (Cambridge: Cambridge University Press, 2002), pp. 212–28.
[15] Juan Antonio de Vera y Figueroa, *Le parfait ambassadeur* (Paris, 1642), p. 476.

of all the news they had received. Indeed, it would have been hard for any ambassador not to use the news acquired through third-party sources. This explains why, from the mid sixteenth century onwards, the links between professional *avvisi* writers and the world of diplomacy grew stronger and closer, until they became almost inseparable. In the case of minor courts, which rarely had their own representatives in foreign capitals, those in power satisfied their need for reliable and up-to-date news by taking out what was almost a yearly subscription with accredited *avvisi* writers in Rome and Venice. In some cases, for example with the republic of Lucca and the duchy of Modena, writers of *avvisi* or similar persons ended up fulfilling the functions of agents, taking on semi-official duties.

However, the sixteenth-century origins of this fully developed system of disseminating news were soon forgotten. The glaring lack of technological innovation and the fact that, despite the Gutenberg revolution, such missives were still handwritten probably impeded people from tracing back the origins of the fast-developing news network and its innovative nature. In 1623, Secondo Lancellotti from Perugia wrote a book which sought to demonstrate that the present was far superior to the past. He argued that the 'genial idea of sending *avvisi* about the successes especially of princes from all over the world, and of thus knowing what is happening in Rome, in France, in Spain, in Germany and elsewhere without spending a halfpenny', was one of the positive elements of modernity. He did, however, admit that he did not know when this system had been invented and merely noted that the collection of *avvisi* in the possession of the Duke of Urbino dated back about seventy years.[16] Ideas about the origins of *avvisi* became even more confused over the next few decades when, just as printed sheets were becoming increasingly common, the historical and etymological origins of the term *gazzetta* began to be studied. By the late sixteenth century the term *gazzetta* had begun to appear in many European languages, as it was considered the only term that truly represented that product. A series of theories about the origins of the word, some

---

[16] Secondo Lancellotti, *L'hoggidì, overo gl'ingegni non inferiori a' passati*, 2 vols. (Venice: Valvasense, 1681; 1st edition: 1623), vol. 2, p. 352.

of which have lasted long enough to be included in the most recent dictionaries of the main European languages, were suggested. In 1676, Ottavio Ferrari, an etymologist from Padua, stated that *gazzetta* was the name of a Venetian coin and that this name had subsequently been adopted to describe the newssheets. A few years later a Frenchman, Gilles Ménage, took up this definition, adding a dubious rider 'that he had often heard said by a gentleman that these sheets had taken the name of this coin because in the past this had been the price demanded from those who bought gazettes'.[17] As time went on, any doubts there may have been about the veracity of this explanation vanished; no one thought it worthwhile to check the accuracy of the 'gentleman's' statement. The main European dictionaries of the eighteenth century adopted the definitions put forward by Ferrari and Ménage. Neither the *Dictionnaire de Trévoux* (French) nor dictionary compilers like Ephraim Chambers and Samuel Johnson (England) ever questioned this explanation. Voltaire even used it in the entry on '*Gazette*' in the *Encyclopédie*. All these great reference works offered a short historical sketch of the concept, mentioning both the etymology and the origins of the word. Voltaire said: 'it was at the beginning of the seventeenth century that this useful custom was invented at Venice, at a time when Italy was still the centre of negotiations in Europe and Venice was still an asylum of liberty'. All attributed the origins of the word to Venice, and basing himself on previously published dictionaries, Voltaire too stated that the word *gazzetta* refers to a low-value Venetian coin, which was what each newssheet used to cost.[18]

Indeed, no one seemed to nurture any further doubts regarding the origins and etymology of the word. The same hypothesis about the origins of the word continued to appear, apparently unchallenged, in all eighteenth-century publications which offered an outline history of the *gazzetta*. Such historical notes usually formed part of an

[17] Ottavio Ferrari, *Origines linguae italicae* (Padua: Frambotto, 1676), p. 156; Egidio Menagio, *Le origini della lingua italiana* (Geneva: Chouët, 1685), p. 247.

[18] 'Ce fut au commencement du xviie siècle que cet usage utile fut inventé à Venise, dans les tems que l'Italie étoit encore le centre des négociations de l'Europe et que Venise étoit toujours l'asyle de la liberté', *Encyclopédie ou dictionnaire raisonné des sciences des arts et des métiers* (Paris: 1751–72), vol. 7 (1767), p. 534.

introductory article written for a new newspaper, for example articles by Scipione Maffei (1710), Gasparo Gozzi (1760) and Antonio Piazza (1787),[19] giving further credit to an idea that has been passed down until now and still appears in the most recent Italian, French and English etymological dictionaries.[20] In some cases the already-traditional explanation of the origins of the term has been adorned by other and even more audacious hypotheses: for instance, the idea that *gazzetta* derives from *gazza* (literally 'magpie' but in slang 'prattler, gossip'); or from the Hebrew *hiš-gad*, which corresponds to the Latin *nuntius*; from medieval Latin *gazetum* which means 'archive, encyclopedia'; or, lastly, from a corruption of the German word *Zeitung*.[21]

Without presuming to resolve the question definitively, one can at least discover how the term has been used over the years. Leaving aside the often imperceptible nuances of the Italian language it would seem that in the period between the sixteenth and the early eighteenth centuries the terms *avviso* and *reporto* were used interchangeably, almost as synonyms to mean a written/printed sheet containing information about current events. During the sixteenth century the term *avviso* was the most commonly used form. In this case, however, the same

---

[19] Scipione Maffei, 'Introduzione', *Giornale de' letterati d'Italia* 1 (1710), 13–16; Gasparo Gozzi, 'Lettera capitata allo stampatore signor Marcuzzi', *Gazzetta veneta* 1 (6 February 1760); Antonio Piazza, 'Parole di chi scrive questo foglio a chi legge', *Gazzetta urbana veneta* 1 (2 June 1787). The articles by Maffei and Piazza have been republished in M. Berengo (ed.), *I giornali veneziani del '700* (Milan: Feltrinelli, 1962), pp. 3–15, 583–5. The article by Gozzi can be found in a reprinted edition of the *Gazzetta veneta*, ed. A. Zardo (Florence: Sansoni, 1915), pp. 5–7. One should add to this classic early reconstruction of journalism the anonymous 'Istoria delle gazzette', published in the almanac *Annuale veneto istruttivo . . . per l'anno 1786* (Venice: Torre, 1786), pp. 174–9, in which the history of journalism in Venice is linked to parallel French and German developments in the field, now republished in G. Pizzamiglio (ed.), *Foglio in cui certamente qualche cosa è stampata* (Venice: Marsilio, 2002), pp. 67–76.

[20] The Italian origins of the term are also mentioned in P. Robert, *Dictionnaire alphabétique et analogique de la langue française*, 9 vols. (Paris: Le Robert, 1987), vol. 4, p. 854, and in *The Oxford English Dictionary*, 20 vols. (Oxford: Clarendon Press, 1989), vol. 6, p. 412.

[21] S. Bongi, 'Le prime gazzette in Italia', *Nuova Antologia* 11 (1869), 314; G. Gaeta, *Storia del giornalismo* (Milan: Vallardi, 1966), 87–9; U. Bellocchi, *Storia del giornalismo italiano*, 6 vols. (Bologna: Edizioni Edison, 1974), vol. 1, p. 87.

term was used indiscriminately both with its generic meaning and specifically to mean the newssheets themselves, a fact which makes it very difficult to accurately determine when and how the genre really developed. It is almost impossible to know whether in the early 1500s, when Marin Sanudo was writing about *avvisi* that arrived in Venice from all over the Mediterranean, he was referring to news sent as part of normal correspondence or to specialised newssheets, which only contained specific types of information. In both the *Arte della guerra* and in *Storie fiorentine*, Machiavelli used the term *avvisi* in its generic sense, as did Guicciardini in his *Storia d'Italia*. Only Pietro Aretino, in the *Dialogo della Nanna e della Pippa* (1536), seems to be using the term in its specific sense when he refers to *Avvisi di Spagna, di Francia e della Magna*.[22] Sanudo used the term *reporto* (variations being *riporto* and, rarely *rapporto*) in the same manner. This term was widely used in Venice until the eighteenth century to mean a bulletin containing a single item of information.

The word *gazzetta* came into widespread use only later. It is true that after 1539 there was a low-value coin in circulation both in Venice and later in the Levant, and that after 1550 this coin was referred to as a *gazzetta* in official documents.[23] It is, however, difficult to make any connection between this coin and the newssheet, especially because the earliest reliable references to the use of this term in connection with newsletters appeared much later and not in documents of Venetian origin. The first time it was clearly used with this connotation was in 1568, when *gazeta* appeared in a poem written and printed in Savoyard dialect entitled *La gazeta de la guerra de zay, zay su zay, zay la vella et zay la Comba*.[24] In Italy, the term began to be adopted more and more frequently after 1577. In that year a Florentine philologist, Vincenzo Borghini, began using the term in his private correspondence[25] and, thereafter, it began to appear increasingly often. The Tuscan poet Giovan Maria Cecchi considered it 'a wicked witch, that goes around

---

[22] Pietro Aretino, *Dialogo Ragionamento* (Milan: Garzanti 1984).

[23] N. Papadopoli Aldobrandini, *Le monete di Venezia*, 4 vols. (Venice: Emiliana, 1893–1919), vols. 2–3 *ad indices*.

[24] This newssheet, lacking a frontispiece, is found in the British Library: T 1589.

[25] *Prose fiorentine*, 4 vols. (Florence: Stamperia granducale, 1745), vol. 4, p. 319.

chattering on and on, and disrespectfully deceives all'.[26] In the same period, the term also appeared in some Roman newssheets, in the dispatches of Venetian ambassadors and in Florentine documents which contain references to *avvisi* sent from Venice.[27]

But not until the following century did the term really come into its own in both French and Italian.[28] In 1602, Tommaso Costo wrote about *avvisi*, which he said are commonly called '*gazzette*'.[29] In 1609, a short poem about a gazette was published in Rouen, in which the anonymous author referred to the characteristics and the functions of these publications. It described the various groups like magistrates, prelates and other office-holders who were the target public of the newssheets and underlined the rapidity with which the gazettes were able to gather information on various aspects of life and present them to this public, satisfying everybody's curiosity.[30]

Over time, the term *gazzetta* – or, more usually *gazzette*, its plural form – began appearing more and more frequently. Paolo Sarpi often used it in his letters around 1609–11, Michelangelo Buonarroti

---

[26] 'La gazzetta è la mala strega / che va ciaramelando tanto tanto, / e che senza rispetto a ognun la frega'. G. M. Cecchi, *Poesie pubblicate per la prima volta da Michele dello Russo* (Naples, 1866). See the item *Gazzetta* in S. Battaglia, *Grande dizionario della lingua italiana*, 21 vols. (Turin: Utet, 1961–2002), vol. 6, p. 624.

[27] Biblioteca Nazionale Centrale di Firenze, Fondo Magliabechi, cl. XXIV, cod. 16, Rome 17 December 1588, also quoted in E. Stumpo (ed.), *La gazzetta de l'anno 1588* (Florence: Giunti, 1988), p. 171; Archivio di Stato di Venezia, *Inquisitori di Stato*, b. 488, 21 July 1586: 'reporti della gazetta'; Archivio di Stato di Firenze, *Mediceo del Principato*, 2940, references to the 'gazzetta di Venezia' in a letter from Marcello Donati to Pietro Usimbardi, 19 March 1588.

[28] L. Trenard, 'La presse française des origines à 1788', in C. Bellanger, J. Godechot, P. Guiral and F. Terrou (eds.), *Histoire générale de la presse française*, 3 vols. (Paris: Presses Universitaires de France, 1969–72), vol. 1, pp. 86–7.

[29] Tommaso Costo, *Lettere* (Venice: Barezzi, 1602).

[30] 'La gazette en ces vers / contente les cervelles / car de tout l'universe / elle reçoit nouvelles... / Gazette aymée des prélats, / des princes et des magistrats: / gazette en vogue incomparable / gazette en science admirable: / Car rien ne se fait, ne se dit, / rien ne va, ne vient par escrit, / en poste, en relaiz, en mazette, / qui ne passe par la gazette... / La gazette a mille courriers, / qui logent par-tout sans fouriers, / et faut que chacun luy responde, / selon sa course vagabonde, / De ça de là diversement / De l'Orient, en Occident, / et de toutes pars de la sphère, / sans laisser une seule affaire, / soit edicts, des commissions.' L. Loviot (ed.), *La Gazette de 1609* (Paris: Fontemoing, 1914).

the Younger in 1611, as well as Boccalini and Della Porta in 1612.[31] Giambattista Marino used the term *gazetier* in 1618.[32] However, it is still not clear what the word *gazzetta* signified precisely, or whether it really was from the outset a true synonym for an *avviso*. Based on what little evidence exists about the ways in which the term was actually employed, it would seem that at least until the early seventeenth century the two words were not always synonymous. While *avviso* was used, technically, only to mean a newssheet that was published regularly, a *gazzetta* could also mean any article about vaguely newsworthy themes, but which did not necessarily appear at regular intervals. This is true not only for the Savoyard *gazzetta* of 1568, but also for other publications. For example, the *Gazette des estats et de ce temps*, printed and published in France in 1614 and presented as a translation from the Italian, was not a periodical but rather a pamphlet dealing with such important contemporary questions as France's possible adoption of the Tridentine decrees.[33] Overall, one gets the impression that the term *gazzetta* was more colloquial, a part of spoken rather than written language. Indeed, it took a long time for the term to appear in any official dictionary; for example, Agostino Mascardi reiterated the concept already used by Tommaso Costo, '*avvisi* or should we use the more vernacular term *gazzetta*'.[34]

Thus it is not surprising that the only sixteenth-century dictionary that actually contained the word and its derivations was the Italian–English *A Worlde of Wordes* (1598) by John Florio, the son of an exiled Protestant from Florence, who translated both Bruno and Montaigne

---

[31] Paolo Sarpi mentioned the *gazzette* or the 'writers of gazzettes' (*scrittori delle gazzette*) in his letters to Jérôme Groslot de l'Isle of 22 December 1609 and 5 July 1611: P. Sarpi, *Lettere italiane . . . al signor dell'Isola Groslot* (Verona, 1673), pp. 182, 372; Buonarroti in the *Fiera* (day 3, act 5, scene 4, 1611); Boccalini used the term quite often in *Ragguagli di Parnaso* (Venice: Farri, 1612); in *Tabernaria*, Giambattista Della Porta wrote 'he will write for the gazzettes' (*scriverà per le gazzette)*: G. B. Della Porta, *Le commedie*, ed. V. Spampanato, 2 vols. (Bari: Laterza, 1910–11), vol. 1, p. 352.

[32] Giambattista Marino, *La galeria* (Venice: Ciotti, 1618).

[33] *Gazette des estats & de ce temps. Du Seigneur servitour de Piera Grosa gio: Traduite d'Italien en François le premier janvier 1614.*

[34] Agostino Mascardi, *Dell'arte istorica* (Florence: Le Monnier, 1859; 1st edition: Rome: Facciotti, 1636), p. 225.

into English and was much more aware of the spoken language and of the words that came from dialect than of those that were part of formal, learned Italian. Florio offered a brief but precise definition of the plural form of the word *gazzette*: 'the daily newes or intelligence written from Italie, tales, running newes'. The as yet ill-defined relation between espionage and information was explicitly mentioned as was the Italian origin of the term. Substantially the same meaning was attributed to the term *gazzettiere* ('an intelligencer or such as have daily occurrences'), while the singular form of the word *gazzetta* was given as either the Venetian coin or a young magpie. The fact that Florio was well aware of how the meaning of words may evolve is clear from the way in which he added a further detail to the entry *gazzette* in the second edition of his dictionary, which was published in 1611. The addition ran: 'flim-flam tales that are daily written from Italie, namely from Rome and Venice'.[35]

It is likely that because the term was considered very colloquial and not academic, it did not appear in any other dictionary of the time. It cannot be found even in the main monolingual dictionaries published in the early seventeenth century: for instance, it does not appear in *Thrésor de la langue française* by Jean Nicot (1608) nor in the first two editions of the *Vocabolario degli Accademici della Crusca* (1612 and 1623). In the third edition (1691), the entry *gazzetta* finally appears, where it is defined as a '*Foglio d'avvisi*' with the already-customary explanation that the name was derived from 'a certain type of coin which was used to buy *avvisi*. A few years later, in 1703, under the entry '*avviso*' in the *Biblioteca universale sacro-profana*, Vincenzo Coronelli explained, '*avvisi* – the gazettes or public news about the affairs of princes, wars, and other notable events, that take place in diverse parts of the world'. The reader was referred to the entry '*Gazzetta*', which however did not exist, perhaps a victim of the vicissitudes of producing a dictionary.[36]

---

[35] John Florio, *A Worlde of Wordes* (London: Blount, 1598), p. 145; John Florio, *Queen Anna's New World of Words or Dictionarie of the Italian and English Tongues* (London: Bradwood, 1611). About the dictionary of John Florio see F. A. Yates, *John Florio: The Life of an Italian in Shakespeare's England* (Cambridge: Cambridge University Press, 1934), pp. 188–212.

[36] Vincenzo Coronelli, *Biblioteca universale sacro-profana antico-moderna*, 8 vols. (Venice: Tivani, 1703), vol. 4, col. 1703.

Basically, the way in which these terms developed reflects the evolution of the documents themselves. One can clearly state that the sixteenth century was the age in which the *avviso* underwent its most significant transformation. It evolved from a generic, not necessarily substantiated, report on a fact or an event, into a well-defined product designed to satisfy the growing demand for specific information that was emerging in certain circles in the more important political and commercial centres of the time. This growing demand for news hastened the development of a market for news and information that could be supplied on a regular basis for more general consumption, no longer reserved for specific consumers. Even though a gazette was still handwritten, it was an *avviso*, capable of enlarging its sphere of readers and arousing interest in political events in the new conditions of the time. It is worth emphasising that these publications were beginning to appear on a regular basis and that this, in itself, created a certain degree of dependence between the means of information and its readers. While it is taken for granted that major political or military events will excite widespread but sporadic interest,[37] the fact that news was offered at regular increments ended up creating a degree of familiarity and interest in ongoing political events, both local and distant, regardless of whether or not they were particularly important. Thus, news from around the world became a part of many people's daily lives. Reading such news reduced distances and offered a means through which both interests and discussion could be broadened. Political events, like religious and military events, became subjects of discussions that evolved as an aspect of socialising with others, offering a chance to compare and contrast ideas, or to argue and disagree.

As news emerged from the corridors of power and became part and parcel of everyday life, it began to affect more evolved urban strata. A series of lively verses, written about 1550 in Rome by the poet Mattio Franzesi, offer a clear idea both of what the desire for information meant then and of how the consequences of this increased access to news were experienced.[38] Franzesi described the anxiety one felt waiting for the courier and the way in which news passed on orally

[37] Cf. the contribution by Barbarics and Pieper to the present volume.

[38] Mattio Franzesi, 'Capitolo sopra le nuove a M. Benedetto Busini', in Francesco Berni, *Il secondo libro delle opere burlesche* (Florence: Giunti, 1555), pp. 58–9.

by the courier would accompany the written news which was eagerly extracted from every letter as soon as it was delivered. The feverish search for information infected everyone, even the lowest and least-educated citizens. News was passed on by word of mouth and everyone became familiar with the main events and personalities involved in the political scene. Truth and lies got mixed up and could no longer be separated. The uncertainty this inevitably created encouraged many people to seek for confirmation elsewhere, in the traditional places where news could be found: among merchants, ambassadors and cardinals. Even though, as the poet Franzesi concluded somewhat moralistically, the news was 'something that concerns ambassadors, great statesmen and governments and not really suitable for lesser citizens',[39] a situation was already forming wherein the relationship between the public and political news was beginning to affect the behaviour and actions of princes when dealing with their subjects.

HANDWRITTEN SOURCES

Archivio di Stato di Firenze, *Mediceo del Principato*, 2940, letter from Marcello Donati to Pietro Usimbardi, 19 March 1588.

Archivio di Stato di Venezia, *Consiglio dei X, parti comuni*, reg. 30, c. 86v; *Inquisitori di Stato*, b. 488, 21 July 1586.

Archivio di Stato di Modena, *Cancelleria ducale, avvisi e notizie dall'estero*, bb. 1–3.

Biblioteca Apostolica Vaticana, Rome (Vatican City): *Urb. Lat.* 1038–1039; *Vat. Lat.* 8223.

Biblioteca Nazionale Centrale, Florence, *Fondo Magliabechi*, cl. XXIV, cod. 16, Rome, 17 December 1588.

---

[39] 'le nuove cose sono da imbasciadore, da huomini grandi di stato e governo e non da quei che van per la minore'.

CHAPTER 2

Handwritten newsletters as a means of communication in early modern Europe

Zsuzsa Barbarics and Renate Pieper

INTRODUCTION

Communication processes between distant regions and different social groups improved during the early modern period. These changes are usually attributed to diffusion of the printing press and increased literacy.[1] Studies analysing printed materials stress the dichotomy between oral and published information.[2] It is assumed that printing not only promoted the spread of reading and writing, but also contributed to the development of a public sphere, thus making the press one of the roots of modern democratic societies.[3] Despite the importance of the new printing technology, traditional forms of communication remained crucial during early modern times.[4] Handwriting, with a long-lasting tradition in the Mediterranean, remained ubiquitous among merchants, urban elites, clergy and nobles, and gained

---

[1] M. Giesecke, *Der Buchdruck in der frühen Neuzeit: eine historische Fallstudie über die Durchsetzung neuer Informations- und Kommunikationstechnologien* (Frankfurt am Main: Suhrkamp, 1998); R. Chartier (ed.), *The Culture of Print: Power and the Uses of Print in Early Modern Europe* (Princeton: Princeton University Press, 1989); E. Eisenstein, *The Printing Press as an Agent of Change: Communication and Cultural Transformations in Early Modern Europe* (Cambridge: Cambridge University Press, 1979).

[2] R. A. Houston, *Literacy in Early Modern Europe: Culture and Education 1500–1800* (London: Longman, 1988); R. Finnegan, *Literacy and Orality: Studies in the Technology of Communication* (Oxford: Blackwell, 1988).

[3] J. Burkhardt, *Das Reformationsjahrhundert: deutsche Geschichte zwischen Medienrevolution und Institutionenbildung 1517–1617* (Stuttgart: Kohlhammer, 2002); Karl Vocelka, *Die politische Propaganda Kaiser Rudolfs II.* (Vienna: Verlag der Österreichischen Akademie der Wissenschaften, 1981).

[4] U. Neddermeyer, *Von der Handschrift zum gedruckten Buch: Schriftlichkeit und Leseinteresse im Mittelalter und in der frühen Neuzeit. Quantitative und qualitative Aspekte* (Wiesbaden: Harrassowitz, 1998).

increasing importance as private and public bureaucracy spread. Thus, older forms of communication coexisted with newer ones.

The development of handwritten and printed newsletters offers a good example of reciprocal influence. Modern scholarship does not differentiate clearly among newsletters as integral parts of correspondence, independent handwritten newsletters and printed ones.[5] In the later Middle Ages, manuscript newsletters formed part of private and public correspondence, a situation which persisted until the early seventeenth century. In addition, a new type of handwritten newsletter appeared during the sixteenth century,[6] offering an independent information medium which remained in use on the eve of the French Revolution.[7] Printed newsletters, first published around 1500, became a regular medium of communication a century later; after a short introductory period, they were issued daily.

With few exceptions,[8] historical studies have analysed printed versions almost exclusively,[9] thereby excluding the majority of

---

[5] J. Wilke, *Grundzüge der Medien- und Kommunikationsgeschichte: von den Anfängen bis ins 20. Jahrhundert* (Cologne: Böhlau, 2000); Th. Schröder, *Die ersten Zeitungen: Textgestaltung und Nachrichtenauswahl* (Tübingen: Narr, 1995).

[6] Th.-G. Werner, 'Das kaufmännische Nachrichtenwesen im späten Mittelalter und in der Frühen Neuzeit und sein Einfluß auf die Entstehung der handschriftlichen Zeitung', *Scripta Mercatorae* 2 (1975), 3–51; R. Grasshoff, *Die briefliche Zeitung des XVI. Jahrhunderts*, doctoral dissertation, University of Leipzig (1877).

[7] J. Mančal, 'Zu Augsburger Zeitungen vom Ende des 17. bis zur Mitte des 19. Jahrhunderts: Abendzeitung, Postzeitung und Intelligenzzettel', in H. Gier and J. Janota (eds.), *Augsburger Buchdruck und Verlagswesen: von den Anfängen bis zur Gegenwart* (Wiesbaden: Harrassowitz, 1997), pp. 683–733; U. Blindow, *Berliner geschriebene Zeitungen des 18. Jahrhunderts* (Berlin and Würzburg: Dissertation-Verlag Karl J. Triltsch, 1939).

[8] Including Mario Infelise, *Prima dei giornali: alle origini della pubblica informazione (secoli XVI e XVII)* (Rome and Bari: Laterza, 2002); Renate Pieper, *Die Vermittlung einer neuen Welt: Amerika im Nachrichtennetz des Habsburgischen Imperiums 1493–1598* (Mainz: von Zabern, 2000); and the unpublished PhD thesis of Zsuzsa Barbarics, 'Tinte und Politik in der frühen Neuzeit: handschriftliche Zeitungen als überregionale Nachrichtquellen für die Machthaber' (Graz, 2006).

[9] W. Harms, 'Das illustrierte Flugblatt in Verständigungsprozessen innerhalb der frühneuzeitlichen Kultur', in W. Harms and A. Messerli (eds.), *Wahrnehmungsgeschichte und Wissensdiskurs im illustrierten Flugblatt der Frühen Neuzeit (1450–1770)* (Basel: Schwabe, 2002), pp. 11–21; H. Lang, 'Die Neue Zeitung des 15. und 17. Jahrhunderts. Entwicklungsgeschichte und Typologie', in E. Blühm and H. Gebhardt (eds.), *Presse und Geschichte II. Neue Beiträge zur historischen Kommunikationsforschung* (Munich: Saur, 1987), pp. 57–60.

newsletters from consideration. Based on the study of several European collections, this chapter concentrates on the general characteristics of handwritten newsletters and the geographical areas they reached, followed by a detailed investigation of a single preserved collection. A third part examines the speed of communication and the validity of information given by handwritten newsletters, using the diffusion of notices about an outstanding event of European importance as an example and tracing the geographical network of these *avvisi* for three subsequent years. Finally, these manuscripts will be compared with the printed news concerning this specific event in order to show the different functions of handwriting and printing.

GENERAL CHARACTERISTICS OF HANDWRITTEN
NEWSLETTERS

Although several studies of various collections of handwritten newsletters exist, there is no general consensus about their nature and function, largely because collections of handwritten newsletters have only been examined separately,[10] making them appear special and unique. Nevertheless, the different collections scattered throughout Europe constitute a single type of sources and were closely related to each other. Although usually seen either as a communication tool for political elites and nobility or as providing information exclusively for merchants[11] or sometimes even considered part of political intelligence services[12], handwritten newsletters were actually subscribed and transmitted throughout Europe by a broad and well-to-do public.

---

[10] E.g., J. Kleinpaul, *Die Fugger\zeitungen 1568–1605* (Leipzig: Verlag von Emmanuel Reinicke, 1921); M. H. Fitzler, *Die Entstehung der sogenannten Fugger\zeitungen in der Wiener Nationalbibliothek* (Baden bei Wien: Rohrer, 1937); Ricarda Huch, 'Die Wick'sche Sammlung von Flugblättern und Zeitungsnachrichten in der Stadtbibliothek Zürich', *Neujahrsblatt* (1895), 1–26.

[11] P. Sardella, *Nouvelles et spéculations à Venise au début du XVIe siècle* (Paris: Colin, 1948); Werner, 'Das kaufmännische Nachrichtenwesen'.

[12] J. Kleinpaul, *Das Nachrichtenwesen der deutschen Fürsten im 16. und 17. Jahrhundert* (Leipzig: Adolf Klein Verlag, 1930); Ágnes R. Várkonyi, 'A tájékoztatás hatalma' (The power of informing), in T. Petercsák and M. Berecz (eds.), *Információáramlás a magyar és a török végvári rendszerben* (Eger: Heves Megyei Múzeumi Szervezet: Dobó István Vármúzeum, 1999), pp. 9–31.

Map 1. Destination of handwritten newsletters in the analysed collections

The collections used here date from the second half of the sixteenth century. They mainly served the German-speaking area, but some are related to Italy (map 1). The south German examples include collections assembled by the Fugger merchant house,[13] the Count of Pfalz-Neuburg,[14] and the Duke of Bavaria,[15] accompanied by two Swiss collections, the *Wickiana*[16] and the *Bullinger-Zeitungen*.[17] In

[13] Österreichische Nationalbibliothek (hereafter ÖNB), Handschriftensammlung, Vienna, Cod. 8949–75.
[14] Bayerisches Hauptstaatsarchiv (hereafter BayerHStA), Munich, Pfalz-Neuburg 918–20.
[15] Bayerische Staatsbibliothek, Munich, Cod. 5864.
[16] Zentralbibliothek Zurich, Handschriftenabteilung, Zurich, MS. F. 12–35.
[17] Zentralbibliothek Zurich, Handschriftenabteilung, Zurich, MS A. 43–69, Staatsarchiv des Kantons Zurich, E II 335–83.

addition, the central European collections of the imperial chancery,[18] the Estates of Inner Austria[19] and of the Hungarian merchant house of Thurzo (who had just become counts of Bethlenfalva and palatines of Hungary)[20] have been investigated. For Italy, we have used the collections of the Duke of Urbino[21] and the Duke of Florence,[22] and some newsletters of the Holy See.[23]

These collections are only a few among a very broad spectrum covering all of Europe. For example, before 1500 the Venetian diarist Marino Sanudo was copying the newsletters he received.[24] Spooner and Braudel analysed handwritten newsletters sent to London during the first half of the seventeenth century.[25] Evidence of sixteenth-century newsletter collections exists at Szczecin, Prague and Simancas, and probably many other places. Their size is very diverse. The *Fuggerʒeitungen* in Vienna's National Library consist of twenty-seven volumes containing several thousands of newsletters each, from which only several dozen survive among the newsletters received by the Thurzos. The collections of the Duke of Urbino, the Duke of Bavaria and the Count of Pfalz-Neuburg are less impressive than the *Fuggerʒeitungen*, but still consist of several books. Letters received by the imperial chancery and the Archduke of Florence were not collected separately and bound in leather, but remained attached to their diplomatic correspondence. Similarly, the newsletters in the *Wickiana* were bound together with personal correspondence in more than twenty volumes. Most of the *Bullinger-Zeitungen* and the newsletters received by the Inner Austrian Estates were separated from diplomatic

---

[18] Haus-, Hof- und Staatsarchiv (hereafter HHStA), Vienna, Geschriebene Zeitungen Fasc. 7a, 8, 10; Böhm 595 W 290.

[19] Steiermärkisches Landesarchiv, Graz, Laa. Antiquum IV, Sch. 98, 99.

[20] Magyar Országos Levéltár, Budapest, Archivum fam. Thurzó, E 196, Sch. 8, Fasc. 28, 29; A Magyar Kamara Archivuma, Lymbus, E 211, Sch. 134, t. 19.

[21] Biblioteka Apostolica Vaticana, Vatican, Cod. Urb. 1040, 1054, 1055.

[22] See for example diplomatic correspondence: Archivio di Stato Firenze, Florence, Mediceo del Principato 4027, 5037.

[23] Archivio Segreto Apostolico Vaticano, Vatican, Avvisi 126.

[24] M. Sanudo, *I diarii*, ed. F. Stefani, 58 vols. (Venice: Visentini, 1879–1903).

[25] F. Braudel, *La méditeranée et le monde méditerranéen à l'époque de Philippe II*, 2nd edition, 2 vols. (Paris: Colin, 1966), vol. 1, pp. 362–7; F. C. Spooner, *L'économie mondiale et les frappes monétaires en France: 1493–1680* (Paris: Colin, 1956).

correspondence, but not made into independent books. Thus, not only the amount of newsletters varied from one collection to the other, but also the form in which they were preserved.

Most of these collections contain newsletters from more than twenty years. Hans Jacob Wick gathered news from 1560 to 1587; the Thurzos assembled theirs from the 1580s until the second decade of the seventeenth century. The Fuggers started to put their newsletters aside in the 1560s. They passed this first part of their collection (which ends in 1604) to the Habsburg emperor; the subsequent seventeenth-century volumes remain in the family archives at Dillingen. Several collections cover almost two centuries. The newsletters received by the imperial chancery were kept from the mid sixteenth century until the second half of the eighteenth; similarly, the Estates of Inner Austria gathered theirs from the 1580s until the end of the reign of Maria Theresa. However, the Duke of Bavaria and the Count of Pfalz-Neuburg both preserved their information for only a few decades after the 1590s.

These thousands of newsletters gathered since the mid sixteenth to the mid eighteenth centuries in numerous European collections shared important characteristics. They were written on one or two sheets of paper that were folded once, making the length of a newsletter vary between three and seven pages. In the case of outstanding news (for example, major military battles, the arrival of a large silver fleet from America, or natural disasters), one may find additional descriptions of several pages and even pictures (fig. 1) attached to the newsletters, giving more detailed information about the event.

In the second half of the sixteenth century, news was usually bundled together with other forms of correspondence. For example, on 13 July 1583 the agent of the Inner Austrian Estates in Augsburg, Mattheus Paller, dispatched handwritten newsletters to the Count of Sarrau together with letters to him from Kaspar Hirsch and Marx Hörwart. Paller's cover letter to the Estates assumed that the correspondence from Hörwart to the Count of Sarrau also contained handwritten newsletters.[26] Some newsletters were dispatched independently and still preserve their seal and the address of the recipient.

---

[26] Steiermärkisches Landesarchiv, Laa. Antiquum IV, Sch. 98, fols. 45r–46v.

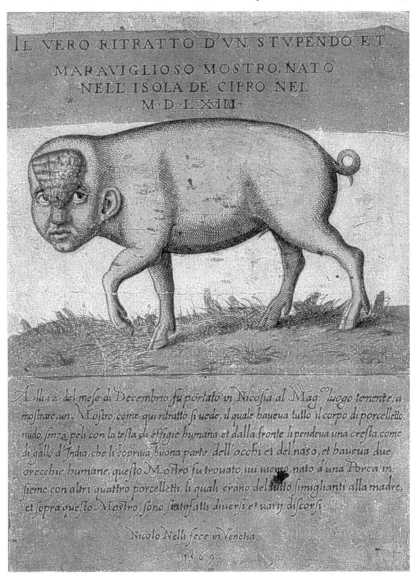

IL VERO RITRATTO D'VN STVPENDO ET
MARAVIGLIOSO MOSTRO, NATO
NELL ISOLA DE CIPRO NEL
M·D·LXIIII·

A lli 12 del mese di Decembrio fu portato in Nicosia al Mag.co Luogo tenente, a
mostrare, un Mostro, come qui ritratto si uede, il quale haueua tutto il corpo di porcelletto,
nudo, senza peli con la testa di effigie humana et dalla fronte li pendeua una cresta, come
di gallo d'India, che li copriua buona parte dell'occhi et del naso, et haueua due
orecchie humane, questo Mostro fu trouato, uiuo, nato d'una Porca, in-
sieme con altri quattro porcelletti, li quali erano del tutto simiglianti alla madre,
et sopra questo Mostro, sono state fatti diuersi et uarij discorsi

Nicolo Nelli fece in Venetia

1569

Fig. 1. Monster born on 12 December 1569 at Nicosia which forecast the conquest of Cyprus by the Ottomans. *Wickiana*, Handschriftenabteilung der Zentralbibliothek Zurich, MS F. 19, fol. 119v

Others were sent as attachments to diplomatic and private letters: Bernardino Rossi, the imperial ambassador in Venice, attached several *avvisi* to his reports in 1593.[27] Likewise, the Protestant humanist Theodore Beza attached handwritten newsletters to his private letters from Geneva to Heinrich Bullinger in Zurich and Tobias Egli in Chur.[28] The Fugger factor in Antwerp, Hans Georg Ött, transmitted parts of *avvisi* to Philipp Eduard Fugger in Augsburg as attachments to his private letters.[29] Only a minor part of this sort of news was directly included as postscripts to private letters. Compared with newsletters around the beginning of the sixteenth century, it becomes clear that such postscripts were forerunners of the independent newsletters that emerged later in the sixteenth century and circulated within Europe for two centuries.

By the late sixteenth century, newsletters were being dispatched once a week. In the 1590s the Fugger merchants received them from Venice and Rome, or from Antwerp and Cologne, on a regular basis. In addition, agents in other European cities sent important information on request. The Styrian Estates ordered newsletters from Venice and Augsburg which were also sent weekly. Even if handwritten newsletters were sometimes delayed by political and natural impediments, recipients expected a regular information service.[30]

Their general pattern of presentation clearly distinguished newsletters from other forms of correspondence. The same model was used almost unchanged for at least two centuries. Its first outstanding feature was that handwritten newsletters were doubly anonymous: they never named the recipient, and they also lacked a signature. This anonymity had at least two advantages. Omitting the recipient's name enabled copies of the same newsletter to be sent to different persons; omitting the author's signature avoided control and censorship by secular or ecclesiastical authorities. Each newsletter began with a heading

---

[27] HHStA, Böhm 595 W 290, vol. 8, fols. 275r–452v.
[28] Handschriftenabteilung der Zentralbibliothek Zurich, MS F 63/1, fols. 57r–58v, Staatsarchiv des Kantons Zurich, E II 342a, fol. 615r–v.
[29] Fitzler, *Die Entstehung*, p. 34.
[30] See the correspondence of the Inner-Austrian Estates with Marx Hörwart and Andrea Dellatori. Steiermärkisches Landesarchiv, Laa. Antiquum IV, Sch. 98, 99.

indicating its place and date of compilation, e.g., 'From Venice, 12 October 1571'.[31] After the heading, a dozen or so news items followed, each paragraph usually mentioning the location and sometimes even the date of origin of its information. Most information provided was rather brief – one or two sentences for a normal event. A newsletter from Cologne dated 3 May 1586, received by the Count of Pfalz-Neuburg, described the sack of Santo Domingo by Francis Drake as follows: 'From Portugal we received news that Captain Drake from England took the island of Sto. Domenigo and distributed weapons to the natives of the island so that they could use them against the Spanish king.'[32] Newsletters introduced a new heading after compiling all notices from a given place. In most cases, newsletters had only two or three headings; a single newsletter distributed reports collected in two or three cities. Some newsletters delivered notices from only a single place, especially those sent from the Iberian peninsula to the Fuggers in Augsburg. Another outstanding characteristic of handwritten newsletters was that they used only the place and date of compilation as formal elements for arranging their contents. Like early modern merchants who traded very large samples of commodities without specialising, the marketing and diffusion of information included a very diverse range of notices, with no order or focus other than their date and place of compilation.

In order to reach the broadest possible European public, most newsletters were written in vernacular languages. At first Italian dominated, but by 1600 newsletters were also being written in other idioms. Hence newsletters acquired different names according to their places of origin: they were called *av(v)isi* in Italy and Spain, *gazettes* in the Netherlands and France, and *Neue Zeitungen* in German-speaking areas.

Their content was extremely diverse, but political and military issues dominated. Besides accounts of battles or descriptions of political unrest and quarrels, they offered information about political and public social life. The arrival of an ambassador was as noteworthy as an aristocratic marriage, the death of a famous person or nominations

---

[31] ÖNB, Cod. 8949, fol. 271r.   [32] BayerHStA, Pfalz-Neuburg 920, fol. 38.

to ecclesiastical and administrative posts. Important economic notices, like the fate of the American treasure fleets or the expectation of exceptionally good or bad harvests, were also reported, as were epidemic diseases or noteworthy natural events like unusual heat or cold. Almost the only omission a modern newspaper reader would really notice is a regular sports report.

The validity of much information distributed by handwritten newsletters was confirmed by other contemporary sources; ambassadors were even blamed because their reports relied too heavily on newsletters.[33] The close relationship between diplomatic correspondence and handwritten newsletters is further shown by the fact that these anonymous letters were often attached to official correspondence.[34] This did not imply that ambassadors simply copied news collected by professional or semi-professional 'journalists'. A comparison of notices from the Iberian peninsula about events in the Americas shows that information given by either diplomatic or merchant correspondence was somewhat longer, slightly more accurate, and sent some days earlier than (or at least simultaneously with) news distributed by these anonymous letters.[35] The authors of the newsletters, diplomats and merchants probably all relied on the same or at least similar sources. Newsletters hint that oral information or incoming correspondence from distant places formed the basis for their notices.[36] Mario Infelise gives a detailed description of the complicated process of gathering fresh and reliable information, showing the variety of methods and sources used by the authors of newsletters in Venice and Rome.[37]

Because handwritten newsletters were usually anonymous, it is very difficult to identify their authors. Nonetheless, one can distinguish two different types of *avvisi* with respect to authorship. The first type, professional newsletters, which appeared in the mid sixteenth century, were compiled and copied at specialised offices. In the German-speaking area, the 'journalists' were called *Avisenschreiber, Zeitunger* or

---

[33] Infelise, *Prima dei giornali*, p. 1.
[34] HHStA, Böhm 595 W 290, vol. 8, fols. 395r–591v.
[35] Pieper, *Die Vermittlung*, pp. 178–210.
[36] *Ibid.*, pp. 211–44.   [37] Infelise, *Prima dei giornali*, p. 53.

Novellisten (from the Italian *novellanti*). Early twentieth-century germanophone historiography supported the idea that postmasters were the persons best suited to compile handwritten newsletters, since they could (mis)use the correspondence they handled.[38] Instead, as Infelise showed for Venice, a wide range of people – none of them postmasters – participated in compiling and copying newsletters. Postmasters apparently restricted themselves to the task of transportation. At Venice and Rome, very humble people (some without regular housing) or scribes were employed as copyists. Clerics and notaries used this possibility to gain extra income by either copying, compiling or gathering news. In Venice, even merchants like the Flemish Nicolas de Stoop became engaged in this business; during the mid sixteenth century, he combined a trade in merchandise with another in information.[39] So did Marx Hörwart in Augsburg. In the last decade of the sixteenth century, he provided handwritten newsletters not only to the Inner-Austrian Estates,[40] but also to the Fuggers and the Count of Ortenburg.[41]

Many people participated in the distribution of newsletters on a reduced scale, but others, like Giovanni Quorli during the mid seventeenth century, specialised and ran large offices. They actively sought every possibility to get fresh news and to have it compiled, copied and distributed to their subscribers (Quorli supplied more than sixty clients).[42] Such newsletter offices were not restricted to Italy, although those in German-speaking areas seem far smaller than Quorli's enterprise. At the end of the sixteenth century, the houses of Jeremias Krasser and Jeremias Schiffle in Augsburg were well known. The former had only ten to fifteen customers ordering his newsletters on a regular basis.[43]

In order to cover the large geographical distances separating authors from readers of newsletters, several persons and offices acted as intermediaries. For some years during the late sixteenth century, the Fugger

---

[38] Kleinpaul, *Das Nachrichtenwesen*, p. 13; O. Groth, *Die Geschichte der deutschen Zeitungswissenschaft: Probleme und Methoden* (Munich: Weinamyer, 1948), pp. 10–11.

[39] Infelise, *Prima dei giornali*, p. 11.

[40] Steiermärkisches Landesarchiv, Laa. Antiquum IV, Sch. 98.

[41] Fitzler, *Die Entstehung*, pp. 75–6.   [42] Infelise, *Prima dei giornali*, pp. 36–9.

[43] Fitzler, *Die Entstehung*, pp. 66–7.

merchants in Augsburg got their Venetian *avvisi* through a German merchant family named Ott living in Venice, who engaged a professional newsletter office: David Ott ordered handwritten newsletters for Philipp Eduard and Octavian II Fugger from two Venetian *novellanti*, Hieronimo Acconzaicco and Pompeo Roma.[44] Foreign ambassadors in Venice and Rome also got their *avvisi* through newsletter offices. Three imperial ambassadors, Vito Dornberg and Bernardino Rossi in Venice and Giovanni Battista Berniero in Rome, attached copies of professional newsletters to their correspondence.[45] Other newsletters were translated into the customer's language by bilingual scribes, either at the place of the newsletter's origin or at an office in the country of destination.[46] Translating Dutch newsletters into German became a major task of Hans Adelgais, the Fugger factor in Cologne.[47]

Another group of newsletters stuck to the traditional pattern. They were written not by professional offices but by friends and relatives, and dispatched irregularly. Newsletters of this type survive in both Swiss collections, the *Wickiana* and the *Bullinger-Zeitungen*. Like Ulrich Zwingli or Philip Melanchton,[48] Zurich's leading Protestant humanists, Hans Jacob Wick and Heinrich Bullinger, exchanged handwritten newsletters with relatives, friends or acquaintances. They or their scribes either copied newsletters they received or compiled them personally. Whereas professional *avvisi* always used vernacular languages, some of the newsletters received by Wick[49] and received or sent by Bullinger[50] were written in Latin.

At the end of the sixteenth century, German princes practised both traditional and modern forms of distribution. The Count of

---

[44] *Ibid.*, pp. 16–18.   [45] HHStA, Böhm 595 W 290, vol. 8, fols. 275r–591v.
[46] Infelise, *Prima dei giornali*, pp. 10, 47.   [47] Fitzler, *Die Entstehung*, p. 28.
[48] L. Weisz, *Der Zürcher Nachrichtenverkehr vor 1780* (Zurich: Neue Zürcher Zeitung, 1954), pp. 12–16; J. Kleinpaul, *Die vornehmsten Korrespondenten der deutschen Fürsten im 15. und 16. Jahrhundert* (Leipzig: Klein, 1928), p. 3.
[49] Handschriftenabteilung der Zentralbibliothek Zürich, Ms. F 19: 'Scriptum ex Nurinburga ad D. Bullingerum . . . 4. Marty 1571', fols. 227r–v; 'Ex Curia Rhatovit 13. Juli 1571', fols. 248v.
[50] Staatsarchiv des Kantons Zürich, 'Ex literas Lipsia datis 13. Oct. 1569', E II 368, fols. 197r–198r; 'Ex Anglia 26. Aug. 1563', 'Ex Frankfortia 12. Sept. 1563', 'Ex Wittemberg 8. Sept. 1563', E II 369, fols. 55r–56v.

Pfalz-Neuburg received professional newsletters and had them copied for the dukes of Bavaria and Württemberg and for the Count of Hessen-Marburg.[51] The Count of Windischgrätz, a customer of Giovanni Quorli, still used a similar procedure in the mid seventeenth century; having the *avvisi* he received from Italy copied for the Estates of Inner Austria.[52] The coexistence of two types of handwritten newsletters illustrates how both change and continuity characterised early modern systems of communication.

Recipients and readers of newsletters belonged to different social and political groups. Besides ruling princes like the emperor, the pope, the dukes of Bavaria, Tuscany, Urbino and Württemberg, members of their chanceries like Fabio de Mondragón at Florence also received handwritten newsletters. Other noblemen, like the counts of Pfalz-Neuburg and Hessen-Marburg, or the members of the Styrian Estates, should be mentioned. Humanists like Hugo Blotius at Vienna,[53] Melanchthon at Wittenberg, Georg Spalatin at Antwerp,[54] or Bullinger and Wick at Zurich exchanged or bought newsletters; so did two citizens of Augsburg, Hans Merer and Hans Heinrich Link.[55] Besides ruling elites and humanists, merchants also subscribed to newsletters. The *Fuggerzeitungen* is the most famous collection; others, like the Thurzo collection, are smaller. With such customers, manuscript newsletters could follow a common pattern and become a successful information medium by the end of the sixteenth century.

A CASE STUDY: THE BATTLE OF LEPANTO IN MANUSCRIPT
AND PRINTED NEWSLETTERS

We propose to begin analysing the evolution of newsletters by examining the information provided about an outstanding event of the second

---

[51] Pieper, *Die Vermittlung*, pp. 204–5.   [52] Infelise, *Prima dei giornali*, p. 39.

[53] E. Rühl, 'Die nachgelassenen Zeitungssammlungen und Gelehrtenkorrespondenz Hugo Blotius' des ersten Bibliothekars der Wiener Hofbibliothek', unpublished PhD thesis, University of Vienna (1958).

[54] K. Schottenloher, *Flugblatt und Zeitung: ein Wegweiser durch das gedruckte Tagesschrifttum* (Berlin: Schmidt, 1922), p. 155.

[55] Fitzler, *Die Entstehung*, pp. 77–8.

half of the sixteenth century, the battle of Lepanto (October 1571), in a single collection, the *Fuggerzeitungen*. The handwritten newsletters sent to the Fuggers residing in Augsburg and Dillingen will be compared with broadsheets describing the same event, published in these towns and preserved in the Austrian National Library in Vienna. A second exercise involves reconstructing the geographical network of newsletters sent to Augsburg during the second half of 1571, using indications at the beginning of each paragraph of a newsletter. Finally, we will survey the geographical areas mentioned in general headings of newsletters over three years (1571-3).[56]

Historians have characterised the collision of the Christian and Ottoman fleets at the bay of Lepanto on 7 October 1571 as one of the greatest naval battles of the early modern age. The resounding victory of the Christian fleet led by Don Juan of Austria, half-brother of the Spanish king Philip II, supposedly signalled a decisive turn in the history of the Mediterranean: it cracked the predominance of Ottoman seapower, stopped the expansion of the 'enemy of Christendom' in the Mediterranean and foreshadowed the decline of the Ottoman Empire.[57] More recent approaches instead stress the psychological significance of a battle which at least temporarily calmed Christian fears of Ottoman invincibility, although it obviously did not open a totally new age in the history of Christendom's wars against the Ottomans.[58] Cyprus remained in Ottoman hands. Despite European expectations, the Ottomans reappeared in the Mediterranean with a new fleet by summer 1572 and occupied Modon one year after the battle of Lepanto. Philip II gave permission to Don Juan of Austria to counterattack only after this event. By this time, Venice had abandoned the Christian alliance on 3 March 1573. Although the Christians seized Tunis and its fort in October 1573, La Goletta fell into Ottoman hands in 1574, enabling them to extend their influence in the western

---

[56] ÖNB, Vienna, Cod. 8949.

[57] K. M. Setton, *The Papacy and the Levant (1204–1571)*, vol. 3 (Philadelphia: The American Philosophical Society, 1984).

[58] H. Pigaillem, *La bataille de Lépante (1571)* (Paris: Editions Economica, 2003); A. C. Hess, 'The battle of Lepanto and its place in Mediterranean history', *Past and Present* 57 (1972), 53–73.

Mediterranean. Nevertheless, their seapower did start to decline – not because of their defeat at Lepanto, but because of their subsequent victories. After reoccupying Tunis in 1574 and defeating the Portuguese in Morocco in 1578, they had attained their goals and made a ceasefire with Spain in 1580. Ottoman naval decline also had inherent causes,[59] but it was shared by other Mediterranean powers as well.[60] After the end of the Venetian–Turkish war in 1573, the Ottomans remained on equal terms with their European enemies until the end of the seventeenth century.

Although the system of handwritten newsletters was then in its infancy, news of the naval victory of the Holy League at the bay of Lepanto on Sunday, 7 October 1571, spread rapidly, and various descriptions quickly reached southern Germany. Due to the considerable participation of the Venetian and Spanish fleet, supported by the papacy, Florence and some Germans, there was lively interest in news about the deeds of the Armada commanded by Philip II's half-brother. Therefore printed broadsheets joined handwritten newsletters in the Fugger collection. Overall, seven newsletters included notices concerning the naval battle. The first, sent from Venice on 12 October 1571,[61] mentions the arrival of a special messenger from Rome bringing news sent from Otranto that the Christian fleet had left Corfu on 29 September for an encounter with the Turkish fleet at the bay of Lepanto. The next newsletter, dated 13 October 1571, came directly from Rome.[62] It refers to news sent from Corfu on 30 September and mentions a council of the commanders of the Christian galleys held the day before. Its content is more detailed than the previous one from Venice. The report from Rome claims that the Venetians wanted to pursue the Turkish fleet, whereas the Spaniards and Don Juan of Austria hesitated because of the approaching autumn.

---

[59] Hess, 'The battle', 63–72; Braudel, *La méditerranée*, vol. 1, pp. 405–44.
[60] J. F. Guilmartin, *Gunpower and Galleys: Changing Technology and Mediterranean Warfare at Sea in the Sixteenth Century* (Cambridge: Cambridge University Press, 1980).
[61] ÖNB, Cod. 8949, fol. 271r.   [62] ÖNB, Cod. 8949, fol. 271r–v.

News of the victory of the Christian fleet on Sunday, 7 October, first reached Augsburg only with the next regular newsletter from Venice, dated Friday, 19 October 1571.[63] A description of the battle was given, covering almost two pages, with a list of the deceased Christian commanders attached. The text reported that news from the battle had been brought by a Venetian commander named Guistiniano, who had arrived with his galley. He said that the battle had begun early in the morning, an hour before sunrise, and that it had been won after three hours of fighting. Some 150 Turkish galleys had been captured, and the rest had been sunk or fled. The Turkish commander had been captured and killed; booty worth 200,000 *ʒecchini* had been found on his battleship. The text claims that 15,000 Turkish soldiers had been killed, another 5,000 captured, and 40,000 Christian galley slaves freed. Twelve Venetian commanders had lost their lives, as well as the Venetian general Barbarigo. The galley of Malta, as well as one from Florence and twelve Venetian galleys, had been lost. Different information was given in the list attached to the newsletter. Whereas the number of Turkish galleys and soldiers captured was identical in the text and on the list, the number of Turkish soldiers killed was twice as great on the list as in the text, but the number of freed Christian slaves was reduced to 14,000. It is obvious that first impressions of the battle were not necessarily accurate.

The next description that reached Augsburg was also from Venice one week later, dated Friday, 26 October 1571.[64] It contained more details about the battle and characterised it as very bloody. This newsletter also mentioned that two sons of the Petrev Pasha were among the prisoners and that the galley of a famous corsair named Antonio Sirocci had been captured. On his ship Christian soldiers found a beautiful young woman, richly adorned with jewels and pearls valued at 60,000 *ʒecchini*. Sirocci, his mistress, and their two sons were prisoners of the Venetian Giovanni Contarini. To celebrate the victory of Lepanto, the newsletter reports, numerous festivities were hold in Venice, with the German residents in the city especially prominent. The Venetian newsletter claimed that Rome lacked any information

[63] ÖNB, Cod. 8949, fol. 272r–v.   [64] ÖNB, Cod. 8949, fol. 273v.

before Sunday, 21 October, when the messenger sent from Venice was expected to arrive only at 10pm. The Roman newsletter dated 27 October states that this special envoy arrived at 4pm on 21 October.[65] According to this report, numerous processions and thanksgivings were held in Rome before notice of the sunken papal galley arrived on Tuesday, 23 October, brought by another messenger from the Venetian Signoria to their ambassador in Rome. An eyewitness was expected to be sent to the pope by the commander of the Christian fleet in the Mediterranean, Don Juan of Austria, but this envoy had not yet arrived when the newsletter was compiled on 27 October.

The last notices concerning the battle of Lepanto were from Venice and Rome, dated Friday and Saturday, 2 and 3 November 1571. The Venetian newsletter mentions the arrival of a second messenger, Giovanni Battista Contarini, from the battle, who reported that Don Juan of Austria had sent envoys to the pope and to the Spanish king. Contarini had left the Christian fleet near Lepanto on 12 October. He gave more details about the captured Turkish galleys, which according to him numbered 161. Furthermore, he corrected some details about the fate of the Turkish and Christian commanders.[66]

The Roman newsletter (3 November) mentions the arrival of the son of the general of the Venetian fleet bringing more details from Lepanto. He entered Rome on Sunday, 28 October, together with López de Figueroa, the messenger sent by Don Juan of Austria to the Spanish king. López de Figueroa was heard immediately by the pope and continued his voyage to the Spanish court that same evening.[67]

These last newsletters with direct references to events at Lepanto described deliberations about how to continue the fight against the Ottomans at great length. The importance given to these considerations indicates very clearly that both the *novellanti* who compiled these newsletters and their informants were acutely aware that the sea war with the Ottoman Empire had not ended, and that the fate of Cyprus as a Venetian possession was still in doubt. These newsletters offered a very clear-cut analysis of the military situation in the Mediterranean at

---

[65] ÖNB, Cod. 8949, fol. 276r.   [66] ÖNB, Cod. 8949, fol. 276v.
[67] ÖNB, Cod. 8949, fol. 277r–v.

their time, a perception far more realistic than that of many historical studies.

In addition to these short reports sent almost every week from Venice and Rome, a lengthy three-page description of the battle was added to the second Venetian newsletter.[68] Whereas ordinary newsletters were written in Italian, this report was a German translation of an Italian text entitled 'Copy of a letter from the Christian Armada from 5 October' (*sic*). It begins with preparations for the battle, mentioning various ships and their commanders involved. According to this information, the battle started on 7 October, two hours after sunrise and lasted five hours. It estimated the number of Turkish soldiers killed in the battle at 18,000 and reported 10,000 Turkish captives and 15,000 liberated Christian galley slaves. Again, considerable booty was mentioned. The most spectacular event was apparently the capture of the galley of the corsair with a beautiful Christian mistress on board, wearing precious jewellery and pearls. The newsletter states that she offered the Christian soldiers a ransom of 60,000 ducats for her freedom. Summarising events, this lengthy report alleges that 20 Venetian nobles and several thousand Christian soldiers died, numbers the captured Turkish galleys at 150, and mentions 60 sunken Turkish ships.

A comparison of the contents of these handwritten newsletters reveals that they did not agree upon the number of captured Turkish galleys, but only on the ransom offered by the Christian woman captured on the ship of the Turkish corsair. The numbers of Turkish and Christian soldiers killed, that of the captives and liberated slaves, or the number of Turkish ships sunk were never identical. Likewise, the names of Christian or Turkish commanders varied: the Venetian newsletter dated 26 October named the famous Turkish corsair Antonio Sirocca, but the lengthy German report first calls him 'Caragossa' and afterwards 'Caragoggia'. A list of leading Turkish commanders (9 Nov., fol. 279v) contains the name 'Caracosa', but not among the corsairs, the captain of whom was named 'Carazali'. Indications of the time and length of the battle also differ.

---

[68] ÖNB, Cod. 8949, fols. 274v–276r.

Despite such inaccuracies, the information given by the handwritten newsletters is more or less correct, although very condensed. Given the means of transportation in the early modern period, the speed of the distribution of news seems relatively fast. Venice was informed about the events in the Mediterranean within twelve to fifteen days, whereas thirteen to sixteen days were needed to contact Rome. From Venice to Augsburg required another fortnight. A special messenger could travel from Venice to Rome in two or three days, a distance normally requiring four or five days. Thus newsletters from Rome reached Augsburg within three weeks; the first containing information about Lepanto was probably received in Augsburg about the end of October or beginning of November, four or five weeks after the battle had taken place.[69]

Besides handwritten information, the Fuggers could also read printed descriptions of the battle of Lepanto. Four of the 93 broadsheets and pamphlets concerning Lepanto now preserved at Vienna's National Library were published in Augsburg[70] and three in nearby Dillingen.[71] Unlike the brief notices of the handwritten newsletters, each printed version had several pages, ranging from six to fourteen or even more. Some broadsheets included a woodcut on the first page. Except one Latin *Oratio* (a copy of a Venetian broadsheet also in Latin),[72] all of these broadsheets were written in German. Broadsheets offered more space than handwritten newsletters, so these printed texts gave more details than such short reports. Obviously these lengthy pamphlets were compiled from different sources. One described the battle of Lepanto together with previous Christian–Turkish battles, especially the Turkish conquest of Cyprus slightly earlier in 1571.[73]

Comparing the contents of handwritten and published news reveals no great difference between them. The information concerning the duration of the battle was identical in both cases, about five hours, but its start varied. According to the printed sources it began at two[74] or

---

[69] Braudel, *La méditerranée*, vol. 1, pp. 333–5, analyses the time needed for distributing newsletters.

[70] ÖNB 74. J. 101; ÖNB 74. J.102; ÖNB 74. J. 103; ÖNB 74. J. 80.

[71] ÖNB 74. J. 87; ÖNB 43. L. 86; reprint: Dillingen 1581, ÖNB 38. D. 60.

[72] ÖNB 74. J. 86.   [73] ÖNB 74. J. 87.   [74] ÖNB 74. J. 101, fol. 7r.

three o'clock[75] in the morning, whereas the handwritten reports gave either one hour before sunrise or two hours after. Concerning booty, two broadsheets assert that 180 Turkish galleys[76] had been captured, while another gave the number as 140.[77] Two different newsletters claimed that 150 galleys had been captured, while a third raised the total to 161. The number of Turkish soldiers killed or imprisoned likewise varied. A broadsheet, which referred explicitly to the newsletter from Venice dated 19 October,[78] had obviously copied only part of the list attached to it, adding information from different sources and changing its original contents. The broadsheet mentioned twenty deceased Venetian commanders; this information did not appear in the handwritten newsletter of 19 October, but in the German copy of the Italian report attached to the newsletter of 26 October. In contrast to the handwritten newsletters, broadsheets were less sceptical and praised Christian deeds far more.

From their very beginnings,[79] it is quite clear that printed reports relied on the handwritten ones and that most differences among them result either from misprints or additional written information which has since disappeared. News from Venice and Rome first reached distant places like Augsburg and Dillingen through handwritten newsletters. Only after several of these were available could they be compiled into a lengthy text and adorned with a woodcut. Using this basis of handwritten information, the printing press could inform a broader local public. Foreign publications could be reprinted or translated, but this process also required additional time. In terms of precision, handwritten newsletters always gave their exact day of compilation, but broadsheets indicated only the year of their publication.

Differences and similarities between the regional distribution of newsletters and broadsheets may be shown by reconstructing their respective networks. The network of newsletters (fig. 2) had its centre in Italy. Notices from the battlefield of Lepanto reached either Otranto or Venice, making these two cities direct links to other places

---

[75] ÖNB 74. J. 102, fol. 3.   [76] ÖNB 74. J. 101, fol. 12; ÖNB 74. J. 103, fol. 4.

[77] ÖNB 74. J. 102, fol. 5.   [78] ÖNB 74. J. 102.

[79] For instance ÖNB 74. J. 102 starts: 'Newe Zeytung auß Venedig vom 19. und 22. October dises 1571 Jars'.

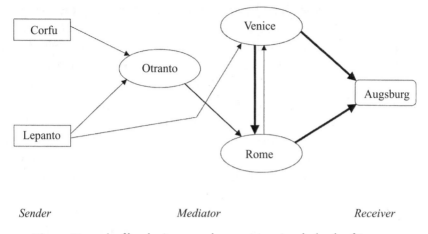

Sender   Mediator   Receiver

Fig. 2. Network of handwritten newsletters concerning the battle of Lepanto

of the network. Rome occupied the second place, whereas places like Augsburg, Lepanto or Corfu lay at the fringes. This impression is confirmed by considering indirect links. They originated from Otranto, the first place receiving news from the eastern Adriatic, which redistributed information to Rome and Venice alike. Next came Rome, the hub of Christendom, with direct or indirect links to all members in the network. Venice, in third place, lacked a connection to Corfu – at least no newsletters mention any. However, considering the number of notices received from or sent to other knots of the network, it was Venice that handled most of the information, Rome holding second place and Otranto only fourth. Combining these three indicators – number of direct links, closeness to other cities and number of notices handled – one might conclude that the network of the newsletters received by the Fugger family in Augsburg concerning Lepanto had its centre in Venice, where information from very different places was collected and distributed to other parts of Europe. Rome was only second in importance, despite the crucial position of the papacy. For the transmission of news from the eastern Mediterranean to the west, and from north to south, the port of Otranto also played an indispensable role. At the fringes of the network lay such senders and receivers of news as Augsburg, Lepanto and finally Corfu.

This impression of a Veneto-Roman system of newsletters can be confirmed by examining the geographical network of all newsletters collected by Octavian II and Philipp Eduard Fugger during the second half of 1571. During this period, the Fuggers received 43 newsletters: 19 from Venice, 18 from Rome, 3 from Antwerp, 2 from Ferrara and one from Vienna. Therefore, almost every week they received a newsletter from Venice or Rome. Many newsletters indicated at the start of each new paragraph where the notices compiled at Venice and Rome originated. The cities and countries mentioned in late 1571 formed a network of 32 places connected by 49 different relations. Its hubs were Venice and Rome, with 19 and 18 connections respectively. Constantinople (the residence of a permanent Venetian ambassador) and Augsburg were each connected to 5 cities. Otranto and Cattaro had 4 direct interconnections; Vienna, Genoa, Corfu and Famagusta 3 apiece. Most cities had a very marginal position within this network, being connected to only one or two other places during these six months.

This impression of clear domination by Venice and Rome is further confirmed by the geographical distribution of notices handled. Venice collected 47 messages; Rome, 43. They distributed 27 and 26 messages respectively. Otherwise, only Constantinople and Otranto handled more than 10 notices; other cities sent and received fewer, most being mentioned only once or twice. Places north of the Alps were mentioned only 17 times, in contrast to 180 times for Italian cities. War with the Turks caused places in the eastern Mediterranean to be mentioned far more often (50 times) than those on the Iberian peninsula (9 times), despite Spanish political importance in Italy.

This picture changed significantly during the following years. We have analysed the headings of all newsletters sent to Augsburg between 1571 and 1573 (map 2). Over three years, the Fuggers collected 567 newsletters. Nearly half still came from Venice (24 per cent) or Rome (22 per cent). However, in contrast to the sample of newsletters from the second half of 1571, almost one-fifth (19 per cent) now came from Antwerp. Vienna sent 5 per cent; Lyon, 3 per cent; and Madrid and Amsterdam, 2.2 per cent each. Over half (56 per cent) of all messages still originated in Italy and its Mediterranean possessions. Cities north of the Alps contributed only one-third of all newsletters; the rest came from France, Spain, or the eastern Mediterranean. Despite Italy's

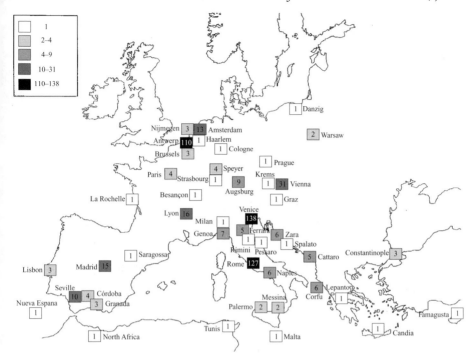

Map 2. Number of handwritten newsletters sent to the Fuggers in 1571–3

central position, the network of the newsletters was very far-reaching, including items from Mexico and Russia.

Although the 1571–3 survey reveals a larger participation of northern Europe, especially Antwerp, in this information network, neither France nor Spain – Europe's two major monarchies, with competing interests on the Italian peninsula – really participated in it. Except for Vienna, places in Germany and Austria were very seldom mentioned. Elizabethan England was completely absent during the whole period. Thus the larger sample shows a growing participation of northwestern Europe during 1572 and 1573, as handwritten newsletters gradually expanded beyond Italy and the Mediterranean.

The network and geographical distribution of the broadsheets concerning Lepanto differ somewhat from those of newsletters (map 3). Notwithstanding their greater weight (pamphlets contained many more pages than handwritten *avvisi*), these printed texts were sent

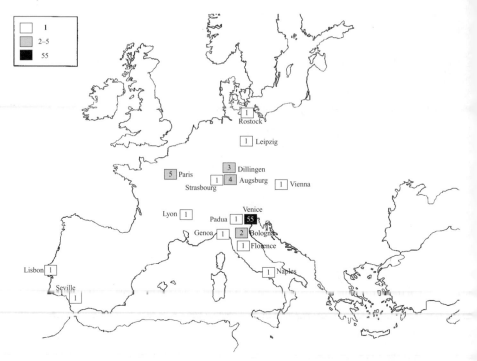

Map 3. Number of broadsheets referring to Lepanto

throughout Europe, normally attached to letters. The broadsheets preserved at the Vienna National Library offer an impression of the distances they covered and their centres of production. In the case of Lepanto, an overwhelming majority were printed in Venice (fifty-five), almost all of them in 1571 and 1572, before news concerning Lepanto virtually stopped being printed. Next in importance came Paris (five), Augsburg (four), Dillingen (three) and Leipzig (one); Bologna published two broadsheets; Florence, Genoa, Naples and Padua, one apiece. Overall, six Italian towns produced broadsheets, while north and west of the Alps eight places issued them (Lyon, Rostock and Strasbourg, besides Vienna and four other cities already mentioned). Broadsheets even appeared in Lisbon and Seville.

Transalpine Europe spread information about Lepanto far more through the printing press than through handwritten newsletters. But if we compare the titles and the centres of the printed pamphlets, it becomes clear that all information was ultimately dependent on printed or handwritten news furnished from Venice. The case of the *Oratio* is a good example. Written in Latin in 1571 by Giovanni Baptista Rosario and published by Vicentius Valgrisius, its title reads *De victoria Christianorum ad Echinadas oratio*. This text was copied the same year in Leipzig and again in Strasbourg in 1572. The Leipzig printer gave a clear hint about the origin of his product by adding *de exemplo Veneto Valgrisiano* to its title. The *Oratio* was also published in Dillingen under a slightly rearranged title: *Oratio de victoria Christianorum ad Echinada*. The sample of broadsheets preserved at the Vienna Library contains only six broadsheets published after 1572, almost all outside Venice.[80] Like handwritten newsletters, printed pamphlets depended on the European political situation. After Venice definitively lost its war against the Ottomans in 1573, no one had any further interest in the battle of Lepanto, which by then seemed an isolated success without lasting consequences.

Thus, in the case of the battle of Lepanto, the network of the printing press had its true centre in Venice. It is noteworthy that not a single broadsheet was published in Rome and only one in Spain. Whereas it is easy to explain the overwhelming interest of Venice in celebrating the victory of Lepanto, it is more difficult to comprehend the silence of its allies. Probably, political differences between the three major Christian participants made it useful for Venice alone to proclaim the victory aloud. Neither the papacy nor the King of Spain had the same vital strategic interests in the eastern Mediterranean as Venice. The reasons why cities and powers north of the Alps issued broadsheets referring to events happening thousands of miles away also require explanation. In the case of Augsburg and Dillingen, where most of the transalpine broadsheets were published, commercial links with Venice and the participation of families like the Fuggers in the Levant trade might offer an explanation. These reasons cannot explain the broadsheets produced at Paris, Leipzig and Rostock. It is even more

[80] Naples 1573, Lisbon 1578, Florence 1581, Venice 1588, Paris 1605, Leipzig 1698.

difficult to understand why broadsheets appeared in Paris and Leipzig after 1600.

We may safely conclude that the system of handwritten newsletters was centred in Venice and Rome in 1571. It already constituted an organised communication business with far-reaching connections. Newsletters provided quick, short and reliable information about outstanding events. By 1571, when this system was still expanding, European regions like the Iberian peninsula, France, German-speaking territories and the British Isles rarely furnished information, and had to read Italian in order to understand a newsletter. During the following decades, two major changes took place. The first was geographical: Antwerp grew in importance, and a north-western European axis developed between Antwerp and Cologne. The second change involved language. Already by the 1570s, newsletters were increasingly written in the language of their recipients. Thus the Italian system of handwritten newsletters became a European network, with two foci: a newer one in Antwerp and Cologne for customers and news from northern Europe supplemented the older one in Venice and Rome for Mediterranean Europe.

Unlike the Italian-centred system of newsletters of 1571, printed broadsheets were published in local vernaculars, or in Latin for learned elites. In the case of the battle of Lepanto, publishing was also centred in Venice, but with a high participation of cities outside Italy, especially in the German-speaking area. Information was exchanged more rapidly through handwriting, but printing had more durable effects. Whereas handwritten information circulated for two months, October and November 1571, printed reports followed at the end of 1571 and throughout 1572; some were even reprinted a hundred years later.

The differences between handwritten newsletters and printed broadsheets can be explained by their respective purposes. The printing press competed with oral forms of communication and often became propaganda for local political purposes. A handwritten newsletter remarked that it still awaited further particulars concerning Lepanto 'because accounts have varied, and the things printed elsewhere are not very exact and differ from each other'.[81] Contemporaries apparently preferred oral statements from eyewitnesses to printed broadsheets. As handwritten newsletters were sent to distant regions beyond the reach of oral communication, they could not be used in the same way. Their notices were too short, almost no images could be included, and their customers belonged to political allies and enemies alike. One must also remember that the Fuggers had strong ties to Habsburg monarchies that increasingly competed with Venice. Therefore, even if Venetian and Roman interests dominated their presentation, newsletters adopted a more moderate tone than broadsheets. Nonetheless, because they could be reprinted frequently and have been conserved better in libraries, printed broadsheets have had more influence on modern historiography. Thus, for a long time, the battle of Lepanto appeared as the start of the definitive victory of Christianity over the Ottoman Empire, since it had been presented this way by the illustrated broadsheets.

---

[81] ÖNB, Cod. 8949, fol. 273v: 'perche si parla variamente, et le stampe, che si sono date fuori non sono molto giuste, et difettive l'una de l'altra'.

CHAPTER 3

Merchants' letters across geographical and social boundaries

Francesca Trivellato

... a Factor is created by Merchant Letters[1]

In his influential book *The Structural Transformation of the Public Sphere*, Jürgen Habermas contrasted medieval business correspondence with the public dissemination of economic news that began in the late seventeenth century, and defined the latter as more central to the development of western capitalism.[2] Several economic historians have endorsed this account. Business newspapers thus add substance to the conventional portrayal of the rise of an open, efficient (modern), Anglo-Atlantic market economy that superseded the medieval, Italian, exclusivist (backward) organisation of trade.[3] This picture, however, rests on a clear-cut and hierarchical opposition between 'private' and 'public' economic information and its means of dissemination that is inconsistent with the commercial practices adopted by European merchants throughout the early modern period.[4] While fast and reliable information is central to all economic activities, it would be wrong

---

[1] Gerard Malynes, *Consuetudo, vel, Lex Mercatoria, or, The Ancient Law-Merchant* (London: Adam Islip, 1622), p. 111. A factor is an agent who worked on commission.

[2] Jürgen Habermas, *The Structural Transformation of the Public Sphere: An Inquiry into a Category of Bourgeois Society* (Cambridge, MA: MIT Press, 1989), pp. 16–21.

[3] For a recent assessment of this view, see John J. McCusker, 'The demise of distance: the business press and the origins of the information revolution in the early modern Atlantic world', *American Historical Review* 110.2 (2005), 295–321.

[4] On the complementarities of manuscript and printed sources of economic information, see Pierre Jeannin, 'La diffusion de l'information', in Simonetta Cavaciocchi (ed.), *Fiere e mercati nella integrazione delle economie europee secc. XIII–XVIII* (Florence: Le Monnier, 2001), pp. 231–62.

to assume that newspapers delivered such information to everyone interested in acquiring it.

Rather, we need to understand the precise content and function of commercial and financial information, how it circulated, and what merchants valued most. The news relevant to merchants often overlapped with news also possessed by diplomats, missionaries, travellers and others – and merchants themselves could simultaneously be missionaries, diplomats, adventurers, pilgrims and similar intermediaries. In Counter-Reformation Italy, for example, 'Lutheran' books were often smuggled by merchants, and business letters contributed to the spread of heterodox ideas.[5] Even restricting our analysis to a purely economic perspective, we must dismiss any simplistic evolutionary depictions of the relation between business correspondence and economic newspapers. By illuminating the principal uses of letters exchanged among merchants involved in long-distance trade, this chapter contends that private correspondence continued to play a fundamental role in the eighteenth century, that is, long after the appearance and diffusion of printed periodicals containing economic information. In so doing, it also throws light on the mercantile culture of early modern Europe even beyond the chronological period examined in this volume.

More specifically, merchants' letters remained uniquely valuable for circulating information about the aptitude and trustworthiness of distant agents. This argument has important empirical and theoretical implications, because as European commerce expanded geographically, business organisation became more complex: new formal institutions such as joint-stock chartered companies and stock markets emerged. Individual family firms and ethnic-religious trading diasporas, however, remained essential protagonists in many branches of commerce, and were also forced to establish durable economic relations with outsiders. Business correspondence, as I will show, was a crucial instrument in forging and maintaining these informal

---

[5] Rita Mazzei, *Itinera mercatorum: circolazione di uomini e di merci nell'Europa centro-orientale, 1550–1650* (Pisa: Maria Pacini Farri Editore, 1999), pp. 189–90.

cross-cultural networks, and thus also constitutes a precious historical source for studying a neglected phenomenon.

BUSINESS CORRESPONDENCE IN LATE MEDIEVAL AND EARLY MODERN EUROPE

In the fourteenth century, offering advice on how to succeed in business, an Italian merchant recommended, 'You should not postpone tending to your correspondence. Paper is cheap, and often brings in good profit.' And he added, 'One must know how to keep books and records; to write and answer letters, which is not a small thing, particularly that of knowing how to dictate letters.'[6] A champion of such recommendations was Francesco, son of Marco Datini (c.1335–1410), a textile merchant–producer from Prato (near Florence), whose suppliers and customers extended from Barcelona to Bruges, Lisbon, Sicily and even further. Through good fortune and his own efforts we possess over 126,000 original commercial letters sent to Datini from 285 different localities, and some 11,000 private letters exchanged between him and his wife, which include many references to his economic activities.[7] To date, this is the largest known collection of business correspondence available to historians of Europe and the Mediterranean. One, two, even three centuries later, merchants still continued to devote considerable time and care to letter writing, although few were as zealous or as fortunate as Datini in their record-keeping. Simon Ruiz of Medina del Campo received more than 50,000 letters between 1558 and 1598;[8]

---

[6] Anthony Molho (ed.), *Social and Economic Foundations of the Italian Renaissance* (New York: John Wiley & Sons, 1969), pp. 55, 57.

[7] Federigo Melis, *Aspetti della vita economica medievale (Studi nell'Archivio Datini di Prato)*, 2 vols. (Siena: Leo S. Olschki, 1962), vol. 1, pp. 13–17; Bruno Dini, 'L'archivio Datini', in Simonetta Cavaciocchi (ed.), *L'impresa, industria, commercio, banca secc. XIII–XVIII* (Florence: Le Monnier, 1991), pp. 45–58; Elena Cecchi, *Le lettere di Francesco Datini alla moglie Margherita (1385–1410)* (Prato: Società Pratese di Storia Patria, 1992).

[8] Henri Lapeyre, *Une famille de marchands: les Ruiz* (Paris: Librairie Armand Colin, 1955); Valentín Vázquez de Prada, *Lettres marchandes d'Anvers*, 4 vols. (Paris: SEVPEN, 1960).

and nearly 80,000 letters were sent to the Roux of Marseilles from 1728 to 1843.[9]

When studying business correspondence, economic historians have mostly privileged the medieval over the early modern period in spite of the large collections of letters surviving from the later period. This preference reflects the importance of merchants' letters in the panorama of sources available to historians of medieval trade. Starting in the sixteenth century, new economic institutions have indeed produced new and voluminous types of records, but reliance on such documents should not obscure the continued centrality of merchants' letters in early modern commercial practices.

Both practical and legal reasons account for the persistent importance of business correspondence in European trade. While merchants became more sedentary, and new legal contracts (such as the *commenda*) ensuring a more efficient division of labour, risk and profit developed in medieval Italy, letters remained the main instruments for a merchant to exert control over his agents overseas.[10] As European commerce expanded, commission agency became increasingly essential for conducting long-distance trade, and business correspondence attained greater rather than lesser significance. In the most famous and widely imitated commercial manual of early modern Europe, Jacques Savary warned against the risks of commission trade, claiming that 'those who do business via commission agency go straight to the poor house'.[11] Savary knew all too well that the age of Europe's travelling

---

[9] Ferréol Rebuffat, *Répertoire numérique des Archives*, vol. II, *Fonds annexes de la Chambre* (Marseille: Imprimerie Robert, 1965), pp. 89–149. The Roux's correspondence is used amply in Charles Carrière, *Négociants marseillais au XVIIIe siècle: contribution à l'étude des économies maritimes* (Marseille: Institut Historique de Provence, 1973), and Charles Carrière, Michel Gutsatz, Marcel Courdurié and René Squarzoni, *Banque et capitalisme commercial: la lettre de change au XVIIIe siècle* (Marseille: Institut Historique de Provence, 1976).

[10] Frederic C. Lane, *Andrea Barbarigo, Merchant of Venice (1418–1449)* (Baltimore: Johns Hopkins University Press, 1944), pp. 97–9.

[11] '... qui fait ses affaires par commission va à l'Hôpital en personne'; Jacques Savary, *Le parfait négociant ou Instruction générale pour ce qui regarde le commerce des marchandises de France et des pays étrangers* (Paris: Jean Guignard fils, 1675), book 2, ch. 47, p. 33; also quoted in Henri Hauser, 'Le "Parfait Négociant" de Jacques Savary', *Revue d'historie économique et sociale* 13 (1925), 1–28, here 16.

merchants had faded away, and that letters were the primary tool for weaving webs of commercial relations across space and social groups. As he recognised, 'nothing preserves commerce as much as commissioners and correspondents'.[12] In addition, beginning in the fourteenth century and becoming standard practice after the sixteenth, merchants no longer needed to certify their papers with notaries.[13] Once business correspondence acquired autonomous legal validity, a merchant's job became simpler and cheaper. Meanwhile, as letters became accepted proof in court, their language necessarily became increasingly formulaic: expressions of gratitude and friendship, for example, acquired contractual meanings.[14] Indeed, the oft-lamented formulaic prose and repetitive content of business letters account for their effectiveness, because rhetorical standardisation rendered contracts and obligations intelligible and enforceable across geographical and social boundaries.

The literature known as *ars mercatoria* mirrors these changes in both the legal and practical functions of business correspondence. Merchants' manuals of the fourteenth and fifteenth centuries rarely mention letter writing, while listing different local units of measurement, currency values and trading customs.[15] From the late sixteenth century onwards, specialised letter-writing models appeared in print while commercial treaties began to devote greater attention to correspondence. The *Formulaire de missives, obligations, quittances, letters de change, d'asseurances* . . . by Gabriel Meurier was published in Antwerp in 1558, followed in 1576 by Gérard de Vivre's *Lettres*

---

[12] 'Il n'y a rien qui mantienne tant le commerce, que les commissionaires ou correspondans'; Savary, *Le parfait négociant*, book 2, ch. 55, p. 143.

[13] Maura Fortunati, *Scrittura e prova: i libri di commercio nel diritto medievale e moderno* (Rome: Fondazione Sergio Mochi Onory per la storia del diritto italiano, 1996).

[14] Fortunati, *Scrittura e prova*, p. 22; Carlos Petit, '*Mercatura y ius mercatorum*: materiales para una antropología del comerciante premoderno', in Carlos Petit (ed.), *Del ius mercatorum al derecho mercantil: III Seminario de Historia del Derecho Privado (Sitges, 28–30 de mayo de 1992)* (Madrid: Marcial Pons, Ediciones Jurídicas y Sociales, 1997), p. 64.

[15] Francesco Balducci Pegolotti, *La pratica della mercatura*, ed. Allan Evans (Cambridge, MA: The Mediaeval Academy of America, 1936); Franco Borlandi, *El libro di mercantie et usanze de' paesi* (Turin: S. Lattes, 1936); Antonia Borlandi, *Il manuale di mercatura di Saminiato de' Ricci* (Genoa: Di Stefano, 1963).

missives and Jean Bourlier's *Lettres communes*.[16] A century later, such compilations had multiplied and now included booklets addressed to tradesmen, shopkeepers and the educated public, such as John Hill's popular *The Young Secretary's Guide: or, A Speedy Help to Learning* (first printed in London in 1680, it had reached its 27th edition by 1764). More specialised bilingual models of business letters appeared, such as the Italian–German edition of Matthias Kramer's *Il segretario di banco* (Nuremberg, 1693). *Il negoziante* by Giovanni Domenico Peri, the most sophisticated seventeenth-century Italian merchants' manual, included sketchy instructions on how to write letters, and referred to the legal standing of business correspondence in a chapter devoted to 'contracts'.[17] In his *Parfait négociant*, Savary urged all merchants to keep copies of the letters they sent, so that they could submit them as evidence in court or could review what they had previously written to their correspondents in order to verify their orders and their answers.[18]

While merchants' manuals took notice of the importance of business letters, by the late sixteenth century and more intensively after 1650, new periodical publications offering economic information became available. First came single-sheet currents (containing lists of local prices and exchanges rates), then more voluminous almanacs and gazettes.[19] These printed materials have provided economic

---

[16] Roger Chartier, '*Secrétaires* for the people? Model letters of the ancient régime: between court literature and popular chapbooks', in Roger Chartier, Alain Boureau and Cécile Dauphin (eds.), *Correspondence: Models of Letter-Writing form the Middle Ages to the Nineteenth Century* (Princeton: Princeton University Press, 1997), pp. 59–111, here p. 68. See also Jochen Hoock, Pierre Jeannin and Wolfgang Kaiser (eds.), *Ars Mercatoria: eine analytische Bibliographie*, 3 vols. (Paderborn: Ferdinand Schöningh, 1991–2001), vol. 1.

[17] Giovanni Domenico Peri, *Il negoziante*... (Venice: Gio. Giacomo Hertz, 1662 [1638]), pp. 11–14, 41.

[18] Savary, *Le parfait negociant*, book 2, ch. 43, p. 8. Similar prescriptions in Samuel Ricard, *Traité général du commerce* . . ., 5th edition (Amsterdam: Aux depens de la Compagnie, 1732), pp. 531–2.

[19] John J. McCusker and Cora Gravesteijn, *The Beginning of Commercial and Financial Journalism: The Commodity Price Currents, Exchange Rate Currents, and Money Currents of Early Modern Europe* (Amsterdam: NEHA, 1991); John J. McCusker, 'The Italian business press in early modern Europe', in Simonetta Cavaciocchi (ed.), *Produzione e commercio della carta e del libro secc. XIII–XVIII* (Florence: Le Monnier, 1992), pp. 797–841.

historians with invaluable information. Michel Morineau, for example, challenged accepted wisdom concerning the arrival of American bullion in Europe on the basis of figures extrapolated from Amsterdam gazettes.[20] We should not, however, conclude that economic periodicals supplanted business letters as the chief source of economic information in the seventeenth and eighteenth centuries. In spite of progress in postal services as well as in overland transportation and sea shipping, no significant remedy existed for slow communication before railways, steamships and the telegraph were invented. In the early modern Mediterranean and Atlantic, couriers became faster and more regular, and average freight costs decreased, but no revolution occurred in maritime or terrestrial transportation.[21]

Economic newspapers thus had no structural advantage over business letters in terms of the rapidity with which they disseminated information. It is often assumed that the public nature of periodicals had a strong impact on market expansion and integration. In practice, however, the publication of prices, exchange, interest and stock rates had only limited effects: it was most effective locally, but did not significantly enhance long-distance trade.[22] While updated lists of stock rates were available to small and medium-sized investors who purchased shares of the Dutch and English East India Companies, they were not able to reduce the asymmetry of information between them and the boards of trustees of these speculative institutions.[23] Admittedly, gazettes and other periodical publications brought remarkable

[20] Michel Morineau, *Incroyables gazettes et fabuleux métaux: les retours des trésors américains d'après les gazettes hollandaises (XVIe–XVIIIe siècles)* (London, New York and Paris: Cambridge University Press and Maison des Sciences de l'Homme, 1985).

[21] Fernand Braudel, *The Mediterranean and the Mediterranean World in the Age of Philip II*, 2 vols. (New York: Harper & Row, 1972–3), vol. 1, pp. 355–74, and *Civilization and Capitalism, 15th–18th Century*, 3 vols. (New York: Harper & Row, 1981–4), vol. 1, pp. 415–30; Russell R. Menard, 'Transport costs and long-range trade, 1300–1800: was there a European "transport revolution" in the early modern era?', in James D. Tracy (ed.), *The Political Economy of Merchant Empires* (Cambridge: Cambridge University Press, 1991), pp. 228–75.

[22] Jeannin, 'La diffusion de l'information', pp. 252–3.

[23] Jonathan Barron Baskin, 'The development of corporate financial markets in Britain and the United States, 1600–1914: overcoming asymmetric information', *Business History Review* 62.2 (1988), 199–237, here pp. 202–3.

innovations in both retail and wholesale marketing. David Hancock has shown how London-based merchants took advantage of the proliferation of newspapers in the first half of the eighteenth century in order to advertise the arrival of their cargo, the auctioning of their goods and the availability of their ships, and promote their affairs more generally.[24] Hancock has also documented how newspapers, correspondence and personal ties all helped expand the market for Madeira wine in North America during the eighteenth century.[25]

Periodicals, however, were less than efficient when it came to informing agents about either the objective or the intangible qualities of their distant correspondents, especially when the latter were neither relatives nor coreligionists. Such goals were best fulfilled by business correspondence. In addition to allowing merchants to deliver orders (purchases, sales, subscriptions of insurance policies, extensions of credit lines, etc.) and serve as proof that such transactions had occurred, letters also transferred information among correspondents about a large variety of topics. Indeed, most letters simply reported facts and opinions without ordering the completion of any specific transactions.[26]

The information transmitted via private business correspondence can be schematically grouped under three headings. The first category included commodity prices, local units of weights and measures, insurance premia, exchange rates, descriptions of the quantity and quality of products available in specific towns or regions, and similar matters. Secondly, news concerning political, military and diplomatic events also abounded. Both types of information helped agents assess

---

[24] David Hancock, *Citizens of the World: London Merchants and the Integration of the British Atlantic Community, 1735–1785* (Cambridge: Cambridge University Press, 1995), pp. 32–3.

[25] David Hancock, '"A revolution in the trade": wine distribution and the development of the infrastructure of the Atlantic market economy, 1703–1807', in John J. McCusker and Kenneth Morgan (eds.), *The Early Modern Atlantic Economy* (Cambridge: Cambridge University Press, 2000), pp. 134–42.

[26] Jeannin, 'La diffusion de l'information', p. 245; Giovanni Levi, 'I commerci della Casa Daniele Bonfil e figlio con Marsiglia e Costantinopoli (1773–1794)', in Stefano Gasparri, Giovanni Levi and Pierandrea Moro (eds.), *Venezia: itinerari per la storia della città* (Bologna: Il Mulino, 1997), pp. 223–43, here p. 225.

short- and medium-term market fluctuations, and thus facilitated their decision-making process. A correspondent often tailored his writing to suit the needs and the requests of his addressees. Naturally, merchants gathered intelligence wherever they could. Strolling along the docks or on the market square was a necessary daily exercise. Sometimes, printed price or stock lists were expedited together with a letter – another testimony to the complementarity of printed and manuscript sources. Gazettes were mostly filled with political and military reports, but did not necessarily offer speed, quality or reliability.[27]

Most importantly, merchants' letters also contained a third type of information, that is, about merchants themselves. This knowledge could be either direct (when, for example, the success or failure of an agent was communicated to correspondents) or indirect (in the sense that letter exchange was itself a form of recognition of reciprocal esteem, or at least tested the possibility of future collaboration). References to personal and family matters in business correspondence, while sporadic, nevertheless nourished social as well as business ties. Any ambitious merchant considered expressing his condolences and greetings to business associates to be part of his duties, and many took up their pens in order to negotiate matters as crucial for their firms as good marriages for their daughters. In addition, bills of exchange, or references to their negotiability, were sometimes included in ordinary business letters. This overlap was due as much to the organisation of private credit at the time as to the inextricable link between an individual's economic and social credit.[28]

Writing to a friend in 1717, an English trader noted, 'To support and maintain a man's private credit, 'tis absolutely necessary that the world have a fixed opinion of the honesty and integrity, as well as the ability of the person.'[29] For this, private business correspondence was definitely

---

[27] As Barbarics and Pieper demonstrate convincingly in chapter 2 of this volume.

[28] This issue is explored, though less in connection to long-distance trade than in relation to local and regional economies, in Craig Muldrew, *The Economy of Obligation: The Culture of Credit and Social Relations in Early Modern England* (New York: St Martin's Press, 1999).

[29] A. A. Sykes, *A Letter to a Friend . . .* (London, 1717), quoted in Peter Mathias, 'Risk, credit and kinship in early modern enterprise', in McCusker and Morgan (eds.), *The Early Modern Atlantic Economy*, p. 29.

more adequate than public sources. Not only did it ensure the secrecy that helped one cope with competition and was necessary in certain dealings, but it also incorporated facts and judgements about other businessmen that rarely found expression in printed materials. By the early eighteenth century the bankruptcy of large merchant houses regularly appeared in a special section of most London gazettes, but this information was fairly selective and standardised, and restricted to a local readership. Private correspondence was the only way in which many merchants could nuance, diffuse, and update information about the reputations of their smaller and distant counterparts. Rich in candid comments about his competitors and filled with a variety of gossip, the letters that Joshua Johnson sent from London to his associates in Maryland in the 1770s, at a time when English trade in North America was the most thriving sector of international commerce, testify to this crucial function.[30]

Letters of introduction provided a common and indispensable tool for any merchant interested in entering a new market or enlarging his network. Conversely, letters could point to the failures of correspondents who did not deliver on their promises or performed below expectations. Always keen to avoid legal troubles, but often unable to bring a distant correspondent to court in cases of malfeasance, merchants used letters to select apt and reliable agents, as well as to check on them. Trust was a precious and fragile commodity; it built on constant reinforcements that buttressed one's reputation and on the multiple cross-references that correspondence networks helped forge. A trader frequently repeated the same information in letters addressed to different agents as a way of stimulating competition and generating vigilance among them. Despite the individual character of each letter, business correspondence should actually be read as a polyphonic conversation rather than a dialogue. In sum, primarily because they conveyed reputations far better than any public information sources, private business letters remained a vital element in the organisation of early modern long-distance trade.

---

[30] Jacob M. Price (ed.), *Joshua Johnson's Letterbook 1771–1774: Letters from a Merchant in London to his Partners in Maryland* (London: London Record Society, 1979).

ECONOMIC HISTORIANS AND MERCHANTS' LETTERS

Merchants' letters have long been a classic source for the study of
European economic history. Scholars have traditionally used them
to document the speed of diffusion of economic information or such
advances in business techniques as the appearance of new forms of
partnership or novel financial and insurance systems.[31] Others have
relied on business correspondence to outline what was once called
'the psychology of merchants', that is, their more or less idealised and
typified sociological traits as a social group. In the words of Robert
Lopez and Irving Raymond, there exists 'no better key to the psychology of the merchant' than business correspondence.[32] A master
of this approach, S. D. Goitein, used merchants' letters to illustrate
the 'sociological' rather than 'economic' aspects of the overseas trade
conducted by a group of North African Jews during the eleventh and
twelfth centuries.[33] In the 1950s and 1960s, under the sponsorship of
Fernand Braudel, various collections of merchants' letters were published with little or no commentary, as if such presumably transparent

---

[31] Pierre Sardella, *Nouvelles et spéculations à Venise au début du XVIe siècle* (Paris:
Librairie Armand Colin, 1948), pp. 56–75; Yves Renouard, 'Information et transmission des nouvelles', in Charles Samaran (ed.), *L'histoire et ses méthodes* (Paris: Editions Gallimard, 1961), pp. 95–142; Melis, *Aspetti*, vol. 1, pp. 13–17; Melis, *Documenti
per la storia economica dei secoli XIII–XVI* (Florence: Leo S. Olschki, 1972), pp. 14–27,
136–229; Melis, 'Intensità e regolarità nella diffusione dell'informazione economica generale nel Mediterraneo e in Occidente alla fine del Medioevo', in *Mélanges
en l'honneur de Fernand Braudel*, vol. 1: *Histoire économique du monde méditerranéen
1450–1650* (Toulouse: Editions Privat, 1973), pp. 389–424.

[32] Robert S. Lopez and Irving W. Raymond, *Medieval Trade in the Mediterranean World:
Illustrative Documents Translated with Introductions and Notes* (New York: Columbia
University, 1955), p. 378. See also Armando Sapori, *Le marchand italien au Moyen
Age* (Paris: Librairie Armand Colin, 1952). Melis, *Aspetti*, p. 4 n. 1, criticised Sapori's
use of Datini's letters and account books for not addressing their technical dimension
more skilfully.

[33] S. D. Goitein, *Letters of Medieval Jewish Traders Translated from the Arabic with Introductions and Notes* (Princeton: Princeton University Press, 1973), p. 11; *A Mediterranean Society: The Jewish Communities of the Arab World as Portrayed in the Documents
of the Cairo Geniza*, 6 vols. (Berkeley and Los Angeles: University of California Press,
1967–93).

primary sources would serve the purpose of a *histoire totale* of the merchants' world.[34]

More recently, economists and economic historians have returned to the study of merchants' letters, this time concentrating on the role of information in pre-modern markets. They are now less preoccupied with the technicalities of its transmission than with its functions in forming solidarities, enforcing contracts and minimising opportunist behaviours. Merchants' letters are thus examined first of all as the means through which an agent's ability and honesty were circulated among his correspondents. The most innovative and influential insights have come from the economist Avner Greif, who for over fifteen years has engaged in theoretical and comparative analysis of the organisation of medieval Mediterranean trade. Through the use of game theory, rational-choice modelling and the new institutional economic history, Greif further refines the opinions of Robert Lopez and Raymond de Roover about the so-called 'commercial revolution' of the Middle Ages, and specifically about the consequences of the routine use of new legal contracts and institutions in the Italian maritime republics of the thirteenth century.[35] Greif's most original contribution concerns the power and limitations of mechanisms of contract enforcement generated solely by reputation control in a context where legal institutions were either weak or absent. He analyses a group of North African Jews active across the Mediterranean as self-interested individuals dependent on information about an actor's past conduct in order to make decisions about whether or not to trade

---

[34] Fernand Braudel, 'Avant-propos', in Micheline Baulant-Duchaillut (ed.), *Lettres de négociants marseillais: les frères Hermite (1570–1612)* (Paris: Librairie Armand Colin, 1953); Ugo Tucci, *Lettres d'un marchand vénitien: Andrea Berengo (1553–1556)* (Paris: SEVPEN, 1957); José Gentil da Silva, *Marchandises et finances: Lettres de Lisbonne 1563–1578*, 3 vols. (Paris: SEVPEN, 1959); Vázquez de Prada, *Lettres marchandes*; Felipe Ruíz Martín, *Lettres marchandes échangées entre Florence et Medina del Campo* (Paris: SEVPEN, 1965).

[35] Raymond de Roover, 'The organization of trade', in *The Cambridge Economic History of Europe*, vol. 3: M. M. Postan, E. E. Rich and Edward Miller (eds.), *Economic Organization and Policies in the Middle Ages* (Cambridge: Cambridge University Press, 1965), pp. 42–118; Robert S. Lopez, *The Commercial Revolution of the Middle Ages, 950–1350* (Englewood Cliffs, NJ: Prentice-Hall, 1971).

with him. Departing from previous interpretations, Greif argues that
they created dependable networks of long-distant agents during the
eleventh and twelfth centuries, not because of their social cohesion
or ethical injunctions, but through individual rational calculation and
collective punishment.[36]

Even a sympathetic reader becomes suspicious of his sharp distinction between economic and social sanctions, since these business
associates were also coreligionists and not infrequently relatives, who
shared much more than an interest in the pursuit of profit. Although
we know that this specific group of North African Jewish traders
cooperated with Muslims as well as with other Jews, Greif claims that
these informal mechanisms of monitoring and information transmission did not extend to members of other communities.[37] This view
reduces business correspondence to a traditional tool of commercial operations incapable of sustaining market expansion, until legally
sanctioned commercial contracts later provided Italian merchants with
the necessary security to venture into business outside their own families and immediate communities.

Historians who have called attention to the role of information in
European commercial organisation are generally more inclined than
economists to acknowledge the social and collective dimensions of
unofficial forms of reputation control. But by and large they too focus
on pre-established groups, whether family clans or religious and ethnic
minorities. Letters are thus considered an asset in the hands of Genoese
merchant-bankers who dominated Iberian finances from the early
sixteenth to the mid seventeenth century.[38] Examining the business

[36] Avner Greif, 'Reputation and coalition in medieval trade: evidence on the Maghribi
traders', *Journal of Economic History* 49.4 (1989), 857–82; Avner Greif, 'Contract
enforceability and economic institutions in early trade: the Maghribi traders' coalition', *American Economic Review* 133.3 (1992), 525–48.

[37] Compare, for example, S. D. Goitein, 'Letters and documents on the India trade
in medieval times', in *Studies in Islamic History and Institutions* (Leiden: E. J. Brill,
1966), pp. 329–50, here p. 350, with Greif, 'Reputation and coalition', pp. 862, 878.

[38] Giorgio Doria, 'Conoscenza del mercato e sistema informativo: il know-how dei
mercanti-finanzieri genovesi nei secoli XVI e XVII', in Aldo De Maddalena and Hermann Kellenbenz (eds.), *La repubblica internazionale del denaro* (Bologna: Il Mulino,
1986), pp. 57–122.

correspondence of two family firms of wholesale traders in Stockholm, Leos Müller demonstrated how intense communication of economic news and social relations had a greater impact than legal enforcement on the stability of commission trade. The activities of these Swedish merchants, however, were restricted in terms of geography, articles and actors, producing remarkable stability in their networks, which revolved around a core of relatives in Amsterdam and a few occasional correspondents.[39]

The function of correspondence can be better tested through commercial diasporas – such as the Sephardic Jews, Huguenots, Quakers, Armenians and later the Greeks – that contributed to disseminating skills and integrating distant markets in various regions of the globe during the European commercial expansion. The geographical expansion of European commerce increased the need for information to travel not only across vast geographical distances, but also across ethnic, religious, cultural and political boundaries. In many instances, specialised groups of brokers and trading diasporas became influential through their ability to facilitate cross-cultural trade.[40] Their strength derived from their internal cohesion and geographical dispersion, which gave them a competitive advantage over individual family firms. Received traditions in the social sciences and the character of most historical records have induced most scholars (whether proponents of a purely economic explanation of trust, or inclined to recognise its social components) to look primarily at how information circulated within the boundaries of closed communities, either locally or globally. But precisely because of their role as cross-cultural agents, trading diasporas had to engage in sustained economic relations with outsiders. Their business letters offer a unique lens through which to observe the workings of these economic relations.

---

[39] Leos Müller, *The Merchant Houses of Stockholm, c.1640–1800: A Comparative Study of Early-Modern Entrepreneurial Behaviour* (Uppsala: Uppsala University Library, 1998).

[40] Philip D. Curtin, *Cross-Cultural Trade in World History* (Cambridge: Cambridge University Press, 1984).

BUSINESS LETTERS ACROSS ETHNIC AND
RELIGIOUS BOUNDARIES

Sephardic Jews were the most global and the most successful trading diaspora of the early modern period, exerting particular influence on international commerce between 1650 and 1750.[41] Especially in the Dutch Atlantic economy, their efficacy was such that on more than one occasion they learned of political or military news before diplomats did, and with this news were able to influence the fluctuations of the Amsterdam stock exchange.[42] They also continued to be dynamic actors in Mediterranean trade throughout the eighteenth century. Like all other merchants of the time, they made use of a combination of printed, manuscript and oral sources of information to devise their strategies. From 1675 to 1690, an entrepreneurial Sephardic Jew of Amsterdam published a periodical in Spanish, called *Gazeta de Amsterdam*, which sent political and economic news to Jews and crypto-Jews across the globe.[43] Not surprisingly given the competition in the information market, the experiment was ineffective. A few surviving collections of letters written by eighteenth-century Sephardic firms in western Europe provide us with a much richer sense of the ways in which they acquired, managed and utilised information. Among these are 13,670 letters written between 16 December 1704 and 4 February 1746 by the Ergas & Silvera partnership of Livorno (known in English as Leghorn) to both coreligionists and non-Jews in numerous ports of the Mediterranean and northern Europe, and even to Goa, the capital of Portuguese India.[44]

[41] Jonathan Israel, *Diasporas within a Diaspora: Jews, Crypto-Jews and the World Maritime Empires, 1540–1740* (Leiden, Boston and Cologne: Brill, 2002).

[42] Israel, *Diasporas*, pp. 453–4.

[43] Henri Méchoulan, *Etre Juif à Amsterdam au temps de Spinoza* (Paris: Albin Michel, 1991), p. 112.

[44] Archivio di Stato, Florence (hereafter ASF), *Libri di commercio e di famiglia* (hereafter *LCF*), 1931, 1935–9, 1941, 1945, 1953, 1957, 1960. The archival classification of these records was recently updated. Here the new one is provided, together with the correct total number of letters included. For more on what follows, see also Francesca Trivellato, 'Juifs de Livourne, Italiens de Lisbonne et hindous de Goa: réseaux marchands et échanges interculturels à l'époque moderne', *Annales HSS* 58.3 (2003), 581–603.

At the turn of the eighteenth century Livorno was the largest Mediterranean port until the rise of Marseille; along with Amsterdam, it was also one of the two largest Sephardic settlements in Europe. Ergas & Silvera was a prominent merchant house, with a branch in Livorno and another one in Aleppo (Syria). Like many of their coreligionists in Livorno, Ergas & Silvera conducted most of their trade with the Ottoman Empire. They imported raw cotton from the Levant, re-exported raw silk from southern Italy, funnelled fine silk textiles from Italy into central and northern Europe, and traded in a large variety of Mediterranean goods. Unlike the Dutch and English Sephardim who made their fortunes in the West Indies, those based in Livorno were not directly involved in transatlantic commerce, although they controlled a large share of the American goods imported into the Italian peninsula, especially tobacco, sugar, indigo, coffee and brazil-wood.

A particular specialty of Livorno's Sephardim was the exchange of Mediterranean coral and Indian diamonds. From the 1660s, this lucrative but risky barter came increasingly under the aegis of the English East India Company, and London became the world market for rough diamonds.[45] The readmission of the Jews to England in 1656 spurred this trade, which in turn stimulated fresh Sephardic migration to London. However, throughout the eighteenth century, and especially until the 1730s (when the English lifted all restrictions on diamond trading and achieved supremacy in the Indian Ocean, while Brazilian diamond mines began to be exploited), the Sephardim of Livorno continued to carry out the exchange of coral and diamonds relying on a Portuguese connection centred on Lisbon and Goa. Indeed, the latter remained a centre of the diamond trade until 1730.[46]

---

[45] Holden Furber, *Rival Empires of Trade in the Orient 1600–1800* (Minneapolis: University of Minnesota Press, 1976), pp. 133–4, 260–2; Gedalia Yogev, *Diamonds and Coral: Anglo-Dutch Jews and Eighteenth-Century Trade* (Leicester: Leicester University Press, 1978); Søren Mentz, 'English private trade on the Coromandel coast, 1660–1690: diamonds and country trade', *Indian Economic and Social History Review* 33.2 (1996), 155–73; Edgar Samuel, 'Diamonds and pieces of eight: how Stuart England won the rough-diamond trade', *Jewish Historical Studies* 38 (2004), 23–40.

[46] Charles R. Boxer, *The Portuguese Seaborne Empire 1415–1825* (London: Hutchinson, 1969), pp. 148–9.

Of the 13,670 surviving letters of Ergas & Silvera, 242 were addressed to Christian (mostly Italian) merchants in Lisbon, and 86 to Hindu merchants in Goa. All their correspondence with both Lisbon and Goa concerns the trade in coral and diamonds. Considering the diversity of the addressees and the lack of an overarching legal authority to which any parties could bring their complaints (aggravated by the banning of Jews from all Portuguese dominions), one naturally wonders how sufficient trust could possibly be built across such geographical and ethno-cultural distances. The answer, I believe, lies primarily in the intense and widespread circulation of business letters among these merchants, which created and nourished informal mechanisms of obligations and reciprocal control. These mechanisms worked because each merchant was not an autonomous entity, a monad, but rather a member of a larger community (which in the case of the Sephardim had a diasporic dimension). Although driven by the search for profit, individual merchants also abided by collective social and normative codes of behaviour impressed upon them by their communitarian organisations. The result was not a series of isolated, occasional transactions, but the development of durable cross-cultural relations of mutual dependence in the context of complex intergroup dynamics made possible by the circulation of information about the reputations of individuals and groups. Ergas & Silvera invested in the Portuguese branch of the exchange of coral and diamonds for a period of over thirty years, between 1710 (when their first shipment of coral to Goa is recorded) and 1741 (when they regularly preferred London and Madras to their previous destinations). They opted for this Portuguese connection because they could rely on a pre-existing network of correspondents in Lisbon and Goa, who also served other Sephardim in Livorno and their coreligionists in Amsterdam and London, and they could use letters to carve their own niche within this network.

In Lisbon, Ergas & Silvera relied primarily on resident Genoese and Florentine merchants, who were active in the trade with the Italian peninsula. The most reliable among these correspondents were the Florentine Enea Beroardi (in partnership until 1738 with another Florentine, Girolamo Paolo Medici) and the Ravara and Cambiaso families of Genoa. In the early eighteenth century, these Italians no longer held the dominant position in Lisbon that they had occupied during the early phase of Portuguese exploration and conquest, but they were still influential, especially in the import of food staples and luxury items from the Mediterranean and the re-export of Portuguese colonial goods to various Italian states. Around 1730, an anonymous traveller to Lisbon noted that the Italians had the biggest commercial houses next to the English, who, together with the Dutch, were the most privileged foreign communities in town, and that some Italian merchants handled a larger volume of transactions than the entire French 'nation'.[47]

All of Ergas & Silvera's letters to Goa were addressed to Hindu Brahamins of the Saraswat caste, the city's leading native elite throughout the four and a half centuries under Portuguese rule.[48] Ergas & Silvera's closest agents were members of the Camotim family (Portuguese for Kamat), probably the richest family in Goa in the 1730s.[49] From this correspondence we learn that the Camotins operated as a united clan,

[47] *Description de la ville de Lisbonne . . .* (Amsterdam: Pierre Humbert, 1730), pp. 249–50.
[48] N. K. Wagle, 'The history and social organization of the Gauda Saraswata Brahmanas' of the west coast of India', *Journal of Indian History* 48 (1970), 7–25, 295–333; Frank F. Conlon, *A Caste in a Changing World: The Chitrapur Saraswat Brahmans, 1700–1935* (Berkeley, Los Angeles and London: University of California Press, 1977); M. N. Pearson, 'Banyas and Brahmins: their role in the Portuguese Indian economy', in *Coastal Western India: Studies from the Portuguese Records* (New Delhi: Concept Publishing Company, 1981), pp. 93–115. Pearson notes that Conlon's 'Saraswat Brahmans' are a small subgroup of the Gaud Saraswat Brahmin caste-cluster; *ibid.*, pp. 111–12 n 5.
[49] Panduronga S. S. Pissurlencar, *The Portuguese and the Marathas* (Bombay: State Board for Literature and Culture, 1975), pp. 277–81; Teotonio R. de Souza, 'Mhamai house records: indigenous sources for Indo-Portuguese historiography', in *II Seminário Internacional de História Indo-Portuguesa: Actas* (Lisbon: Instituto de Investigação Científica Tropical, 1985), pp. 933–41; Teotonio R. de Souza, 'French slave-trading in Portuguese Goa (1773–1791)', in de Souza (ed.), *Essays in Goan History* (New Delhi: Concept Publishing Company, 1989), pp. 119–31; Celsa Pinto, *Trade and Finance in Portuguese India: A Study of the Portuguese Country Trade, 1770–1840* (New Delhi: Concept Publishing Company, 1994), pp. 53–6; Charles J. Borges, SJ, 'Native Goan participation in the Estado da Índia and the inter-Asiatic Trade', in Artur Teodoro de Matos and Luís Filipe F. Reis Thomaz (eds.), *A Carreira da Índia e as rotas dos estreitos: Actas do VIII seminário internacional de história indo-portuguesa* (Braga: Angra do Heroísmo, 1998), pp. 672–83.

careful about the good standing of their members and eager for the continued delivery of new orders from Livorno. Writing to Gopala and Fondu Camotim in January 1727, Ergas & Silvera complained to them about the lack of return cargoes and letters from their relative Nillea Camotim. At the same time, they wrote to a Genoese in Lisbon, Lazzaro Maria Cambiaso, enquiring about the opinion that his 'friends', recently returned from Goa, held of this Nillea.[50] Ergas & Silvera's correspondence indicates that cross-checks worked to threaten negligent agents. It mentions no cases of actual expulsion from the network by reputation mechanisms, although it allows us to examine the circumstances under which some names appeared and disappeared from the pool of Ergas & Silvera's agents. Greif found very little evidence of misconduct in his analysis of the documents concerning the medieval 'coalition' of North African Jews.[51] Similarly, the heterogeneous network of Sephardic, Catholic and Hindu traders in which Ergas & Silvera participated showed a remarkable level of cohesion and continuity, which can be attributed to the pressure exerted by letter writing.

Considering the nature of the coral and diamond trade, business correspondence proved much more efficient than public sources of economic information. Livorno was then a centre for the production and dissemination of economic information, where a commodity price current was first printed in 1627 and exchange rate lists began in 1663 and became a regular biweekly publication by the mid eighteenth century.[52] Every Monday, Wednesday and Friday, the postal service delivered foreign mail, from which it was possible to ascertain price variations elsewhere.[53] Finally, numerous manuscript *avvisi*, which included information about commercial activities, were sent to the

---

[50] ASF, *LCF*, 1939.

[51] Greif, 'Contract enforceability', p. 528 n 8; Greif, 'Cultural beliefs and the organization of society: a historical and theoretical reflection on collectivist and individualist societies', *Journal of Political Economy* 102.5 (1994), 924 n 13.

[52] McCusker and Gravesteijn, *The Beginning*, pp. 253–63; Elena Gremigni, *Periodici e almanacchi livornesi secoli XVII–XVIII* (Livorno: Tipografia San Benedetto, 1996).

[53] ASF, *Mediceo del principato* (hereafter *MP*), 2275 (letter of Giacinto del Vigna to Marquis Rinuccini, 18 January 1723).

Medici grand dukes in Florence and circulated widely.[54] Presumably, Ergas & Silvera consulted these *avvisi* regularly, and their papers show that they subscribed to various gazettes, some of which they sent to their coreligionists in Aleppo, who eagerly awaited these publications in order to catch up on world news.[55] But private business correspondence was definitely their primary source of information, certainly when it came to coordinating their long-distance trade.

The difficulty of bringing a lawsuit to court in a port many months distant and the unpredictability deriving from the coexistence of various statutory and customary laws both conferred even greater importance on merchants' letters as tools to monitor the good standing of distant agents. As we have seen, this information travelled across local or transnational merchant communities, and thus contributed vigorously to the formation of cross-cultural trading networks. Nevertheless, the role of each community in implementing conformity among its members should not be disregarded. For a minority group such as the Sephardim, constantly vulnerable to stereotypical anti-Semitic accusations of illicit speculation, for example, collective credibility was an indispensable asset. More generally, peer pressure and normative sanctions concurred with rational calculation to minimise misconduct in all merchant communities. In other words, the self-policing mechanisms enacted by each merchant family, community and diaspora were inseparable from the rational pursuit of profit. Cross-cultural networks such as the one in which Ergas & Silvera participated should thus be regarded as networks of communities rather than networks of individuals. Each merchant involved in the exchange of coral and diamonds via Livorno, Lisbon and Goa was related to other members of the network by 'multiplex relationships', which provided sources of potential conflict as well as added strength.[56]

---

[54] ASF, *MP*, 2328A ('Avvisi di Livorno', 1686–1704); ASF, *MP*, 1540–61 and 1612–28 ('Avvisi di mare', 1664–1715); ASF, *MP*, 4277–8 ('Avvisi da Costantinopoli e da altre località del Levante', 1543–1625); ASF, *MP*, 1605–6 ('Avvisi di Levante, India et Barbaria', 1665–93).

[55] ASF, *LCF*, 1942, fols. 28, 32; ASF, LCF, 1938, letter to Isaac and Joseph Belilios in Aleppo (25 February 1724).

[56] Max Gluckman, *The Judicial Process among the Barotse of Northern Rhodesia (Zambia)* (Manchester: Manchester University Press, 1955), p. 19.

The interconnectedness of the Sephardic diaspora across Europe was an essential component in the stability of a cross-cultural network that also included Italians and Hindus. Notarial records in both Livorno and Amsterdam reveal that the same correspondents who served Ergas & Silvera in Lisbon and Goa also acted on behalf of several other European Sephardim.[57] The interdependence of this diaspora was highlighted in 1722: upon hearing the news of the seizure of the Portuguese ship *Nossa Senhora do Cabo* off the Mascarene Islands, Ergas & Silvera initially feared that the diamonds it carried would never be recovered, and lamented to a coreligionist in Genoa the suffering this loss would cause to 'our nation' (the Sephardim) both 'here' (meaning in Livorno) and in Amsterdam.[58]

The reliability of this intercontinental, informal network of Sephardic, Catholic and Hindu merchants was so well recognised and noteworthy that the Portuguese government entrusted it with the transfer of public funds. After losing the Northern Provinces of its Indian territories to the Marathas (1736–40), the Portuguese crown appealed to Sephardic bankers for a loan of about 90 million *réis* (the equivalent of about 450,000 *livres tournois*) to finance a military counter-offensive. The state bonds that were issued refer to 'the money that is borrowed from the merchants of the Portuguese Kingdom, Livorno and Amsterdam'[59] – an expression that clearly alludes to Portuguese 'New Christians' and Jews. But the identity of these bankers had to be protected from the Inquisition, and the money had to be made available in Goa. Once more, it was the Italians of Lisbon

---

[57] For Livorno, see ASF, *Notarile Moderno. Protocolli* (hereafter *NMP*), Agostino Frugoni, 24732, fols. 15v–16r, 90v–91r, 141v–143r; 24733, fols. 43v–46v; 24736, fols. 4r–5r; 24737, fols. 151r–152r, 162v–163v; ASF, *NMP*, Giovanni Battista Gamerra, 25265, fols. 77v–78r, 46r–v; ASF, *NMP*, Filippo Gonnella, 27193, fols. 1v–2r. For Amsterdam, see Gemeentearchief, Amsterdam, *Notarieel Archief*, 11291, fol. 34; 2943, fol. 34; 6036, fol. 58; 2943, fol. 13. Occasionally, as in 1728, Italian merchants in Lisbon also served leading Sephardic merchants in London; Stephen H. E. Fisher, *The Portugal Trade: A Study of Anglo-Portuguese Commerce 1700–1770* (London: Methuen, 1971), pp. 55n, 57.

[58] 'Que el Dio tenga piedad y restaure a los perdientes que bastantes ai de nostra nacion aqui y Amsterdam'; ASF, *LCF*, 1938, letter to Abraham Lusena in Genoa (22 April 1722).

[59] '. . . o dinheiro que se toma por empréstimo aos mercadores do Reyno, Leorne e Amstardão'.

and the Camotins of Goa who supplied the link to the Sephardic diaspora. In 1742 Italian merchants like Enea Beroardi, Giovanni Battista
Ravara, Lazzaro and Gianandrea Cambiaso – all prominent members
of Lisbon's Italian community and regular correspondents of Ergas &
Silvera's – bought these state bonds and thus served as intermediaries
in their repayment in Lisbon.[60]

The heterogeneity of addressees in Ergas & Silvera's correspondence is hardly exceptional. The letter books of two Sephardic firms
in eighteenth-century Bordeaux, Gabriel de Silva (*c*.1683–1763) and
Abraham Gradis (*c*.1695–1780), also reveal that they employed non-
Jews whenever it seemed most advantageous to do so. De Silva specialised in the banking sector. His correspondents included Christians
in both Amsterdam and Paris, and especially influential Huguenots
in the French capital.[61] As the Gradis family expanded the scale and
scope of their operations in the 1740s, they also strengthened their ties
with the Parisian and provincial nobility as well as the ministers of the
French crown in the West Indies. Although Abraham had relatives
in the Caribbean, the position of the Jews in the French Antilles was
fragile. If the Gradises became increasingly involved in the Atlantic
trade, it was through forming partnerships with non-Jews and developing connections with public officials in the colonies, particularly in
the slave and Canadian trade.[62] Like Ergas & Silvera or de Silva, the
Gradises cultivated agents who they expected would deliver the best
services, regardless of their religious affiliation. Their letters open up a
rare window into some prolonged business associations between Jews
and non-Jews.

CONCLUSION

On the basis of the records left by North African Jewish traders in
the eleventh and twelfth centuries, Avrom Udovitch maintained that

[60] Arquivos Nacionais / Torre do Tombo, Lisbon, *Chancelaria D. João V*, livro 18, fols.
269r–270r; livro 22, fols. 123r–125r; livro 22, fols. 143r–144v.
[61] Jose do Nascimento Raposo, 'Don Gabriel de Silva: a Portuguese-Jewish banker in
eighteenth century Bordeaux', unpublished PhD thesis, University of York, Ontario
(1989), pp. 89–90, 97, 248–61.
[62] Richard Menkis, 'The Gradis family of eighteenth century Bordeaux: a social and
economic study', unpublished PhD thesis, Brandeis University (1988), pp. 130–1,
154–77.

'Business letters were more than just a means of communication; they served as sinews holding together the entire organic structure of medieval Islamic long-distance trade . . .'[63] The same conclusion applies to European commerce, and far beyond the Middle Ages. Despite the creation of such new economic institutions as joint-stock chartered companies and stock markets, and the birth of so-called economic journalism, letters remained the single most important source of information for merchants involved in long-distance trade throughout the early modern period. Even Max Weber, who never failed to stress the precocious evolution of western capitalistic institutions, admitted that newspapers began to play an important role in the diffusion of economic information only in the nineteenth century, when the publication of stock prices became the rule. He concluded that 'in the eighteenth century, business depended on the organized exchange of letters'.[64]

The centrality of business letters persisted for several reasons. Slow progress in transportation systems affected private and public sources of information alike. The different kinds of news contained in printed and manuscript sources made correspondence a decisive tool to minimise the risks involved in agency relations (that is, the relations between a 'principal' and his 'factors' or agents). Improvements in the legal validity of merchants' records and the development of a customary, internationally recognised commercial law did not eliminate the perils of commission trade, especially when conducted outside familial circles. Correspondence was simply more efficient than periodicals when it came to circulating information about the aptitude and trustworthiness of private traders: and the circulation of this information made commission agency viable. The same anonymous fourteenth-century Italian merchant who urged his fellows to tend with care to their correspondence also proclaimed, 'one must take good account

---

[63] Avrom L. Udovitch, 'Formalism and informalism in the social and economic institutions of the medieval Islamic world', in Amin Banani and Speros Vryonis Jr (eds.), *Individualism and Conformity in Classical Islam* (Wiesbaden: Otto Harrassowitz, 1977), p. 63.

[64] Max Weber, *General Economic History* (New Brunswick and London: Transaction Books, 1981), p. 295.

of the types of people one deals with, or to whom one entrusts one's goods, for no man is trustworthy with money'.[65] The ability to provide and obtain information about an agent's competence and solvency was the best way for merchants to reduce hazards in a world where uncertainties loomed large and the means to tame them were restricted. In their letters, merchants conveyed agreements of reciprocal assistance, promises of future profits and outrage about fraud. In so doing, they wove a net of legal and practical enforcing mechanisms that could not have emerged otherwise.

If reputation was a merchant's social capital, business letters offered the most viable channel for reinforcing and spreading it. Business correspondence thus served as an instrument to control flows of information that were both a strategic economic advantage and a form of social control. Both features were not necessarily confined to the limited world of family firms or even to a single trading diaspora. Merchants' letters could become connective links between trading networks which transcended cultural barriers that are generally presumed to jeopardise forms of reciprocity and trust perceived to be 'natural'. As evidenced in the exchange of Mediterranean coral and Indian diamonds conducted by the Sephardim of Livorno via Lisbon and Goa, business correspondence was the glue that kept together a network of communities who lived in distant regions and were also separated by dramatic ethnic and religious divides. While the prospect of future profitable transactions helped to contain dishonesty, institutional coercion was often feeble or sometimes altogether absent. It was the regular and wide circulation of information, enhanced by the global nature of the Sephardic diaspora, which created a set of durable and effective informal mechanisms of reputation control that allowed cooperation to develop across geographical and cultural borders.

[65] Molho, *Social and Economic Foundations*, p. 55.

CHAPTER 4

Correspondence and natural history in the sixteenth century: cultures of exchange in the circle of Carolus Clusius

Florike Egmond

INTRODUCTION

'Your friend to my utmost powers . . .' is the telltale ending of one the letters that are the subject of this essay.[1] Those six words suffice to evoke the notions of friendship and mutual exchange to which a discussion of sixteenth-century correspondence among naturalists almost inevitably leads.

Inspired by the work of Giuseppe Olmi, this chapter focuses on the European-wide correspondence network of Carolus Clusius (1525–1609), one of the foremost botanists of the sixteenth century.[2] After taking a look at some general characteristics of the network of Clusius's correspondents and their letters, we will explore various aspects of correspondence and exchange while zooming in on examples from individual letters. We will not use the Clusius correspondence to reconstruct or analyse his social network (important as it was), nor will we study exchange as an economic phenomenon. The perspective here is

---

[1] Letter in Dutch dated 23 March 1601 from Pieter Garet in Amsterdam to Clusius in Leiden. Unless otherwise indicated all of the original letters to or from Clusius mentioned or quoted in this chapter are in the University Library of Leiden (hereafter ULL). Details about dates, places and language of the individual letters mentioned below will be given in the footnotes. All quotations are my translations into English. For their comments, advice and support I would like to thank all the friends from our present-day virtual European community, especially Sabine Anagnostou, Irene Baldriga, Francisco Bethencourt, Peter Mason and Francesca Trivellato.

[2] See Giuseppe Olmi, *L'inventario del mondo: catalogazione della natura e luoghi del sapere nella prima età moderna* (Bologna: Il Mulino, 1992) and especially his '"Molti amici in vari luoghi": studio della natura e rapporti epistolari nel secolo XVI', *Nuncius. Annali di Storia della Scienza* 6 (1991) fasc. 1, pp. 3–31.

Fig. 3. Portrait of Carolus Clusius by Martinus Rota, sixteenth-century engraving. Courtesy of Leiden University Library (PK I 152 Rot 1)

distinctly cultural and the main themes are styles of correspondence and (gift) exchange among naturalists at a time when European society had in many respects already become geared to merchant enterprise, the market and commodities.[3] This implies, for one thing, that the

---

[3] Most of the present-day discussions among historians about gift exchange go back to issues raised in Marcel Mauss, *The Gift: The Form and Reason for Exchange in Archaic Societies* (London: Routledge, 1990; originally published as 'Essai sur le don: forme et raison de l'échange dans les sociétés archaïques', *L'Année Sociologique*, 2nd series, 1 (1923–4)); see also Nathalie Zemon Davis, *The Gift in Sixteenth-Century France*

letters themselves are not just seen as carriers of information. We will look at their appearance as well as their contents and briefly discuss the acts of writing, sending and reading them. These letters were at the same time containers of information, objects of intrinsic value and means to the manifold ends that their writers had in mind. Apart from the obvious, intentional aspects of letter writing – to recommend a friend, provide and ask for information, show interest, obtain a publication, reassure your loved ones, maintain friendships, etc. – the letters exchanged in Clusius's large European network had other functions and effects which often went beyond the immediate purposes of the senders or recipients. To those we will turn in the last section of this essay.

Although scholarly interest in early European natural history has increased enormously since the late 1980s (repeating an earlier 'wave' during the 1920s and 1930s), not much new research has as yet been done concerning the correspondence of sixteenth-century experts in this field. While lists and (partial) editions of the correspondence of scholars or scientists such as Lipsius, Scaliger, Grotius and Huygens are available, for the contents of the naturalists' letters we have to rely in most cases on older (generally nineteenth-century and early twentieth-century) editions of small selections of their correspondence while, of course, the original letters themselves remain scattered in libraries and archives all over Europe. Even surveys listing the letters and correspondents of individual naturalists remain scarce.[4] Clusius's famous counterpart, the Swiss polymath, physician, bibliographer and natural historian Conrad Gessner (1516–65), whose influence on both learned and popular European culture can hardly be overestimated, forms an exception – up to a point. Many of his letters were published in the late sixteenth century, shortly after his death, and additional

(Oxford: Oxford University Press, 2000); Pamela H. Smith and Paula Findlen (eds.), *Merchants and Marvels: Commerce, Science and Art in Early Modern Europe* (New York and London: Routledge, 2002); and Peter Mason, 'Troca e deslocamento nas pinturas de Albert Eckhout de sujeitos brasileiros', *Estudos de Sociologia. Revista do programa de pós-Graduação em sociologia da UFPE* 7, 1 and 2 (2001), 231–49.

[4] In this respect internet search instruments specialising in manuscripts and letters, and the catalogues or lists put on the internet by European libraries (Bologna, Aldrovandi) promise to be a major improvement.

material was published during the 1950s and 1970s.[5] By now, publications more than 400 years old are almost as inaccessible as the original letters, and Gessner's correspondence is certainly worth a new look. The situation with respect to Clusius's correspondence is similar to the extent that a number of letters to and from him have been published, some in the seventeenth century, more in the nineteenth and twentieth centuries.[6] Given the considerable size of the Clusius correspondence (to which we will come back below), it is understandable that the bulk has never been published, but even a survey listing the individual letters was lacking until very recently.[7]

Older editions of letters between sixteenth-century naturalists — and this seems to apply to other early modern scholars as well — have, moreover, often been inspired either by a very basic biographical interest in the naturalist himself (or in some of his correspondents) or else by a desire to uncover more information about his scholarly ideas and knowledge. Much of Clusius's correspondence, for instance, was consulted by his biographer F. W. T. Hunger before World War II and the letters that have appeared in print are almost without exception letters from correspondents who were famous in their own right.[8] Thus, interest generally has focused on a limited part of the contents

---

[5] See R. J. Durling, 'Konrad Gessner's Briefwechsel', in R. Schmitz and F. Krafft (eds.), *Humanismus und Naturwissenschaften*, Beiträge zur Humanismusforschung 6 (Boppard: Boldt, 1980), pp. 101–12; also G. Rath, 'Die Briefe Conrad Gessners aus der Trewschen Sammlung', *Gesnerus* 7 (1950), 140–70, and 8 (1951), 195–215; and Claude Longeon (ed.), *Conrad Gesner: vingt lettres à Jean Bauhin fils (1563–1565)* (Université de Saint-Etienne, 1976).

[6] A few examples: J. Lluís Barona and X. Gómez i Font (introd. and trans.), *La correspondencia de Carolus Clusius con los científicos españoles* (Valencia: Seminari d'Estudis Sobre la Ciència, Universitat de Valencia, 1998); Ans Berendts, 'Carolus Clusius (1526–1609) and Bernardus Paludanus (1550–1633): their contacts and correspondence', *Lias* 5 (1978), 49–64; Piero Ginori Conti, *Lettere inedite di Charles de l'Escluse (Carolus Clusius) a Matteo Caccini, Floricultore Fiorentino: contributo alla storia della botanica* (Florence: Olschki, 1939); G. B. de Toni, *Il carteggio degli Italiani col botanico Carlo Clusius nella biblioteca Leidense* (Modena: Società Tipografica Modenese, 1911).

[7] This survey will be available via Leiden University Library.

[8] Of Hunger's biography one volume is in Dutch and the other in German: F. W. T. Hunger, *Charles de l'Escluse (Carolus Clusius) Nederlandsch Kruidkundige, 1526–1609*, 2 vols. (The Hague: Martinus Nijhoff, 1927 and 1942).

of such letters or on their biographical references, rather than on the exchange itself or the larger network. Here, as elsewhere in this volume, our interest mainly concerns these latter issues.

All of the remaining letters to Clusius in Leiden University Library form the basis for this chapter, especially where quantitative matters are concerned. The whole corpus is currently being reviewed and a full list of the correspondents and the languages is available, while a survey of the dates and places for each letter is in the making. For more detailed analysis and examples I have concentrated on letters written to Clusius by a dozen male and two female correspondents. None of them belonged to the category of famous humanists; for that very reason, they seemed particularly important for a topic central to our subject: the formation of a virtual community of European natural historians. All of them united the roles of aficionados, experts and intermediaries in the expanding network of naturalists. Our examples from their letters were selected for their 'high specific gravity': their quality of presenting and revealing several distinctive traits that (I believe) can be discerned *throughout* the culture of exchange in sixteenth-century natural history.[9] Exploring these characteristics may raise questions about similarities and differences between the exchanges of naturalists and those of the better-known republic of letters with which the networks of naturalists partly overlapped.[10] Whether such exchanges differed from those in other groups of sixteenth-century specialists, such as merchants, courtiers, politicians, astronomers or mathematicians cannot be answered in this chapter. But a comparison with the other contributions in this volume should reveal at least some possible variations.

[9] On case studies, high specific gravity and microhistory see Florike Egmond and Peter Mason, *The Mammoth and the Mouse: Microhistory and Morphology* (Baltimore and London: Johns Hopkins University Press, 1997) and Florike Egmond and Peter Mason, 'A horse called Belisarius', *History Workshop Journal* 47 (1999), 240–52.

[10] Hans Bots and Françoise Waquet, *La République des Lettres* (Paris: Belin / De Boeck, 1997) forms an implicit point of reference throughout this chapter. See also *Les correspondances: leur importance pour l'historien des Sciences et de la Philosophie. Problèmes de leur édition* (*Revue de Synthèse*, 3rd series, 97) (Paris: Editions Albin Michel, 1976), pp. 81–2; and for a much later period Anne Goldgar, *Impolite Learning: Conduct and Community in the Republic of Letters, 1680–1750* (New Haven and London: Yale University Press, 1995).

FASHIONABLE NATURE

During the sixteenth century, a great many changes occurred in the study, classification and representation of plants and animals. If the term 'scientific revolution of the seventeenth century' had not originated as part of a Whiggish and evolutionist style of historiography, or led to so much unfortunate reification, it would have been tempting to describe the changes of the sixteenth century as a first phase of the scientific revolution or even as an (earlier) revolution in the life sciences. Travel, observation, description and the development of new systems of classification were of central importance in sixteenth-century botany and zoology. The discovery of the New World and the transportation of exotic naturalia to Europe from all over the world helped to trigger new kinds of interest in naturalia which, between around 1530 and 1600, stimulated the development of natural history as a scholarly discipline (or at least a field of expertise) and of botany as a specialised branch of medicine.[11]

This growing interest in nature focused mainly on plants and gardens and to a somewhat lesser extent on animals, which were much more difficult and expensive to keep. Two major manifestations were the creation of numerous private gardens all over Europe and the collection of naturalia (such as plants, shells and parts of animals) and their visual representations in drawings, watercolours, woodcuts, engravings or even illustrations from printed works. Nature very quickly became fashionable in Europe. In the rich, aristocratic

---

[11] On the connections between the voyages of discovery, the New World and natural history see Olmi, *L'inventario del mondo*, esp. pp. 211–55; and Henry Lowood, 'The New World and the European Catalog of Nature', in Karen Ordahl Kupperman (ed.), *America in European Consciousness, 1493–1750* (Chapel Hill and London: University of North Carolina Press, 1995), pp. 295–323. For the creation of a field of expertise see especially Paula Findlen, 'The formation of a scientific community: natural history in sixteenth-century Italy', in A. Grafton and N. Siraisi (eds.), *Natural Particulars* (Cambridge, MA: MIT Press, 1999), pp. 369–400 (she prefers the term discipline). See also her excellent *Possessing Nature: Museums, Collecting and Scientific Culture in Early Modern Italy* (Berkeley: University of California Press, 1994). See also Karen Meier Reeds, *Botany in Medieval and Renaissance Universities* (New York and London: Garland, 1991).

and princely collections of the period naturalia often formed part of much larger *Kunst- und Wunderkammern*. Almost every self-respecting nobleman owned a garden and showed off exotic flowers to his visitors.[12] Some even owned a maze or a private menagerie. An example of an aristocrat with a particularly varied collection was Charles de Saint Omer, Lord of Moerkercke and Dranoutre. His collection comprised books, tapestries, a menagerie, gardens, a maze, prints, paintings and coins, naturalia and other curiosa. He was one of the first patrons of Clusius.[13]

Commercial, scientific and 'cultural' interests often coincided. The Spanish king Philip II, who sent out the Spanish physician Francisco Hernandez to investigate, describe and depict the flora of Mexico, was very much alive to the possibility of creating plantations in the New World to grow medicinal plants for commercial purposes.[14] Economic motives were even more prominent in the early explorations of the Dutch in the East Indies. The instruction to the commanders of the first Dutch ships sent out to the East Indies to explore and bring back herbs, fruits and spices from the Far East may have been of help to botanists, but it was mainly inspired by the expectation of enormous profits in the spice trade. At the same time European universities claimed prestige and status by creating botanical gardens (the oldest

[12] For gardens of this period see, for instance, Ursula Härting (ed.), *Gärten und Höfe der Rubenszeit: im Spiegel der Malerfamilie Brueghel und der Künstler um Peter Paul Rubens*, exhibition catalogue, Gustav-Lübcke-Museum Hamm and Landesmuseum, Mainz (Munich: Hirmer Verlag, 2000); and Roy Strong, *The Renaissance Garden in England* (London: Thames & Hudson, 1979). For science at an Italian court see Dario A. Franchini, Renzo Margonari, Giuseppe Olmi, Rodolfo Signorini, Attilio Zanca and Chiara Tellini Perina, *La scienza a corte: collezionismo eclettico natura e immagine a Mantova fra Rinascimento e Manierismo* (Rome: Bulzoni, 1979).

[13] Results of ongoing archival research by Jacques de Groote concerning his life, possessions and role in the making of the Libri Picturati A.16–18 with watercolours of plants and animals can be found on the following website: www.tzwin.be/sint-omaers.htm (in Dutch).

[14] Henry Kamen, *Philip of Spain* (New Haven and London: Yale University Press, 1997), p. 91; and for Hernández: José Pardo Tomás (with José María Lopez Pinero), *La influencia de Francisco Hernández (1515–1587) en la constitución de la botánica y de la materia médica modernas* (Valencia: Universitat de Valencia – CSIC, 1996).

of which originated between 1520 and 1610[15]) – showing not only that they took their teaching of medicine and medicinal herbs seriously, but also vying with each other and with aristocratic gardens by growing rare exotic plants whose medicinal value was often irrelevant.

The fascination with nature did not only affect the rich or the learned, however. The origins of many smaller and more specialised collections comprising naturalia and their pictures can be traced to the decades between 1540 and 1590 and to men (and a few women) who belonged to the professional middle classes or even the artisanal ones. They too could own a (small) garden and grow new plants from seeds or cuttings obtained by barter. The fascination with nature and curiosities was shared almost from its earliest phase (i.e. roughly the second quarter of the sixteenth century) by people who belonged neither to the aristocracy nor to the limited circle of university-trained specialists.[16]

EXPERTS

During the sixteenth century, natural history formed a varied field of practice which was inextricably connected with elite collecting, gardening, the universities and the great voyages of discovery, as well as with the more mundane worlds of apothecaries, farmers and folk healers. Expertise in nature therefore belonged to men and women from enormously different backgrounds. Unlike law or medicine – fields in which a relatively clear distinction existed by this time between university-trained experts of high status and people who had gained their experience in practice – in natural history such distinctions were only then just beginning to be drawn. Scholars such as Clusius and the people who acted as specialised and highly expert information brokers

---

[15] Alicja Zemanek, 'Renaissance botany and modern science', in Zbigniew Mirek and Alicja Zemanek (eds.), *Studies in Renaissance Botany*, Polish Botanical Studies, Guidebook Series 20 (Cracow: Polish Academy of Sciences, W. Szafer Institute of Botany: 1998), pp. 9–47.

[16] Whether this holds equally true for Mediterranean and north-western Europe awaits further investigation.

in this field, helped to select, channel, organise and translate some of this knowledge and elevate it to the level of specialist expertise.

Of the men considered the principal experts in natural history of the sixteenth century in Europe north of the Alps – such as Leonhart Fuchs, Otto Brunfels, or Hieronymus Bock during the 1530s–40s and Pierre Belon, Guillaume Rondelet, Conrad Gessner, Carolus Clusius, Rembertus Dodonaeus and Kaspar Bauhin during the 1550s–1610s – almost none had been trained as a botanist, zoologist or naturalist, because there was no formal training yet in this field. Nearly all of them had studied medicine and made themselves experts in natural history in the course of their lives. Some obtained posts at universities; others were employed as expert advisors by rich patrons and several held both types of positions alternately. Few were rich enough to possess large private gardens, but most of them owned smaller plots of land and many had access to both university botanical gardens and the private gardens of princes, aristocrats or rich bourgeois. It is among the latter, members of the elite who owned parks or gardens and had a passion for growing exotics, that we should look for a second category of experts in natural history. Quite a few of them took gardening and botany very seriously indeed, owned rich collections of naturalia and illustrations and read as widely as possible on the subject. They became genuine experts capable of conversing and corresponding about plants on an almost equal footing with experts like Clusius.

The most important non-elite collectors and aficionados of natural history all over Europe were apothecaries, perfumers and druggists.[17] As yet they have hardly been taken seriously in this role by historians of science, but some well-documented examples show that their interest

---

[17] There is a large quantity of extremely fragmented information on apothecaries, and their interest in nature has (as far as I know) yet to produce a synthetic essay. See Peter Dilg, 'Apotheker als Sammler', in Andreas Grote (ed.), *Macrocosmos in Microcosmo: die Welt in der Stube. Zur Geschichte des Sammelns 1450 bis 1800*, Berliner Schriften zur Museumskunde 10 (Opladen: Leske und Budrich 1994), pp. 453–74. For Jesuits as apothecaries in America see Sabine Anagnostou, *Jesuiten in Spanisch-Amerika als Uebermittler von heilkundlichem Wissen*, Quellen und Studien zur Geschichte der Pharmazie 78 (Stuttgart: Wissenschaftliche Verlagsgesellschaft mbH, 2000).

in nature went far beyond mere professional (medicinal) requirements and manifested itself in ways that came close to scholarly or elite forms and practices of knowledge. Some owned small experimental gardens, grew exotics, compiled encyclopaedic surveys of information about nature, and had portraits of plants or animals painted. Apothecaries such as Hugh Morgan, James Garet Jr and Thomas Penny in England, or their continental counterparts Peeter van Coudenberghe, Thomas de la Fosse, Jean Mouton and Christiaan Porret (in the Low Countries) became famous as the first to grow certain exotic plants and to experiment with highly prized new varieties of non-indigenous flowers. As their letters to Clusius demonstrate, the gardens owned by these men and their more upper-class counterparts were visited both by foreign travellers, aristocratic collectors (like Princess Marie de Brimeu or Sir Philip Sidney), scholars (like Lipsius or Lobelius), and by miscellaneous friends and relatives who all shared an interest in plants, animals, exotic naturalia, or 'curious simples' (as they were often called at the time). Though they were certainly not public domains, the comparatively democratic openness of these gardens to visitors of various classes and backgrounds contrasts with the relatively closed character of most *Kunst- und Wunderkammern*, which were visited, it seems, mainly by other members of the elite.

The wider context of the Clusius correspondence is thus an early modern European milieu of collecting and exchanging naturalia, and of botanical gardens, medicine and pharmacy in the social settings of courts, universities, urban patriciate and middle-class professionals. To call it a European setting might in fact underestimate its range: the exchanges in which Clusius and many other sixteenth-century naturalists took part were actually worldwide, since they involved exotica from the New World and the Far East as well as naturalia from the Middle East, southern and central and eastern Europe.[18]

---

[18] For example, the letters sent to Clusius by Esaia Le Gillon from Prague cover topics about Hungary, Turkey and Persia. The Garets' letters to him contain many references to the voyages of discovery and exotica brought back from both the East Indies and the New World (see also below), while all captains of outward-bound Dutch East Indiamen received a request from Clusius to bring back seeds and cuttings.

CLUSIUS AND HIS CORRESPONDENCE NETWORK

One reason why Carolus Clusius is now known as possibly *the* foremost botanist of the sixteenth century was his European stature. It
rested on three pillars: his travel and investigations in several European
countries; his publications and innovative approach to botany; and his
far-flung network of correspondents. Clusius was born in Arras in
the southern Netherlands, studied both there and in Germany and
France, travelled and did botanical field research in Spain, Portugal,
the southern Netherlands, Austria, Hungary, Germany and England,
lived, studied and worked in the southern Netherlands, at the universities of Paris, Montpellier and some German towns, at the Habsburg
court in Vienna, on an aristocratic estate in Hungary, in Frankfurt and
at the University of Leiden. He maintained exchanges by letter with a
very large network of friends, collectors, fellow experts and others for
at least half a century, from the early 1560s until his death in Leiden
in 1609.

About 1,500 letters remain from this correspondence, the bulk of
them (more than a 1,300) in Leiden's University Library with about
200 at the library of Erlangen in Germany.[19] Of this total, about 1,150
letters were addressed to Clusius; the remaining 350 were sent from
Clusius to various correspondents. A still-unknown number of letters (probably dozens rather than hundreds) is scattered throughout
libraries and archives all over Europe. Next to the correspondences of
Conrad Gessner and Ulisse Aldrovandi the Clusius correspondence
probably constitutes the most valuable collection of correspondence
in the field of early European natural history. The reason why far
more letters *to* Clusius than letters written *by* him to others have been
preserved is simple: while the letters he sent were dispersed all over
Europe, the letters sent to him came to one person. Clusius obviously
took very good care of them; they not only formed a permanent and
rich source of information for his own research and the manifesta-
tion of important friendships, but also provided material evidence of a

[19] These numbers remain imprecise because of double counts, and many identifications
and datings remain uncertain. A survey of all extant letters, starting with the Leiden
collection, is available on the website of Leiden's University Library.

virtual European community of naturalists and of his own central position within that growing community. Between around 1560 and 1609 Clusius corresponded with at least 300 different persons throughout Europe. Given the fact that a considerable number of them were expert botanists, collectors, and garden owners who in their turn commanded large and partly overlapping networks of friends, acquaintances and fellow experts, the reach of Clusius's network of information and exchange is amazing. His correspondents stretched from England to Hungary, from Greece to Poland and from Spain and Portugal to the northern Netherlands, Germany and Norway. In a geographical sense his network was truly European.

Among Clusius's correspondents we find aristocratic collectors, courtiers and rich patrons (such as the Count of Aremberg, Lamoraal van Egmont and Charles de Saint Omer, Lord of Moerkercke, in the southern Netherlands, Sir Philip Sidney and Lord Zouche in England, Ludwig I, Duke of Württemberg, and Ludwig VI, Elector of the Palatinate, in Germany, the Hungarian Count Batthiany, Princess Marie de Brimeu from the Netherlands); famous humanists such as Benito Arias Montano and Justus Lipsius; fellow botanical experts such as Felix Platter, Joachim Camerarius, Matteo Caccini, Ulisse Aldrovandi and Simon de Tovar; printer-publishers and artists such as Christoph Plantin, Franciscus Raphelengius and Anselmus de Boodt; diplomats such as Ogier Ghislain de Busbeq; and apothecaries such as the Garet family, Jean Mouton, Christian Porret and Hugh Morgan; but also relatives and many others. The better known Clusius became as a leading botanical expert, the more his epistolary contacts proliferated. His network snowballed.

Two points, Clusius's correspondence with women and the different languages used in his correspondence, are of special interest because of the widespread but often implicit assumption that correspondence among early modern experts of this scholarly type was generally in Latin, only involved men (i.e., learned humanists or scientists), and usually had a relatively stylised and 'public' character somewhere between individual information exchanges, a non-printed newsletter and a pre-publication.[20]

---

[20] Cf. Bots and Waquet, *La République des Lettres*.

Clusius never married and we know of no affairs, lovers or children. His many longstanding friendships with men throughout his life
suggest a closer affinity with men than with women, but he also maintained close friendships with women and corresponded with some
of them for decades.[21] For instance, ten letters to him from Anna
Starzerin Aicholtz survive (for the years 1588–92), while twenty-five
letters from Anna Maria von Heusenstain to Clusius testify to a longstanding friendship spanning the years 1588–1606. His best-known
and almost lifelong female friend, however, was Princess Marie de
Brimeu (c.1550–1605).[22] Of her letters to Clusius, twenty-seven have
been preserved, dated between 1571 and 1607. She was the aristocratic
owner of a superb garden in Leiden and a keen grower of tulips and
other exotic flowers and shrubs. Nearly all of Clusius's correspondence
with women awaits analysis, but it is clear that he did not only discuss
household or family matters with them. In fact, Clusius conversed
about botany with at least some of these women on the same footing
as with some of his male correspondents who were also friends and
garden owners. Even a brief perusal of their letters shows that many of
these ladies asked Clusius for instruction in growing and maintaining
(exotic) plants. But it is equally clear that, however modestly they
write about themselves, many of them, including Anna Maria von
Heusenstain and Princess Marie de Brimeu, became experts themselves in such matters and sometimes advised Clusius, also sending
him cuttings, seeds, bulbs and tubers. Upon receiving a letter from
Clusius accompanied by a large basket full of bulbs, seeds and roots,
Marie de Brimeu replied as follows:

I will receive them certainly with complete affection, as much because of the
rarity of all these as for the opportunity that you say you have had to send
them to me knowing how much I enjoy gardening. That pleasure, I confess to
you, is certainly great but is as yet more enjoyment than science because I have
neither many hours to spend on it and become more expert as I would want,

---

[21] Until now we know fourteen women who corresponded with Clusius. Sometimes
only one letter remains.

[22] For an excellent biographical essay which uses her correspondence to Clusius, see
J. L. van der Gouw, 'Marie de Brimeu: een Nederlandse prinses uit de eerste helft
van de tachtigjarige oorlog', *De Nederlandsche Leeuw* 64 (1947), 5–49.

ILLVSTRISSIME ET EX.^{ME} DAME MARIE DE BRIMEV,
Heritiere de ladt. Maison, Contesse de Meghem, Vis contesse de Dourlans, Baronnesse d'Humbercourt,
Dame de Houstlam, Coullemont, Constardles, Mondicourt, Ransthon, Pimeraff, Hurtebise, Gorges on, Rochefay,
Esperleques, Gezmcourt, Gorges, Yoncourt, Montigny, Noa l'hospital, Houlica, Sorus, Zelucques, Brimeu, &c.

Premiere femme du susdict Messire
Charles de Croy, premier Duc de
Croy, et quatriesme Duc d'Arscot.

Fig. 4. Portrait of Princess Marie de Brimeu. From J. L. van der Gouw, 'Marie de Brimeu: een Nederlandse prinses uit de eerste helft van de tachtigjarige oorlog', *De Nederlandsche Leeuw* 64 (1947), 5–49

nor a teacher who can instruct and assist me, as you do who are, as I have well
understood from Monsieur Lipsius, the father of all beautiful gardens in this
country, and this both because of the knowledge you have of the plants and
because of the generosity which you have displayed towards many, and now
towards me . . .[23]

Botany, plants and gardens offered one of the few semi-public domains
in which both men and women could legitimately (be seen to) participate. Women could become experts and be addressed as such in these
fairly private exchanges.[24]

None of these undoubtedly learned and well-educated women of
generally high social position corresponded with Clusius in Latin.
Marie de Brimeu wrote to him in French, Anna Starzerin Aicholtz
and Anna Maria von Heusenstain wrote in German. His other female
correspondents likewise used the vernacular, such as Eva Ungnadin
(German), Louise Boisot (French), Anne de Thiennes (French) and
Cathryna Quadt (German). The reason might simply be that women
at the time did not have access to universities or other forms of higher
education, but some women could and did learn Latin. Besides, many
of Clusius's male correspondents likewise preferred the vernacular.
Their choice of language seems to have been only partly related to
their social or educational status. His Polish or Hungarian correspondents, coming from regions whose vernaculars were almost unknown
in western Europe, wrote in Latin, which indeed remained a *lingua
franca*. Most of the humanists (such as Lipsius), all of Clusius's friends

---

[23] Letter sent from Leiden to Clusius, probably in Frankfurt, September 159(1?): 'je le
recevray cependant dentiere affection tant pour la rarete dicelluy que pour loccasion
que dites avoir eu a me lenvoir a scavoir le plaisir que jaij de jardiner. Lequel certes je
vous confesse estre grand mais de joli et non encore des science pour navoir jusques
ores en moien de mij emploijer a bon escient comme je voudrois ny en maistre pour
mij introduire et assister comme vous que jaij bien entendu par monsieur Lipsius
estre le pere de tous les beaux jardins de ce paijs et ce tant pour la connaissance quaves
des simples que pour la liberalite dont aves use envers plusiers et maintenant envers
moij . . .'

[24] Bots and Waquet, *La République des Lettres*, pp. 96–8, discuss women as absent
from the republic of letters, with a few exceptions, and do not mention their role in
botany. Although the connection between women and botany seemed an obvious
one, the relevant literature concentrates completely on the eighteenth and nineteenth
centuries.

from his student days at Paris as well as many German, French, Dutch and English physicians wrote in Latin. But some of the learned correspondents in Italy (such as Ferrante Imperato, Hieronimo Calzeolari, Giacomo Cortuso and Giuseppe Benincasa/Casabona) preferred Italian, while several other men who must have known Latin preferred French. On the other hand Dutch, German and possibly Spanish seem to have been used mainly by correspondents who did not know Latin. A few correspondents even used more than one language, either in one and the same letter or successively, changing back and forth. For instance, Johannes van Hoghelande, a rich bourgeois garden owner from Leiden, mixed French and Latin; a German or Austrian Christian von Ecgk wrote in French for some years, then changed to German and later turned back to French; and the German-Hungarian Joannes Lewenklau alternated between Latin and Italian. Personal preference overrode any rules or regularities in this respect. A good example comes from a letter from Christiaan Porret, a Leiden apothecary, to Matteo Caccini in Florence, discussing Clusius just after the latter's death. It concludes: 'I have written in French because the Italian language is rather difficult for me to understand and even more to write'.[25]

Judging from the information presently available about most of the letters sent to Clusius, about half were in Latin, while the others were in French, Italian, German, Spanish or Dutch (roughly in that descending order). Clusius himself was a polyglot. He read and wrote an impressive number of languages: besides Latin, Dutch and French, he was fluent in German, Italian and Spanish. He could probably read and understand Portuguese, read (classical) Greek and may have understood some Hungarian. One of the few languages he never managed to master well was today's *lingua franca*, English.

The issue of language use in Clusius's correspondence suggests that Latin was apparently less of a *lingua franca* at the time than has been assumed. We may infer that Clusius's correspondents generally wrote to him in the language of their choice, since Clusius was at home in so many vernacular languages. Should we interpret the possibility

---

[25] Dated 6 January 1610: 'Jaij escrit en franchoijs pour mestr la langue Italienne ung peu fascheuse a entendre et encores plus a escrire.'

offered by Clusius to his correspondents to use the language of their choice as part of a code of civility? It presumably had this effect on some of his less-educated correspondents, who obviously felt comfortable writing to Clusius in their vernacular (or even dialect) and in scripts that bore very little resemblance to the beautifully fluid and easily legible 'Italianate' forms customary among humanists. For instance, the interesting letters from an apothecary from Brigg, Fabianus Ilger, are difficult to decipher, while those from Anna Maria von Heusenstain pose problems mainly because of the Viennese dialect which she used. Half a sentence is enough:

Ih pit den hern halt gar herʒlih schan wan er etwas selcʒam pekhumbt von rasen od nägl und was ist von sam und stöckhlwerg der herr wöll mein nit vergösen[26]

(I ask Sir with all my heart that Sir will not forget me when he receives something rare such as roses or carnations and whatever in the shape of seeds or stocks)

Nonetheless, it seems implausible that Clusius learned so many languages just in order to be polite. Moreover, it seems significant that Clusius himself did not invariably adapt to his correspondents' choice of language. In the correspondence (1550–78) with Hubertus Languetus, a friend from his student days in Paris, Languetus always used Latin while Clusius consistently replied in French – perhaps for nostalgic reasons. Clusius had obviously learned Latin and knew Dutch and French, the languages of his childhood in the southern Netherlands. His knowledge of German and Spanish was directly connected with his subsequent work and travels, although not everyone would have learned good Spanish just by travelling in Spain for some months. The case of Italian is more intriguing. Clusius always wanted to visit Italy but never managed to do so. He nonetheless wrote good Italian. As he explains in one of his letters, he picked up Italian mainly from reading.

Although his linguistic proficiency may be partly explained in terms of practical circumstances, therefore, it still raises a further question.

---

[26] Dated 9 January 1589, sent from Starhemberg to Frankfurt. The German word *stock* can be used also in a wider sense, for cuttings or for a plant with many flowers that can be cultivated in a pot or in the garden (my thanks to Sabine Anagnostou).

Could the fact that Clusius learned so many different languages imply that Latin was not enough for his purposes, and that communication in the vernacular with informants and patrons from other countries was essential to his type of research? Did this apply to other natural historians too? And if so, was there a difference in style of communication between naturalists and other scholars? This point deserves further investigation and should perhaps be connected with an issue raised above. As a new field of expertise, botany was more 'socially fluid', less closed off by scientific disciplinary boundary markers to women, non-university-trained persons or non-elite practical experts than many other sciences.[27] Moreover, botanical expertise consisted, to a considerable extent, of local knowledge and first-hand observation. Both his printed works and his correspondence show that Clusius was seriously interested in 'ecology' and 'folk' nomenclature of plants and the latter's possible relevance to their classification.[28] Therefore, Clusius's multilingualism might well be a clue to his innovative research methods and, vice versa, to the way in which the vernacular languages and 'folk expertise' were making their way into and contributing to the discipline of botany.

FORM AND CONTENTS

Most letters to Clusius do not look as if any *very* special care had been taken about the composition, layout or handwriting. Although the handwriting of most is orderly (though by no means always clear), it is very hard to decipher indeed in some cases. In only a small percentage of the letters the handwriting looks almost 'printed'. Many letters are characterised by unpredictable and inconsistent spelling as well

---

[27] About the continued 'openness' of botany to amateurs, see James A. Secord, 'The crisis of nature', in N. Jardine, J. A. Secord and E. C. Spary (eds.), *Cultures of Natural History* (Cambridge: Cambridge University Press, 1996), pp. 447–59. For brief discussions of the vernacular and botany see Lowood, 'The New World and the European Catalog of Nature'; and David Freedberg, *The Eye of the Lynx: Galileo, his Friends, and the Beginnings of Modern Natural History* (Chicago and London: University of Chicago Press, 2002), pp. 192–4.

[28] Andrea Ubrizsy Savoia, 'Environmental approach in the botany of the 16th century', in Mirek and Zemanek (eds.), *Studies in Renaissance Botany*, pp. 73–86.

as minimal punctuation – all perfectly ordinary characteristics at the time. The frequent absence of full stops or other markers at the end of a sentence and the near absence of paragraphs often make it hard for any reader to know where to look for the beginning of new topics. Although many writers express their concern for his health, hope that Clusius may live long and emphasise their warm feelings and respect, hardly any letters open or close with elaborate statements of deference. Formal salutations only seem to occur in exchanges between Clusius and humanists or diplomats who approached him for the first time. Clusius must either have been a very easy person to approach, or the rules of deference in the circles of naturalists were less strict than among diplomats or famous humanists. Both the frequent use of the vernacular and this relative lack of emphasis on deference may reflect the mixed composition of the naturalists' networks in terms of status and prestige.

Anarchy seems to reign in the Clusius correspondence concerning the topics that could be discussed and the order in which to do so. Apart from the fact that information about previous letters and packages sent can nearly always be found in the first few lines, while greetings to family members, friends and other naturalists are usually reserved for the last sections, no order seems to have been prescribed. Demands for seeds, information about new plants, bad growing seasons, new publications, complaints about servants and the postal service, information about political events and military campaigns, issues of health and illness, information about one's own journeys and those of friends, enquiries after new patrons, business and financial information, news about children, gossip, a request for some new shoes to be sent, news about the big voyages to the East and West Indies, gardening items and other matters are mentioned indiscriminately. Here we are a long way removed from the Ciceronian models of written eloquence.

The minimal punctuation, almost complete lack of paragraphs and the fact that in some letters almost every sentence broaches a new subject, while knowledge of many things is taken for granted, tell us a lot. Clearly, many of Clusius's exchanges were matter of fact and informal to a considerable extent. They formed part of exchanges between persons who shared the same interests and similar types (if not levels) of expertise, and they belonged to ongoing conversations in which many things no longer needed to be explained. Clearly these letters were never meant for publication or even circulation on a larger scale, although some were shown to relatives and friends who shared the passion for botany. In this respect their form and contents match. They neither look nor read like the semi-public type of correspondence intended to be passed on or read aloud, which one encounters in the later circles of Peiresc, Huygens or Mersenne.[29] The informality of these exchanges is also evident from the implicit references to previous letters and gifts, and the fact that correspondents more than once forget to finish a sentence. Perhaps the most striking and interesting general characteristics of these letters, however, are their liveliness and practical orientation and the wide range of topics they cover.

Another detail of the physical appearance of these letters illustrates their practical nature. On the outside of the letter near the address – envelopes did not yet exist – Clusius (like many of his contemporaries) meticulously wrote down the dates on which he received and answered that particular letter. Similarly, quite a few of his correspondents confirm in their first few lines the receipt (and sometimes the dates) of previous letters, mention via which route or carriers their own letter should (have) travel(led), or indicate that previously sent packages or letters had been lost or stolen. Their principal reasons for doing so were practical: to ensure that lost letters were at least known to have been lost, to explain to the receiver to which letters the sender was replying and to tell him or her which packages containing seeds, bulbs, roots or pictures of plants were on their way. European postal services were still in the early days of their development, although they could be remarkably efficient over short distances – for instance between the towns of Holland – and during the drier season. Most long-distance letters and packages required weeks if not months to deliver, however, and Clusius's correspondents often used the services of merchants, ships or private couriers employed by acquaintances. There was no guarantee that any package would arrive intact. Many letters contain warnings against a specific route or recommendations to use a particular service or person. Thus, while these letters were themselves sources of information and a means of exchange, they also accompanied the exchange of objects, discussed that exchange itself

[29] Bots and Waquet, *La République des Lettres*, pp. 129–30.

and attempted to guarantee that objects were not lost or stolen. In all
of these respects the letters as well as the objects they accompanied
formed part of an ongoing gift exchange.

EXCHANGE AND FRIENDSHIP

Because friendship is explicitly mentioned in almost every single letter, we should take a closer look at the relatively informal character
of the exchanges between the naturalists in Clusius's network and the
rules governing these exchanges. Friendship was a concept – a topos –
frequently used in the early modern period, especially by humanists. It not only played an important part in humanist correspondence
of the seventeenth century, however, but also in the more mundane
exchanges of, for instance, early modern merchant families. Its meaning covered a much wider range than modern 'friendship' and could
include mutual assistance and kinship, while implicitly or explicitly
carrying overtones of the classical rhetorical concept. As the following quotations show (and similar expressions can be found in almost
any letter to Clusius), the concept of friendship was often linked with
the idea of disinterested services and gifts to a friend.

In 1601 the Flemish merchant Hendrik Bloeme wrote from Frankfurt to Clusius in Leiden:

I send you in this box three leaves of my Indian fig[30] and two of my aloë
americana plants. If I had had any larger ones I would have sent them to you,
but I have shared all of them with friends who also desired them and don't
have any more at the moment . . . I thank you very warmly for the gift that
it has pleased you to make to me of your Historia plantarum and of the book
by monsieur de St Aldegonde and consider it a great favour. I have always
regarded myself as very much obliged to you for the many courtesies that I
have received from you over such a long period and have often wished for an
occasion that would enable me to do just something in return, but continuing
to burden myself with new favours (without using any ceremony) I ask you
affectionately whether there is anything with which I can serve you, or whether
there is anything here that would be pleasant to you; please ask me directly.[31]

---

[30] An opuntia cactus.
[31] From Hendrik Bloeme in Frankfurt to Clusius in Leiden, 13/23 April 1601 (in
French): 'vous envoije en ceste cassetta 3 feuilles de mon figuijer d'inde avec deux
plantes de mon Aloë Americana, si je les eusse en plus grandes je les vous envoijeroije,

Clusius's old friend Jean de Brancion also wrote to him about their friendship:

but I beg you not to use the formalities that you put in your letter, because you know well that I am not taken in by them and that I am and always will be a true and devoted friend and that on my side I need nothing but a reciprocation of that friendship.[32]

Sharing was regarded as a virtue, a means of giving pleasure, and a sign of friendship. Among both men and women, liberality and generosity – to share and be seen to share – were very important in the virtual community of sixteenth-century naturalists. The apothecary Thomas de la Fosse wrote to Clusius in 1596 that he hoped to share a special plant named 'lenticus' with as many friends as possible who were worthy, and emphasised that he would be pleased to be of service to Clusius because he valued his friendship.[33] Although written in a rather less elegant style, the message from Anna Maria von Heusenstain was similar. To her and many others, Clusius was first and foremost a generous benefactor, giver and provider of plants, exotica, botanical knowledge and friendship. Heusenstain's letters show that receiving gifts from Clusius raised a garden owner's status immediately to that of special favourite in the circles of plant lovers, neighbours and fellow garden owners, circumstances which could provoke considerable envy, as these quotations from Heusenstain's letters show:

mais les ayant tous participe avec amis qui la desiroijent n'en aij pour le present aultres . . . Je vous remercie bien affectueusement de la presentation qu'il vous a pleu faire tant de votre Historia plantarum que du livre de feu monsieur de St. Aldegonde, l'estimant un tres grand faveur. Je m'aij toussiours estime estre fort oblige envers vous pour tant de courtoisies des long temps receu et en aij souvent fois desire quelque occasion pour aulcunement vous en pouvoir gratifier, mais me chergeant continuellement de nouvelles faveurs (sans user de ceremonies) vous prie tres affectueusement s'il ia perdeca en quoij je vous pourroij servir, ou que desiriez quelque chose dici que vous seroit agreable . . .'

[32] From de Brancion in Malines to Clusius in Paris, 3 August 1571 (in French): 'Mais je vous prie n'user plus des ceremonies que mettez en v-re l-re, car vous scavez bien que je n'en suijs refaict et que je vous suijs et seraij toujours vraij et entier amij et qu'il ne fault en mon endroit aultre recognoissance sinon la reciprocque.'

[33] From de la Fosse in Middelburg to Clusius in Leiden, 12 July 1596 (in French): 'J'aij espoir de le sy bien conserver que je le poldraij tenir et en participer avecq le tans les bons amys qui en sont dignes.'

I ask you Sir, . . . In return let Sir ask from me whatever he wants. When I obtain some rarity which according to my opinion Sir does not have, then I will send it to Sir. But since Sir has been gone from here, nobody will give me anything. They just say to me, ask Sir Clusius, let him give it to me.[34]

And a year later:

I have heard that Sir has sent beautiful things to Frau Ungnadin and I thought that I too meant something to Sir and I still think so.[35]

She obviously minded very much that Clusius might think of her as ungenerous, as (she implies) had been suggested to him by some false friends:

I am really worried that Sir might feel animosity towards me, because he does not even want anything from me and writes to me in his previous letter that I have many more things in any case than Sir himself and give nothing to anybody. I just believe that there are people who want to stir up trouble between me and Sir, so that Sir does not send me anything. But I hope Sir will not do that nor believe that I give things to just anyone. That I do not, my garden is not producing enough. Nobody gives me anything anyhow, apart from the rarities that Sir sends me.[36]

As the last quotation demonstrates, the Clusius correspondence contains many clues about the informal but very important rules of

---

[34] From Heusenstain in Starhemberg to Clusius in Frankfurt, 9 January 1589 (in German): 'Ich bitte den Herr . . . Dagegen verlanghe der Herr auch von mir, was der Herr will. Bekomme aber ich etwas seltenes von dem ich der Meinung bin, der Herr habe es nicht, so will ichs dem Herrn schicken. Aber seit der Herre weg ist, gibt mir kein Mensch etwas. Sie sagen nur, ich solle es dem Herrn Clusius sagen, das er mirs gebe.'

[35] From Heusenstain in Vienna to Clusius in Frankfurt, 18 July 1590 (in German): 'Ich habe gehört, der Herr habe der Frau Ungnadin schöne Sachen geschickt und ich habe gemeint, ich gelte auch etwas bei dem Herrn und es dünkt mich noch so.'

[36] From Heusenstain in Vienna to Clusius in Frankfurt, 15 August 1591(?) (in German): 'Ich habe rechten Kummer [weil ich denke] der Herre sei mir feindlich (gesinnt), weil er so gar nichts von mir begehrt und mir im nächtsvorhergegangenen Brief schreibt, ich hätte sowieso viel mehr Sachen als der Herr und gebe niemandem etwas. Ich glaube nur es seien Leute, die mich gerne mit dem Herrn verfeinden willten, damit der Herr nichts schickt. Aber ich hoffe der Herre wird es nicht tun und nicht glauben dass ich jedermann gebe; dat tue ich nicht, es leistet mein Garten nichts. Er gibt mir auch niemand etwas, als was mir der Herr Seltenes schickt.'

behaviour governing these apparently liberal exchanges. Naturally, such unwritten rules were never spelt out in the correspondence, since those who participated were expected to know and abide by them. Yet, we can infer most of them from asides, hints, brief remarks and especially from situations where something went wrong or someone deliberately or inadvertently broke them. For instance, James Garet Sr wrote to Clusius about the rich bourgeois garden owner Johannes van Hoghelande in whose garden he had seen some beautiful flowers that were presents from Clusius himself: 'he is so possessive and I could not get any out of his hands, patience'.[37] A remark by his son Pieter in a letter to Clusius also reveals that sharing was certainly not done indiscriminately:

Paludanus[38] begged me to give it [i.e. a special type of gum used by Indians to waterproof their canoes] to him or at least part of it but I refused hearing that he wanted to describe it, and I told him that if you wanted him to have part of it you would make a present of some to him.[39]

In other words, when Pieter Garet discovered that Paludanus wanted to 'steal' the honour from Clusius of being the first to describe or publish a special gum, he protected Clusius – and thereby his own good relationship with him, also leaving the option open for Clusius to show his generosity and give some of the gum to Paludanus.

Once a person was recognised as 'a friend' (meaning in this case a fellow member of the network of naturalists), it was not done to

---

[37] From James Garet Sr in London to Clusius in Frankfurt, 4 April 1592 (in Dutch).

[38] Bernardus Paludanus (1550–1633), a physician and collector, from Enkhuizen in North Holland. His collection of curiosities was famous throughout Europe north of the Alps; many foreign guests of high rank visited his collection and private botanical garden. He travelled widely, but from his international correspondence very few letters survive and he published nothing. There is no monograph about him. See H. D. Schepelern, 'Natural philosophers and princely collectors: Worm, Paludanus and the Gottorp and Copenhagen collections', in Oliver Impey and Arthur MacGregor, *The Origins of Museums: The Cabinets of Curiosities in Sixteenth and Seventeenth-century Europe* (Oxford: Oxford University Press, 1985), pp. 121–7.

[39] From Pieter Garet in Amsterdam to Clusius in Leiden, 30 January 1602 (in Dutch): 'Paludanus heefter mij seer om gebeden ofte ten minsten een stuck daervan dwelck ick geweijgert hebbe hoorende dat hij het wilde bescrijven, dan hebbe hem geseijt soo het UL geliefde dat ghij hem een stuck soude willen vereeren.'

withhold information or lie about it, refuse to give counter-gifts, be stingy, steal bulbs or seeds (or have them stolen by servants), publish someone else's results or discoveries without any form of recognition, bribe agents or brokers in order to obtain rare naturalia that were destined for someone else, or plagiarize (although the definition and the notion of authorship were not identical with modern ones). Transgressions of these rules of civility and courtesy resulted in conflict, broken friendships, denial of access to further information, loss of reputation and status in the virtual community of scholars.[40] Ultimately, probably, an offending person could be ostracised from this virtual community. The extent of irritation, jealousy and even exclusion from the 'exchange circle' entailed by breaking these rules emerges from a letter to Clusius from Jacques Plateau, a rich garden owner at Tournai in the southern Netherlands. He describes the visit of Jehan Robin, Parisian apothecary, creator of the botanical garden of Paris (in 1597) and *hortulanus* of the French king, to the Low Countries. At Tournai Robin visited:

... all the gardens of the town, both those of the church dignitaries and those of the apothecaries, from whom he amassed a large quantity of ordinary plants. I asked him why he was putting himself under an obligation to so many people when he could have had the same plants from a single garden owner. He told me that he would go from Tournai to Ghent, then to Bruges, Antwerp, Malines, Brussels, Mons, Valenciennes, Cambrai and from there to Paris. I expect that he did the same thing there as he did in Tournai, putting himself under an obligation to an infinite number of persons. Since his return to Paris I have received two letters – the messenger told me that there were as many as 8 or 10 letters for Tournai alone – ... in which he asked for new plants. I don't think he will have received many. From me he had not a single one. For more than 15 or 16 years I haven't received a single plant from him. I also don't feel obliged to him because he asks for such a large number of plants all at once that it makes one feel disgusted; if any other person asked for one, he would ask for 10 or 12. Seeing that he did not get from me what he desired, he has asked whether I wanted to sell him some. I have replied to him that they were not for sale, since

---

[40] Cf. Bots and Waquet, *La République des Lettres*, pp. 124–6; and for a later period Goldgar, *Impolite Learning*. For a comparison and differences between northern Europe and Italy see Findlen, 'The formation of a scientific community', esp. pp. 383–9.

then I have had no news from him . . . I have little confidence in the French, given the fact that it would neither be the first nor the second time that I have been deceived by them.[41]

It was bad enough that Robin over-asked and gave nothing in return. The penultimate sentence of this letter shows how he made matters even worse by offering to buy plants from Plateau, who replied disgustedly that they were not for sale. This whole episode beautifully illustrates the point that the type of 'free' exchange of naturalia described in these examples existed exclusively *within* a community of naturalists who regarded each other as friends and were bound by the rules of civility and honour.

By the later sixteenth century, European society was geared to merchant enterprise, markets and commodities. A large number of naturalia were not only of academic interest, but also formed part of the market economy as (potential) drugs, spices or valuable rarities. Many people had an eye for their commercial value: bulbs were regularly stolen from gardens and from packages to or from Clusius. The market value of plants would become much more evident some decades later, during the early seventeenth century, with the famous tulip craze of the 1630s when prices of tulips reached astronomical proportions, the growing market for medicinal herbs, and the fortunes made in the spice trade (nutmeg, pepper, ginger and cinnamon). During the 1580s and

---

[41] From Plateau in Tournai to Clusius in Leiden, 8 February 1602 (in French): 'Il a visite tous les jardins de la ville tant de gens d'église que d'apothicaire, desques il a amasse grande nombre de plantes communes. Je luy dit pourquoy il s'obligoit a tant de personne voyant que une seule personne luy pouvoit furnir. Il me disoit quíl alloit de Tournay a Gand puis a Bruges, Anvers, Malines, Bruxelles, Mons, Valenchienne, Cambray et la a Paris. Jestime quil aura faict le mesure ausdictes villes comme en Tournay s obligeant a un e infitie de personnes. Depuis son retour a Paris j'ay receu deux lettres le messager quoy me delivre sa lettre, me dit quil avoit bien 8 ou 10 stant seulement pour Tournay . . . pour plantes nouvelles je ne pense point quil en aura eu beaucoup quant est de moy il n'en a eu une seul. Il y a plus de 15 ou 16 ans et davantaige que je n'ay receu plante de luy aussi je ne me demande estre oblige a luy pour cause quil demande si grande nombre de plante a une fois que lon en est degoute, sil en encore une il en demandere 10 ou 12 voyant quil n'a sceu avoir de moy ce quil desiroit, il m'a prie luy en vouloir vendre aucunes, Je luy ay respondu quelles nestoient a vendre depuis je n'ay eu des ses novelles . . . Jay peu de fiance aux Franchois ce me seroit pas le premier, ne seconde fois quil m'auroient trompe.'

1590s the persons who probably best realised the economic potential of special plants were those naturalists who (also) acted as brokers and were involved in commerce themselves.

The Garet family provides a good example.[42] James Sr and his sons James Jr and Pieter worked as apothecaries and spice traders. Originally from Antwerp, they fled the southern Netherlands in 1569–70, no doubt for both religious and economic reasons, and moved to London, where they joined the Dutch Reformed Church at Austin Friars. Pieter later moved to Amsterdam. The Garets combined scholarly and economic interests. The London Garets grew European and exotic plants in their gardens, experimented with them and exchanged information with fellow botanists, druggists, perfumers and spice traders. They received and corresponded with many learned guests from the continent, besides forming part of a highly specialised circle of botanists, physicians and apothecaries in London, including Hugh Morgan, Thomas Penny, John Gerard, Thomas Moffet, Jacob Cole (Ortelianus), Richard Garth, Mathias de L'Obel and John Rich, many of whom likewise corresponded with Clusius. Both the younger Garets developed a passion for exotic naturalia. James Jr was especially interested in new varieties of tulips and lilies. In 1589–90 he also grew potatoes, a most exotic plant that had just been imported from Peru, in his garden. He was closely in touch with such famous overseas adventurers as Sir Francis Drake and Thomas Cavendish, and it was through James Garet Jr that Clusius gained access to some of the newly discovered drugs and plants brought from Roanoke and Virginia.[43] Together with his fellow London apothecary Hugh Morgan, 'royal druggist' and likewise correspondent of Clusius, James Jr pioneered the importation of drugs and the cultivation of plants from the New World in Britain.[44]

[42] The Garets, to whom I will devote a fuller study, also figure in Deborah E. Harkness, '"Strange" ideas and "English" knowledge: natural science exchange in Elizabethan London', in Smith and Findlen (eds.), *Merchants and Marvels*, pp. 137–60.

[43] Leslie G. Matthews, *The Royal Apothecaries* (London: Wellcome Institute, 1967).

[44] Margaret Pelling and Charles Webster, 'Medical practitioners', in Charles Webster (ed.), *Health, Medicine and Mortality in the Sixteenth Century* (Cambridge: Cambridge University Press, 1979), pp. 165–235, here 178. See also R. S. Roberts, 'The early history of the import of drugs into England', in F. N. L. Poynter (ed.), *The Evolution of Pharmacy in Britain* (London: Pitman Medical Publishing, 1965), pp. 165–86.

In Amsterdam Pieter also owned a garden where he grew exotica and in his turn maintained close contacts with the first Dutchmen who explored the East Indies, such as Wybrant van Warwijck and Jacob van Neck. He may even have had a contract with the East Indies Company to provide the outward-bound ships with drugs for their medicine chests. Although a merchant himself, Pieter complained bitterly to Clusius when he discovered that upon the return of several ships from the East Indies, buyers from the emperor's court in Vienna or Prague were ready to board the ships in the harbour of Amsterdam, in the middle of the night if necessary, and pay enormous sums for exotica – thus preventing him from obtaining anything special for Clusius or for himself.[45] Thus, an economy of free exchange and barter among experts overlapped and sometimes clashed with a market economy. The two were certainly not mutually exclusive, but belonged to different 'registers': non-market exchange going with hospitality, gift, generosity, friendship and reputation; market exchange with the money economy, capital, profit and commodification.[46] No wonder that Plateau was so offended by Robin's behaviour!

FRIENDS AND EXPERTS

Having explored some of the elementary rules of exchange in this virtual community of sixteenth-century naturalists and the relatively informal character of the correspondence, we may try to tease out a link between them, illustrating the formation of a European community of scholars and the establishment of a new field of expertise.

Friendship was a topos, but we should not underestimate its real effects on exchanges in these circles. Up to a point friendship and sharing the same passion for nature could efface (or perhaps suspend or overrule) some of the social and gender differences that undeniably existed between Clusius and quite a few of his correspondents. This could work in more than one direction. The Garets ranked below Clusius in terms of status and education, although probably not in

---

[45] From Pieter Garet in Amsterdam to Clusius in Leiden, 9 February 1605 (in Dutch).
[46] Smith and Findlen (eds.), *Merchants and Marvels* largely ignores the fact that these two types of economy could coexist and were not necessarily mutually exclusive – and that most naturalists participated in both.

terms of wealth. None of them had gone to university, while as businessmen they belonged to the world of trade rather than study. This is also apparent from the respectful tone of the Garets' letters and their frequent demonstrations of willingness to be of assistance. Nonetheless, the Garets and Clusius were friends and that term was not a merely rhetorical one. Their gift exchanges were mutual. Respect and affection obviously existed on both sides. Clusius visited them in London, recognised them as experts in their own right, and they were mentioned as friends and experts in letters from other correspondents of Clusius. The fact that three members of one family living in different countries and belonging to two generations maintained a correspondence from 1583 to 1605 also demonstrates a mutual and longstanding friendship.

In terms of social status and wealth Clusius himself, in turn, stood definitely below such aristocrats as Princess Marie de Brimeu, Charles de Saint Omer or the Duke of Aremberg. Education and his growing prestige as scholar probably acted to some extent as a counterweight. Clearly the differences in status between patrons and their protégés could be overcome up to a point – even if only during certain circumstances and in certain cases – by friendship, shared affinities and their sheer pleasure in discoveries and the beauty of nature. This connection between patronage, friendship and expertise in the field of natural history should certainly be explored further, especially since this was one of the few domains where women could shine both as patrons and as experts. Moreover, botany was not only a passion shared by those who already were friends; it could and did create new friendships between people from different countries and different classes, as the Clusius correspondence makes clear. In the continuous search throughout Europe for new and rare discoveries, friends of friends continually recommended each other as new contacts for exchange. Frequently new friendships grew out of such contacts, thus promoting the growth of the virtual community of naturalists.

The Clusius correspondence also provides ample evidence that pleasure, the enjoyment of nature and emotional responses to it were felt long before the Romantic era. It cannot be a coincidence that Clusius's near-contemporary, the Swiss naturalist Conrad Gessner was probably the first European to write (1541) about the beauty and majesty of the Swiss mountains, which he explored during herbalising trips.[47] Such herbalising excursions and journeys, which became part of the training of many students of natural history during the later part of the sixteenth century, may have had an important effect on the appreciation of nature in an aesthetic, non-utilitarian and also non-religious and non-symbolic way.[48] Expressions of enjoyment can be found not only in the letters from such wealthy and aristocratic owners of private botanical gardens as Princess Marie de Brimeu, but also in those from modest middle-class garden owners. A touching example of an owner's emotional attachment to his garden comes from two letters written to Clusius by the apothecary Thomas de la Fosse about his deceased uncle Jean Mouton, likewise an apothecary, who had transmitted his pleasure in plants to his nephew, or as de la Fosse said 'is the cause of my total delight and pleasure in plants'. Mouton had for many years been one of Clusius's regular correspondents and shared the latter's love for plants down to the last day of his life. Even in his final months, when he was extremely weak and paralysed from the neck down, one of Mouton's main delights and preoccupations in life was his garden: 'still he was taking care of his garden and had plants moved because of the cold and other things done as if he was not ill at all . . .'.[49]

This emotional involvement with nature and gardens could have a complex background; for at least some men and women it was deeply

---

[47] In a treatise about milk and milk products published at Zurich in 1543: *Libellus de lacte et operibus lactariis, philologus pariter ac medicus. Cum epistola ad Jacobum Avienum de montium admiratione.* See H. Wellisch, 'Conrad Gessner: a bio-bibliography', *Journal of the Society for the Bibliography of Natural History* 7 (1975), 151–247, especially 159 and 180–1. Cf. Joaneath Spicer, 'Roelandt Savery and the discovery of the Alpine waterfall', in Eliška Fučíková et al. (eds.), *Rudolf II and Prague: The Imperial Court and Residential City as the Cultural Heart of Central Europe* (Prague, London and Milan: Prague Castle Administration, Thames & Hudson, Skira Editore, 1997), pp. 146–56, quoting a letter from Gessner on this topic.

[48] I am not arguing here that (some of) these naturalists were a-religious, but that they started writing and, as it seems, feeling about nature in terms of beauty and not necessarily of religion or symbolism.

[49] 'Qui est cause que j'ay entierement delectassion et plaisir aulx simples.' 'Encore avoit il soing de son jardin faisant transporter les plantes pour la froidure et faire autres chozes comme s'il n'eut este aucunement malade' (letters dated respectively 12 July 1596, from de la Fosse in Middelburg to Clusius in Leiden, and 31 August 1589, from de la Fosse in Tournai to Clusius in Frankfurt).

connected with the experience of danger. Olmi argues, for instance, that Ulisse Aldrovandi's shift from medicine and philosophy to natural history after his imprisonment by the Inquisition and during the Counter-Reformation was decisively influenced by the uncontroversial nature of natural history.[50] For many expert sixteenth-century naturalists 'nature' formed a safe enclave and a hide-out. Quite a few of them were Protestants or even Calvinists. Nearly all had personally experienced the effects of warfare and persecution in a Europe deeply divided by wars, conspiracies and religious controversy.[51] As they could see in their immediate surroundings, many fields of knowledge were dangerous. Theology and alchemy literally cost some experts their lives and apothecaries in particular could be suspected of knowing too much for their own good about drugs and poisons. The fate of William Turner, the English naturalist and author of *Libellus de Re Herbaria* (1538), was particularly dramatic. He joined the Reformation, was banished from England, lived in Italy and Switzerland around 1542–3 (where he became a close friend of Conrad Gessner), and travelled in the Low Countries and Germany. His works were prohibited by Henry VIII, but he returned to England upon the accession of Edward VI. During the first year of Queen Mary's reign, Turner lost his job and almost his life, and had to flee once more to the continent. His works were prohibited a second time before he finally returned after Elizabeth I became queen in 1558.[52] A rare example in which this image of natural history and botany as a safe shelter in dangerous times was made explicit occurs in a letter from the southern Netherlandish nobleman Philip de Marnix de Saint Aldegonde to Clusius:

The French king himself, who is great lover of plants, desires nothing but quiet after the furors of these civil wars, so that he can renew botany in France with the help of such men as I have described to you.[53]

---

[50] Giuseppe Olmi, *Ulisse Aldrovandi. Scienza e natura nel secondo cinquecento* (Trento: Libera Università degli Studi di Trento, 1976), pp. 45 and 57.

[51] Reeds, *Botany in Medieval and Renaissance Universities*, pp. 13–14.

[52] Whitney Jones, *William Turner: Tudor Naturalist, Physician, Divine* (London: Routledge, 1988), esp. pp. 17–25.

[53] From Saint Aldegonde in Souburg in the province of Zeeland to Clusius in Frankfurt, 8 November 1590 (in Latin): 'Rex certe ipse qui hortulariae rei est amantissimus nihil

The emphasis on disinterested friendship and a 'free' exchange of gifts may have been especially strong in the European 'virtual' community of naturalists which had only started to develop from the 1530s on. It was very much a new community trying to establish a new type of expertise and carve out its own niche in a social and cultural domain in which many different parties operated – from university academics, physicians, surgeons, and aristocratic garden owners, to apothecaries, explorers, peasants and local healers – and where different economies overlapped and clashed. Not only did their domain lack clear boundaries, the status of their expertise also remained uncertain.

Getting muddy, digging up roots, pruning trees, gathering mushrooms, being out in the fields in all seasons and types of weather were not regarded as particularly prestigious activities at the time. Nature did become fashionable in the sixteenth century, while hunting and the outlay of private gardens had long been pastimes suitable for princes and aristocrats, but the arduous activities that accompanied such interests were generally looked down upon and usually left to servants. For a Renaissance way of thinking, 'low' activities involving both manual work and contact with lower-class persons implied low-quality knowledge, unless it was transformed and elevated by scholarship. For instance, the status of both the knowledge and the social position of surgeons – who dirtied their hands by manipulating human bodies – were much lower than those of the physicians, who did no such things and desperately tried to maintain a big barrier between themselves and the surgeons.[54] It is no coincidence therefore, that many botanical publications of the early modern period abound in derogatory remarks about information and plants obtained from rustics, old women and other socially undesirable persons. In the preface to his *Cruydtboeck* (1554) the famous southern Netherlandish botanist

nisi ab his bellorum intestinorum furoribus otium exoptat ut eiusmodi virorum qualem te praedicavi opera, rem herbariam in Galliae possit instaurare.' The rest of the letter makes clear that Aldegonde had Clusius himself in mind for such a job, since he enquired whether Clusius might be interested in a connection with the French court.

[54] See Erwin Huizenga's excellent study, *Tussen autoriteit en empirie: de Middelnederlandse chirurgieën in de veertiende en vijftiende eeuw en hun maatschappelijke context* (Hilversum: Verloren, 2003).

(and friend of Clusius) Rembertus Dodonaeus states, for instance, that the knowledge of plants and herbs had long been despised in the circles of physicians, who regarded it as a demeaning manual activity and a domain only suited to lesser figures, such as 'apothecaries and other untrained persons, who search for herbs on a daily basis in the woods and fields, and that it would have been dishonourable for themselves and a useless burden to acquire and investigate the knowledge of herbs'.[55] The research methods of the emerging botanical experts required at least some physical contact with nature, however, and they must have been careful about defining their own position between lowly manual labourers and aristocratic garden owners. The well-known botanising trips by sixteenth-century French and Italian naturalists and their (medical) students consisted primarily of teaching and social expeditions during which most of the hard work seems to have been done by servants.[56] It would be interesting to know whether Clusius did much manual work himself during his early field trips.

Between 1530 and around 1600, experts in natural history lacked the prestige of the old and established disciplines. They were scattered throughout Europe, moreover, and only rarely had access to organisations or locations where they could meet or deposit their information.[57] This situation changed – up to a point – in the course of the seventeenth century, when many European countries created academies and royal societies that helped to channel research in natural history; but these institutions also demanded new loyalties that may have made them less international and European than the preceding virtual communities. During most of the sixteenth century, however, 'naturalists' could only advance by working together and

---

[55] Quoted (in Dutch) in A. Schierbeek, *Van Aristoteles tot Pasteur: leven en werken der groote biologen* (Amsterdam: Versluys, 1923), p. 41: 'Omdat zij meijnden dat alsulcken scientie ofte kennisse haer niet en betaemde, maer alleen toebehoorde den apotekers oft sommighen anderen ongheleerden, die daghelijcx die cruyden in die bosschen, ende op die velden soecken, ende dat huerlieden oneere gheweest soude hebben oft anders een noodeloose sorghe die kennisse vanden cruyden te leeren ende te ondersoecken.'

[56] Findlen, *Possessing Nature*, pp. 164–70.

[57] Mario Biagioli, 'Etiquette, interdependence, and sociability in seventeenth-century science', *Critical Inquiry* 22 (1996), 193–238.

sharing information. None could acquire prestige or even become a real expert without the help of others. 'Free' gift exchange was in everyone's interest: it helped increase expertise and raise the general status of the discipline – and by extension that of its members. The idiom of friendship acquires fresh meaning in this context. In terms of function it both expressed and underpinned the value of free exchange, which itself helped to create a virtual community of natural history experts throughout Europe. As we have seen, the correspondence about natural history in Europe (of which Clusius's huge collection forms only a small part) belonged to an ongoing exchange which comprised both material objects (plants, seeds, pictures of plants and books) and non-material gifts, such as pleasure, assistance, knowledge, respect, time, friendship. Perhaps the most valuable gift of all expressed and made through these letters was the feeling of belonging to a virtual but very real and far-flung community of friends and naturalists. Today, these letters help us to reconstruct that community of exchanges; at the time they both embodied and helped to constitute that community.

CONCLUSION

Correspondence formed only one means of exchange among early modern experts in natural history: there were face-to-face meetings, travel, social gatherings, the participation in a court or aristocratic setting as either patron or protégé, printed books and treatises, herbalising expeditions, diplomatic missions, voyages of discovery, meetings of academies, university gatherings and so on. Yet, correspondence offers the unique advantage of being not only a means of conveying information *about* all of these other aspects of exchange but also itself a means of information exchange; in addition, it is an instrument in the creation of both a community of scholars and a new field of expertise. We can only begin interpreting correspondence in this way, however, once we have shifted from the individual, biography and the history of ideas – which has underlain many older publications about correspondence among scholars and scientists – to communities, group culture and styles of exchange. The latter perspective has also determined the choice of the examples and correspondents in this essay, and has made us transfer our attention (at least partly) from well-known humanists and famous men to brokers, apothecaries, women and some aristocratic garden owners and experts. The latter often become the more interesting figures, while the former continue to be crucial as points of entry into the community of exchange.

In studying Clusius's correspondence we should, finally, ask ourselves what this correspondence meant to Clusius, the spider in this European web of a virtual community. Since he kept these letters carefully, they must have been dear to him, for emotional reasons, because of the information they contained, and as a kind of personal archive. Perhaps a partial answer comes from looking at a man who operated in a similar way three centuries later: Charles Darwin. As Janet Browne brilliantly writes:

> Systematically, he turned his house into the hub of an ever-expanding web of scientific correspondence , , , He relied on these letters for every aspect of his evolutionary endeavour, using them not only to pursue his investigations across the globe, but also to give his arguments the international spread and universal application that he and his colleagues regarded as essential footings for any new scientific concept. They were his primary research tool . . . If there was any single factor that characterised the heart of Darwin's scientific undertaking it was this systematic use of correspondence.[58]

APPENDIX: LETTER FROM JAMES GARET JR IN LONDON TO CLUSIUS IN FRANKFURT, 28 AUGUST 1590

Monseigneur Clusius, I have received everything you sent me up to 26 April. I have also received the book on Virginia in French for which I thank you many times. I am afraid that the person who has published them will receive nothing from Sir Walter Rawleijg, because it seems to me that the said Rawleig is displeased that he has had the said books printed without his approval. I enclose with this letter the portrait of the pepper of Rana and also how the branches look, and I also send you

---

[58] Janet Browne, *Charles Darwin: The Power of Place*, volume 2 of a biography (London: Jonathan Cape, 2002), pp. 11–12.

some grains of the said pepper so that you can describe them better. I also send you a little box with some bulbs of which only two are of carnation-coloured hyacinths and the rest are blue, and the other bulbs are pseudo-daffodils – I am not sure whether you had asked me for the latter last year. Six weeks ago I had dug up in my garden 6 bulbs of carnation-coloured hyacynths to send them to you, and because I had to leave immediately for the countryside with Mr Edward Wotton (whom you know well) because of his wife who had ulcerous veins – where I stayed for a whole month without moving from there and since then, having returned, I had to leave once more for another place, staying there for 15 days, not having spent more than one day in my own home – seeing that the said bulbs had been left above ground I had them put back into the ground until my return, and I ordered my servant to mark the place where he put them with a stick. He had put them in so well that my wife had the earth turned in my absence to sow vegetables and thus my 6 bulbs were lost, and since then a friend has given me another bulb of the carnation-coloured hyacinth of which I have sent you three in all. They multiply better in gardens than they do in the fields; further I send you enclosed a letter that Monsr Wotton has asked me to have delivered safely to his brother who lives in Altorff near Nuremberg as indicated in the address. I beg you to take care that the letter will be delivered safely because it contains a bill of exchange for the said scholar and if you could [. . .?] the answer and send it to me, it would please me; I do it to please Mr Edward Wotton who certainly takes good care of his brother. I think that he will be the Queen's secretary, replacing Monsr Walsingame; he would have obtained this position a long time ago, but he refused it because he has means enough to live on without involving himself in such inconvenience. The Queen has ordered him to appear at court and it is precisely for this reason, and I have understood that she wants him to accept the post. I send you also a little bit of aethiopian pepper, so that you can see it. I hope to send you with the next letter the portrait of Hysopus Tennig and another portrait of a plant that I have grown from the seeds that I found among the gardening things of [. . .], which is a rare plant. The person who has drawn all the portraits

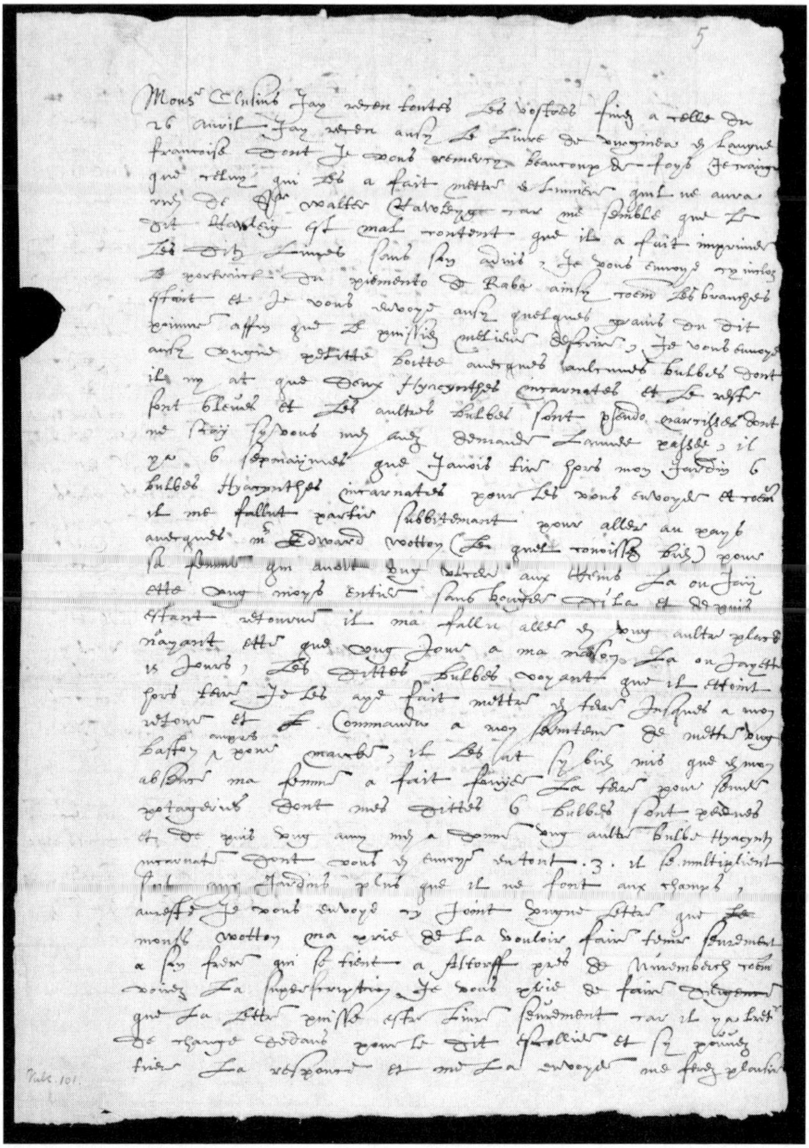

Fig. 5. Letter from James (Jacques) Garet Jr to Clusius, 28 August 1590. Courtesy of
Leiden University Library, VUL 101

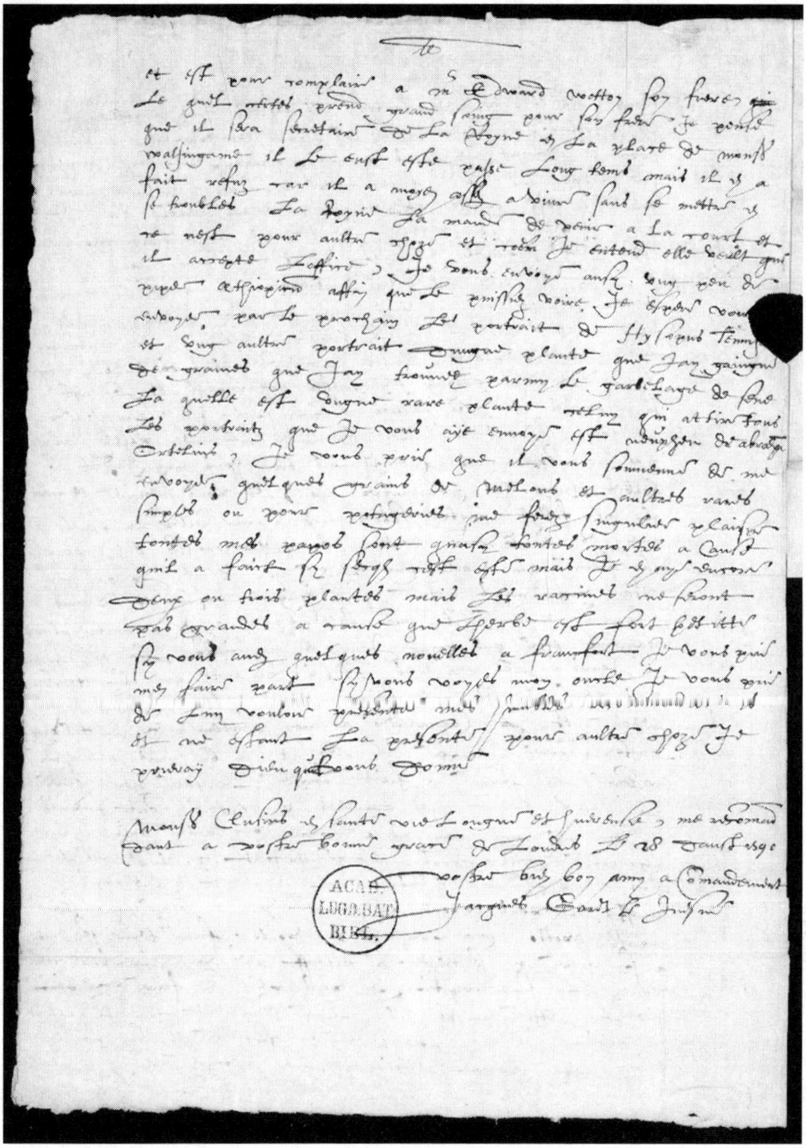

Fig. 5. (*cont.*)

that I have sent you is the nephew of Abraham Ortelius. I beg you not to forget to send me some seeds of melons and of other rare plants or for vegetables; it would give a singular pleasure. All my papos [= potatoes] are almost dead because it has been so dry this summer, but I still have some two or three plants, but the roots will not be very big because the leaves have remained rather small. If you hear of any news in Frankfurt please let me know; if you see my uncle please present him my humble respects; that being all for the present I pray God that he give you, Monsr Clusius, a healthy, long and happy life, recommending myself to your good grace, from London, 28 August 1590.

Your very good friend at your command Jacques Garet the Younger.

PART II

Uses and meanings of correspondence: artists, patrons, collectors

CHAPTER 5

Letters and portraits: economy of time and chivalrous service in courtly culture

Fernando Bouza

A character in a play by Pedro Calderón de la Barca, D. Álvaro de Acuña in *Fuego de Dios en el querer bien*, complains of the tiresome burden of having to write. He grumblingly recalls the words of a famous courtier who prophesied that if a letter shop existed it would be the securest and most thriving business in the world.[1] Such establishments undoubtedly existed, for in Lisbon, London, Seville, Rome, Paris and Madrid it was possible to acquire letters that were ready written and awaiting a buyer.[2] However, much to his regret, Don Álvaro had to devote his energies to letter writing, as he could hardly show himself to be a true gentleman unless he at least finished off the correspondence he signed with a few lines in his own hand.

This research was funded by Project BHA2000–03328, 'Cultura erudita y poder en el Siglo de Oro. Lucha política, comunicación y república de las letras en torno a la crisis ibérica de 1640', Ministerio de Educación, Ciencia y Tecnología del Reino de España, and is part of its activities. The initial results were incorporated in a paper entitled 'Words of art: virtuosi, court politics and artistic language in the 16th –17th century Spanish Monarchy' presented at the Cultural Exchange in Europe *c.*1400– *c.*1700 Plenary Conference, European Science Foundation, Naples, 1 October 1999, which provided a partial basis for a chapter by F. Bouza, *Palabra e imagen en la corte: cultura oral y visual de la nobleza en el Siglo de Oro* (Madrid: Abada Ediciones, 2003).

[1] 'What fatigue is so honourable, / but fatigue nonetheless, as that of writing! As rightly said / by a discreet Courtier, / if there were a shop, where / some shrewd merchant / were to sell written letters, / it would be the securest business / in the world . . .' ('Qué fatiga es tan honrada, / pero fatiga en efecto, la de escrivirl. Bien dezía / un Cortesano discreto, / que si huviese tienda, donde / algún mercader de ingenio / vendiesse cartas escritas, / fuera el más seguro empleo / del mundo . . .'). P. Calderón de la Barca, *Fuego de Dios en el querer bien*, II, p. 11.

[2] This market is dealt with in F. Bouza, *Corre manuscrito: una historia cultural del Siglo de Oro* (Madrid: Marcial Pons, 2001).

Reading the letter collections of nobles of the early modern age provides, first and foremost, a huge amount of information on the customs and changeable situation of the court. Through these letters, which are closely linked by a thread despite being delicately woven from loose pieces, their writers sought to convey the ever-changing circumstances of court politics to their absent correspondents. The letters were thus filled with news, their main merchandise.

But reading these letter collections also allows us to shape a particular theory on courtly life by analysing at length the use of key devices such as courtesy, reciprocity or concealment, as Nicoletta Bazzano has recently done with excellent results in connection with the correspondence of Marco Antonio Colonna between 1556 and 1577.[3]

Like other manuscripts related to embassies, governments or negotiations, correspondence was undoubtedly an essential aspect of a noble's education in the various practices and groups engaged in the political struggle at the court. The letters of the most outstanding courtiers were accordingly disseminated to an extent in manuscript copies, though correspondence was mainly housed in nobles' archives and libraries as testimonies of the family's history and grandeur and as a reference for future readers.

Aristocratic letter-writing customs clearly attest to a particular type of sociability based on manuscript correspondence. As stipulated by the rules of conversation, whose standards it set out to imitate, letter writing was governed by canons of *style* that dictated all aspects ranging from the courtesies that should be used to appropriate subjects for letters, not to mention whether or not the signatory of the letter should write in his own hand.

However, at this point we do not wish to focus on the aforementioned informative and formative aspects of correspondence, but rather on the fact that letters were intended to overcome the distance which temporarily or permanently separated the writer from those he considered his equals. In a world as codified as letter writing,

---

[3] Nicoletta Bazzano, '"A Vostra Eccelenza di buon cuore mi offero e raccomando": il linguaggio della politica attraverso il carteggio di Marco Antonio Colonna (1556–77)', in M. A. Visceglia (ed.), *La nobiltà romana in età moderna: profili instituzionali e pratiche sociali* (Rome: Carocci, 2001), pp. 133–64.

structured as it was into genres, treatments and formulas, writing partially or fully in one's own hand instead of using scribes or penmen can be regarded not only as a sign of deference towards one's correspondents but also as a wish for conversation and representation, if not in person at least in writing.

Despite his multiple occupations, in 1544 Antoine Perrenot de Granvelle wrote in his own hand to the Aragonese Martín de Aragón, Duke of Villahermosa, to inform his correspondent that he was sending a portrait he had recently had painted in Brussels. With certain misgivings about the artist's skills, Granvelle apologises to his friend and wonders 'whether there will be anything in it to remind Your Lordship of me'.[4] In this case we are dealing with both a handwritten letter and the sending of a portrait, a manner of keeping the friendship alive despite the distance and furthermore a sign of deference which Granvelle himself describes as a *service*, an essential term in courtly culture of the period.

Courtiers' correspondence is thus a specific genre governed by the conventions of the age and can be interpreted as an external sign of courtly culture, both in its rhetorical devices and in the nature of its content and outward gestures of deference, such as writing in one's own hand. The correspondence between Granvelle and Villahermosa, which is fully autograph and deals mainly with artistic issues, is the central focus of this chapter.

From this extensive correspondence, which was written during the middle decades of the sixteenth century and includes letters sent from various parts of the continent, it can be inferred that Granvelle made of his own time – as opposed to ritual or ceremonial time – a gift which he gave freely and generously as a sign of distinction towards those who deserved his respect and affection. This time, which he snatched from his many activities as a statesman in the service of Charles V's empire, was displayed in his generous and constant sending of letters and portraits. Both were manners of serving his friends, though Granvelle

---

[4] Granvelle to Martín de Aragón, Duke of Villahermosa, Metz, 23 July 1544, 'Correspondencia Perrenot/Villahermosa', Montijo, Caja 34–1, § xxvii, Archivo de los Duques de Alba, Madrid (hereafter ADA).

was not the only courtier of his age to resort to paintings and letters in order to shape, maintain and express the categories of courtly culture.

PORTRAIT LETTERS: SEE AND BE SEEN THROUGH CORRESPONDENCE

In 1616, the European courts followed with utmost interest the case of the Earl and Countess of Somerset, a court scandal, involving a conspiracy, with almost theatrical or novel-like overtones. The Lord Chamberlain, Robert Carr, and his wife, Frances Howard, whom James VI/I's favourite had recently married following her much talked-about divorce from Robert Devereux, were tried for the murder of Sir Thomas Overbury in the Tower of London.[5] That same year, writing from Madrid, the Duke of Infantado thanks the Count of Gondomar vigorously for sending him 'the portraits of the Earl and Countess of Somerset', and furthermore asks him to send his 'own account of the crime of the earl and countess', which he is keen to be able to read as soon as possible.[6]

Juan Hurtado de Mendoza *kissed the hands* of Sarmiento de Acuña in recognition of the service he had rendered him by sending him the portraits of the Earl and Countess of Somerset, the central figures in that tremendous scandal. This attests to the *circulation* of portraits in response to the demand for news, in parallel to the sending of notifications and accounts of events. Naturally, this was not the first time that Diego Sarmiento de Acuña provided his friends a prompt *service* by supplying them with paintings.

A letter he was sent from the court in 1593 portrays him as ever-diligent and also provides interesting information on the art market at the end of the sixteenth century.[7] It instructs the future Count

---

[5] On the case and the ways in which it was disseminated see A. Bellamy, *The Politics of Court Scandal in Early Modern England: News Culture and the Overbury Affair, 1603–1660* (Cambridge: Cambridge University Press, 2002).

[6] Juan Hurtado de Mendoza, Duke of Infantado, to Diego Sarmiento de Acuña, Count of Gondomar, Madrid, 21 July 1616, ms. II-2170, 10, Real Biblioteca, Madrid (hereafter RB).

[7] Anonymous correspondent to Sarmiento de Acuña, Madrid, 2 November 1593, ms. II-2149, 82, RB.

of Gondomar to enquire discreetly in Valladolid about a *Sleeping Venus*, some Flemish *Landscapes* painted in oils and a portrait of the *Queen Doña Isabel* that had belonged to Cristóbal de Santisteban. Having identified the works in the usual manner of the period, without mentioning the artist but conveniently describing their subject matter, frames and, as appropriate, provenance, the letter bids Don Diego to find out 'without [the then owner] realising who they are for, if he wishes to sell' the paintings and, having done so, 'to ascertain how much he wants for them and if he is willing to be owed for them for a year and a half'.

Despite the request for absolute discretion, the material aspects of the potential sale are not omitted, as the correspondent insists he try to bargain as much as possible in order to reach a convenient price. As we can see, this is a business transaction proper, involving covert negotiation of the terms and manner of payment and price, and the appropriate bargaining with the owner, even though the *goods* include an evocative *Sleeping Venus*. In this connection it is interesting to recall the extraordinary letter in which Jean Baptiste Colbert warns the Marquis of Villars of certain practices of Spanish collectors of the Baroque age inherited from their forefathers of the 1500s.[8]

As is known, in 1672 Louis XIV sent the painters Gabriel Blanchard and Joseph Cussat to the court of the child king, Charles II, in order that they 'choose the fifty most beautiful' paintings of Gaspar de Haro y Guzmán, Marquis of Carpio, to take back to France, for which they could pay up to a quarter of a million *livres*. Colbert points out to the French ambassador to Madrid that 'His Majesty wishes that above all you agree on the price with him [Carpio] or with whoever the Count has empowered to negotiate', but furthermore warns him to take extreme care to ensure that 'all the pictures are genuine', because:

it is sometimes feared that they have had copies made of the best pictures, which are so well done that they can scarcely be distinguished from the originals, and that after showing the true originals, on occasions they replace them with copies without one realising.[9]

[8] Colbert to Villars, Versailles, 8 September 1672, in P. Clément (ed.), *Lettres, instructions et mémoires de Colbert* (Paris: Imprimerie impériale, 1868), vol. 5, pp. 333–4.
[9] Clement (ed.), *Lettres, instructions*, p. 333.

Blanchard and Cussat returned to France without finalising what would undoubtedly have been one of the most important art sales of the seventeenth century. Without going into the highly complex world of copying and forgery in the Golden Age, we should perhaps now focus on these material aspects of collecting and patronage among sixteenth- and seventeenth-century nobility. Relations between nobles and artists were continuous and fruitful, but were not always bathed in the selfless glow of the benevolent *kunstfreund*. If, for example, we consider the sums of money that a good many nobles owed Juan Pantoja de la Cruz for various works, which are carefully listed in the will that the court painter to Philip II and Philip III made in 1599, we have the overwhelming impression of a nobility unconcerned about meeting their obligations towards artists.[10]

The will is also a more than eloquent testimony to Spanish nobles' constant recourse to *portrait painters* and to artists in general. The nobility's longstanding relationship with works of art was aptly defined with glaring simplicity by the Jesuit Lorenzo Ortiz when he stated in 1677 that 'to have a fair idea of painting is a sign of having been born between well-adorned walls'.[11]

However, returning to the letter asking the future ambassador to the court of James I to mediate in the purchase of that *Sleeping Venus*, perhaps the most curious aspect is the terms in which the request is addressed to Diego Sarmiento: 'I beg Your Honour to grant me this favour, which would be very great, and beg you to excuse this task; I shall not fail to serve Your Honour in return for it.'[12]

One task for another, one favour for another: his mediation in the sale of the paintings was interpreted as a *service* rendered by a well-educated gentleman capable of acting with the necessary discretion so as not to reveal the name of the buyer and even of keeping up a pretence in order to ensure as *convenient* a price as possible. The

---

[10] 'Testamento de don Juan Pantoja de la Cruz. (Pintor de Cámara de Su Majestad). (23 de julio de 1599)', in Antonio Matilla Tascón (ed.), *Testamentos de 43 personajes del Madrid de los Austrias* (Madrid: Instituto de Estudios Madrileños, 1983), pp. 101–9.

[11] L. Ortiz, *Memoria, entendimiento y voluntad: empresas que enseñan y persuaden su buen uso en lo moral y en lo político* (Seville: Juan Francisco de Blas, 1677), fol. 26r.

[12] Anonymous correspondent to Sarmiento de Acuña, ms. II-2149, 82, RB.

Count of Gondomar's career was full of services of this kind, in which a gentleman of his stature could display his generosity, particularly, as is known, by opening the doors of his magnificent library to writers and other people with an interest.[13] And what greater gesture of chivalry than offering a portrait of oneself as a gift.

In recognition of his support lent in the capture of the rock of Vélez de Gomera in 1564, Philip II had *delivered* to Francisco Barreto, the former governor of the Indies and *capitão-mor* of the Portuguese galleys at the time, 'a portrait of myself on a chain'.[14] The chronicler Diogo do Couto, who gives an account of this in his *Decada Nona de Asia*, adds that it consisted of a sheet of gold with a ring and sturdy chain, and it must therefore have been similar to the 'portraits on a medal' which are frequently mentioned in records and also appear in portraits of the period. However, what makes this case particularly interesting is that Couto also transcribes the letter which the king sends Barreto together with his self-portrait. In the letter Philip II himself explains the significance of his gift:

The good success of the Rock expedition I attribute more to your fortune than to my power; I always believed, as was confirmed to me, that Don García de Toledo was helped by your favour. I am very grateful to the part you played in it and am accordingly greatly indebted to you, and until now I did not know how to pay and thank you but by sending you a portrait of myself on a chain in order that I be bound to you every day of your life, for whatever you wish.

By sending Barreto his portrait on a sheet of gold, Philip was primarily rewarding the man who had served him well and, to judge by the four thousand *cruzados* at which Diogo do Couto estimated its price, this was a splendid reward indeed. But over and above the considerable value of the metal and workmanship, this precious gift should be interpreted as a personal debt of gratitude which Philip II openly acknowledged owing to Francisco Barreto. Thereafter, for want of a better expression, Barreto would wear his Catholic Majesty,

---

[13] Ian Michael, 'O primeiro Conde de Gondomar (1567–1626): home e imaxe', in *Mar por medio. V Xornadas de cultura galega: unha visión de Galicia dende o Reino Unido* (Lugo: Diputación provincial de Lugo, 2000), pp. 81–96.

[14] Diogo do Couto, *Decadas da Asia* (Lisbon: Domingos Gonsalves, 1736), vol. 9, p. 552.

as depicted on the portrait the king himself had given him, hanging on a sturdy chain, 'in order that', as the king himself wrote, '*I be bound to you every day of your life*, for whatever you wish'.[15]

Such a testimony reminds us once again that portraits, whether or not of the king, could serve purposes other than the merely representative in European early modern age culture – what is more, this was rarely their sole use.[16]

Undoubtedly, some portraits of the age were designed to record individuals' *vera facies*, their features considered almost materially, such as the portraits that were sent to borders and ports to help officers identify fugitives or persons sentenced to exile or expulsion. Such were the portraits of the Spanish American prince Don Diego Luis, a descendent of Montezuma banned from 'returning to the Indies' by the Prudent King, who accordingly gave orders for the portraits to be displayed 'at ports lest he should pass through and reach them'; one still survived in La Coruña in 1682, according to a vindicatory memorial written by Countess Jerónima María de Moctezuma, who claimed to be the 'fourth granddaughter of the emperor' of Mexico.[17] We imagine that identification was also the purpose of portraits such as those of 'two men who say they want to kill the King', which were sent to Louis XIII from Holland in 1617 and of which Ferdinand von Boischot informed the Count of Gondomar in an eloquently ciphered letter.[18]

Apart from these portraits that sought absolute likeness, there was a broad genre characterised by lifelike portrayal and rhetorical adaptation between the sitter's class and status and their visual representation. This explains why portraits generally *concealed* in some way the true appearance of the persons portrayed; we might cite the perhaps

---

[15] Couto, *Decadas*, vol. 9, p. 552. Our italics.
[16] J. Portús, 'Soy tu hechura: un ensayo sobre las fronteras del retrato cortesano en España', in Fernando Checa (ed.), *Carlos V: retratos de familia* (Madrid: Sociedad Estatal para la Conmemoración de los Centenarios de Felipe II y Carlos V, 2000), pp. 181–219; L. Campbell, *Renaissance Portraits: European Portrait-Painting in the 14th, 15th and 16th Centuries* (New Haven and London: Yale University Press, 1990); and Carlo Ginzburg, 'Le peintre et le bouffon: le *Portrait de Gonella* de Jean Fouquet', *Revue de l'Art* 111 (1996), 25–39.
[17] Ms.-9/3633, 16, Real Academia de la Historia, Madrid.
[18] Boischot to Gondomar, Paris, 14 June 1617, ms. II-2124, 213, RB.

extreme and well-known case of the portraits of the Prince Don Carlos of Austria. In a letter accompanying a recently completed portrait of the prince painted by Alonso Sánchez Coello and commissioned by Maximilian of Austria, who is shortly to become Maximilian II, Adam von Dietrichstein describes to Maximilian in full detail the true appearance of Don Carlos and, lest his words should not be sufficient, asks the gentleman Herberstein to again give an account of all the differences between the sitter's real appearance and how he is portrayed by the artist upon delivering the portrait in Vienna.[19] However, the case of the *portrait medal on a chain* that Philip II sent to Francisco Barreto furthermore underlines the potential of royal portraits, on the one hand, as instruments of kingly policy and, on the other, as aspects of a specific courtly culture, as it is the monarch himself who bestows an extra-artistic value upon his portrait.

Together with the notions of friendship and service,[20] European early modern courtly culture took pleasure in the idea of the *gift*, which it raised to a key status in the particular mental *habitus* of the age.[21] Generosity was a virtue to be displayed at all times by the gentleman, who, devoid of self-interest in his innocence, generously *served* those whom he regarded as his equals or friends or those to whom he was indebted: his superiors or others who had rendered him services with the same generosity. In this culture of the gift as such, presents were a gesture that was almost necessary as they expressed friendship and service.[22]

---

[19] Dietrichstein to Maximilian of Austria, Madrid, 4 July 1564. Now in Friedrich Edelmayer (ed.), *Die Korrespondenz der Kaiser mit ihren Gesandten in Spanien*, vol. 1: *Der Briefwechsel zwischen Ferdinand I., Maximilian II., und Adam von Dietrichstein 1563–1565* (Munich: Oldenburg, 1997), no. 43. This is the portrait of Don Carlos now in the Kunsthistorisches Museum in Vienna, which was documented in H. Zimmermann, 'Zur Ikonographie des Hauses Habsburg. II. Angebliche und Wirkliche Bildnisse des Don Carlos', *Jahrbuch der Kunsthistorischen Sammlungen des Allerhöchsten Kaiserhauses* 28 (1909–10), 153–70.

[20] Cf. S. Deswarte, *Il 'perfetto cortegiano' D. Miguel de Silva* (Rome: Bulzoni, 1989).

[21] A. M. Hespanha, 'La economía de la gracia', in *La gracia del derecho: economía de la cultura en la Edad Moderna* (Madrid: Centro de Estudios Constitucionales, 1993), pp. 151–76.

[22] Natalie Zemon Davis, *The Gift in Sixteenth-Century France* (Oxford: Oxford University Press, 2000).

Handwritten letters and portraits – the latter in any possible medium – appeared to be a particularly appropriate means of meeting this obligation to present gifts, especially in the case of people separated by distance, for whom letters served as a second-best substitute for private conversation, and portraits for personal contact. In the aforementioned case of Francisco Barreto, Philip II resorted to the usual device employed by the courtier who needs to return a generously granted service that cannot be repaid in money but rather by means of a letter and a portrait to make his presence doubly felt. The extreme largesse of his rank (*maxima largitio*) called for a portrait painted on gold, but the gesture of sending it – of *sending himself* – could have been shared by a good many of his courtiers.

Hans Khevenhüller, imperial ambassador to the court of Philip II, acted as the agent, for want of a better word, of Archduke Ferdinand of Tyrol, who wished for new pictures to complete his gallery/armoury of 'princes, lords and gentlemen distinguished in war'. On returning in 1583 from the Portuguese expedition on which he had accompanied the Empress Maria, he wrote the following letter to Pietro de' Medici:

His Most Serene Highness Archduke Ferdinand is amassing with great curiosity and diligence as many portraits as possible of princes, lords and gentlemen distinguished in war, together with the arms with which the aforementioned served and fought on some expedition, in order that all these mementoes may adorn a very rich hall; and in the past days he has thus written to me requesting me to ask Your Excellency on his behalf to kindly provide him with your portrait and the weapons you have brought back and with which you have served his Catholic Majesty on this Portuguese expedition, as his Lordship the Duke of Alba also did some months ago, giving his Highness those with which he served in the war of Germany. I beg Your Excellency to please His Highness by granting this request and to arrange for them to be sent to me, as such are my instructions, for in addition to pleasing him greatly, Your Excellency would be granting me a very special favour. May Our Lord preserve Your Excellency and may you prosper as we your greatest servants wish. From Madrid.[23]

---

[23] Hans Khevenhüller to Pietro dei Médici, Madrid, n.d. [c.1583], ms./II 409, fol. 72r–v, Universitätsbibliothek Wien (hereafter UW).

Don Pedro and the Grand Duke of Alba would serve Archduke Ferdinand by obliging his *curiosity* and would act like true gentlemen by sending him their portraits and the weapons they had carried, one on the Portuguese campaign against the Prior do Crato, the other against the Schmalkaldic League.

As is known, Jakob Schrenck von Notzing published a list of the contents of Ferdinand of Tyrol's 'very rich hall' in 1601, thereby disseminating the extraordinary collection of weapons and portraits that the archduke had amassed at his *Armamentarium heroicum* at Ambras and, with it, the deeds and gentlemanly generosity of those who, like the Duke of Alba, had kindly supplied weapons and portraits.[24]

The Marquis of Santa Cruz was also asked to contribute to one of these collections of military heroes, though in his case the invitation was made by Emperor Rudolf II through Count Trivulcio. To commemorate this gesture, a book was printed with an *ad hoc* eulogy of Cristóbal Mosquera de Figueroa, the cover of which, naturally accompanied by the compulsory portrait, proclaimed the honour bestowed upon Álvaro de Bazán and the generous service he rendered to the emperor:[25]

Count Trivulzio, Master of the Horse to the Empress, asked His Excellency the Marquis of Santa Cruz for his portrait and arms on the orders of His Majesty Emperor Rudolf the Second of Germany and king of Bohemia and Hungary. And on this occasion the present eulogy or commentary was composed. Praise for the portrait of His Excellency Don Álvaro de Bazán, Marquis of Santa

---

[24] *Augustissimorum imperatorum, serenissimorum regum, atque archiducum, illustrissimorum principum, necnon comitum, baronum, aliorumque clarissimorum virorum qui aut ipsi cum imperio duces fuerunt, aut in iisdem praefecturis insignioribus laudabiliter functi sunt, verissimae imagines & rerum ab ipsis domi, forisque gestarunt succintae descriptiones. Quorum arma aut integra aut horum partes, quibus inducti, usique adversus hostem heroica facinora patrarunt aut quorum auspiciis tam prospera quam adversa fortuna res magnae gestae sunt, a Serenissimo Principe Ferdinando, Archiduce Austriae . . . opus* (Oeniponti: Agricola, 1601). Indeed there is a likeness of Fernando Álvarez de Toledo in the *Armamentarium heroicum* entitled 'Ferdinandus Toletanus Albae Dux', unnumbered.

[25] C. Burlingham, 'Portraiture as propaganda: printmaking during the reign of Henry IV', in Karen Jacobson (ed.), *The French Renaissance Prints from the Bibliothèque Nationale de France* (Los Angeles: Grunwald Center, 1994), pp. 139–51.

Cruz, lord of the townships of Viso and Valdepeñas, Comendador mayor of
León, of his Majesty's Council and his Captain General of the Ocean Sea and
of the armies of the Kingdom of Portugal.[26]

Writing from Florence little more than thirty years previously with
the news of having acquired an image of Our Lady 'with great luck,
painted by Michelangelo's master of painting, which I believe will
be to Madame's [Margaret's] liking as it is very devotional and very
different from the ways in which they paint Our Lady nowadays',
the ambassador Francisco de Toledo announces to Antoine Perrenot
de Granvelle that he is having a portrait of his copied, stating that
'I will send the original, as the portrait will be sufficient to move
me to contemplation.'[27] This shrewd observation of mid-sixteenth-
century 'ways' compared to a fifteenth-century Madonna, perhaps
by Ghirlandaio, must have provided food for thought for Granvelle,
one of the most important mid-sixteenth-century art collectors and
patrons and an indefatigable writer of letters on artistic matters.[28]

Between 1542 and 1581, Cardinal Granvelle and Don Martín de
Aragón, Duke of Villahermosa, who were linked by a courteous
friendship, kept up an extraordinary correspondence in which they
frequently exchanged news of portraits and painters.[29] Despite his
many occupations, Granvelle appears to have acted almost as the
duke's agent in much of Europe, where he looked after his commissions (carvings, books, prints, paintings), strove to find ways of serving
him and his first wife Doña Luisa de Borja and furthermore always
found time to write to them in his own hand as a token of the deference
they deserved.

[26] S.l. a.n. [1586].
[27] Francisco de Toledo to Antoine Perrenot, Florence, December 1554, ms. II-2286,
fol. 255r, RB.
[28] Joanna Woodall, 'Patronage and portrayal: Antoine Perrenot de Granvelle's relationship with Antonis Mor', in Krista De Jonge and Gustaaf Janssens (eds.), Les
Granvelle et les anciens Pays-Bas. Liber doctori Mauricio Van Durme dedicatus (Louvain:
Universitaire Pers Leuven, 2000), pp. 245–77.
[29] Autograph correspondence of Antoine Perrenot de Granvelle with Don Martín de
Aragón and Doña Luisa de Borja, Duke and Duchess of Villahermosa, 1542–81.
Montijo, Caja 34–1, ADA.

Writing from Mantua in January 1543, the then bishop of Arras confesses that 'so hurriedly are we passing through Italy . . . that not only am I unable to see anything or search for paintings for Your Lordship, but I scarcely have the time to write this.' However, writing from Cremona in June, he stresses to the duchess that 'Your Ladyship should not hesitate to send me precise instructions of the painting you wanted and of the size, because they will be carried out most willingly, like any orders Your Excellency should wish to give me.' He always finds time to send some gift with which to *serve* them, be it a *scatula* containing medals, including one of plaster 'of our lord the prince [Philip II] which my brother made the day those of the kingdom of Aragon swore allegiance to his highness at Monzon . . . [and] it is as white as his highness was that day' (Barcelona, October 1542), or 'a silver lizard' (Mons, October 1543), 'a silver serpent and lizard', which 'I believe you will find well made' (Brussels, December 1543) or a *caxeta* (casket) 'in which there is a game of draughts, some medals and powder for making medals of plaster, wood or other materials that appear to be copper' (Pavia, June 1543).[30]

It seems that some of these objects were the work of Granvelle himself, a true virtuoso, such as the 'lizards . . . which can be placed on cups, jugs or bowls' that he sent from Brussels in March 1549 and about which he wrote: 'I have learnt much since the last time I saw you, but it is slipping away as my business does not allow me to set to work.'[31] However the main object of these exchanges is undoubtedly portraits. For example, Granvelle wrote from Nuremberg in April 1543:

As for the portrait of mine, I had said that it would be ready by the time we go to Flanders, God willing, and in order for it to be completed sooner I have arranged for six to be done here yet none resembles me; I am having another three done, and if any of them turns out well I will send it to Your Lordship. Do not fail to keep your promise of sending me that of her Ladyship Doña Luisa and your sisters, as I shall treasure them.[32]

---

[30] Granvelle to Villahermosa, 26 (Mantua, 3 January 1543); 35 (Cremona, 22 June 1543); 58 (Brussels, 30 October 1542); 29 (Mons, 16 October 1543); 30 (Brussels, 24 December 1543); 28 (Pavia, 12 June 1543).

[31] Granvelle to Villahermosa, 41 (Brussels, 24 March 1549).

[32] Granvelle to Villahermosa, 15 (Nuremberg, 28 April 1543).

Needless to say, Granvelle not only speaks of portraits but also of artists, particularly the one he repeatedly calls 'my painter', who is undoubtedly Anthonis Mor. Writing from Brussels in March 1549, he gives the Duke of Villahermosa the first news of 'a painter I have found here', regretting that the duke and his wife are not accompanying him, as he would instruct the painter to portray 'your whole household . . . perhaps better than Titian'. A year later, writing from Augsburg, he informs the duke that 'the Queen has borrowed my painter to send him to Portugal', nonetheless offering that 'if she does not object I will instruct him to call by here on his return'. Although the painter has been *borrowed* by Mary of Hungary, Granvelle nonetheless stresses over and over again that he will instruct *his* painter to call at the duke and duchess's small provincial court in Pedrola, not far from Saragossa, once he has completed the portraits commissioned in Portugal.[33]

A letter sent from Brussels on 20 December 1549 illustrates very well Granvelle's constant references to painting and to *his* painter in his correspondence with the Duke and Duchess of Villahermosa: after giving an account of the recent marriage of Thomas Perrenot, Seigneur de Chantonnay, to Hélène de Brederode and other family news, the bishop of Arras writes:

The things that I am going [to] send you from here are trivial and better ones could be made there, if only God should allow us to go there some day, and I hope that once there we would not be short of time and I could persuade my painter to go with me and we would be able to put right some things at Pedrola, though I know that all is in order; meanwhile, I beg Your Lordship not to forget to send me as soon as possible the portrait of Doña Luisa which I very much wish for. That of the Duchess of Lorraine which [is] here belongs to her and she writes to me every day saying that she wants to send for it and she has entrusted it to me making me swear not to allow another to be made, not even for me, and granted it to me as I gave my word that I did not even wish to leave it with Prince N. S. for 6 days although he insisted greatly, unless the duchess gave her permission. As it is very large my painter will not be able to paint it in two months and meanwhile we will leave, and Your Lordship would not like it very much not having ever seen it, and I promise that I am not even keeping it for myself and furthermore I am not happy about the smaller copies my painter

---

[33] Granvelle to Villahermosa, 41 (Brussels, 24 March 1549); and 42 (Augsburg, 7 October 1550).

makes, but let me know if you wish for another portrait that can be painted; I will arrange for it to be painted and indeed, he does a marvellous job in a large size and neither Your Lordship nor I have ever seen a portrait equal to his and his art is portrait painting rather than anything else.[34]

In addition to the repeated reference to a possible trip to Pedrola with Mor, Granvelle resorts to his status as artist's patron to *serve* the Duke of Villahermosa as he deserves – on this occasion, with a portrait of Christina, Duchess of Milan, which the daughter of Christian II of Denmark and Isabella of Austria is unwilling to have copied unless she gives her express consent. Although he has borrowed it under oath, Mor in fact copied it in 1549.[35] The precise references to the painter's skills are a natural part of this correspondence between virtuosi, in which Anthonis Mor is presented as the product of Granvelle's teaching, though Granvelle comes to admit that, despite continuing to pay the artist's wife her husband's annual wages, 'he did not work for me' during the years his services were required by Mary of Hungary (Brussels, August 1553).[36]

Becoming a patron of artists was thus a natural facet of the profile of the gentleman connoisseur and virtuoso, and included a touch of emulation and rivalry between patrons and collectors that was characteristic of the sixteenth century and which Granvelle does not conceal when he mentions that the queen has *borrowed his painter*, that extraordinary artist who 'is the best I have seen for portraits after Titian'.[37]

Even the trials and tribulations caused by these masters, who were skilled but very unreliable, find their way into the correspondence as yet another sign of the patience that is an attribute of the code of ethics of the gentlemanly patron of the arts. Writing from Augsburg in October 1547, Granvelle complains about the silversmiths because 'they are so slow . . . that I dare not give a time by which they will have finished' the pitcher and cup the Villahermosas have entrusted him with; three years earlier, in a letter written from Metz concerning

---

[34] Granvelle to Villahermosa, 50 (Brussels, 20 December [1549]).
[35] A. Jordan, *Retrato de corte em Portugal: o legado de António Moro (1552–1572)* (Lisbon: Quetzal, 1994), p. 102, n. 62.
[36] Granvelle to Villahermosa, 48 (Brussels, 22 August 1553).
[37] Granvelle to Villahermosa, 42 (Augsburg, 7 October 1550).

some reliquaries for Luisa de Borja, he criticises the Brussels masters 'because there are few of them as almost all have gone to war and those that remain are so unwilling to work what with the sound of the drums that they never finish anything'. In 1560, Perrenot describes his negotiations, his *dispute*, with Franz Floris, as follows:

I arranged for frank flores [*sic*] to do the canvases of the planets and I was in dispute with him for four months before he was willing to take them on. He gave the excuse of having a lot of work on his hands. I do not know if it was to cover up his lack of practice in this, though he will have time to learn if he does not know how to complete the work.[38]

Even Mor, the magnificent *portrait painter*, is reprimanded by his patron for failing to reply to his letters: 'In two years since he left, there has been no word of him save from his wife, who does not forget to come to my house for his wages every year, though I have answered that unless her husband replies and does what I instruct him he can get lost.'[39]

In short, the patron compensates for the self-interest, slowness, volubility or disobedience of the artists and, partly thanks to them, emphasises his own eminence, generosity, willingness to serve and constancy. At best, he is a protector of men of art, taking them under his wing or writing letters of recommendation, such as the one Hans Khevenhüller sent Gabriel de Zayas supporting Hernando de Ávila's wish to take over from Cristino de Amberes as his majesty's equerry painter, 'it seeming to him that he has sufficient merits and references for this position, as no doubt it will seem to Don Luys Manrique, who has used him frequently, and I do the same as I consider him a good man of his trade'.[40] And, with childish eloquence, Giovanni Paolo Poggini appeals to the protection of Granvelle, the 'father of the poor virtuosi who work only for glory and honour' in a letter of 1557 requesting his intercession.[41]

[38] Granvelle to Villahermosa, 76 (Brussels, 1 November 1560).
[39] Granvelle to Villahermosa, 5 (Augsburg, 20 October 1547); 21 (Metz, 23 July 1544); and 64 (Villach, in Carinthia, 2 June 1551).
[40] Hans Khevenhüller to Zayas, Madrid, s.d., UW, mss./II 409.
[41] Brussels 7 August 1557, in *Lettere di artisti italiani ad Antonio Perrenot di Granvella. Tiziano, Giovan Battista Mantovano, Primaticcio, Giovanni Paolo Poggino ed altri* (Madrid: Istituto Italiano di Cultura, 1977), p. 80.

The lengthy correspondence between Granvelle and Villahermosa is a magnificent example of how art became a primordial subject of courtly letter writing. In these letters, painters, antiques, engravings, paintings, medals and other kinds of art objects, and even artists play a role as items of exchange between equals.

This applies particularly to portraits, which were a sort of means of making oneself present despite the distance, of bearing news and of personal representation. The service rendered is the image itself but also time – the time spent seeking out the best gifts to be sent, posing for artists who were often slow and idle, and, in Granvelle's case, fashioning with his own hands precious metal objects that were the greatest gift that could be made as he employed his own time to write about and design them.

A MECHANICAL *POSTSCRIPT*

In December 1843, Alphonse Giroux & Cie presented their clients with a novel mechanical automaton capable of writing and drawing at the request of any member of the public attending. The directors of the establishment at 7, Rue du Coq Saint-Honoré invited the city's families, accompanied by their children, to admire the amazing invention by Jean-Eugène Robert-Houdin, at the time merely a 'mechanic, inventor . . . of many marvellous discoveries in clock making'. Alphonse Giroux thus pursued his dream of showing 'everything that Parisian fashion and industry can offer',[42] the same wish which had spurred him, for example, to sell the first devices enabling photographs to be taken using Daguerre's method a few years previously.

Robert-Houdin's mechanical device was in fact the last in a long line of writing and drawing androids built throughout the 1700s, a century fascinated by the possibility of developing automatic writing and drawing.[43] In 1774, the workshop of Pierre Jacquet-Droz at Neuchâtel produced an automaton called *L'écrivain*: 'a small figure

---

[42] *Etrennes de 1844. Salons de MM. Alph. Giroux & Cie* (s.l. [Paris]: s.n., s.a. [1843]). I quote from the copy of the prospectus formerly belonging to María Cristina de Borbón, queen regent of Spain, and now in the Escrigas Galán collection, Madrid.

[43] A. Chapuis and E. Gélis, *Le monde des automates: étude historique et technique* (Paris: s.n., 1928), vol. 2, § xxiv, 'Les androïdes écrivains et dessinateurs'.

at his desk, with quill pen in hand; he is a young prodigy capable of writing without making ink blots'.[44]

Together with two other automatons, called *Le dessinateur* and *La musicienne*, the eighteenth-century child writing machine toured the European courts, from Paris and Brussels to London and Madrid, to the surprise and enthusiasm of all those who witnessed their marvellous demonstrations.[45] No doubt the same astonishment with which in 1760, Emperor Franz I's courtiers received the letters composed by a mechanical device built by Friedrich von Knauss, which were signed with a ceremonious 'the most loyal of secretaries'.[46]

Having become the star attraction of a Parisian store during the Christmas sales period, the writing and drawing devices had found their way from the classical *salons* to the modern *magasins*. The history of court correspondence is perhaps not very different. Its ceremonial etiquette and somewhat convoluted conventions became widespread, used by all. Though perhaps Don Álvaro de Acuña from Calderón's play would have liked to come by one of these automatons as it would have relieved him of the tiresome burden of writing.

---

[44] Chapuis and Gélis, *Le monde des automates*, pp. 231–2.

[45] Now housed in the Musée d'Art et d'Histoire de Neuchâtel. Roland Carrera, 'Pierre Jaquet-Droz: l'uomo a orologeria', *Art. FMR. Secolo* XVIII (Milan: Rizzoli, 1990), vol. I, pp. 237–56.

[46] Chapuis and Gélis, *Le monde des automates*, p. 228.

CHAPTER 6

The letter as deferred presence: Nicolas Poussin to Paul Fréart de Chantelou, 28 April 1639

Peter Mason

PAINTING AND WRITING

If correspondence has come to occupy a privileged position in present-day historiography, combining the personal dimension of the writer, the social dimension of the shared world of writer and recipient, the formal dimension of the conventions of letter writing, and the technical dimension of the means of communication,[1] little attention has been paid to the physical dimension: the tangible and visible form of the written word on the page. This is all the more important when the writer happens to be an artist.

In the case of the French artist Nicolas Poussin (1594–1665), there is a particularly close relation between painting and writing in his painted works and drawings, from the succinct but enigmatic letter E inscribed on a stone tower in the background of *Ordination* from the second series of *The Seven Sacraments* to the letters ET IN ARCADIA EGO of the two paintings of *The Arcadian Shepherds*; from the writing activities of the evangelists in *Landscape with St John on Patmos* and *Landscape with St Matthew* to the reading figures of the man reading a book in the left-hand background of the earlier *Ordination*, the holy organist reading the musical notes in *St Cecilia*, or the Virgin distracted from reading in the London and Munich *Annunciations*; from the filled roll of parchment held aloft by Christ in a drawing *for The Seven Sacraments: Ordination* to the Hebrew

---

[1] Fernando Bouza, *Corre manuscrito: una historia cultural del Siglo de Oro* (Madrid: Marcial Pons, 2001), p. 138. The present chapter has benefited from conversations not only with Fernando Bouza, but also with Irene Baldriga, Florike Egmond, Ruth Mohrman, Francisco Bethencourt and fellow Poussin devotee Frank Müller.

lettering laboriously inscribed on the head coverings of the Pharisees in *Penitence* from the second series of *The Seven Sacraments*; and from the trompe-l'oeil *cartellino* in the London *Annunciation* containing the words POUSSIN. FACIEBAT. ANNO. SALVTIS. MDCLVII. ALEX. SEPT. PONT. MAX. REGNANTE. ROMAE. to the proud inscription EFFIGIES NICOLAI POVSSINI ANDELYENSIS PICTORIS. ANNO AETATIS. 56 ROMAE ANNO IVBILEI 1650 on the *Self-Portrait* in the Louvre.[2] Indeed, the finger of the shepherd who is tracing the outline of the inscription ET IN ARCADIA EGO in the second *The Arcadian Shepherds*, just like the finger of the Pharisee in the Louvre *Christ and the Woman Taken in Adultery* pointing to the sand in which the finger of Christ – which it imitates – has written, directly replicates the artist's own brushstrokes in the delineation of those written characters.[3] In such a case, it seems justified to go beyond the evidence of the paintings and drawings alone to include another category of writing by the same artist: his correspondence. In particular, taking Poussin's famous injunction to 'read the story and the painting' literally can help us to understand how the temporality of letter writing and exchange in many ways resembles the temporal structure of a painting and the

[2] The words 'De lumine et colore' on the spine of the book held in the hand of the artist in the Berlin *Self-Portrait*, as well as the inscription NICOLAVS POVSSINUS ANDELYENSIS ACADEMICVS ROMANVS PRIMVS PICTOR ORDINARIVS LVDOVICI IVSTI REGIS GALLIÆ. ANNO DOMINI 1649. ROMAE. AETATIS SVÆ. 55 in the same painting, although they also appear in the engraving after the portrait made during the painter's lifetime by Jean Pesne, are no longer considered authentic; see P. Rosenberg (ed.), *Nicolas Poussin 1594–1665*, exhibition catalogue, Galeries Nationales du Grand Palais (Paris: Réunion des Musées Nationaux, 1994), p. 426.

[3] All of these works, except the *St Cecilia* now in the Prado in Madrid, were included in the exhibition 'Nicolas Poussin 1594–1665' in the Grand Palais, Paris, in 1994, and are illustrated in the catalogue to that exhibition, P. Rosenberg (ed.), *Nicolas Poussin 1594–1665*, as follows: *The Seven Sacraments: Ordination* (second series), cat. no. 111; *The Arcadian Shepherds* (Chatsworth), cat. no. 11; *The Arcadian Shepherds* (Louvre), cat. no. 93; *Landscape with St John on Patmos* (Chicago), cat. no. 94; *Landscape with St Matthew* (Berlin), cat. no. 95; *The Seven Sacraments: Ordination* (first series) (Belvoir Castle), cat. no. 67; *Annunciation* (Munich), cat. no. 216; *Annunciation* (London), cat. no. 227; *The Seven Sacraments: Ordination* (second series), drawing (pen, brown ink, brown wash), (Louvre), cat. no. 127; *The Seven Sacraments: Penitence* (second series) (Edinburgh), cat. no. 110; *Self-Portrait* (Louvre), cat. no. 190; *Christ and the Woman Taken in Adultery* (Louvre), cat. no. 214.

time it takes a viewer to take it in. Though reference will be made to quite a number of Poussin's letters, the focus of attention will be on one letter in particular: the letter to Paul Fréart de Chantelou dated 28 April 1639. As will emerge from the discussion, such a concentration on a single letter is very akin to Poussin's own recommendations on how to read his paintings.

PAINTING, WRITING AND PRESENCE

Poussin's correspondence must have been extensive; the phrase 'I have many letters to write ... which is why I beg you to be content with these two lines for now' [121][4] is indicative. The only complete, scientific edition of his correspondence, edited by Charles Jouanny in 1911,[5] comprises 215 items: letters and other documents written by Poussin, and a few letters sent to him by his correspondents. The majority consist of the 136 letters and 6 statements of account sent by Poussin to Paul Fréart de Chantelou (1609–94); regrettably, no letters from Chantelou to Poussin have survived. They are written in Poussin's hand, their orthography betraying the shakiness of his hands from which he was already suffering at this time.[6] (In an exchange between Bernini and Chantelou, when the former pointed to his forehead and commented, 'Il signor Poussin is a painter who works from there', Chantelou replied that 'his works came from the head, having always had bad hands'.)[7] They were discovered in 1857, and are now in the

---

[4] In every case except that of the last letter which Poussin ever wrote, I have followed the numbering of *Correspondance de Nicolas Poussin*, ed. Charles Jouanny, Archives de l'art français, nouvelle période, vol. 5 (Paris: F. de Nobele, 1911). The numbers in square brackets correspond to the numbers of the letters in that edition.

[5] The date is significant, as it coincides with the first signs of the revival of interest in the French painter on the part of the modernists, particularly Paul Cézanne. See R. Verdi (ed.), *Cézanne and Poussin: The Classical Vision of Landscape*, exhibition catalogue, National Gallery of Scotland (Edinburgh, 1990).

[6] In a letter to Cassiano dal Pozzo written in June 1642, Poussin comments on a sketch for a composition representing the episode of Scipio Africanus and the pirates, that he will do it 'as best as my shaky hand permits' [69]. Compare [85] (to Chantelou, 2 July 1643).

[7] Milovan Stanić (ed.), *Chantelou, Journal de voyage du Cavalier Bernin en France* (Paris: Macula, 2001), p. 112.

Bibliothèque Nationale de France. A number of Poussin's letters to Cassiano dal Pozzo, the famous lawyer, collector and patron who played such a prominent part in the aristocratic and intellectual life of Rome, have survived in manuscript form.[8] André Félibien, one of Poussin's biographers, cited from letters of Poussin to Sublet de Noyers, Chantelou and Jacques Stella.[9]

The letter that concerns us here is an autograph letter, and is one of the earliest of Poussin's letters to have been preserved [11]. It is dated 28 April 1639. Its addressee, Paul Fréart de Chantelou, was a cousin and agent of François Sublet de Noyers, the principal adviser on the arts to Cardinal Richelieu. Together they made every effort to bring Poussin back from Rome to Paris to contribute to the elaborate artistic programme designed to enhance the prestige of Louis XIII and his court. When the French art market first began to show an interest in Poussin's work in the early 1630s, Chantelou was one of the first to commission works from him, starting with the *Israelites Gathering the Manna* (Louvre),[10] which Poussin must have already conceived in 1637.[11] During the course of the lifelong and warm friendship between the two men, Chantelou commissioned a number of paintings, including the second series of *The Seven Sacraments* now in the Duke of Sutherland collection (Edinburgh).[12] Chantelou himself

---

[8] On the figure of Cassiano dal Pozzo (1588–1657) see especially D. L. Sparti, *Le collezioni dal Pozzo: storia di una famiglia e del suo museo nella Roma seicentesca* (Modena: Franco Cosimo Panini, 1992), and the two exhibition catalogues edited by Francesco Solinas under the same title, *I segreti di un collezionista: le straordinarie raccolte di Cassiano dal Pozzo 1588–1657*, Galleria Nazionale d'Arte Antica, Palazzo Barberini (Rome, 2000) and Museo del Territorio Biellese (Biella, 2002). Cassiano's combined interest in literary and scientific matters is neatly illustrated in a painting of coral fishers, drawing on Ovid's *Metamorphoses* as well as catering to Cassiano's taste for scientific inquiry, that was executed for him by Pietro da Cortona around 1619–22: see Francesco Solinas, 'La Pêche du Corail de Pierre de Cortone retrouvée à Tsarskoïe Selo', *Gazette des Beaux-Arts* 138 (2001), 233–49. On dal Pozzo's archaeological interests see Ingo Herklotz, *Cassiano del Pozzo und die Archäologie des 17. Jahrhunderts*, Römische Forschungen der Bibliotheca Hertziana 28 (Munich: Hirmer Verlag, 1999).

[9] Stefan Germer (ed.), *Bellori, Félibien, Passeri, Sandrart, Vies de Poussin* (Paris: Macula, 1994), pp. 151–281.

[10] P. Rosenberg (ed.), *Nicolas Poussin 1594–1665*, no. 78.

[11] This can be deduced from letter [2].

[12] Besides the *Seven Sacraments*, the *Israelites Gathering the Manna* and the *Self-Portrait* discussed here, he also had a *Hercules and Deianira* (originally painted for Jacques

provided a written description of how the works were displayed in his residence in the rue Saint-Thomas du Louvre on the occasion of Bernini's visit there on 25 July 1665. Indeed, the journal that Chantelou wrote covering Bernini's stay in Paris may well have been intended as a disguised plea for Poussinesque values at a time when Paris was in the grip of a conflict between the 'poussinistes', led by the very influential figure of Charles Le Brun, and the 'rubénistes', associated with Le Brun's rival Pierre Mignard.[13]

The following is the text of the letter, deliberately done in a rather literal translation in order to avoid putting words into Poussin's mouth:

To Monsieur de Chantelou, Agent of Monseigneur de Noyers at Court.
Monsieur,
I shall wait to be with you by the grace of God in order to recognise the obligations that I owe you, not with words but directly, if you shall judge me worthy. For the moment I shall not fatigue you with a long letter; I shall inform you only that I am sending your painting of the manna via Bertholin, the carrier from Lyon: I have mounted it carefully and believe that you will receive it in good condition. I have included another small one that I am sending to Monsieur Debonaire, master of the king's robes, not having had any other opportunity until the present to convey it to him. You will therefore allow him to take it because it is his.

When you have received yours, I beg you, if you find it good, to give it a frame with a slight profile, for it is required, in order that in viewing it in all its parts, the rays of the eye are concentrated on it and are not allowed to be dispersed outside, receiving the impressions of the other adjacent objects which, when mingled with the things in the painting, confuse the lighting.

It would be very advisable for this frame to be gilded with matt gold in a simple fashion, for it blends very well with the colours without disturbing them.

Stella and now lost) and *Transportation of St Paul* (now in Sarasota, Florida), as well as a number of copies after Poussin (three *Bacchanals*, a *Nativity* and a *Flight into Egypt*). Mme de Chantelou owned *Rest during the Flight to Egypt* (now in the Hermitage) and *Christ and the Samaritan* (now lost). See Alain Schnapper, *Curieux du grand siècle: collections et collectionneurs dans la France du XVIIe siècle* (Paris: Flammarion, 1994), pp. 234–5 and Isabelle Pantin, *Les Fréart de Chantelou: une famille d'amateurs au XVIIe siècle entre Le Mans, Paris et Rome* (Le Mans: C&R, 1999), pp. 135–47.

[13] See Javier Portús, 'España y Francia: dos maneras de convivir con la pintura', in F. Checa Cremades (ed.), *Cortes del Barroco: de Bernini y Velázquez a Luca Giordano*, exhibition catalogue, Palacio Real de Madrid and Palacio Real de Aranjuez (Madrid: SEACEX, 2003), pp. 99–112, esp. 104–6. For Bernini's visit to Chantelou's collection see Stanić (ed.), *Chantelou, Journal de voyage du Cavalier Bernin*, pp. 87–90. This work also contains nine letters by Chantelou (398–408).

For the rest, if you remember the first letter I wrote you, concerning the movement that I proposed to give the figures, and if at the same time you view the painting, I believe that you will easily recognise those who are languishing, struck with amazement, take pity, perform acts of charity, of great necessity, of a desire to feed their hunger, to console, and others, for the seven main figures on the left will tell you everything that is written here and all the rest is of the same fabric: read the story and the painting, to judge whether everything is appropriate to the subject.

And if, after having contemplated it more than once you will have derived some satisfaction, please let me know, without concealing anything, so that I may rejoice in having satisfied you the first time that I have had the honour to serve you. If not, I am ready to make all amends, begging you to consider that the spirit is willing but the flesh is weak.

I have written to Monsieur Le Maire about the principal matter that keeps me here for the summer; I therefore beg you (Monsieur) to convey with him my excuses to Monseigneur de Noyers so that, when this courtesy is added to the others that I receive daily from you, I may be all my life the person most obliged to you in the world.

POUSSIN

Rome, 28 April 1639.

I shall write to Monsieur Stella, who I believe is in Lyon, to convey the painting to you as soon as it arrives.

Before showing it, it would be very advisable to have it framed a little more elaborately. It should be placed only a little above eye level directly opposite.

To start at the beginning of the document as we know it, means to start with the summary that Chantelou methodically wrote at the head of each letter before filing it. In this instance he wrote '28 April 1639. This letter accompanied the painting of the Manna. M. Poussin. 28 April sending me the Manna'. This cannot have been the case. Firstly, the letter itself is clearly addressed to 'Monsieur de Chantelou, Commis de Monseigneur de Noyers en Court', while Poussin makes it clear in a postscriptum that the painting itself is being sent to Jacques Stella in Lyon.[14] Secondly, it would have been unusual, not to say redundant, for Poussin to include a description of the painting in the letter if the two items had been posted together; in a letter to Chantelou of 1645

---

[14] The artist Jacques Stella, by the way, was an intimate friend of Poussin; he may have been instrumental in introducing Poussin to France and in securing commissions for him from Richelieu; see Schnapper, *Curieux du grand siècle*, p. 230.

[131], he writes that the painting *Confirmation* is finished, and adds: 'I shall not make any effort to describe it to you because it is a thing that has to be seen.' Being able to see a painting takes precedence over, makes redundant, a written description of it.

Between Chantelou's summary and Poussin's postscriptum, then, there is a disjunction: the painting and the letter are not in the same place, and it is the *absence* of the painting which justifies Poussin's recourse to verbal description on this occasion.

This is not the only absence. Not only is the painting absent, but so is its maker. The letter – any letter – owes its raison d'être to absence for the obvious reason that you only write to someone if that person is (physically or mentally) remote – what Lope de Vega called a 'mental prayer to the absent'.[15] Poussin's written words are a substitute for his physical presence.

He makes this point in the very first sentence: 'I shall wait to be with you by the grace of God in order to recognise the obligations that I owe you, not with words but directly, if you shall judge me worthy.' The opposition between words (*paroles*) and direct action (*effet*) on which he plays here betrays the same suspicion of words that he showed in opposing 'describe' (*dépeindre*) to 'see' (*voir*) in the later letter to Chantelou cited above. Once again, verbal (textual) representation is viewed as inferior to the directness of vision and physical presence.[16] It should also be noted that this deprecatory attitude towards words casts its shadow on the rest of the letter, which, by its very nature, consists of nothing but words – it will and can only be a poor substitute for something else.

---

[15] Cited in Fernando Bouza, *Comunicación, conocimiento y memoria en la España de los siglos XVI y XVII* (Salamanca: Seminario de Estudios Medievales y Renacentistas, 1999), p. 27. The author's refreshingly 'anti-actualista' discussion of the relations between the oral, the visual and the written is relevant to many of the considerations of the present chapter.

[16] In his *Primera parte de las excelencias de la virtud de la castidad* (Alcalá, 1601), José de Jesús María wrote that 'words paint something that is absent or already past, but paintings render it as present' ('las palabras pintan una cosa ausente o ya pasado, pero las pinturas la figuran presente'), cited by Javier Portús Pérez in Miguel Morán Turina and J. Portús Pérez, *El arte de mirar: la pintura y su público en la España de Velázquez* (Madrid: Istmo, 1997), pp. 233–4.

This first sentence also links the theme of presence–absence to time: proximity to Chantelou (*auprès de vous*) will be a thing of the future ('I *shall* wait'). The letter is marked by time at a number of points. First of all, below the signature and the place of writing (Rome) comes the date: '28 April 1639'. In a slightly earlier letter to Chantelou [10], dated 19 March 1639, Poussin had written: 'I have already let you know that your painting is finished.' We thus have a temporal sequence of at least two letters prior to the present one that all bear on the painting of the *Israelites Gathering the Manna*. Indeed, in the present letter Poussin asks Chantelou to recall an earlier one ('the first letter') touching on 'the movement that I proposed to give the figures'. This letter has been lost, but some idea of its contents can be gained from a letter to Jacques Stella preserved in Félibien's life of Poussin [2]:

> I have found a certain distribution for the painting of M. de Chantelou, and certain natural attitudes that show the misery and hunger to which the Jewish people were reduced, as well as the joy and happiness that have come over it; the astonishment with which it has been struck, the respect and reverence that it has for its legislator, with a mixture of women, children and men of different ages and temperaments; things, as I believe, that will not displease those who know how to read them properly [*qui les sauront bien lire*].

The letter to Chantelou is marked by a present (the date); it refers to the past (previous correspondence with Chantelou); and it anticipates the future (the use of the future tense). These temporal modalities are all linked to the painting and the painter: both of them are absent (from Paris) at the moment – their *hic et nunc* is Rome – and they will be present (in Paris) in the future.

The timing of this letter is crucial for the light it casts on Poussin's motivations.[17] Four years earlier, Richelieu had ordered three *Bacchanals* from Poussin for his recently constructed château in Indre-et-Loire.[18] In an attempt to emulate the successful policy of the Barberini

---

[17] For the sequence of events here see Francis Haskell, *Painters and Patrons: A Study in the Relations between Italian Art and Society in the Age of the Baroque* (New Haven and London: Yale University Press, 1980), p. 176.

[18] These were *The Triumph of Bacchus* (Kansas City), *The Triumph of Pan* (National Gallery, London) and *The Triumph of Silenus* (National Gallery, London). See S. Loire, 'La dispersione delle collezioni Gonzaga in Francia', in Raffaella Morselli (ed.), *Gonzaga: La Celeste Galeria. L'esercizio del collezionismo*, exhibition catalogue, Palazzo Tè – Palazzo Ducale, Mantova (Milan: Skira, 2002), pp. 262–3.

in Rome, Richelieu and Sublet de Noyers began to put serious pressure on Poussin to leave Rome and return to Paris. Poussin was understandably worried by these developments. He had been in Rome for fifteen years, had married Anne-Marie Dughet there in 1630, and had turned his back on grandiose courtly commissions to devote himself to painting for connoisseurs and collectors (his proud motto was 'my ambition is to satisfy art, you and me'). A generation earlier, when the young Rubens was torn between staying in Antwerp or returning to Rome for good, he had expressed a similar reluctance to 'become a courtier again' for the Archduke and the Infanta in a letter to the professor of medicine, collector and member of the Accademia dei Lincei Johannes Faber dated 10 April 1609. Rubens decided to stay in Antwerp, even though he concluded the same letter with greetings to friends in Italy 'whose good conversation makes me often long for Rome'.[19] Poussin's letters from the beginning of 1639 on, especially the one to Jean Le Maire [7] that he mentions in the concluding paragraph of the letter under consideration here, reveal the same concern and his continual attempts to postpone the move as long as possible. When invitation turned to threat ('kings have very long arms'), he no longer felt able to refuse. In May 1640 Chantelou was sent to Rome to bring Poussin back with him, and in December of the same year the painter arrived in Paris. He was to stay there for twenty-two months. On the pretext of going to visit his wife, he returned to Rome in the autumn of 1642. There were no reprisals; fortunately for Poussin, the death of Richelieu on 4 December 1642 and that of Louis XIII the following May, as well as the fall from favour of Sublet de Noyers,[20] changed the French artistic and political constellation and removed the pressure from him.

[19] There is an English translation of the letter in *The Letters of Peter Paul Rubens*, ed. Ruth Saunders Magurn (Evanston: Northwestern University Press, 1991), pp. 52–3. The original text is reproduced in Irene Baldriga, *L'occhio della lince: i primi lincei tra arte, scienza e collezionismo (1603–1630)* (Rome: Accademia Nazionale dei Lincei, 2002), pp. 292–3. See too her valuable discussion of the interest in Neostoicism that was shared by Faber and the Rubens brothers and, we might add, Nicolas Poussin.

[20] After the death of Richelieu, Sublet de Noyers failed to win the confidence of Mazarin. He was dismissed on 10 April 1643 and his place was taken by Michel Le Tellier. Sublet died on 20 October 1645. See Pantin, *Les Fréart de Chantelou*, p. 79.

Seen in the light of this train of events, Poussin's letter of 28 April 1639 belongs to a period of *temporisation*.[21] He was playing for time. That is why in the concluding paragraph of the letter he appeals to Chantelou to apologise on his behalf to de Noyers for his delay in setting out for Paris. It is surely symptomatic that in the preceding sentence Poussin makes use of the biblical figure 'the spirit indeed is willing, but the flesh is weak'.[22] Though Poussin tacks it on to the end of a sentence about the possibility that Chantelou may not be entirely satisfied with the painting, it also anticipates the concerns evinced in the concluding paragraph, for it is the artist's 'weak flesh' that he uses as an excuse not to leave Rome immediately. Biblical allusions are extremely rare in Poussin's correspondence (the only other instance is an Old Testament reference in a letter to Chantelou dated 3 July 1645 [125], where the injunction 'Put not your trust in princes, nor in the son of man, in whom there is no help'[23] takes on a particular relevance if we bear in mind the nature of Poussin's association with the French court). So the presence of such an allusion here is symptomatic[24] and justifies our paying extra attention to it. At about the same time, Poussin deployed a related figure in a letter to Sublet de Noyers [9]: 'I shall therefore hasten as much as possible to go and serve you, for what remains here now is only the more material part, the spirit having already been transported to you to pay you humble reverence.' The opposition between Poussin's physical presence in Rome and his spiritual transportation to Paris plays on the same kind of antithesis. However, as we have seen, Poussin valued physical, material presence above mediation. The excuse presented to de Noyers rings hollow, and Poussin's use of the matter/spirit opposition betrays the insincerity of his pleading.

It is at this point in our reading of the letter that the absences converge: the absence of Poussin from where Chantelou is, which creates the need to send a letter in his place; the absence of the painting,

---

[21] For the different stages and ploys of this temporisation, see Jacques Thuillier, *Nicolas Poussin* (Paris: Fayard, 1988), pp. 165–211.

[22] Matthew 26: 41.   [23] Psalms 146: 3.

[24] On the application of this Freudian concept to the art of painting see especially Georges Didi-Huberman, *Devant l'image* (Paris: Editions de Minuit, 1990).

Fig. 6. Nicolas Poussin, *Israelites Gathering the Manna in the Desert*, oil on canvas, 149 × 200 cm, 1639. Courtesy of Musée du Louvre, Paris, inv. 7275 ©Photo RMN

for which the letter is a feeble and temporary substitute; and the absence of Poussin from where de Noyers is. The last of these absences is the most delicate, and the most difficult to broach. Its implications are the most threatening to Poussin. Nevertheless, in writing about the *Israelites Gathering the Manna* (perhaps we could even say: under cover of writing about the *Israelites Gathering the Manna*), he gives voice to his predicament in the hope that his appeal to his friend Chantelou will not fall on deaf ears.

PAINTING AND READING

'The spirit indeed is willing, but the flesh is weak' implies a division between the inside and outside (of the body) that recurs in another passage of Poussin's correspondence in which the notion of writing (and therefore reading) is not very far away. André Félibien has preserved a passage from one of his letters in which the artist claimed that, as the twenty-four letters of the alphabet serve to shape our words and to express our thoughts, so the lineaments of the human body serve to express the diverse passions of the soul in order to show externally (*au-dehors*) that which is in the spirit.[25] It is interesting to note that this inner/outer dichotomy is here linked to the theme of writing (and therefore, by implication, of reading). While the discussion so far has been about reading texts, Poussin here seems to imply that the notion of reading can be extended from texts to paintings. Indeed, in the very letter on the *Israelites Gathering the Manna* Poussin enjoins Chantelou to read both the story and the painting (*lisés l'istoire et le tableau*). What did he mean by this? Whether we take *l'istoire* to mean either 'history' or 'story', the reference is to a textual source. *Le tableau* can only refer to the painting. Poussin is calling upon Chantelou to read the painting and to read the (hi)story. Unless one of the two terms is redundant, there are two activities to be carried out.

To start with what at first sight appears to be the easiest one, as the title of the painting makes clear, its subject is the divine gift of manna to the Israelites during the exodus from Egypt. We may take Poussin to be asking the reader to identify the various representations of emotions and to make a comparison with the written text as an exercise in intellectual discrimination.[26] One would expect the written text in this case to be a biblical one, namely chapter 16 of the Old Testament book of Exodus. But the painting is not an illustration of that text. Poussin invents the emotions of the persons from the biblical story, for they are

---

[25] Anthony Blunt (ed.), *Nicolas Poussin: lettres et propos sur l'art* (Paris: Hermann: 1989). The notion of reading off the passions, vices and virtues of a person from a portrayal of his physical features can already be found in the sixteenth century. For an example – that of the physician Juan Cornejo, who claimed to be able to carry out medical diagnoses on the basis of portraits, provided they were accurate – see Fernando Bouza, *Palabra e imagen en la corte: cultura oral y visual de la nobleza en el Siglo de Oro* (Madrid: Abada, 2003), p. 106.

[26] Oskar Bätschmann, *Nicolas Poussin: Dialectics of Painting* (London: Reaktion, 1990), pp. 114–15; Richard W. Lee, *Ut pictura poesis: humanisme et théorie de la peinture XVe–XVIIIe siècles* (Paris: Macula, 1991), p. 67.

not mentioned in the written account.[27] This is precisely why there is no redundancy in the expression 'read the history and the painting', for neither act of reading can be reduced to the other. Poussin does not create a painting 'in the air', as it were, on which to display his invention. He grounds it in a written account, taken from the Old Testament. But it diverges considerably from that starting point.

'The spirit is indeed willing but the flesh is weak' is a citation from the New Testament. Many of the emotions listed by Poussin in the letter and depicted in the painting correspond to New Testament values as exemplified, for example, in the Sermon on the Mount.[28] So here – as in so many of Poussin's paintings based on themes from the Old Testament – the story is the Christian doctrine of salvation in which the Old Testament is considered to adumbrate the New, the New to fulfil the Old. The life-saving manna of the Old Testament becomes the body of Christ which brings salvation. The distinct temporal modes of the two testaments have been conflated; time has been condensed.

However, the 'archaeology' of the temporal strata underlying the composition of the painting is even more complex than that.

In the foreground on the left-hand side of the painting we see a group consisting of a woman offering her breast to an old woman and denying it to a child. Though charity is a Christian virtue, the textual source for this particular scene is not the Bible but classical antiquity, namely the chapter on filial piety (*De pietate in parentes*) in the *Dictorum factorumque memorabilium libri* V written around AD 29 by Valerius Maximus. In that work the Roman historian successively describes two versions of filial piety, one in which a girl nourishes her imprisoned mother, and one in which it is the imprisoned father who is succoured by his daughter. The anecdote is repeated by other classical authors; sometimes a baby is present in their versions, sometimes not. The version with father and daughter became popular in the sixteenth and seventeenth centuries on medals, prints and in decorative cycles,

---

[27] For another instance of the artist's going beyond Exodus, compare his *Moses Changing Aaron's Rod into a Serpent* (Louvre), which, like its companion piece *Moses Trampling on Pharaoh's Crown* (Louvre), draws on the *Jewish Antiquities* of Flavius Josephus. Rosenberg (ed.), *Nicolas Poussin 1594–1665*, nos. 152 and 153.

[28] Matthew 5–7.

though it was comparatively rare at first in independent easel pictures.
The title *Caritas Romana* is first found in the seventeenth century in
what has been called a 'chauvinistic recasting' of the original *Greek*
version featuring Pero and her father Cimon.[29] It is typical, given his
penchant for recherché subjects, that Poussin here opts for the version
which was much less common as a pictorial theme, namely the piety
of the daughter towards her *mother*. It is also noteworthy that Valerius
Maximus does not actually describe the historical incident itself, but
a *painting* of the scene. How characteristic it is of Poussin to derive
his inspiration for this figural group from a *textual* description of an
ancient painting!

This classical textual source should thus be considered rather as a
classical visual source, albeit one embedded in and mediated through
a text. A classical visual source of an unmediated kind served as the
source of inspiration for the hollow rock formation in the upper left-
hand part of the painting. As Blunt pointed out,[30] Poussin was aware of
its ancient model: the rocky outcrop in a representation of beasts in the
highlands of Ethiopia (appropriate enough to convey an impression
of the Egyptian landscape through which the Israelites sojourned) as a
detail of a large mosaic pavement dating from around 120–110 BC that
became known to artists in Rome in the seventeenth century through
Prince Federico Cesi. Cesi saw and recorded the pavement in situ at
Palestrina (ancient Praeneste), where it had originally decorated the
floor of the nymphaeum of one of the public buildings in the town
centre, and in the course of the 1620s the pavement was transported
to Rome. Cassiano dal Pozzo commissioned nineteen coloured copies
of the mosaic, which was subsequently restored to Palestrina and set
in place in the Palazzo Barberini there.[31]

---

[29] Elizabeth McGrath, *Rubens Subjects from History*: *Corpus Rubenianum Ludwig Burchard XIII (I)*, vol. 2: *Catalogue and Indexes* (London: Harvey Miller, 1997), p. 99.
For a full discussion of the iconography of Pero and Cimon see pp. 97–114.

[30] Anthony Blunt, *Poussin* (London: Pallas Athene, 1995), p. 271.

[31] The coloured copies have been attributed to Bernardino Capitelli by Nicholas Turner
in *Quaderni Puteani 4: The Paper Museum of Cassiano dal Pozzo* (Milan, 1993), p. 115.
During the re-restoration of the mosaic after its return to Palestrina, the rocky
outcrop was separated into two pieces that were set at opposite ends of the mosaic.
The fullest recent discussion is Paul G. P. Meyboom, *The Nile Mosaic of Palestrina:
Early Evidence of Egyptian Religion in Italy* (Leiden: Brill, 1995), to which should

The painting also draws on classical visual sources in the round. Around 1626, Poussin and the sculptor François Duquesnoy were living in the same house in the Via Paolina (today the Via del Babuino) in the quarter of Rome between the Piazza del Popolo and the Piazza di Spagna, which was a favourite haunt for generations of artists. The French artist and the Flemish sculptor worked together on measuring the proportions of the ancient statues in Rome and carried out a profound and detailed study of the Greek style. Before the end of the decade, they were being employed by Cassiano dal Pozzo to continue their researches and to make copies for the benefit of his Museo Cartaceo.[32] Awareness of the different proportions appropriate to different figures in the Greek style is evidenced in the *Israelites Gathering the Manna*. For instance, the woman in the *Caritas Romana* group is modelled on the marble group of Niobe and her children, now in the Uffizi in Florence, which served as a model for the rendering of a wellborn woman of middle age.[33] The old man on the ground to her right is modelled on the black marble so-called Seneca in the Borghese Collection in the Louvre, now generally considered to be a second-century Roman copy of a Hellenistic statue of a fisherman.[34] Incidentally, their use of the 'Seneca' figure is another of the elements that Poussin and Rubens have in common.[35] Rubens drew extensively on the drawings after the antique that he made during his stay in Italy, and particularly

[32] Poussin was to make use of his stay in Paris between 1641 and 1642 to further the ends of the Museo Cartaceo. Through the intercession of Sublet de Noyers and Chantelou, he obtained permission from the Duchess of Savoy to have copies made of the fifteen codices by Pirro Ligorio in the ducal library in Turin which Cassiano dal Pozzo had coveted for some time. See Francesco Solinas, *L'Uccelliera: un libro di arte e di scienza della Roma del primi Lincei* (Florence: Leo Olschki Editore, 2000), pp. 22–3. He continued to work for the Museo Cartaceo after his return to Rome, though his exact role in the enterprise is controversial; see the brief discussion by Nicholas Turner, 'Some of the copyists after the antique employed by Cassiano', *The Paper Museum of Cassiano dal Pozzo*, pp. 31–2.

[33] See Germer (ed.), *Bellori, Félibien, Passeri, Sandrart, Vies de Poussin*, p. 240.

[34] Poussin drew on the same 'Seneca' for the figure in the foreground of the *Baptism of Christ* (Philadelphia); see Rosenberg (ed.), *Nicolas Poussin 1594–1665*, no. 219.

[35] Rubens drew on the same source for his *Death of Seneca* (Munich, Alte Pinakothek), but replaced the African features of the fisherman with those of his own bust of 'Seneca' (itself a Roman copy of a Hellenistic bronze of an unidentified individual).

Rome, most evidently in the cycle of twenty-four paintings which Marie de Médicis commissioned in 1622 for the Palais du Luxembourg in Paris.[36] Poussin was also working at the Palais du Luxembourg at that time, where he executed a few small panels under the direction of Duchesne, and would thus have been able to see some of the first of Rubens's canvases, though not the complete series, before he left for Rome at some date before the end of 1623.[37] The painter Charles Le Brun, who went back to Rome with Poussin in 1642, described the proportions and contours of the human figures in his *Israelites Gathering the Manna* as constituting a virtual visual compendium of the famous ancient statues which were to serve as the basis of taste for the next couple of centuries. Though following his Greek models for proportion and contour, Poussin has not slavishly copied them; instead he has adapted their postures to the action of the painting.[38]

So the phrase 'read the history and the painting' evokes a number of different textual and mediated or unmediated sources that go into

See Christopher White, 'Rubens and Antiquity', in Peter C. Sutton, *The Age of Rubens*, exhibition catalogue, Museum of Fine Arts, Boston (Ghent: Ludion, 1993), p. 151, and Kristin Lohse Belkin and Fiona Healy, *A House of Art: Rubens as Collector*, exhibition catalogue (Antwerp: Rubenshuis and Rubenianum, 2004), no. 65.

[36] See Fiona Healey, 'Drawings after the Antique and the "Rubens Cantoor"', in *A House of Art*, pp. 298–9, and Alexis Merle Du Bourg, 'De Florence à Cologne, Marie de Médicis et Pierre Paul Rubens (1600–1642)', in P. Bassani Pacht and T. Crépin-Leblond (eds.), *Marie de Médicis, un gouvernement par les arts*, exhibition catalogue, Château de Blois (Paris. Somogy Éditions d'art, 2003), pp. 94 109. On the genesis of the cycle, and in particular on the role of Nicolas Fabri de Peiresc, friend of both Rubens and Cassiano dal Pozzo (not to mention Charles de l'Ecluse), in a number of practical, scholarly and personal ways, see Stephanie-Suzanne Durante, 'The Medici cycle', in *Peter Paul Rubens: A Touch of Brilliance*, exhibition catalogue, Courtauld Institute of Art London (Munich, New York and London: Prestel, 2003), pp. 86–8. Several of Rubens's drawings after the antique are reproduced and discussed in Anne-Marie Logan (ed.), *Peter Paul Rubens: The Drawings*, exhibition catalogue, Metropolitan Museum of Art, New York (New Haven: Yale University Press, 2005), pp. 106–17.

[37] Blunt, *Poussin.* p. 35.

[38] See Elizabeth Cropper and Charles Dempsey, *Nicolas Poussin: Friendship and the Love of Painting* (Princeton: Princeton University Press, 1996), pp. 24–34, and Blunt, *Poussin*, p. 230. On the repertoire of classical statues that had such an important *Nachleben*, see Francis Haskell and Nicholas Penny, *Taste and the Antique* (New Haven and London: Yale University Press, 1981); the Niobe group is their no. 66; the so-called Seneca is their no. 76.

the making of the *Israelites Gathering the Manna*. Just as the letter to Chantelou proves to be marked by a series of different temporalities extending over past, present and future, the various iconographical elements that are a part of the composition unite the times of the Old Testament, classical antiquity and the New Testament, along with the New Testament's appropriation of the future within a perspective of salvation.[39]

Blunt made the point most forcefully:

This idea of reading the picture is fundamental in Poussin's conception of painting. A composition is to be studied figure by figure, and each one will express its role in the story exactly, as does an actor on the stage, without the use of words but with an equally effective means of expression, the alphabet of gesture.[40]

This conception of painting evidently entails that the act of reading a painting cannot be instantaneous, but will have a temporality of its own. Poussin emphasises 'after having contemplated it more than once'. Writing to Chantelou in March 1642, he uses the expression 'to read properly' (*bien lire*) with reference to the enjoyment of fine works of art, and repeats the need to take one's time in examining them:

I am convinced that what you say will be true that this time you will have culled the flower of the beautiful works with more pleasure than before when you only saw them en passant without *reading them properly* [*sans les bien lire*]. The things in which there is perfection should not be viewed hastily, but with *time*, judgement and intelligence. [56][41]

---

[39] Another example of this interlocking of different temporalities can be seen in the painting *The Vision of Sta. Francesca Romana*, which Poussin painted for Cardinal Giulio Rospigliosi in 1657. For a long time this work was only known from engravings. It is now in the Louvre, where it was exhibited for the first time in 2001. Although relating to a figure born in the fourteenth century – Francesca dei Ponziani (1384–1440), who founded a female Benedictine order in the Tor de' Specchi – the painting's immediate temporal reference is to the plague in Rome in 1656–7. Spanning two centuries, the painting abolishes the distance between them. See Marc Fumaroli, *Nicolas Poussin: Sainte Françoise Romaine* (Paris: Réunion des Musées Nationaux, 2001).

[40] Blunt, *Poussin*, p. 223.

[41] It should not be forgotten that, before Bernini's famous sculpture of the revelation of Truth by Time (Villa Borghese, Rome), Poussin had done a painting of the same subject, which is only known from a copy and a print. With a characteristic

Chantelou was impressed by the time and attention that Bernini spent on examining each of his *Seven Sacraments* by Poussin, and Bernini himself stated that he could look at the same *Seven Sacraments* for six months without losing interest, though his own extreme piety will have played a role here too.[42] There is an art of reading – one can do it badly or one can do it well – and it takes time. Thus in the same letter to Chantelou [56], and in his letter to Stella [2], Poussin notes that the depictions of the different emotions in the *Israelites Gathering the Manna* 'will not displease those who know how to read them properly'.[43]

Not only should the reader of the painting consider it more than once. Chantelou is also advised to start on the left, 'for the seven main figures on the left willl tell you everything that is written here and all the rest is of the same fabric'.[44] If we do the same, the first figure we see is a man gazing in wonder at the scene of *Caritas Romana*. As Louis Marin perceptively pointed out,[45] this spectator is the artist

volte-face, however, in the letter to Chantelou the lofty injunction to view with time, judgement and intelligence is followed by a reference to the good-looking girls of Nîmes, a tell-tale residue from Poussin's libertine past which was also the cause of his tremulous hands. On the dating of his venereal infection see Thuillier, *Nicolas Poussin*, pp. 104–5.

[42] Stanić (ed.), *Chantelou, Journal de voyage du Cavalier Bernin*, pp. 88–9 and 246.

[43] Poussin's notion of reading that extends beyond the written or printed page has a long history. For discussion of the *longue durée* of this conceit/concept see my 'Lecciones superficiales: transparencia y opacidad en las Américas, siglo XVI', *Aisthesis: Revista Chilena de Investigaciones Estéticas* 31 (1998), 76–88; 'Pretty vacant: Columbus, conviviality and New World faces', in Joanna Overing and Alan Passes (eds.), *The Anthropology of Love and Anger* (London: Routledge, 2000), pp. 189–205; and 'Reading New World bodies', in Florike Egmond and Robert Zwijnenberg (eds.), *Bodily Extremities: Preoccupations with the Human Body in Early Modern European Culture* (Aldershot: Ashgate, 2003), pp. 148–67.

[44] F. H. Dowley, 'Thoughts on Poussin, time, and narrative: The Israelites gathering manna in the desert', *Simiolus* 25.4 (1997), 329–48, claims that 'a text has a sequential order in one direction left to right, in contrast to a picture which can be "read" from any direction, and can represent its meaning all at once to the perception of the observer' (p. 335). Poussin explicitly states that this picture cannot be read from any direction and that it cannot represent its meaning all at once to the perception of the observer.

[45] Louis Marin, *Sublime Poussin* (Paris: Seuil, 1995), pp. 28–9.

himself showing Chantelou how to look at the painting.[46] In other words, the external relation between the viewer and the painting has been internalised within the painting; what was a relation of depth has undergone a process of *lateralisation*.[47]

As for the precise specifications for the frame that Poussin prescribes in his letter, even returning to them in the final postscriptum, they too serve as indications of how to read the painting. It is a self-contained unity, and should be read and re-read as such. The eye must not be allowed to wander beyond the frame, or to be confused by what is extraneous to it; there can be no *parergon* for Poussin.[48] We can compare Poussin's approval of Chantelou's idea of covering each of the seven *Sacraments* with a curtain so that they could be shown one by one – which is how they were shown to Bernini in 1665[49] – 'because seeing them all together would be too much for the senses' [162]. In fact, the frame could be said to reinforce the presence of the painting by reducing the distraction produced by proximity, leaving only the option of presence or absence, of inside the frame or outside the frame. This to and fro between Poussin's letters and his paintings is enabled by the literal-mindedness or absence of metaphor in his concept of reading. To read a text or to read a painting are one and the same activity.

The profound unity linking text and image is expressed most clearly in the famous *Self-Portrait* (Louvre) that he painted for Chantelou in 1650.[50] In a chapter tellingly entitled 'Presence-absence', Bätschmann refers to Leon Battista Alberti's *Della pittura*, where at the opening of book II the Renaissance humanist boldly claims: 'Painting possesses a truly divine power in that not only does it make the absent present (as they say of friendship), but it also represents the dead to the living

[46] We can detect the presence of a similarly 'deictic' figure in Poussin's Raphaelesque *Esther before Ahasuerus* (Hermitage, St Petersburg), where the Persian slave, half-hidden by a column in the centre of the painting, directly engages the viewer's gaze.

[47] Louis Marin, *Détruire la peinture* (Paris: Galilée, 1977), p. 71.

[48] For the parergon as that which lies beyond the frame, see Jacques Derrida, *La vérité en peinture* (Flammarion: Paris, 1978).

[49] Stanić (ed.), *Chantelou, Journal de voyage du Cavalier Bernin*, p. 88.

[50] Rosenberg (ed.), *Nicolas Poussin 1594–1665*, no. 190.

many centuries later . . . Through painting, the faces of the dead go on living for a very long time.'[51] This power, Bätschmann argues, brings out the paradoxical nature of the portrait: 'Will the newly created presence make one forget the real absence of the represented person, or will this presence be a reminder of the absence?'[52] The inscription painted on an empty, primed and framed canvas in the *Self-Portrait* runs 'EFFIGIES NICOLAI POVSSINI ANDEL:/YENSIS PICTORIS. ANNO AETATIS. 56/ ROMAE ANNO IVBILEI/ 1650.' We can read 'EFFIGIES' as the title of the painting that we see, a rough Latin equivalent of 'Self-Portrait'. But we can also read it as stressing the fact that what we see is a representation, a present image that is a substitute for an absent presence, like the wax effigies of themselves with which the leading citizens densely populated the church of Santissima Annunziata in Alberti's native city of Florence.[53]

The absent presence that will, at some time in the future, become a present presence is thus a deferred presence. The deferred presence – of the painting of the *Israelites Gathering the Manna* in the letter to Chantelou, of Nicolas Poussin himself, present in Rome and absent from Paris – articulates time and space, a space that is elsewhere, a space whose presence is deferred by time. In his last painting, the enigmatic *Apollo and Daphne* (Louvre), which the many preparatory drawings show to have undergone a gestation period of at least four years,[54] Poussin carried disjunction to its limit. Apollo and Daphne are as removed from one another as can be on the canvas. Daphne's eyes are closed, she does not want to look at Apollo. The god seems

---

[51] Leon Battista Alberti, *On Painting*, translated by Cecil Grayson (Harmondsworth: Penguin, 1991), p. 60.

[52] Bätschmann, *Nicolas Poussin: Dialectics of Painting*, p. 49.

[53] See Aby Warburg, *The Renewal of Pagan Antiquity* (Los Angeles: Getty Research Institute for the History of Art and the Humanities, 1999), pp. 189–90; Didi-Huberman, *Devant l'image*, 262ff.; Giovanni Ricci, *Il principe e la morte: corpo, cuore, effigie nel rinascimento* (Bologna: Il Mulino, 1998), pp. 119–25; Adriano Prosperi, *Dare l'anima: storia di un infanticidio* (Turin: Einaudi, 2005), pp. 285–94.

[54] Pierre Rosenberg and Louis-Antoine Prat (eds.), *Nicolas Poussin: la collection du musée Condé à Chantilly*, exhibition catalogue, Musée Condé, Château de Chantilly (Paris: Réunion des Musées Nationaux, 1994), pp. 144–5.

absent, isolated, enveloped in his own world.[55] Presence (and with it, conjunction) is, endlessly, deferred. In this painting, too, reading is reduced to its most illegible: we cannot even be sure that what the shepherdess is tracing on the tumulus of earth beside the dead Leucippus are words.[56]

Poussin did not complete *Apollo and Daphne*. On 26 July 1665 he wrote to l'Abbé Nicaise: 'I have abandoned the brushes for ever. All I have left is to die, it will be the only remedy for the ills that afflict me. May God will that it be soon, for life is too heavy for me. You will show these two lines to the seigneur [M. de Chamilly], whom I beg to excuse me if I write no more.'[57] No more painting, no more letter writing. Less than four months later, Nicolas Poussin was dead. Like its pendant in Berlin,[58] the Louvre *Self-Portrait* had become a memorial.

APPENDIX: THE AUTOGRAPH LETTER AND TRANSCRIPTION

Transcription (from *Correspondance de Nicolas Poussin*, ed. Charles Jouanny, Archives de l'art français, nouvelle période, vol. 5, Paris: F. de Nobele, 1911)

A Monsieur de Chantelou, Commis de Monseigneur de Noyers en Court.
Monsieur,
J'atendray que dieu me face la grase d'estre auprès de vous pour recognoistre les obligations que je vous dois, non avec des paroles, mais par effet, si vous

---

[55] Rosenberg (ed.), *Nicolas Poussin 1594–1665*, no. 242. On this painting see also David Carrier, 'Blindness and the representation of desire in Poussin's paintings', *Res* 19–20 (1991), 31–52.

[56] On the identification of these figures see Cropper and Dempsey, *Nicolas Poussin*, p. 307.

[57] This letter, which was printed for the first time in 1947, is therefore not to be found in the collection edited by Jouanny. It is here cited from Blunt, *Nicolas Poussin: lettres et propos sur l'art*, pp. 176–7.

[58] Cropper and Dempsey, *Nicolas Poussin*, p. 188: 'If for Alberti painting could make the absent present and bring life to the dead, Poussin seems to insist instead here that in painting, and especially self-portraiture, no matter how much it may triumph over sculpture, the living voice is silent, and absence is commemorated as in a kind of tomb.'

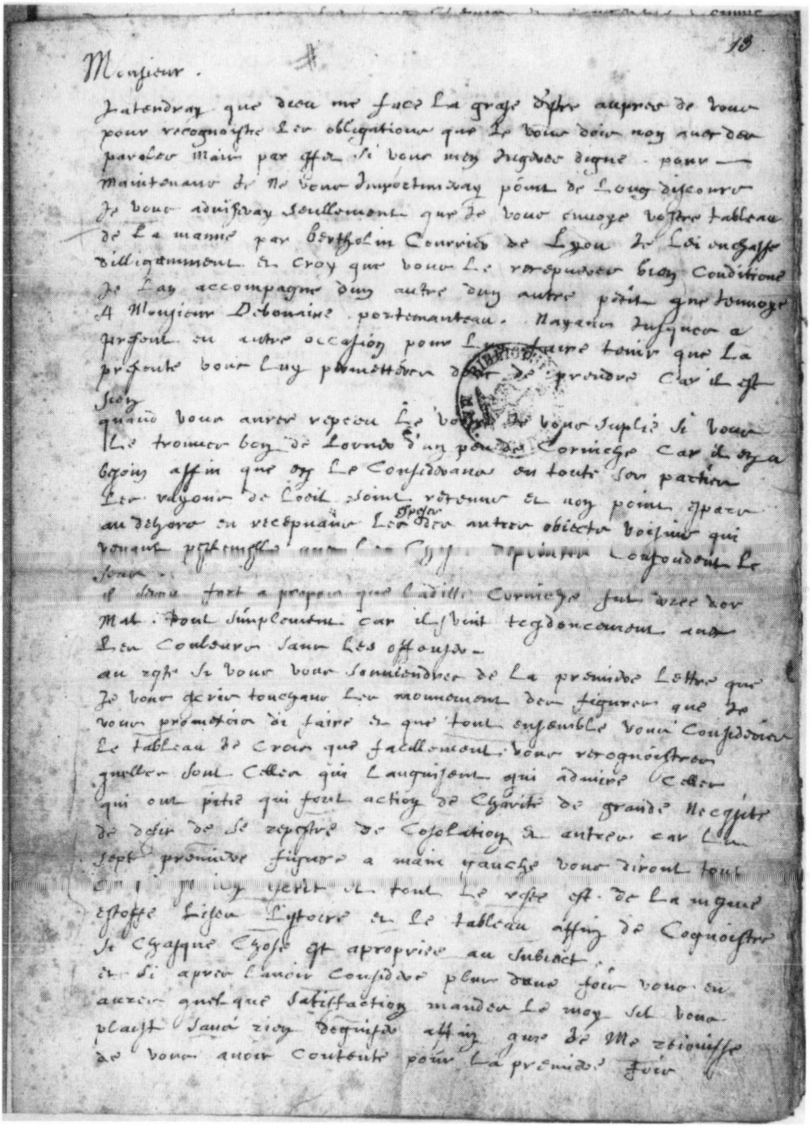

Fig. 7. Letter from Nicolas Poussin to Paul Fréart de Chantelou, 28 April 1639. Courtesy of Bibliothèque Nationale de France, MS fr. 12347, fol. 13

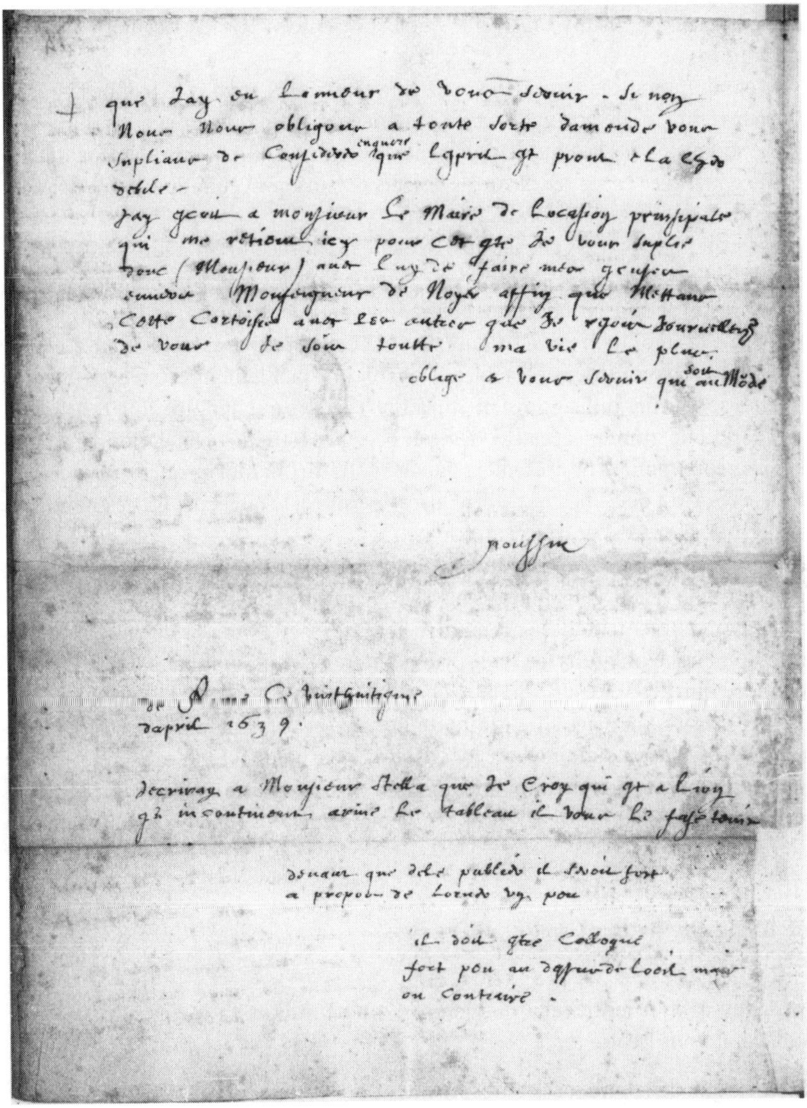

Fig. 7. (*cont.*)

m'en jugerés digne. Pour maintenant je ne vous importuneray point de long discours; je vous aduiseray seullement que je vous enuoye vostre tableau de la manne, par bertholin, Courrier de Lyon: Je l'ay enchassé dilligemment, et croy que vous le recepurés bien conditioné. Je l'ay accompagné d'un autre petit que j'envoye à Monsieur Debonaire, portemanteau, n'ayans jusques à présent eu autre occasion pour luy faire tenir que la présente. Vous luy permetterés donc de prendre car il est sien.

Quand vous aurés repceu le vostre, je vous suplie, si vous le trouués bon, de l'orner d'un peu de corniche, car il en a besoin, affin que en le considérans en toute ses parties les rayons de l'oeil soient retenus et non point espars au dehors en recepuant les espèses des autres obiects voisins qui venant pesle-mesle, avec les choses dépeintes confondent le jour.

Il seroit fort à propos que laditte corniche fut dorée d'or mat tout simplement, car il s'unit très-doucement avec les couleurs sans les offenser.

Au reste, si vous vous souuiendrés de la première lettre que je vous escris, touchans les mouuement des figures que je vous prometois di faire, et que tout ensemble vous considériés le tableau, je crois que facillement vous recognoistrés quelles sont celles qui languisent, qui admire, celles qui ont pitié, qui font action de charité, de grande nécessité, de désir de se repestre de consolation, et autres, car les sept première figure à main gauche vous diront tout ce qui est icy escrit et tout le reste est de la mesme estoffe: lisés l'istoire et le tableau, afin de cognoistre si chasque chose est aproprié au subiect.

Et si, après l'auoir consideré plus d'une fois vous en aurés quelque satisfaction, mandés le moy s'il vous plaist, sans rien déguiser, affin que je me réiouisse de vous avoir contenté pour la première fois que j'ay eu l'onneur de vous seruir. Si non nous nous obligons à toute sorte d'amende, vous supplians de considérer enquore que l'esprit est pront et la cher débile.

J'ay escrit à monsieur Le Maire de l'occasion principale qui me retient icy pour cet été; je vous suplie donc (Monsieur) avec lui de faire mes escuses envers Monseigneur de Noyers affin que, mettant cette cortoisie avec les autres que je resois journellem[t] de vous, je sois toutte ma vie le plus obligé à vous seruir qui soit au Monde.

POUSSIN

de Rome ce vingthuitiesme
d'apvril 1639.

J'écriray à Monsieur Stella que je croy qui est à lion qu'incontinent arivé le tableau il vous le fase tenir.

Deuant que de le publier il seroit fort à propos de l'orner un peu.

Il doit estre colloqué fort peu au dessus de l'oeil mais au contraire.

CHAPTER 7

The role of correspondence in the transmission of collecting patterns in seventeenth-century Europe: models, media and main characters

Irene Baldriga

> If the pictures of our absent friends are pleasing to us, though they
> only refresh the memory and lighten our longing by a solace that
> is unreal and unsubstantial, how much more pleasant is a letter,
> which brings us real traces, real evidences, of an absent friend! For
> that which is sweetest when we meet face to face is afforded by the
> impress of a friend's hand upon his letter-recognition.[1]
>
> *Seneca*

COLLECTING AND CORRESPONDENCE

In 1663 the Jesuit Father Athanasius Kircher published one of his
most praised books: the *Polygraphia, seu artificium linguarum quo
cum omnibus mundi populis poterit quis respondere*. In his dedication
to the emperor, Ferdinand III, Kircher announced the invention of
a universal method of communication.[2] Even more interesting is the
fact that – in Kircher's view – the new system could allow everyone to
exchange letters with correspondents in all countries without knowing
any other language than their own. Such an ambitious project not only
seems to stem directly from the needs created by the republic of letters,
but it also appears particularly striking for having been postulated
by one of the most eclectic and brilliant collectors of the seventeenth
century. The revolutionary nature of Kircher's invention was not
ignored by his readers: after having received a copy of the volume, an

---

[1] Lucius Annaeus Seneca, *Epistulae Morales ad Lucilium*, IV, 40,1. Seneca, *Epistles*,
trans. R. M. Gummere, 3 vols. (Cambridge, MA: Loeb Classical Library, Harvard
University Press, 1917), pp. 263–5.
[2] 'Linguarum omnium ad unam reductio.'

enthusiastic supporter of the Father complimented him on 'teaching how to correspond, by letters, with all the Nations of the World'.[3]

In the evaluation of this cultural event, we should not avoid stressing the role played by collecting in the general scope of Kircher's activities. The goal that Kircher hoped to achieve by publishing the *Polygraphia* went beyond the interests of an erudite linguist. As the dedication of the volume clearly explains, he had actually been engaged in the creation of a universal system of communication which could make a letter understandable in every corner of Babel's tower.

By the time that Kircher had been entrusted with the task of creating the Jesuit Museum at the Collegio Romano in 1651, collecting had become a widespread activity all over Europe. More precisely, as I shall try to show, it had become a 'European' practice. Geographical and cultural boundaries had been crossed, in large part, thanks to the creation of a capillary web of connections which found its principal means of communication in correspondence. Thousands of letters were sent all over the continent in order to describe museums and galleries, to allow people to visit collections, to deliver items of various kinds, or simply to share the pleasures of collecting.

The importance achieved by correspondence not just as a way to communicate but also as a fundamental part of collectors' lives is testified by Kircher's experience as well. In the catalogue of the Collegio Romano museum published by Giorgio de Sepi in 1678, the twelve volumes of letters collected by Kircher over about forty years were considered as one of the most precious treasures to be held in the Jesuit Gallery.[4] Not only had the letters contributed to create the museum by enlarging the knowledge of its owner and the range of his relationships; they had become a part of the museum itself as they were turned into objects to be shown to the visitors. As a result, we can assume that correspondence was considered at this time to be a measure of the importance of a collection.

[3] Letter sent from Castiglione to Rome (Athanasius Kircher), 1663: 'coll'insegnamento di corrispondersi, per lettere, con tutte le Nationi del Mondo'.
[4] The importance of the fact has been stressed by Paula Findlen, 'Un incontro con Kircher a Roma', in E. Lo Sardo, *Athanasius Kircher: Il Museo del Mondo*, exhibition catalogue (Rome: De Luca, 2001), pp. 39–47.

The fortune of a collection was, in large part, determined by the wideness of acquaintances and contacts of the owner, not just in order to promote the museum but mainly in order to purchase or simply to get information about rarities of various kinds. This is the reason why, very often, letters were not simply containers of news, but more precisely accompanied items and gifts addressed to naturalists and connoisseurs. The diffusion of such a practice seems to show the many inadequacies of the market with regard to the needs of a large number of collectors.[5] Commenting on the pains suffered by the botanist and the collector of flowers in order to obtain rare seeds and bulbs, Giovanni Battista Ferrari wrote in his famous *Flora* (1633) that the best way to purchase 'foreign specimens' was to resort to 'friendly letters, with promises to exchange some other plants or, if necessary, to offer money'.[6]

The idea of sharing interests and research findings by exchanging information and objects seems to nourish a general project aimed at the creation of a universal museum which would grow by itself: the system of an efficient correspondence led to a sort of virtual, circulating museum whose fortunate visitors were the erudite members of the republic of letters.

A further consideration should also be taken into account with regard to the importance of correspondence as a pivotal element of seventeenth-century collecting: the influence of Lipsian Neostoicism in the general context of the republic of letters. The role played in Lipsius's philosophy by epistolary contacts certainly influenced the profile of erudite communication of that time,[7] especially in the context of scientific collections. This has clearly emerged in the case of the Italian Accademia dei Lincei, which found in Neostoicism a very

---

[5] The analysis of seventeenth-century correspondence allows us to conclude that this latter consideration can be extended to the distribution of books.

[6] G. B. Ferrari, *De Florum Cultura* (Rome, 1633).

[7] M. Morford, *Stoics and Neostoics: Rubens and the Circle of Lipsius* (Princeton, NJ: Princeton University Press, 1991). Clear evidence of the perception of the republic of letters as a common, virtual space devoted to knowledge and science comes from a letter sent from Queen Christina of Sweden to Kircher: 'While I have a great desire to know what you are handling at the moment in the subjects of the humanities, I wonder what you are managing for the well-being of the Republic of Letters.'

important element of identification.[8] The consideration of correspondence as valuable documentary evidence is a quite recent development in the history of collecting. In this chapter, I would like to examine correspondence not just as a means of communication but, more widely, as an instrument of exchange and transmission of collecting patterns on a European scale.

First of all, it is possible to distinguish between 'private and/or specialised collections' and what I will call 'dynastic collections'. In the first case we are dealing with individual collections of a small or medium size which are often characterised by a certain specialisation and are sometimes connected to a precise research activity. 'Dynastic collections' are often the fruit of a secular process of accumulation, mainly due to the social status and to the political role of the owners. Following such a classification, we can also distinguish different kinds of correspondence. Letters connected to private collecting are very different in style, aim and purpose from those which were produced in a dynastic context. To begin with the former, a large part of the huge correspondence of the Gonzaga court has been recently published thanks to the dedication of a group of brilliant researchers led by Raffaella Morselli.[9] This impressive documentation will certainly be examined from a number of different and very specific perspectives; in this humble contribution I would like to underline a few aspects which I consider to be particularly interesting with regard to the history

---

[8] See I. Baldriga, *L'occhio della lince: i primi lincei tra arte, scienza e collezionismo* (Rome: Accademia Nazionale dei Lincei, 2002).

[9] See the series of books concerning the Gonzaga collection, published under the direction of Raffaella Morselli, i.e. B. Furlotti, *Le collezioni Gonzaga: il carteggio tra Bologna, Parma, Piacenza e Mantova (1563–1634)* (Cinisello Balsamo: Silvana Editoriale, 2000); E. Venturini, *Le collezioni Gonzaga: il carteggio tra la Corte Cesarea e Mantova (1559–1636)* (Cinisello Balsamo: Silvana Editoriale, 2002); R. Piccinelli, *Le collezioni Gonzaga: il carteggio tra Firenze e Mantova (1554–1626)* (Cinisello Balsamo: Silvana Editoriale, 2000); B. Furlotti, *Le collezioni Gonzaga: il carteggio tra Roma e Mantova (1587–1612)* (Cinisello Balsamo: Silvana Editoriale, 2003); D. Sogliani, *Le collezioni Gonzaga: il carteggio tra Venezia e Mantova (1563–1587)* (Cinisello Balsamo: Silvana Editoriale, 2002); M. Sermidi, *Le collezioni Gonzaga: il carteggio tra Venezia e Mantova (1588–1612)* (Cinisello Balsamo: Silvana Editoriale, 2003); R. Piccinelli, *Le collezioni Gonzaga: il carteggio tra Milano e Mantova (1563–1634)* (Cinisello Balsamo: Silvana Editoriale, 2003).

of collections as a whole. As this chapter is mainly focused on the topic of European cultural relations, I will take into account only the correspondence between Mantua and the court of Emperor Rudolph II during the rule of Duke Vincenzo Gonzaga I.

First of all, we should stress the strikingly different nature of the correspondence which linked Mantua with the imperial court. The vast majority of letters were sent and addressed from or to official representatives of the Gonzaga family in Prague. It is widely known that political and diplomatic relations at this time were often facilitated by means of precious gifts; in the case of Rudolph II, paintings and rare specimens could be the only way to win the favour of such a capricious emperor. Nevertheless, Rudolph's eagerness was completely out of control: letters from Prague often contain precise requests for masterpieces to be found on the market, to be purchased from other collectors, or to be taken directly from the duke's gallery. Rudolph's requests were clearly an abuse of his power. At the other end, Vincenzo tried to defend his interests and property with excuses (these are sometimes very interesting, as on the occasion when he refused to give a painting in order to avoid 'altering' the order of the gallery where it had been hung), or simply by proposing valuable (in his opinion) alternatives or, more boldly, copies after the originals. The latter strategy could be very dangerous. In 1602, the emperor commented on a painting already owned by Cardinal Montalto in Rome and sent to Prague at Rudolph's direct request: 'which is something of no importance and a bad copy'.[10] He wondered how Vincenzo 'could send you such rubbish'.[11] The relationship between Rudolph and Vincenzo appears to be unique: the exchanges between these exceptional collectors, who shared many interests but did not occupy the political scene at the same level, are often characterised by very unbalanced relations and betray the profiles of the most unscrupulous museum owners. This correspondence teaches us a lot, for instance, about the commission of copies within important collections like that of the Gonzagas. Vincenzo was extremely jealous about his gallery and tried

---

[10] 'che è cosa di nessun momento e copia mal fatta'.
[11] 'le mandi simil coglionerie'. Letter from Aderbale Manerbio to Annibale Chieppio, Prague. Cf. Venturini, *Le collezioni Gonzaga*, pp. 509–10, doc. 883.

strenuously to avoid its dispersal. On the other hand, the importance of his collection and the fame it had gained over the centuries led to some embarrassing situations, such as the one mentioned above. Having a good painter at his disposal who was able to reproduce faithfully the masterpieces of the collection could be a solution to the problem. The young Rubens, active for the court at the beginning of the century, played this delicate role. In 1605 the Flemish painter was asked to make copies for Rudolph II after two paintings by Correggio.

The case of the correspondence between Mantua and Prague brings to light the 'official' dimension of the collection and its official involvements. What it does not reveal is the intimate life of collectors and the nature of their mutual exchanges as a part of their activity as accumulators. This different, more fascinating aspect of the subject is more evident when we take into consideration the phenomenon of private collecting. Here we are dealing with isolated, passionate owners whose principal public is the virtual space of the republic of letters. The role played by correspondence in this case seems to be very different from its role in the 'dynastic' context. Correspondence becomes a fundamental strategy aimed at gaining new objects for the collection or, in many cases, at collecting information and clues about the meaning and value (historical, but also economic) of new, unknown, specimens. This aspect is particularly suitable to the genre of collections of scientific objects and antiquities, where the 'discovery' of objects and their examination appears as a crucial part of the profession of the collector. This was the case, for instance, with the correspondence by Peiresc and Rubens on the famous Portland Vase, one of the most precious examples of ancient glass cameo, dating back to 25 BC.[12] Peiresc had seen the item in 1600 in Cardinal del Monte's collection in Rome, as he mentioned in a letter of 1633, and he could not avoid inserting it in the illustrated volume dedicated to antique cameos that he and his close friend Rubens started to plan in the 1620s.[13] The story of the Portland Vase involved a large number of letters sent from France to Italy and

---

[12] See D. Jaffé, 'Peiresc, Rubens and the Portland Vase', *The Burlington Magazine* 131 (1989), 554–9.

[13] M. van der Meulen, *Petrus Paulus Rubens Antiquarius: Collector and Copyist of Antique Gems* (Alphen aan de Rijn: Canaletto, 1975).

to Flanders, mostly aimed at investigating and discussing the nature of the object, but also at commissioning good reproductions, not only on paper (drawings and etchings from Cassiano dal Pozzo's Museum Chartaceum atelier) but also in cast.

The crucial role of correspondence in the development and transmission of collecting patterns becomes even clearer when we consider the specific context of scientific collecting. In an important contribution, the historian Giuseppe Olmi focused attention on a striking passage taken from a letter sent in 1596 by the Bolognese scholar Ulisse Aldrovandi to the Dutch doctor Evert van Vorsten: 'in this knowledge of nature it is important to have many friends in different places, since the same land does not produce everything'.[14] In that letter, Aldrovandi thanked his Dutch friend for a description of Paludanus's museum in Enkhuizen and asked for a catalogue listing the objects it contained, offering in exchange a catalogue of his own collection. There could not be a more eloquent testimony to the role played by letters in the spreading of European scientific research in the sixteenth and seventeenth centuries. It has been estimated that the exchange of objects of scientific interest (bulbs, seeds, fossils, minerals, etc.) gave birth to a real flux of material communication between different European countries, but mainly between southern and northern Europe.

THE LETTER AS A LITERARY GENRE IN THE CONTEXT OF ART COLLECTING

The seventeenth century marked the absolute ascendancy of epistolary literature as an autonomous genre. This becomes particularly clear when we consider the number of published volumes containing selected letters. This phenomenon has its roots in the classical tradition, particularly in Seneca's *Letters to Lucilius*, and emerges clearly in Neostoic Lipsian circles, where the function of letters becomes

---

[14] 'In questa cognitione della natura bisogna havere molti amici in varij luoghi, cum non eadem ferat omnia tellus.' See G. Olmi, 'Molti amici in varij luoghi: studio della natura e rapporti epistolari nel secolo xvi', *Nuncius. Annali di Storia della Scienza* 6 (1991), 3–31, esp. p. 7.

crucial in the establishment of long-distance relationships and friendships formed to pursue the superior goal of *contubernium*. It was not
by chance that Lipsius, like Erasmus before him, wrote an essay on
correspondence as a writing genre, discussing methods, patterns and
techniques of letters (*Epistolica Institutio*). There would be much to
say about such a fascinating topic, but I shall now simply recall that
the principal categories of letters classified by Lipsius were the 'seria',
the 'docta' and the 'familiaris'.[15]

It is noteworthy that one of the most famous seventeenth-century
artistic texts, written by the Genoan collector Vincenzo Giustiniani,
has the format of a letter. This is the 'Letter on painting' addressed to
Dirck van Ameyden (Teodoro Amideni) and dating from the first half
of the century.[16] As is typical of this kind of literature, the text begins
with a practical, probably fictitious, reference: Vincenzo mentions
the pitiful quality of the manner of a Flemish painter[17] and takes the
opportunity to outline twelve different 'manners' of painting, from
the easiest to the most difficult. No doubt we are here dealing with the
'docta' category of letters mentioned by Lipsius. The importance of
the 'Letter' lies not only in the extraordinary value of the information
given by the author with regard to the evaluation of painting at that
time; what makes this document so unique is the fact that it was not
written by a lettered artist but, on the contrary, by a collector or,
more appropriately, by a virtuoso. The letter, which is written by one
virtuoso and is addressed to another, should be considered not only –
as it has been traditionally examined – for its general art-historical
value but, more specifically, as a unique source of information about
the attitude and taste of seicento collectors.

---

[15] For a profound and erudite discussion of the topic, see Morford, *Stoics and Neostoics*.
[16] Giustiniani is also the author of a 'Letter on sculpture', which is far less known.
[17] 'Vincenzo Giustiniani to Teodoro Amideni: I confirm to you that I have information
that the Flemish painter in question is worse than mediocre; and to make my response
better understood, I will distinguish various ranks of painters' ('Vincenzo Giustiniani
al signor Teodoro Amideni: Confermo a Vostra Signoria che ho relazione che quel
Fiammingo è pittore più che mediocre; e per maggior intelligenza di questa risposta,
farò alcune distinzioni, e gradi di pittori . . .'). See G. Bottari, *Raccolta di lettere sulla
pittura, scultura ed architettura scritte da' più celebri personaggi dei secoli XV, XVI, e XVII /
pubblicata da Gio. Bottari e continuata fino ai nostri giorni da Stefano Ticozzi* (Milan:
Per Giovanni Silvestri, 1822), vol. 6, p. 121.

Why, first of all, did Giustiniani choose the format of the letter to express his preferences with regard to painting? Generally speaking, two main purposes could lie behind such a choice: to qualify the text by virtue of the authority of its addressee, and to widen the range of its potential audience by transforming a traditionally private relation (the relation between correspondents) into a sort of open letter made available to a number of potential readers. Consequently, I would venture to propose that the 'Letter on painting' might have originally been intended for publication. I am not aware that this hypothesis has ever been suggested, but I believe it to be worthy of consideration, especially if one bears in mind the variety of erudite interests cultivated by the Marchese.

As the subject of the present chapter is the relation between collecting and correspondence, I shall focus my attention on the use of the 'Letter' as the means chosen by Vincenzo to spread his ideas on art or, as he explains in the text, on 'the different ways to paint, on the basis of the knowledge I acquired thanks to a basic practice of this profession'. The genre of the didactic letter had a very long tradition, but it must be stressed that the format preferred by scholars in order to advance new theses and ideas was, generally, the 'dialogue' or 'conversation'. The latter permitted a dialectical treatment of a topic, which considered all the pros and cons and made it possible to root out any doubt. This was the format most appreciated among philosophers and scientists: Galileo Galilei wrote his most famous treatise in the form of a dialogue, *Dialogo sopra i massimi sistemi* (Dialogue concerning the two chief world systems). On the other hand, even Federico Cesi suggested to his fellows Linceans that they compose their writings in the format of the letter: his *Lettera sulla fluidità del Cielo* (Letter on celestial fluidity), addressed to Cardinal Bellarmino and written in 1618, is widely known.

GENESIS OF A STATUS SYMBOL: THE COLLECTION

During the seventeenth century a common feeling of desire to achieve the status of the collector seems to have become more and more diffused among the upper and middle classes of Europe. It is important to consider that, beyond the objective differences which distinguished the economic and social realities of many European countries during the seventeenth century, the establishment of certain attitudes, which soon became clichés, contributed to stimulate the diffusion of collecting on the basis of cultural itineraries outlined below. We will see, for instance, how the preferred space devoted to collections of statues and paintings within a short period of time became what we call the gallery, following a model that originated in France and then spread to Italy and England.[18] At the same time, we will see how the 'paper museum' became the most popular means of self-celebration adopted by the European aristocracy; we find it at the same time in England, Italy, France and the Netherlands. Some models of collecting took a long time to cross the borders of some countries. Private collecting ('bourgeois' collecting), for instance, which emerged in the Netherlands in the seventeenth century and was described by the English traveller John Evelyn, did not gain a footing in the rest of Europe, which lacked the economic and social conditions from which it had sprung (the presence of an art market, middle-class economy, and so on). Nevertheless, written communication widely contributed to disseminating the knowledge of different patterns and models of collecting. With regard to the diffusion of a new attitude towards collecting as a status symbol, it is extremely important to consider the role played by the birth of a market for *naturalia* and *artificialia* which made it easy to obtain objects of beauty and rarity, even without assimilating all the knowledge and erudition traditionally associated with the practice of creating museums.[19]

[18] See W. Prinz, *Galleria: storia e tipologia di uno spazio architettonico*, ed. C. Cieri Via (Modena: Panini, 1988). The first example of a real gallery devoted to housing an art collection is the corridor created at Fontainebleau by François I. At the same time, while he was creating a model of ideal architectural space, François was the first to import a taste for Renaissance Italian art into France. See also R. Lightbown, 'Charles I and the tradition of European princely collecting', in A. MacGregor (ed.), *The Late King's Goods: Collections, Possessions and Patronage of Charles I in the Light of the Commonwealth Sale Inventories* (London and Oxford: MacAlpine, 1989), pp. 53–72.

[19] Interesting contributions to this topic are contained in P. H. Smith and P. Findlen (eds.), *Merchants and Marvels: Commerce, Science and Art in Early Modern Europe* (New York and London: Routledge, 2002).

The history of collecting is a relatively recent branch of art history and is not often associated with the strategies of the history of culture. Nevertheless, the possible connections between different countries may appear particularly evident and striking when examined from such a perspective. This is the case with the relatively unknown mutual relationship between the Italian and English cultural contexts in the seventeenth century. The sharp religious gap which divided the two countries from the time of Henry VIII on threw up a barrier to considering the cases of Italy and England as part of a single history. By contrast, I want here to draw attention to a specific case which could be an interesting starting point for reconsidering such assumptions.

The opinion expressed by some scholars that modern collecting was born in England, thanks to the extraordinary activity of Thomas Howard, second Earl of Arundel, is widely shared.[20] Arundel was able to collect an enormous number of paintings, drawings and statues, many of which were bought in Italy by his agents. On the other hand, in considering the history of his collection, Arundel's travels in Italy have not been sufficiently taken into account. Above all, during his stay in Rome, Arundel must have had the opportunity to meet one of the most interesting of Italian collectors of the day: the Marchese Vincenzo Giustiniani. The Giustiniani collection, which in 1638 comprised some 1,800 statues and 600 paintings, would soon become legendary. At the time of Arundel's visit to Rome, the collection was about to be arranged, especially with regard to the statues, busts and reliefs which Giustiniani was so eager to buy. It is likely that Arundel was influenced by Giustiniani's passion for antiquities and painting, and there are clues which point to such an influence and bear on the relation established later between the two noblemen.

First of all, there is a striking similarity between the famous portrait of Arundel painted by the Dutch painter Daniel Mijtens (fig. 8) and the description of a lost portrait of Giustiniani by Baldassare Galanino which is contained in the 1638 inventory of the Italian collection. The

---

[20] On Arundel, see M. F. S. Hervey, *The Life, Correspondence & Collections of Thomas Howard, Earl of Arundel* (Cambridge: Cambridge University Press, 1921); D. Howarth, *Lord Arundel and his Circle* (New Haven and London: Yale University Press, 1985).

Fig. 8. Daniel Mijtens, portrait of Thomas Howard, second Earl of Arundel. London, National Portrait Gallery

portrait of Giustiniani is described as follows: 'a half-figure portrait of the Marchese Vincenzo Giustiniani, with the view of a gallery of statues, painted on canvas by Baldassare Galanino from Bologna'. Both paintings thus show a long gallery of statues behind the figure of the collector, who is represented in the foreground and celebrated for his ability and taste as a buyer and connoisseur. It can hardly be denied that the two paintings are connected and that one of them must have been the model for the other. The success of this kind of portrait was so great that a later example was made for Cardinal Mazarin in France. This similarity suggests more than a simple coincidence: I would venture to say that there is a sort of a sequence among the portraits Giustiniani–Arundel–Mazarin, a sequence which becomes a tradition or the transmission of a pattern. Not only are these noblemen and this cardinal asserting their wealth, nobility and elegance by stressing the importance of their collections: more specifically, they have chosen to be represented against an unusual background, that of a gallery filled with ancient statues.

The particular nature of the Arundel–Giustiniani relationship is based on the fact that the two collectors seem to have influenced each other. In the case of Cardinal Mazarin, who lived in Rome in a palace of his own and bought a number of paintings and statues in order to transfer an Italian collection to French soil, we can talk about a one-way influence, where the pattern is without any doubt Italian. By contrast, in the case of Arundel the patterns imitated have as a counterpart some other patterns which are also imitated. Although the contacts between the English nobleman and Vincenzo Giustiniani still require further investigation, it can be stated that the two collectors met in Rome at the beginning of the century, that they probably shared the same agent to buy Roman antiquities and that, probably, they both patronised artists like Joachim von Sandrart and Gerrit van Honthorst. Thanks to the writings of the German painter Sandrart we know, for instance, that he visited Arundel Castle: in his *Teutsche Academie* he also described the famous gallery of statues represented in Mijtens's portrait.

In his constant desire to achieve the status of a modern Italian-style collector, Arundel certainly had an objective limit: he could not be considered, as far as we know, as a member of the republic of letters.

His interpretation of collecting was mainly self-oriented and aimed at the private accumulation of pieces, while the spirit of the virtual community of letters had its roots in a generous and mutual sharing of things and ideas.

At this point it should be stressed that, although correspondence undoubtedly played a crucial role in the development of the European phenomenon of collecting, letters could be used to achieve two very different goals: the material purchase of things destined to be housed in private museums, or the pure satisfaction of heterogeneous curiosities ranging from archaeology to philology, the natural sciences, and so on. This perhaps over-simple distinction also involves a precise conception of what we call the 'spirit' of the republic of letters: nowadays, we would define this unbordered community as a non-profit, non-organised and informal erudite fellowship. The desire to share and spread knowledge was the main goal of this unwritten project: no selfish concept of accumulation, whether material or not, could be reconciled with such an ambitious attitude.

ON 'PAPER TRANSMISSION': EDITORIAL MEDIA, TRAVELLERS' DESCRIPTIONS AND CORRESPONDENCE

During the period under consideration, communication on paper was, obviously, the main – in some cases the only possible – means of information. It is therefore necessary to devote some attention to the genre of the virtual paper museum that circulated. Correspondence among scholars soon became the most effective instrument to promote these initiatives. In addition, the more effective the promotion was, the more it stimulated imitation.

On 4 September 1636, Pieter Paul Rubens wrote to Nicolas de Peiresc to inform him about the brand-new publication of the *Galleria Giustiniana*, a two-volume collection of engravings representing the most important statues, busts and bas-reliefs which were held at that time in the Giustiniani Palace in Rome.[21] In Rubens's words we

---

[21] 'I have also seen letters from Rome that mention that the Galeria Justiniana has come out, at the expense of the Marchese Justianino, that is considered a most noble work,

recognise the anxiety of a passionate collector; most of all, the desire to examine directly this rare collection of precious ancient marbles. The two volumes of the *Galleria* were published separately, and we know from a number of sources that this was actually viewed as a very important event not only by 'virtuosi' and collectors, but also by many artists. The letter of Rubens to Peiresc puts this publishing initiative within a wider European setting and indicates the fame achieved by the Giustiniani collection well beyond the confines of Italy. This example is particularly suitable for illustrating a specific kind of cultural model which seems to become familiar to a large part of the European class aristocracy in the seventeenth century: the paper museum, a pattern which was not limited to the famous example of Cassiano dal Pozzo's collection of drawings and sketches after the antique, but was an effective medium through which to advertise and diffuse particular collections.

It was not by chance that this kind of publishing initiative was promoted by different subjects and in different countries more or less at the same time. This brings us back to Vincenzo Giustiniani and the Earl of Arundel, since they both patronised the publication of illustrated catalogues of their respective collections: by the time Vincenzo Giustiniani had published his *Galleria*, Thomas Howard already had his own lavishly bound *Marmora Arundeliana*. The scientific approach on which the history of culture is based does not admit any coincidence, so I cannot help stressing the relevance of such a similarity of events. Some years later (during the 1650s), we come across a similar kind of initiative with the publication of Gerard Reynst's collection of paintings and antiquities in the form of two richly illustrated volumes.[22] Furthermore, we should not forget to underline the international

and I hope that within a few months some copies will also be available in Flanders, but I do believe that every new product ends up in your own museum' ('Ho visto ancora lettere di Roma che dicono esser uscita in luce la Galeria Justiniana, a spese del Marchese Justianino, che si pretia un'opera nobilissima, e spero che capiterà fra pochi mesi qualche esemplare in Fiandra, ma ben credo che ogni frutta nova capita nel museo di V. S.'), quoted in I. Cotta, *Lettere italiane / Pietro Paolo Rubens* (Rome: Istituto della Enciclopedia Italiana, 1987), p. 486.

22   A. M. S. Logan, *The Cabinet of the Brothers Gerard and Jan Reynst* (Amsterdam: North Holland Publishing Company, 1979).

importance quickly gained by Howard's *Marmora Arundeliana* and followed by the *Galleria Giustiniana*. Once again, a precious piece of evidence concerning Howard's success comes from correspondence. This time it is a letter sent by Nicolas Fabri de Peiresc to the Frères Dupuy in 1629 which shows the growing desire to obtain a copy of this rare volume:

And when a copy of this book with the title Marmora Arundelliana arrives, via Holland or Germany, *I am dying for it*, I would be infinitely obliged if you would get me one, the sooner the better, and I am surprised that not one of your booksellers has taken care to order one from those places. Because it is a long time ago that one has been seen in Rome.[23]

On the basis of this document, nobody should wonder why – seven years after the Dupuy brothers received this letter – Rubens addressed his request for a copy of Giustiniani's *Galleria* to Monsieur Peiresc.

Even more interesting is the fact that, like Arundel, Giustiniani thought of another paper gallery devoted to his collection of paintings. Of the latter, we know only very few etchings, representing – among others – the *Virgin and Child* by Ludovico Carracci. The series dedicated to the Giustiniani paintings was never completed, probably because of the death of the collector in 1638. It should be stressed that Arundel and Giustiniani were actually the first collectors who thought to promote their galleries of paintings by means of printed catalogues. Strangely enough, scholars usually refer in this connection to the example of David Teniers's *Theatrum Pictorium* for Archduke Leopold (1658) as the first case of an illustrated catalogue of a collection of paintings. Economic reasons will have prevented patrons from commissioning engravings after their collections. In the Italian context, Pope Urban VIII Barberini has been considered as the

---

[23] 'Et quand il viendrà, soit par la Hollande, ou par l'Allemagne, quelque exemplaire de ce livre intitulé Marmora Arundelliana, *j'en suis si affamé*, que vous m'obligerez infiniment de m'en faire avoir un, le plustost qu' il se pourrà, m'estonnant que quelqu'un de voz libraires n'aye prins le soing d' en faire venir de ces lieux-là. Car il y a longtemps qu'on en a eu dans Rome'; P. Tamizey de Larroque (ed.), *Lettres de Peiresc aux frères Dupuy. Janvier 1629–décembre 1633*, Collection de documents inédits sur l'histoire de France, 2nd series (Paris: Impr. Nationale, 1890).

forerunner of this kind of commission.[24] Nevertheless, a deeper analysis of Arundel's and Giustiniani's experience would seem to allow us
to set the birth of the illustrated catalogue of collections of paintings at
least three decades earlier. Not only would I stress the significance of
the cultural path which clearly connects these extraordinary European
collectors, but I am also interested in investigating some similarities
between the two projects.

The notion of reproducing and documenting works of art is in a
way more typical of northern than Italian culture and comes from the
tradition of the books of sketches done by enthusiastic travellers, eager
to bring home the images of monuments which they could not possess
by other means. The practice of printing and publishing etchings after
original paintings and sculptures – an effective way of satisfying the
vanity of the powerful – is based on this tradition. That is why we
should not be surprised by the fact that a mutual influence seems
to connect northern and southern European countries, especially in
the case of the birth of the genre of the Museum Chartaceum. Clear
evidence of such a phenomenon is the fact that the main characters of
the story I am trying to tell frequently shared the same artists, namely
artisans who were particularly skilled in the art of illustration. This is
what happened in Rome, where a number of documents suggest that
the workshop active for Cassiano dal Pozzo was strongly connected
with the one which worked on the *Galleria Giustiniana* of Vincenzo
Giustiniani. There was a sort of osmosis between these two workshops.
Even more extraordinary is the fact that at least one of the artists
involved in the two projects, Anna Maria Vaiani, was called to London
to make some floral drawings for Lady Aletheia Arundel, wife of the
earl, Thomas Howard.

At a time when creating a collection began to be considered not
just as the acquisition of a social status but also as a cultural process
with a value of its own (a surplus-value, determined by the individual

---

[24] Cf. E. Borea, 'Stampa figurativa e pubblica dall'origine all'affermazione nel Cinquecento', in *Storia dell'arte italiana*, part I, vol. 2: *L'artista e il pubblico* (Turin: Einaudi,
1979), pp. 389–90. See also A. M. Talamo, 'I Gonzaga e le incisioni', in R. Morselli
(ed.), *Gonzaga. La Celeste Galeria. L'esercizio del collezionismo*, exhibition catalogue
(Milan: Skira, 2002), vol. 2, pp. 139–49, esp. p. 144.

contribution of the owner, who shapes the collection itself and thus creates a system of connections among the works of art which form the museum), there are a number of further conclusions we could draw. How could a collector preserve his principal 'work of art' (which means the result of his choices, taste, accumulation, compositions, and so on)? In Italy there was, first of all, a form of legal protection called *fidecommisso*: the mandatory rule under which, after the death of the owner, a collection passed to his elder son and thus prevented him from selling the heritage. Nevertheless, so many dangers could undermine the integrity of a collection, and the risk of dispersal was always possible. During the first half of the seventeenth century a tragic event quickly became a warning for all collectors in Europe: the sale of the celebrated Gonzaga collection to Charles I of England. We will later examine this extraordinary event and its consequences for cultural transmission, but I want to stress here the incredible, shocking effect which it had among the most famous collectors of the time. By selling one of the most spectacular collections ever assembled to the Flemish merchant Daniel Nys, Vincenzo Gonzaga II lost not only the possession of a vast number of masterpieces but, even worse, a unique web of mutual relations which were intertwined with the collection itself. The 'Celeste Galeria' in Mantua did not have any printed catalogue or series of engravings to document its content or appearance. The inventories compiled after the death of Vincenzo I, which are now an incomparable source for all those interested in studying the collection, were just legal documents, and were not intended to disseminate or promote the splendour of the museum. As a result, the precious but intangible masterpiece compiled over the course of about two centuries by the Gonzaga family was lost for ever.

We can hardly deny that such a dramatic event stirred the emotions of tactful museum-makers all over Europe: a mixture of envy (of the buyer, for the inestimable paintings sold) and sympathy (for the former owner) must have filled their minds. In my opinion, the creation of the first illustrated catalogues of museums was probably motivated by the desire for the collection to survive beyond the material proximity of its pieces: the ideal connecting link which had held the pieces of the puzzle together, at least in the brain that devised it.

THE LETTER IN IMAGE: COLLECTORS AND PAINTED
CORRESPONDENCE

In the diary he wrote during his Italian stay, the English traveller Richard Symonds took note of a portrait by Domenichino of the well-known collector Giovanni Battista Agucchi, holding a letter in his hands. It is possible that this painting, admired by Symonds in the collection of Francesco Angeloni, can be identified as the canvas now in the City Art Gallery of York[25] (fig. 9). The reddish-bearded, middle-aged man looks at the beholder, wearing a white shirt and black jacket and holding a letter whose content remains – unfortunately – illegible. As the identification of the man portrayed is taken for granted, we should instead wonder why he is represented in the act of reading his private correspondence, without any other hints which could enhance his social status and his appearance. No rings, no objects, not even items of furniture are represented to identify him: just his physical appearance against a bare black background. The painting is thus inhabited by two characters: the reader and the letter, the latter a wide, white sheet whose sharp folds are so clearly outlined that we can imagine the gestures required to open it.

The representation of letters in painting is certainly worth a proper study, as it appears to be quite a frequent topic in western art.[26] One can think of famous examples such as the many paintings by Johannes Vermeer representing young women reading or writing. Nevertheless, as Lipsius taught us, there are different kinds of letters, and there are therefore different kinds of painted letters too. Vermeer's characters are caught in private, intimate sketches of life: in those paintings, letters have the role of absorbing the total attention of the people portrayed and of enhancing our sense of being admitted to their private, secret, world. In Agucchi's portrait, on the contrary, the subject is looking at

---

[25] See the catalogue entry by R. E. Spear in C. Strinati and A. Tantillo (eds.), *Domenichino, 1581–1641*, exhibition catalogue (Milan: Electa, 1996), p. 420.

[26] But see the very interesting discussion of the topic in S. Alpers, *The Art of Describing: Dutch Art in the Seventeenth Century* (London: Murray, 1983), especially where the author quotes Carel van Mander's *Schilderboeck* with regard to 'letters as silent messengers'.

Fig. 9. Domenichino (or Annibale Carracci), portrait of Giovanni Battista Agucchi.
York Museums Trust (York Art Gallery)

us, as if he were reading the letter when he was momentarily distracted by our presence. The painter does not invite us to spy on the man portrayed; the letter has here a different function. It is a symbol, or rather, it is a status symbol. Giovanni Battista Agucchi is considered one of the most important theoreticians of seicento classicism and one of the principal sources of inspiration of Domenichino's art.[27] The

---

[27] S. Ginzburg Carignani, 'Domenichino e Giovanni Battista Agucchi', in Strinati and Tantillo (eds.), *Domenichino*, pp. 121–37.

bulk of his ideas on painting are contained in a treatise discovered by Sir Denis Mahon but also, and not by chance, in a very famous letter sent by Domenichino to the collector Francesco Angeloni in 1632.[28]

What I want to discuss here is the iconography of the painting in York: why would a scholar and art lover like Agucchi want to be represented reading a letter instead of, more traditionally, surrounded by precious canvases and antiquities or in a sophisticated posture? The association between patron and letter was, actually, quite frequent: one can think of famous cases such as the portrait of Pope Innocent X Pamphilij, painted by Velázquez holding a letter of presentation from the painter himself. In that case, the artist wanted – and the man portrayed allowed him – to establish a relationship game with his subject, inviting the beholder to witness the very moment of a private meeting. Again, a sketch of private life becomes public by means of the painting: in the Velázquez painting the paper is clearly readable and leaves no space for our interpretation. We can assume that, in Agucchi's portrait, it is the mere presence of the letter (which we are unable to read) and the very attitude of the reader that are sufficient to show the cultural engagement of the man portrayed. A precise relation between letters, in both their tangible and non-tangible form, and collecting may be recognised even in the representations of cabinets like Frans Francken II's *Art Gallery* (Vienna, Kunsthistorisches Museum, c.1636, fig. 10) where, in the foreground on the left, a folded letter is represented among coins, prints and shells. The presence of the letter is sufficient to allude to the huge web of contacts which allowed the creation of the collection itself. What we are here invited to think of is the fact that painted letters, in these specific contexts, assume the role of cultural status symbols, far from the connotation of love that they otherwise often have.

The letter can also function as a complement to the portrait itself. Lipsius wrote that letters allow us to keep in touch with people who are far from us, letting us know their very thoughts ('scriptum animi nuntium ad absentes aut quasi absentes'). As the portrait permits our image to travel and to join others without our actually moving, so the

---

[28] Bottari, *Raccolta di lettere*.

Fig. 10. Frans Francken II, *Art Gallery*. Vienna, Kunsthistorisches Museum

letter communicates our feelings, thoughts and desires everywhere. For this same reason letters often travelled along with portraits, conveying the image and soul of the sender.

FROM IMITATION TO APPROPRIATION: BUYING THE 'AURA' OF A MUSEUM

Modern studies have revealed a lot about the history of the Gonzaga collection in Mantua, especially with regard to the events which led to its sale and its eventual dispersal. It is well known that growing rumours concerning the sale of the collection spread all over Europe after the death of Federico Gonzaga. The news of the sale was received by the citizens of Mantua as a real tragedy; Vincenzo II quickly became a sort of devil in the eyes of many. From our perspective, what is most interesting is not the Italian reaction, but the participation of the English cultural circle that was closest to the king at the time he was handling the affair. The opportunity offered by Nys to Charles I was much more than that of buying the bulk of the most famous art collection in Europe: it constituted not just a number of authentic masterpieces, but the invaluable fascination of story and tradition, the fame of a family that had devoted its best energies to the creation of a museum.

There are many pieces of evidence which can be listed here to support this idea. First of all, it is extremely interesting that – on the occasion of her stay in Mantua in 1623 – Lady Aletheia Arundel asked for a wooden model of the Palazzo del Tè. We know that her mission to Mantua was aimed at investigating the possibility of buying the duke's collection, and it is now possible to argue that she was acting on behalf of the English court.[29] The interest of Aletheia in the setting of the collection within its original space gives us an extremely important clue to better understand the wide range of motivations which actually led to the acquisition of the museum. The idea of buying a collection not just to own the works it is composed of but also to gain possession of its order changes the traditional perspective of this kind of transaction. Charles I was eager to wear the cloak of dignity and austerity which only an Italian Renaissance collection (the most famous in the world) could give him. Keeping this idea in mind, we should also remember that in these very years, Charles received from Sir Richard Wynn a detailed description of the Escorial collection: this is just a further demonstration of the deep desire of the king to emulate absolute examples of princely collecting.[30]

But how was it possible to maintain quite unaltered and for such a long period the 'aura' of a collection which had never been reproduced in print and whose pieces could hardly be copied? How was it possible to nourish the thirst for information concerning this unique mass of masterpieces? Travellers and official visitors could

---

[29] L. Whitaker, 'L'accoglienza della collezione Gonzaga in Inghilterra', in Morselli (ed.), *Gonzaga. La Celeste Galeria*, vol. 2, pp. 233–49.

[30] Cf. Lightbown, 'Charles I and the tradition', esp. p. 64.

certainly contribute to enhancing the curiosity surrounding the Gonzaga gallery, but the role of correspondence was certainly much wider and played a major part in defining the collection as an absolute model for all collectors.

The incredible story of the Gonzaga collection appears, in the particular context of the transmission and translation of patterns, as a multifaceted phenomenon. In fact, not only were the Gonzagas able to create something absolutely unique in the history of collecting, attracting the attention of all art lovers and collectors in Europe, but they also showed an extraordinary sensibility towards different models of collections. More than his predecessors, Duke Vincenzo Gonzaga I (1587–1612) tried to emulate the example of the Habsburg collections, particularly Rudolph II's in Prague, Archduke Ferdinand's in Schloss Ambras, and Philip II's at the Escorial. Such unusual attention to foreign models led Vincenzo to show a deeper interest in northern painting and to summon artists from the (southern) Netherlands (Pieter Paul Rubens, Frans Pourbus).

The irresistible appeal of Italian collections attracted not only the English court but, generally speaking, the most important European aristocracies. We can take the example of France, where – with the exception of François I – a tradition of collecting only began during the reign of Maria de' Medici in the 1620s.[31] Schnapper has argued that, although the interest of French monarchs in art was after this time much closer to the Italian model, it cannot be denied that in their view painting was just a minor aspect of patronage and that, in the economy of a cultural project aimed at enhancing the authority of the crown, sustaining an ambitious architectural policy was a more effective strategy.[32] Nevertheless, we cannot ignore the fact that, in creating a sort of

[31] P. Bassani Pacht and T. Crépin-Leblond (eds.), *Marie de Médicis: un gouvernement par les arts*, exhibition catalogue (Paris: Somogy, 2003).

[32] A. Schnapper, 'The king of France as collector in the seventeenth century', in R. I. Rotberg and T. K. Rabb (eds.), *Art and History: Images and their Meaning* (Cambridge: Cambridge University Press, 1986), pp. 185–202, esp. p. 198: 'The collecting of paintings, then, was a brief interlude in the King's long reign, and by no means his most important royal artistic activity. Paintings were considered a suitable adornment of a great king, but contributed to his glory only in a vague, indefinite way, especially when compared with buildings.'

museum in the Galerie des Ambassadeurs (or Galerie de Diane) in the Louvre between 1666 and 1671, the royal patron chose as a decoration a copy of the Farnese Gallery in the Palazzo Farnese in Rome, while a select variety of paintings by the most appreciated Italian Renaissance and Baroque masters was hung on the walls. Schnapper mentions this episode of Louis XIV's patronage as a clear demonstration of the fact that the king did not consider collecting as a means of propaganda: this would be the reason why in the context of an 'international space' like the Galerie des Ambassadeurs the king chose Italian works of art instead of promoting French national painting. On the contrary, it should be considered that such a choice (certainly not a fortuitous one) could hide a precise desire to emulate the model of the Italian collection, a model which at this time had become international. As they walked through the gallery, foreign visitors would appreciate the eclectic and open-minded taste of the king, who could be proud to show such extraordinary masterpieces in his residence.

Even more, the setting of the Galerie des Ambassadeurs also appears as the definition of an international taste which significantly matches Italian tradition, and this not just in terms of quality or style but also as an appropriate choice aimed at avoiding other cultural alliances that might be difficult to justify or to maintain. At this time the Italian states had lost any autonomous political power: the celebration of Venetian or Tuscan painting would hardly suggest approaches of a different nature other than simply cultural. That is why showing Italian pictures in an extra-territorial space like the Galerie des Ambassadeurs (which it was important to maintain as a neutral space) was the safest way to avoid both self-celebration and any suggestion of partnership with other nations.

It would be easy, at this point, to conclude that – in the context of a mutual and incessant system of transmission of models which seems to span a large part of the old continent – Italy played a major role as the *alma mater* of the collecting of paintings and antiquities but even more as the historical and uncontested holder of the dignity and nobility of a superior 'aura'; at the same time, Italian collectors could not avoid looking at the rest of Europe which held the fascination of an effective and active aristocracy, with crowned heads of state.

In the light of these considerations, we should now consider the role played by written correspondence in the creation and mostly in the preservation of the patterns described. Letters could keep alive the tradition of collections that had disappeared in reality but still survived in the minds of buyers and amateurs. It was mainly thanks to the transmission of written information that a high level of interest in general cultural patterns, but also even in remote but specific collections, could be maintained for a long time. In fact, not only was the sale of the whole Gonzaga collection mainly conducted by means of correspondence; later, the fame of the paintings involved was kept alive largely thanks to the tom-tom signals produced by the exchange of letters among scholars and merchants. It is not a question of the simple use of correspondence in the international art market; dealers and artists often specialised in the field of foreign art and they were obviously used to obtaining their information and making their offers by letter. What I would like to stress is that the circulation of letters, especially in the Lipsian format of 'docta' and 'seria', would enhance the aura of ideal and real models of collecting (in the specific case of the present section: the genre of the Italian gallery, as adopted at the Louvre, and the actual case of the Mantuan 'Celeste Galleria').

PROMOTING YOURSELF AS A COLLECTOR: *CABINETS D'AMATEURS* AS AN INSTRUMENT OF PROPAGANDA

During the very first years of the seventeenth century, a new kind of genre appears in Flemish painting: the representation of real or invented collections, which soon becomes a sort of specialisation for artists particularly skilled in the reproduction of details and in realistic imitations. It cannot be denied that such a bizarre fashion was closely connected with the evolution of the practice of collecting. Furthermore, we should also realise that the genre of the *cabinet d'amateur* painting was born in Flanders, a country which was a newcomer to the field of collections.

Commissioners of this kind of work were mostly members of the *haute bourgeoisie*: rich people eager to rise to the ranks of the highest levels of society, who needed to promote themselves in order to be accepted by the aristocracy. This is the main reason why many of these paintings not only reproduce walls filled with canvases but also represent visits of important people (kings, when possible) to these private galleries. In this perspective, the *cabinet d'amateur* becomes a sort of a real-life photograph taken to attest the entry of the owner to the Olympus of patrons and collectors. For us, it is also important to realise that in establishing the characteristics of this kind of painting, artists (and patrons with them) used to imitate the model of the Italian gallery of art in the form that had been imported to Flanders by Pieter Paul Rubens.[33] Furthermore, it is also a fact that most of the paintings represented on the walls of the *cabinets* are works of Italian Renaissance and Baroque masters. It has been recently pointed out that, in the famous painting that Willem van Haecht did for Cornelis van der Geest, *The Studio of Apelles* (The Hague, Mauritshuis), the commissioner (and collector) intended to imitate the famous Gonzaga collection in Mantua. Among the many paintings owned by Van der Geest, the painter inserted some famous masterpieces which were actually kept in the Gonzaga gallery.[34]

As the genre of the *cabinet d'amateur* painting is a specific product of the Flemish area, we should try to reach some conclusions concerning its connections with the rest of the European tradition. The *cabinet d'amateur* is, first of all, the portrait of a collector and his museum. If we want to make a comparison between this kind of portrait and the traditional model of paintings representing collectors, we immediately notice a remarkable difference: the *cabinet d'amateur* insists mostly on the quantity of pieces and tries to dazzle the viewer by displaying a huge number of masterpieces, even trying to challenge his skill as a connoisseur by inviting him to recognise the paintings so beautifully

---

[33] J. M. Muller, *Rubens: The Artist as a Collector* (Princeton, NJ: Princeton University Press, 1989), and, more recently K. Lohse Belkin and F. Healy (eds.), *A House of Art: Rubens as Collector*, exhibition catalogue (Antwerp: Rubenshuis and Rubenianum, 2004).

[34] A. M. Ambrosini Massari, 'La solitudine dei capolavori', in Morselli (ed.), *Gonzaga. La Celeste Galeria*, vol. 2, pp. 1–38, esp. p. 1 ('Diventare come uno dei Gonzaga, i più grandi collezionisti d'Europa: a tanto doveva aspirare Cornelis Van der Gheest quando Willem Van Haecht dipinse per lui *L'atelier di Apelle*, ... un modello assoluto di raccolta d'arte e di collezionismo e anche un'aspirazione sociale . . .').

reproduced in the canvas; the 'traditional' portrait shows the collector mostly as a nobleman, tactful and inspired, and gives the viewer just a few clues to recognise the nature of his passion: one or two objects (a mere coin, a bust, a marble) to evoke an entire collection.

The *cabinet d'amateur* marks, in a sense, a vulgarisation of the practice of collecting and its entry into the marketplace: the painting becomes a sort of (real or invented) catalogue and is often commissioned in order to promote the collection and its owner. This aspect becomes particularly interesting if we realise that in the sixteenth and seventeenth centuries Antwerp was the main centre of production of copies after famous works of art (paintings, specifically).[35] The *cabinet d'amateur* could be considered as the promotion of an imaginary gallery, which you could probably create by simply commissioning (at an affordable price) decent copies after the originals from the specialists in the field. Patrons and collectors debated the permission to imitate the precious originals held in their private residences: an indiscriminate reproduction of images corrupted the aura and reduced the value of the paintings. On the other hand, in the eyes of the middle class – mostly composed of ambitious bourgeois wanting to breathe the precious atmosphere of a princely collection – a gallery of imitations would not appear so dull and offensive. The existence of such a lively market of copies was probably largely supposed to satisfy the desires of these capricious but easygoing patrons. Even famous collections had, of course, plenty of imitations, but it must be stressed how meticulous the descriptions of copies were in the inventories of such museums: the Giustiniani inventory of 1638 even distinguishes between copies made directly after the original and copies of unknown manufacture.

Coming back to the main topic of this chapter, I strongly believe that the birth of the bourgeois galleries also involved a severe change

---

[35] The presence of copies in seventeenth-century collections was considered normal. We should remember this fact in order to better understand the sense of the *cabinet d'amateur* genre. In some cases, it is possible that – far from the ambitious idea of realising imaginary collections filled with masterpieces which were actually held in different collections – these paintings represent the actual contents of *quadrerie* which included copies of famous canvases and panels.

in the close relation we have been outlining between collecting and correspondence. When the practice of creating 'ready-made' museums became established, with the consequence of denying or simply bypassing the importance of the uniqueness of museums, the role of correspondence decreased. The visual transmission of collecting patterns evidenced in the paintings of *cabinets d'amateurs* signals a commercial approach which does not need the subtle and sophisticated connections required by the previous era.

GRAPHIC SIGNS: FROM MEANS TO ITEMS

The breadth of the topic I have been trying to outline in this chapter led me to take into consideration different aspects of the letter in terms of meaning and function but also in terms of material content. I want now to conclude by coming back to the phenomenon I mentioned at the beginning, with regard to the importance accorded the correspondence in Kircher's museum. When we deal with letters, we should always remember that we are talking about graphic signs on paper. There is, thus, a visual aspect that should not be forgotten.[36] In the internet era we are more and more appreciating the value of correspondence 'on paper': receiving material letters becomes all the more special just because of the feelings which calligraphy is still able to produce. The emotions provoked by letters through their capacity to convey signs produced by human hands were equally strong in the past. A touching letter sent by Lipsius to his close friend Plantijn in 1589, who was dying at the time, clarifies the concept I am unfolding: 'never has a letter of yours brought more pleasure or heaviness than this last one. *I kissed your writing repeatedly, written by your feeble hand...*'.[37] Like footprints left by our feet on the ground, writings are signs of thoughts imprinted on the paper by our hands. In this way, letters become simulacra of our feelings and establish a contact which is far from being simply sensible

---

[36] On the 'visual value' of letters see the considerations of Comenius (cf. Alpers, *The Art of Describing*).

[37] 'Languida manu scriptionem tuam nimis exosculatus sum ....' See Morford, *Stoics and Neostoics*.

but which is also sensorial (in the sense of being visible, tactile and thus material).

In their objective value as items, letters established a relation with the practice of collecting which is very different from the patterns we have discussed up to now: in some cases letters actually entered the collections as things to be preserved for their unique value as historical and most of all human documents. A particular interest soon developed in letters written by artists, so that a specific kind of collecting focused on this research from the seventeenth century on.[38] The phenomenon did not involve only artists' correspondence but represented, apparently, a general transformation or development of the function and meaning of letters: from mainly being a means of communication to being items of material and unique value. As a result, the instrument which had permitted, or at least helped, the formation of many collections itself became a collectible. The desire to possess (rare specimens, precious works of art) and to create something of unique value (the collection) involved the appreciation of the historical, but still sentimental, value of letters.

[38] It has been estimated that Cesare Malvasia possessed about 900 letters of artists. Cf. G. Perini, 'Le lettere degli artisti da strumento di comunicazione, a documento, a cimelio', in E. Cropper, G. Perini and F. Solinas (eds.), *Documentary Culture: Florence and Rome from Grand-Duke Ferdinand I to Pope Alexander VII* (Bologna: Nuova Alfa Editoriale, 1992), pp. 165–83.

PART III

Uses and meanings of correspondence: noblemen, peasants, spies

CHAPTER 8

The political correspondence of Albuquerque and Cortés

Francisco Bethencourt

Qué importa que el entendimiento se adelante si el corazón se queda?

Baltasar Gracián

Political correspondence reveals the agency of different powers, the purposes and positions of the agents involved in different levels of political administration, the type of relationship established between them (close or distant, intimate or professional, symmetrical or hierarchical) and the tension between role-playing and the writer's real feelings. While chronicles provide a superficial sequence of so-called major events, political correspondence discloses decision-making processes where forms of persuasion, creation of trust, definition of priorities, expectations and demands are all at stake. Sometimes, the culture of specific political organisations can be better defined through the analysis of correspondence, where forms of action, jurisdictional limits and hierarchical control are all inscribed.

Comparing the correspondence of Albuquerque and Cortés to their respective kings reveals much about the European political atmosphere in the first quarter of the sixteenth century, during the process of expansion undertaken by both main Iberian powers, Portugal and Castile. In fact, both sets of letters already define the main issues involved in the foundation and development of the two empires. Albuquerque and Cortés offer two invaluably rich case studies, because they not only acted as conquerors but also reflected on the political issues resulting from their actions. Cortés fought for political legitimacy, Albuquerque for political support. But they shared a common inheritance, even if they belonged to different traditions of expansion and dealt with different realities in the field. The initial phase of European expansion cannot be treated as a peripheral and compartmentalised area of early modern history, but must be brought into the centre of historiography because it shaped Europe more than nationalistic academic divisions recognise. Our focus is not on the history of American or Asian people affected by European expansion, but on European history, and more specifically on correspondence as a major tool of European cultural exchange.

Between 1510 and 1515, Albuquerque conquered Goa (a main port on India's west coast), Malacca (the key port of south-eastern Asia, controlling the passage from the Indian Ocean to the Pacific Ocean) and Hormuz (an island which dominated the maritime trade of the Persian Gulf) for the Portuguese crown, thereby establishing the basic network which structured the Portuguese Empire in Asia for over a century.[1] In 1521, Cortés conquered the Aztec 'empire', enlarging the area dominated by the Spaniards in Central and North America in the following years. He established a pattern of dominion over local populations and territories that lasted several centuries, even if the modes and forms of control were soon changed through the crown's decisive intervention.[2]

The founders of these Iberian empires were acting in the same conjuncture, even if Albuquerque preceded his counterpart by more than a decade, a fact that corresponds to the generational gap between them. They had totally different social backgrounds and political training. Albuquerque belonged to the high nobility of Portugal: his great-grandfather had been head secretary to King João I (1385–1433), and his grandfather and father had held the most senior positions in the royal court. Afonso de Albuquerque himself was born around 1460 in Alhandra, in the province of Lisbon and raised in the household of King Afonso V (1438–81) as a companion to Prince John (future King João II, 1481–95). He belonged to the prince's personal guard and fought with him in Castile at the battle of Toro (1476). He later

[1] Albuquerque has few biographers. See the useful but uncritical synthesis by Geneviève Bouchon, *Albuquerque: le lion des mers d'Asie* (Paris: Editions Desjonquères, 1992).

[2] For a very accurate biography, see José Luis Martínez, *Hernán Cortés* (Mexico: Fondo de Cultura Económica, 1990).

participated in the naval expedition to relieve Otranto from a Turkish siege (1480), and served the king in the captaincies of North Africa, participating in the constant fighting against local Muslim powers. In 1503, King Manuel (1495–1521) sent Albuquerque to India for the first time as captain of a small fleet of three ships. In 1506, he returned to India as captain of five ships, with the official mission of reconnoitring the Red Sea and the Persian Gulf, and the secret mission of succeeding the first governor of India, Francisco de Almeida, appointed in 1505 for a three-year term. Albuquerque never returned to Portugal, dying in 1515.

In contrast, Cortés was born into minor nobility around 1485 in Medellín, near Badajoz, in the province of Extremadura; his father was probably a squire. He had no real attachments to the royal court – a cousin and royal official, Francisco Núñes, agreed to become his legal representative to the emperor – and was trained as a notary in Salamanca or Valladolid. Cortés's first post in Hispaniola, after arriving with an expedition under its new governor Nicolás de Ovando in 1505, was as notary of the new city of Azúa, where he obtained a house and land. In 1511, he accompanied Diego Velázquez, entrusted by Admiral Diego Colón with the conquest and government of Cuba, maintaining his function as notary in the new city of Santiago, where he was twice nominated *alcalde* (military governor). Nobody could have predicted that Charles V would one day appoint him governor and captain-general of New Spain, or that he would be elevated to the high nobility of Spain under the title of Marquis del Valle de Oaxaca. In 1547, Cortés died in Castilleja de la Cuesta, near Seville, leaving a huge patrimony in Mexico.

POLITICAL SUPPORT

The correspondence between Afonso de Albuquerque and King Manuel was intense.[3] There are 116 extant letters from Albuquerque,

---

[3] Bulhão Pato and Henrique Lopes de Mendonça (eds.), *Cartas de Affonso de Albuquerque, seguidas de documentos que as elucidam*, 7 vols. (Lisbon: Academia Real das Sciencias, 1884–1935).

written between 1507 and 1515; nearly all are in complete form, with just three summaries. Three letters were written in 1507, nine in 1510, fifteen in 1512, twenty-seven in 1513, fifty-seven in 1514, and three in 1515; two have no date. Understandably, Albuquerque's correspondence increased significantly after assuming governmental power in October 1509, and there is an obvious lack of some correspondence from previous years, when Albuquerque was fighting to assert his authority over the first viceroy who refused to leave the job for a full year, until Marshal Fernando Coutinho arrived from Portugal to reinforce successive orders from the king. Only twelve letters survive from Manuel to Albuquerque; the total number was clearly much higher, probably about the same as those received, because Albuquerque replied to numerous questions or comments from the king, who sent several packs of letters, entrusted to different captains, in every fleet of the *carreira da Índia*. The lost letters written by Albuquerque can also be reconstituted through chronicles, mainly the history of his actions in India composed by his only (illegitimate) son and heir, Brás de Albuquerque.[4]

Throughout the year, Albuquerque dictated notes for the future letters to his secretaries, reporting on the political problems he faced or narrating events in which he was involved, including military actions. Most of his letters are dated October or November, because they took their final form during the last months before the annual fleet departed for Lisbon, generally in December or at the latest in January. Despite the vast number of accumulated letters (the fifty-seven from 1514 must have been close to the real annual average), we must keep in mind that they were sent only once a year and generally took six months to

---

[4] João de Barros, *Ásia*, ed. António Baião and Luís F. Lindley Cintra, 2 vols. (Lisbon: Imprensa Nacional, 1932–74); Fernão Lopes de Castanheda, *História do descobrimento e conquista da Índia pelos portugueses*, ed. M. Lopes de Almeida, 2 vols. (Porto: Lello, 1979); Gaspar Correia, *Lendas da Índia*, 4 vols., ed. M. Lopes de Almeida (Porto: Lello, 1975); Damião de Góis, *Chronica do felicissimo rei Dom Emanuel*, 4 vols. (Lisbon: Francisco Correia, 1566–7); Jerónimo Osório, *De rebus Emmanuelis regis Lusitaniae invictissimi virtute et auspicio gestis* (Lisbon: António Gonçalves, 1571; translated into French in 1581 and English in 1752); Brás de Albuquerque, *Commentaries of the Great Afonso de Albuquerque* (original Portuguese edition 1557), trans. Walter de Gary Birch, 4 vols. (London: Hakluyt Society, 1875–80).

reach Europe. Monsoons complicated matters further; their rhythms imposed a gap of twenty months in the elapsed time of communication between Lisbon and Goa. In a standard voyage, the fleet sailed from Lisbon in March and arrived at Goa in September. It could not start its return journey until December, reaching Lisbon in June. Thus King Manuel could only reply to Albuquerque's letters in March of the following year and his wishes would not be known until September. The result of this real-time distance was that royal reactions to important events, already reported with considerable delay, sometimes remained unknown two years after they happened. Within this cycle of communication, the king or the governor could use the traditional land routes from Europe to India via the Middle East for truly urgent information.

A governor thus had an extraordinary margin for decision-making which could be abused, as in the case of the first viceroy, Francisco de Almeida. Yet governors or captains were also in a position of weakness during a crisis of authority, for example when Albuquerque was imprisoned by his rival. We know that Albuquerque wrote the king careful reports about all his actions in Oman and the Persian Gulf in August and September 1507, when he destroyed or subjugated six ports, including Musqat and Hormuz. In January 1508, Albuquerque faced a major crisis after his captains deserted and sailed to India without notice, leaving him with only three ships to oppose the rebellious city of Hormuz and a strong Muslim fleet. In February 1508, Albuquerque reported these events to the viceroy in three letters, asking that the captains who had forced him to withdraw be punished.[5] Although he also wrote a complaint to the Portuguese king, only these letters have survived. The captains deserted because their long stay in Hormuz prevented them from intercepting the rich traffic to Mecca in the Red Sea, and from benefiting from loading the *carreira da Índia* in Cochin. They also complained about receiving no benefit from the tribute paid to the Portuguese king by Hormuz, and argued that Albuquerque could not hold them for such a long time while involved in a fierce dispute with the vizier of Hormuz, Khâja Atâ, over building a fort which was against the viceroy's strategy.

[5]   *Cartas*, vol. 1, pp. 6–19.

This was a typical conflict of interests. Albuquerque wanted to complete the fort in Hormuz, but had no intention of returning to India before the first viceroy's governorship ended in October 1508. Even when forced to withdraw from Hormuz, he sailed to the island of Socotra under pretext of rescuing its Portuguese garrison and stayed in the region for several months, until a new fleet arrived from Portugal, allowing him to return to the Gulf with more ships, manpower and artillery. He obviously had no intention of giving up his political and military autonomy from the Portuguese king to operate in that region; Albuquerque only remembered hierarchy when his captains fled to the viceroy, putting his entire operation at risk. The captains presumably understood Albuquerque's hidden agenda, which would have forced them into war for another year and a half without sufficient reward. The runaway captains managed to win protection from the viceroy, who needed their support to counter news of Albuquerque's appointment as his successor. Accepting the charges brought by the deserting captains against their captain-general, Almeida started legal proceedings and sent a messenger to Hormuz to relieve Albuquerque of his command.

Divergent political strategies over the means of Portuguese expansion in India during the first twenty years of the sixteenth century underpinned this conflict of interests. Almeida, supported by some captains and officials, preferred a strategy of exclusively maritime warfare to gain control over interregional and long-distance trade. Meanwhile, Albuquerque adopted the opposite strategy, arguing that maritime control could not be achieved without domination over key ports; access to the spice market and the subjection of major ports could never be secured through maritime power alone. The forts built at Cochin, Cannanore and Quilon to protect trade after the destruction of the Portuguese factory at Calicut in 1500 already defined a middle course between maritime trade and military presence on the coast through the construction of strongholds. However, the precarious situation of these forts, which depended on local alliances, became abundantly clear at Hormuz, where Albuquerque faced fierce local resistance to his projected fortress; indeed, he had to abandon it after most of his captains broke away. At the end of 1509, the destruction of the Portuguese factory in Malacca, compelling its captain to retreat and leaving several Portuguese imprisoned by the sultan, strengthened arguments in favour of increased military action. In January 1510, the defeat of the Portuguese troops in Calicut was a major blow that defined Albuquerque's subsequent strategy.

Although the letters that Albuquerque wrote the king explaining the defeat at Calicut have been lost, the chronicles suggest their content, since Albuquerque emerges from the event completely blameless. They report that Marshal Fernando Coutinho insisted on destroying the city, claiming that he had precise orders from the king to do so. Coutinho asked for help from Albuquerque, who used all his ships and military forces in the operation. Due to the marshal's failures as a military commander, their landing at Calicut was quite chaotic. Coutinho wanted to be in the front line and had a violent argument with Albuquerque, who watched the first groups of Portuguese land in disorderly fashion and engage in military action with the local troops. The marshal rejected Albuquerque's advice to rest before assaulting the city. Instead, having landed far away, he and his troops had to make an exhausting hour-long march along the beach to the city. Nonetheless, they managed to force their way in. Coutinho, depicted as a stubborn, arrogant and unfit man who had to be carried by two soldiers, rested in the sabay's palace while his troops sacked the city and burned the main buildings. After several unheeded warnings, Albuquerque personally had to order the marshal's immediate withdrawal because the Portuguese were outnumbered by local reinforcements. Their retreat was chaotic; the marshal was killed along with several Portuguese noblemen among a total of eighty Portuguese fatalities. Albuquerque managed to escape, but his left arm was severely wounded.[6]

It was Albuquerque's first military action as India's governor. Even if the fleet remained untouched and only a minority of the troops had been killed (most of them the marshal's dependants), Albuquerque had received a major blow to his pride and knew that Portuguese prestige in India had been shaken. What amazes us is the speed of his recovery,

---

[6] Barros, *Ásia*, vol. 2, bk. IV, ch. 1; Lopes de Castanheda, *História do descobrimento*, bk. III, chs. 1–3; Gaspar Correia, *Lendas da Índia*, vol. 2, chs. 1–3.

as also happened after Cortés was expelled from Tenochtitlán. Albuquerque immediately proposed an alliance with the King of Vijayanagara to defeat the sabay of Calicut while reorganising his fleet and troops for renewed military action – this time in the Red Sea, as King Manuel had instructed. In February 1510, already en route to Socotra, Albuquerque learned from local people that there were Turkish troops in Goa, provoking dissension between Hindus and Muslims. These Hindu mediators offered their assistance for a military operation. After consulting the captains of the fleet, Albuquerque decided to change course and invade Goa, which surrendered immediately. However, expelled by the reaction of Idal Khan, the regional ruler, Albuquerque stayed in Goa's waters with his fleet until he could pass the bar, which only happened in August. After waiting for new reinforcements from Portugal in Cannanore, he organised a new fleet with twenty-three ships and 2,000 men and successfully re-invaded Goa in November 1510.

In this period, Albuquerque's correspondence is quite scarce, with no reports on the first conquest and retreat from Goa. His first known letters to the king were written from Cannanore and dated 16, 17 and 19 October 1510, before sailing to Goa.[7] He justified the conquest of Goa by arguing that it was essential for Portuguese security in India, because of the constant presence of Turkish troops (a 'defensive' argument used by all politicians engaged in military offensives to this day). He emphasised Goa's agricultural wealth – it could feed an army more easily than other ports – its industrial shipbuilding capacity from specialised craftsmen, and its position as a main trading port for wood, iron and saltpetre. As we know, the official decision to conquer Goa was taken in February 1510. The final conquest, on 25 November 1510, happened just in time to send the news back via the *carreira da Índia* ships anchored at Cochin. His final letter of that year, written on 22 December, mentions a previous long report on the conquest of Goa, adding details about persecuting the Turks, the alliance with local 'gentiles', administrative decisions, military booty sent to the king, and the marriage of more than 200 Portuguese men

[7] *Cartas*, vol. 1, pp. 19–25.

with (unwillingly) converted Muslim women, whom he described as 'white and good-looking'.[8]

The arguments in favour of the operation and the final result of the military actions were sent with the same fleet, and the king's reaction would not be known in India before September 1512, although news travelled fast through the Middle East. Albuquerque thus enjoyed a huge autonomy to take extremely dangerous decisions, which threatened the very existence of the Portuguese 'enterprise' in India. In the meantime, he was much more dependent on approval from his captains than from his king. But because royal approval was ultimately essential for keeping his office and maintaining his authority, Albuquerque's letters to the king gave detailed information about his military and diplomatic actions, the political situation in the Indian Ocean, and various administrative and commercial problems. He needed to persuade King Manuel of his mastery of intelligence, strategic vision, commercial wisdom, and decision-making capacity. Briefly, he needed political support to implement his vision of 'Portuguese India'.

The conquest of Goa proved an ambiguous achievement. Albuquerque's activities in the Persian Gulf during 1507 could be justified as implementations of direct instructions from the king (previously convinced by Albuquerque himself), but the conquest of Goa had not been mentioned in any royal instructions. Although Albuquerque managed to assert his political authority in India in the eyes of the other powers and also of the Portuguese, he still faced strong criticism over the political and financial impact of his achievement. Albuquerque's letters before and after the conquest demonstrate a full awareness of the criticisms addressed to the king by the captain, factor, vicar and secretary of Cochin, who viewed the possible transfer of Portugal's political, commercial and financial centre to Goa as a threat.[9] They pointed out the excessive expenses involved in maintaining troops and keeping the territory under control. Thus, the conquest of Goa renewed an old divide between those favouring a commercial enterprise, based on military control of the maritime trade routes (and permanent corsair booty) and those favouring the conquest of key

---

[8] *Ibid.*, p. 27.   [9] *Cartas*, vol. 3, pp. 48–51, 337–56, 380–406.

ports to reinforce a monopoly of maritime trade, with a *Pax Lusitana* based on permanent offices distributed by the king or the governor.

Even before its conquest, the political battle was to convince the king to maintain Goa. This is obvious from the letters written by Albuquerque early in November 1510, before the final invasion. He drew up a global blueprint for the future Portuguese presence in India, advising the king to conquer four key ports (Aden, Diu, Hormuz and Goa), build four factories (Khambhat, Hormuz, Cochin and Malacca), and use three ports to load ships (Cochin, Cannanore and Quilon).[10] Albuquerque explicitly contested the arguments in favour of a Portuguese presence in India based strictly on naval power, stating that it involved immense cost for reduced results, leaving the factories permanently vulnerable. He insisted that territorial conquest would generate increased financial resources, as well as better distribution of manpower and military resources. He maintained pressure on the king to send arms, mainly spears, pikes and shields, more men, and 'Swiss captains' to discipline the troops. Most of Albuquerque's requests were satisfied, including Swiss-style captains and German canon-makers and operators,[11] allowing him to develop military campaigns during the most intense period of Portuguese conquests in the Indian Ocean. However, Albuquerque's political position was not secure, and he bitterly felt the criticism from high officials in Cochin.

In view of this political context, and given his real-time distance from Portugal, Albuquerque's decision to conquer Malacca, implemented in July 1511, comes as no surprise. He was exploiting the conquest of Goa, which obviously galvanised his soldiers, but he was also deliberately creating another *fait accompli* to avoid any possible royal decision to abandon territorial conquest. In this case, he disobeyed explicit orders from the king, who had sent Diogo Mendes de Vasconcelos with a small fleet to end the conflict around the factory in Malacca. First Albuquerque used Vasconcelos's troops and ships to conquer Goa, then left Vasconcelos as captain in Goa and decided to command the conquest of Malacca himself. This time, his critics emphasised the way Albuquerque abandoned the factories in India,

[10] *Cartas*, vol. 1, p. 419. [11] *Ibid.*, pp. 83, 105.

removing troops and making the Portuguese enterprise vulnerable – similar criticisms to those levelled at Cortés when he decided to explore Central America. There is another gap in the corpus of letters written by Albuquerque, despite some indication that he sent the king a report about the conquest of Malacca in October 1511. His letter to the king in April 1512 is a bitter one; for the first time, he criticised officials in Cochin (and Goa) for not executing his orders to maintain and repair the ships left, for opposing marriages between Portuguese men and local women, for allowing Portuguese to escape to enemy territory, and for deliberately damaging his authority by spreading rumours of the arrival of a new governor.

For the first time, Albuquerque even made a veiled criticism of the king, lamenting his preference for defending territories conquered by his predecessors over the new acquisitions that augmented the king's reputation.[12] Albuquerque was obviously referring to the North African forts, which King Manuel was launching major efforts to consolidate and expand in 1513 and 1514. The governor was well informed in India, even if he exaggerated his information for propaganda purposes. The same letter further criticised the king for his contradictory instructions, such as restricting war and making peace with the Muslims while simultaneously ordering forts to be built and maritime trade with Jeddah, Mecca and Cairo to be destroyed.

Albuquerque's letters to the king between August and December 1512 showed their author in a mellow mood. In recognition and reward for the conquest of Goa, Albuquerque had been made a member of the royal council; moreover, he had received substantial reinforcements of men and arms, allowing him to plan new expeditions. He replied to several enquiries on administrative appointments, revealing the king's intention to monopolise the power of appointment. Albuquerque also reported on the provision of forts such as Cochin, and the destruction of the fort at Socotra, which he had suggested to the king. Having decided to expose the incompetence of the royal factor at Cochin, Albuquerque also wrote extensively about commercial matters like the loading of the *carreira da Índia*. He developed his vision of the

---

[12] *Ibid.*, pp. 33–4.

future of Portuguese rule in India, providing new information on the political situation in the region and responding to royal instructions to block maritime trade to the Red Sea. In addition, he reported the conquest of a fort near Goa, which could threaten the city's security. Finally, he insisted on correcting the real number of the Portuguese in India: there were 1,200 before the arrival of the fleet in 1512, most of them without arms.

His mood had changed radically in his letters written between November 1513 and January 1514. In March 1513, Albuquerque had been defeated in Aden; worse still, when he returned to Goa in September, he received several letters from the king, who apparently accused him of bad management and of abandoning India for the conquest of Malacca. The king summoned a council of all the captains and high officials to hear their opinions on maintaining Goa, and forbade further weddings between Portuguese men and local women. These instructions, which explicitly contradicted his policies, exasperated Albuquerque. Weddings were an important issue; to Albuquerque, they were a sign to natives that the Portuguese wanted to settle permanently. It had political importance; Albuquerque's correspondence clearly recognised that the Portuguese did not have the 'strength' (here meaning manpower) to build a structured power in India without local alliances involving native people. His policy of weddings, launched immediately after the conquest of Goa and offering rewards (lands, rents, jobs) for these new couples, was a practical expression of Albuquerque's vision for a future *Estado da Índia*. If opposition to this policy revealed deep racism against local women, Albuquerque replied at the same level, maintaining that the weddings involved only white Muslim and Brahman women and not 'morally corrupt' (*sic*) black Hindu women.[13]

In April 1512, Albuquerque reported that there were 200 (mixed) couples in Goa and another 100 in Cochin and Cannanore. His purpose was to create a new Christian elite who would gradually control land and property, while his opposition maintained a policy which envisioned a purely Portuguese maritime enterprise. Acknowledging

[13] *Ibid.*, pp. 27, 31, 63, 338.

the king's express order, the governor declared that no new weddings would take place.[14] Yet the issue was not closed, because the king returned to it the following year; and Albuquerque, while submitting again to his orders, offered new arguments in support of his previous policy. Moreover, he found an interesting solution: new mixed weddings would occur only with rich widows, to avoid scandals, where royal finances were not at stake.[15] This is a typical example of how the governor could twist a direct order from the king, because what is implicit is that if there was no involvement of royal finances, such weddings could take place.

Albuquerque implicitly made the link between this racist issue and Jews in a letter dated 1513: 'I wish to know', he asked, 'if you consider it to be in your service to let Castilian and Portuguese Jews circulate in India via Cairo, or if Your Highness wants me to snuff them out [*apagar*] one by one wherever I find them.'[16] This brutal phrase must be understood within an extremely tense political context, because the Portuguese captains and governors of the *Estado da Índia*, including Albuquerque, always used Jews as informants and translators. Comparing this phrase with others written by Albuquerque – for instance, when he outrageously asked the king whether new appointments should be examined by himself or by his critics[17] – enables us to conclude that this is a clear case of Albuquerque's speaking freely in order to express contempt for royal policies.

Autumn 1513 marked a turning point in Albuquerque's relationship with his critics. Deciding that the time for dissimulation and soft words was over, he openly denounced the captains and high officials at Cochin and Cannanore who were involved in the intrigue against him as liars, incompetent, traitors and corrupt. Moreover, he accused them of revealing secrets of the *Estado da Índia*, serving the interests of the Rajah of Cochin, being paid by Muslims, and using royal revenues for their own profit and trade.[18] His letters make it clear that Albuquerque had decided to strike back and attack officials who opposed his policies. He announced to the king that he had removed Duarte Barbosa, the

[14] *Ibid*, p. 191.   [15] *Ibid*., p. 298.   [16] *Ibid*., p. 244.
[17] *Ibid*., p. 187.   [18] *Ibid*. pp. 122–32.

factor of Cannanore and ringleader of all the revolts, from his office.[19] He wrote that if he had had the monarch's complete trust, he would have placed the heads of those officials on the walls of Calicut, but he had been forced to restrain himself because they had royal support.[20] In his last letter, written on 1 January 1514, Albuquerque revealed that he had found the 'mine' that drafted the letters which his critics had sent to the king. He expressed surprise that they dared to write so many lies, and directly criticised the king for encouraging dissent, saying that he was only surprised that with such informants, the king had not decided to 'burn' the entire enterprise. Albuquerque's reaction to those documents revealed his character: he organised an assembly of noblemen and officials, and published those letters accusing him of the worst crimes. António Real, captain of Cochin, after swearing on the Gospels that these letters contained only lies, accused two other accomplices, Diogo Pereira (the royal factor) and Gaspar Pereira (the governor's royally appointed secretary).[21]

This move was quite risky, because Albuquerque was explicitly attacking high officials with royal protection. Yet he had no choice, because the survival of his government and of his policies was at stake. Perhaps he knew that the king's character was vulnerable to political pressure: certainly King Manuel's policies offer an example of zigzagging imposed by a balance of power, not only in overseas expansion, but also in his policies towards Jews and 'New Christians'.[22] His decision to smash the 'Cochin group' (which represented a matter of personal interest, not just an expression of divergent political strategy)[23] was a victory for Albuquerque, because maintaining his conquests would never again be disputed. However, the eventual price was his replacement. Albuquerque's letters went further, implicitly railing against the king's right to appoint officials in India; he complained that he could

[19] *Ibid.*, p. 134.   [20] *Ibid.*, p. 137.   [21] *Ibid.*, p. 260.

[22] Francisco Bethencourt, 'A expulsão dos judeu', in Diogo Ramada Curto (ed.), *O Tempo de Vasco da Gama* (Lisbon: Difel, 1998), pp. 271–80.

[23] This criticism is directed against the anachronistic interpretation of Inácio Guerreiro and Vítor Luís Gaspar Rodrigues, 'O "grupo de Cochim" e a oposição a Afonso de Albuquerque', *Studia* 51 (1992), 119–44, opposing the 'Cochin group' as an expression of a 'liberal' or 'free-trade' policy, to Albuquerque's 'state-oriented' policy, even defined as an 'authoritarian state' aiming to 'conquer the Muslim empire'.

not even nominate a ship's notary, because every position, from the captain of a fort to a notary, was appointed by the king[24] – although in the same letters Albuquerque reported his appointments of captains for both ships and forts.

Taking control of the new offices created by Asian conquests, King Manuel decided to appoint new men who, on arrival in India, would replace the captains and factors appointed by Albuquerque. One can easily imagine the conflicts aroused by this practice. The governor rewarded men who had fought and sometimes been wounded in India with new responsibilities, which they must relinquish to new arrivals from Portugal. The political struggle was a very common one: the king wanted to assert his power at a great distance by controlling the main source of authority, the creation of offices and the appointment of clients; meanwhile, Albuquerque, as governor, could make rapid nominations to avoid a power vacuum and remove other people from office on the grounds of incompetence. However, there were political limits on the governor's autonomy, especially if he wanted to stay in office beyond the traditional three-year mandate. Albuquerque stated in one letter that he wished to die in India serving the king, and also dramatised his reduced powers, while assuring the king that all royal appointments had been provided.[25]

The king also established some control over administrative issues by reducing Albuquerque's autonomy while increasing the authority of captains and factors. All twelve known letters from the king focus on such administrative issues, filled with minutiae about appointments, payment of salaries and distribution of such privileges as private space in the royal navy for carrying merchandise. Although a king should ideally think in strategic terms, it is undeniable that such constant pressure on the governor of the *Estado da Índia* implied the establishment of a permanent hierarchy and respect for different competences and regular administrative procedures. This explains why Albuquerque was never in charge of the *carreira da Índia*, which was instead the responsibility of the royal factor in Cochin. The governor was even supposed to avoid Cochin when the ships were loaded – a measure

[24] *Cartas*, vol. 1, p. 142.   [25] *Ibid.*, p. 185.

that Albuquerque accepted gladly, because it gave him an opportunity to undertake new expeditions and escape local intrigue. Nonetheless, he still managed to inform the king about such matters as the administration of tribute, war booty and rents from conquered territories. The problem was that the king was not totally coherent. He accepted the intrusion of senior officials in the governor's policies and asked the governor to guarantee the good loading of the *carreira da Índia*. This latitude allowed Albuquerque to criticise the royal factors' incompetence, make long reports on trade, and even advise the king that he would be better off being robbed by two Florentines than served by his factors.[26]

The main issue in the set of letters from autumn 1513 was the meeting about maintaining Goa. Albuquerque was obviously furious, but nevertheless dealt with the problem with political tact. He informed the king that he had executed the consultation exactly as ordered, but he could not hold a public council that would provoke unrest and threaten the preservation of the *Estado da Índia*. Instead, he asked for an oath of secrecy from all captains, one by one, who were asked to write and sign their opinion on the subject. If the matter was discussed at a public council, he as governor would have to present his opinion and thereby influence some people. He reminded the king that the conquest of Goa had been decided only after four consultations with the captains, who had signed documents (which Albuquerque had already sent) in favour of the enterprise.[27] Interestingly, this procedure killed the issue, and was significantly complemented in the following years by the removal of his main critics.

One of those letters records the defeat at Aden. Albuquerque described his attempt to take the castle and the destruction of the ladders, isolating the Portuguese who had already scaled the walls. He blamed his ultimate withdrawal on a lack of military equipment; but the question is why Albuquerque did not make a clear breach by bombarding the walls, as his captains suggested after the attack failed. He also indicated the vulnerability of future actions because of the absence of water around Aden. After Albuquerque's expedition burned all the

---

[26] *Ibid.*, p. 155.　　　[27] *Ibid.*, p. 184.

ships anchored at Aden, his fleet became the first European military force to enter the Red Sea. Making the island of Kamaran his centre of operations, Albuquerque sent a caravel to explore the archipelagos of Dahlak and Suakin. He included several descriptions of the area to complete his report on the political situation on both banks from Aden to Suez. Albuquerque's writing skills are evident in this report, which managed to transform a military defeat into a useful operation in which a Portuguese fleet blockaded maritime traffic in the Red Sea, provoking huge damage at Jeddah, Mecca and Cairo. He advertised the future uses of the information gathered in the Red Sea; he further proposed to return to Aden and build a fort at Massawa, which was controlled by Muslims but situated near the kingdom of Prester John.[28]

It was probably during these dark days in autumn 1513 that Albuquerque wrote letters to Duarte Galvão and Martinho de Castelo Branco, his greatest friends at the Portuguese court. He complained about intrigues, defended himself against such accusations as neglecting India to conquer Malacca, and argued that any decision to abandon Goa should be taken only after the king sent four major advisers to see the city's value for themselves. Albuquerque also elaborated on the military and diplomatic strategies he proposed for India.[29]

His correspondence from autumn 1514 reveals a certain appeasement. News of the king's approval of the conquest of Malacca must have had a major impact on Albuquerque's mood.[30] Making an important reinforcement in Albuquerque's authority, the king had authorised the governor to fill certain administrative and military posts,[31] allowing Albuquerque to distribute privileges in the king's name up to the considerable value of 8,000 *cruzados* per year. The governor thanked the king for this major favour in colourful language: 'people felt I had better face and better eyes' ('pareceu à gente que eu tinha melhor rosto e melhores olhos') and 'I now look more beautiful, and people work better to please me' ('lhes pareço já agora mais formoso, e se trabalham mais por me comprazer').[32] The king also elevated

---

[28] *Ibid.*, pp. 209–39.   [29] *Ibid.*, pp. 395–414.   [30] *Ibid.*, pp. 304–5.
[31] *Ibid.*, p. 363.   [32] *Ibid.*, pp. 294 and 363.

António Fonseca, Albuquerque's private secretary, to the status of royal esquire.[33] In a relaxed way, Albuquerque could point out to the king that the galardões (new positions and privileges) created by the expansion in India 'remove many obligations from you' ('vos tiram de muita obrigação'),[34] underlining the role of the conquests in the king's distributive functions of rewarding vassals and reinforcing patronage ties.

His reinforced prestige at court encouraged Albuquerque to pursue his critics. He wrote a long letter accusing Gaspar Pereira, the royally appointed governor's secretary, of taking bribes from notaries and (like the 'Cochin group') loading ships with his own copper and pepper against royal regulations. Albuquerque described Pereira's many shortcomings as secretary in order to justify his decision to expel him from office and send him back to Lisbon.[35] Pereira's disgrace had the king's implicit authorisation, since he left Albuquerque free to decide the matter as he wished, and asked his opinion about naming a new secretary. In response, Albuquerque requested someone virtuous and competent, who gave good advice and kept secrecy, to be appointed.[36] Yet the governor did not dare punish his critics in India further. He wanted to marginalise the 'Cochin group' in public opinion,[37] remove them from office and send them back to Lisbon, defining a paradigm of action for future governors.

Obviously affected by his defeat at Aden, for the first time Albuquerque stayed in India for almost eighteen months, from September 1513 to February 1515. In autumn 1513, he negotiated peace with the new sabay of Calicut, despite opposition from the captain and senior officials in Cochin. Albuquerque defended this act by showing the contradictions in previous royal instructions on the matter, and eventually obtained royal approval. Albuquerque now worked mostly as a diplomat and as a politician who wanted to control his administration in India. He reported extensively on commercial matters, recommending

---

[33] Ibid., p. 292.   [34] Ibid., p. 293.   [35] Ibid., p. 291.   [36] Ibid., pp. 284–9.

[37] Bernard Guenée, L'opinion publique à la fin du moyen Age, d'après la 'Chronique de Charles VI' du Religieux de Saint Denis (Paris: Perrin, 2002), proves that 'public opinion' was not an invention of the Enlightenment, but existed since at least the Middle Ages.

lists of products to be sent to different ports, and gave new advice on negotiations at Khambhat, Surat, Sofala, Pegu and Sumatra. While improving administrative methods and introducing greater control over rents and tribute, Albuquerque never stopped criticising the king for trusting his trade and factories to courtiers rather than intelligent and knowledgeable merchants.[38]

During this period, Albuquerque reacted strongly against any slur on his reputation. One charge levelled at him by the 'Cochin group' was the supposed sale of slaves to men who would marry them; he immediately opened an inquiry to clear his name.[39] In November 1514, Albuquerque revealed that he had decided to sail to the Persian Gulf instead of the Red Sea, as he had previously said,[40] in order to take supplies to people at the factory and consolidate Portugal's grip on an island which he considered the key to India. He expressed himself thus: 'I am determined to sail to Hormuz to find the means to eat' ('estou determinado cometer o caminho d'Ormuz para termos que comer'), meaning that he intended to increase revenues and achieve Portuguese economic self-sufficiency in India. He was proved correct, because Hormuz remained one of the most profitable factories in the *Estado da Índia* until 1622, when it was invaded by the British in coalition with Persian forces.[41]

Albuquerque's final period in India was essentially characterised by administrative reorganisation. He replaced Pereira with Pero Alpoim, whom the king had sent as an *ouvidor* (judge). This position was given back to Vasco de Vilhena, member of the Order of Christ and 'good Latinist' ('homem latino').[42] The governor also decided to remove Garcia Coelho, notary of the royal finances in Cochin, accusing him of corruption and mismanagement, and appointing Pero Barreto to replace him.[43] Albuquerque also intervened in favour of

---

[38] *Cartas*, vol. 1, p. 274.   [39] *Ibid.*, p. 337.   [40] *Ibid.*, pp. 345–6.

[41] Vitorino Magalhães Godinho, *Les finances de l'état Portugais des Indes Orientales (1517–1635)* (Paris: Fundação Calouste Gulbenkian, 1982); Francisco Bethencourt, 'O Estado da Índia', in Francisco Bethencourt and Kirti Chaudhuri (eds.), *História da expansão portuguesa*, vol. 2 (Lisbon: Círculo de Leitores, 1998), esp. pp. 294–303 on receipts and expenses.

[42] *Cartas*, vol. 1, pp. 351–2.   [43] *Ibid.*, pp. 364–5.

Pero Alvares, who was married to his niece but had been ignored in royal appointments.[44] The most significant letter of the year concerned Albuquerque's own advancement. He complained that despite thirty-eight years of military service (since 1476, at the battle of Toro) he had never obtained the reward he deserved from successive kings and declared that his conquests in India should be motive enough for the king to elevate his status: 'ela por si obriga Vossa Alteza fazerdes grande quem assim conquistou'.[45] It is obvious that Albuquerque wanted a noble title because he boasted that he already possessed a coat of arms and lineage. But in contrast to Cortés, who had a much humbler social background, Albuquerque never received a title. Albuquerque was the anchor and founder of a grandiose but insecure enterprise, whose questionable merits would change radically over time. He could not have imagined the standard practice in the seventeenth and eighteenth centuries, when viceroys negotiated new titles with the king before accepting the post.

Albuquerque wrote only three letters to the king in autumn 1515. The first, dated September, reported the construction of the fort at Hormuz and the administrative situation in the *Estado da Índia*, including a list of ships' captains; the second was a recommendation on behalf of one of his captains; the last, written on his way back to Goa and dated 6 December 1515, reported his suffering and was dictated from his death-bed. One of the shortest letters he ever wrote to the king, it declared that he was going to die, leaving only his (illegitimate) son 'for his memory' and declaring him his sole heir. Albuquerque asked the king to transfer his *tenças* (rents on royal revenues) to his son and make him a grandee, thereby compensating for the service that he himself, the governor, had given in India. Albuquerque briefly referred to his achievements: 'the things from India will speak for me . . . I leave it with the main heads conquered, in your power, with no open issue except control of the strait [Red Sea].'[46]

Since at least the beginning of November, Albuquerque had known that he had been replaced in the government of India by one of his enemies, Lopo Soares de Albergaria. Reportedly, he even received a

[44] *Ibid.*, pp. 353–5.   [45] *Ibid.*, p. 360.   [46] *Ibid.*, pp. 380–1.

letter from the ambassador of Shah Ismael inviting him to become a leading lord in Persia.[47] Albuquerque's illness was reported as early as September 1515. Feeling himself near death, he drew up his will, appointed the captain and senior officials of Hormuz, and organised a final council with his captains to decide the main matters affecting the *Estado da Índia*. He died within sight of Goa. His body, dressed in the habit of the Order of Santiago, was carried in procession beneath its pall to the chapel of *Nossa Senhora da Conceição*, followed by all the noblemen, clergy and people in a highly emotional scene of mourning and weeping. The 'gentiles' were reported as saying 'it could not be that he was dead, but that God had needed him for some war and had therefore sent for him'.[48]

King Manuel's zigzagging policies continued, still trapped by the constraints of real-time communication between Lisbon and Goa. Hearing rumours that the Sultan of Cairo was preparing a huge army to prevent the conquest of Hormuz, he organised a new fleet for India in March 1516, dispatching a letter to the new governor ordering that Albuquerque, if he was still in India, should remain as commander-in-chief of the troops facing the sultan's army. According to this letter, Lopo Soares de Albergaria would become governor of Cochin and Malacca, with control over the *carreira da Índia*, while Afonso de Albuquerque would be the governor of all other forts, with control over the army.[49] Albuquerque's death prevented certain dissent in the *Estado da Índia*.

In the six years of his government, Albuquerque never managed to win solid or consistent political support from the king, but he could nevertheless implement the policies he defined in the field, imposing them on the royal court. Albuquerque also failed to obtain a title for himself or his son Brás, although he only requested one at quite a late stage. Renamed Afonso by the king, Brás received 180,000 *cruzados*, part of the huge amount of money that the crown owed his father, plus a permanent *tença* of 300,000 *réis* annually. This man of letters wrote a biography of his father the governor, built two famous Italian-style

[47] Brás de Albuquerque, *Commentaries*, vol. 4, p. 195.
[48] *Ibid.*, p. 198.   [49] *Ibid.*, pp. 200–4; *Cartas*, vol. 4, pp. 30–1.

palaces (*Casa dos Bicos* in Lisbon and *Quinta da Bacalhoa* in Azeitão), was employed on diplomatic missions and became president of the Lisbon senate. Although Afonso de Albuquerque never benefited personally from his conquests, his descendents or 'clan' (families to which he was connected, like the future dukes of Aveiro and counts of Linhares) occupied the highest posts at the royal court as well as in India, Brazil and Africa.

POLITICAL LEGITIMACY

The standard edition of letters sent by Cortés to Emperor Charles V consists of five long reports written between July 1519 and September 1526.[50] The second, third and fourth letters were printed almost immediately in Castilian, then rapidly disseminated throughout Europe in Latin, Italian, German, French and Flemish. Cortés's letters were reprinted in the following centuries, but with a hiatus in Spain from 1525 until 1749 due to a royal order dated March 1527, prohibiting their publication and sale.[51] The first and the last letters were discovered only in the nineteenth century, defining the standard one-volume edition.

The first *carta de relación* was not printed in Spain by Cortés's agents because it was disguised as a letter from the new municipal council of Vera Cruz, a mainland community created by Cortés's expedition 'in the name of the king' to evade the political hierarchy and legal control of the governor of Cuba, Diego Velázquez. This first step revealed Cortés's intelligence and his knowledge of medieval Castilian laws, which recognised communities' autonomous initiative to create their own settlements and request recognition from the king. Having been

---

[50] Hernán Cortés, *Letters from Mexico*, ed. Anthony Pagden, introd. by J. H. Elliott, 2nd edn (New Haven: Yale University Press, 1986); *Cartas de Relación*, ed. Angel Delgado Gómez (Madrid: Castalia, 1993). Both editions boast extremely accurate introductions, notes and comments, with a good critical approach. For an extended edition of letters by and to Cortés, including government decisions, instructions, petitions and succession documents, see Hernán Cortés, *Cartas y documentos*, ed. Mario Hernández Sanchez Barba (Mexico: Porrua, 1963).

[51] Marcel Bataillon, 'Hernán Cortés, autor proibido', in *Libro Jubilar de Alfonso Reyes* (Mexico: Porrúa, 1963), pp. 77–82.

'elected' by his men as judge and captain, Cortés could address the emperor directly on behalf of that community, signing the letter alongside Alonso de Avila and Alonso de Grado, its 'elected' treasurer and financial supervisor 'of the king'. The *relación* was dated 10 July 1519 (five months after setting sail from Cuba) and reached the emperor in Valladolid at the beginning of April 1520. This delay cannot be attributed to the great distance between Mexico and Spain: Cortés's agents (Alonso Fernández Puerto Carrero and Francisco Montejo) embarked at Vera Cruz on 16 July and arrived at Sanlucar de Barrameda, Seville's seaport, in early October. They would have completed the standard two-month return trip had they not stopped over in Cuba, against their instructions. Although the real-time distance from Mexico to Seville (via Vera Cruz, which soon became Mexico's key port) was considerably less than the real-time distance from Goa to Lisbon (aggravated by the monsoon season), it still took several years to organise a regular circuit of communication. The subsequent five-month wait before Cortés's agents met the emperor was partly due to their ship and freight, including gifts for the king, being confiscated by the *Casa de Contratación* in Seville. The institution had accepted a request to do this from Velázquez's chaplain, who was in the city and accused Cortés and his men of robbery and betrayal. Cortés's agents had to convince the emperor's staff of the seriousness of their purpose.

Puerto Carrero and Montejo, assisted by Martín Cortés, the *conquistador*'s father, were acting in a politically complicated period. Charles V had summoned the *Cortes* (parliament or assembly of the three orders) to Santiago de Compostela, near La Coruña, where he would embark for Flanders and, from there, travel to Aachen, where he would be invested as emperor. The king's absence, combined with the threat of Spain's political subordination to imperial concerns, spread discontent in both Castile and Aragon; it reached a climax some months after Charles's departure with the outbreak of the *Comunero* revolt in Castile, and a year later with the *Germanías* revolt in Valencia and the Balearic Islands. Despite the tangle of conflicting political issues at that particular conjuncture, Cortés's agents (presumably aided by rumours of the wealth involved) managed to obtain the release of the ship and its freight. When they were finally granted a meeting, the gifts they had brought (which included pure gold, huge sculpted gold and silver plates, and a large quantity of jewellery, feather-work and cloth) had already been delivered to the emperor, who took them with him to Flanders. In Brussels, they were apparently exhibited to a select group of people, including Albrecht Dürer, who called them the most wonderful objects he had ever seen.[52]

The impact of these 'marvels' should not be underestimated: in sending Charles V all his best 'acquisitions', Cortés had made the correct decision. Although Puerto Carrero and Montejo failed to obtain the emperor's support for Cortés's project, they did manage to have the accusation of treason suspended, despite protests from the governor of Cuba, supported at court by Juan Rodríguez de Fonseca, Bishop of Burgos, the councillor responsible for affairs in the Indies, thus keeping the emperor 'neutral' while awaiting the final result of Cortés's enterprise.

Thus the first letter must be placed in conjunction with the objects sent at the same time and with the agents who reported the facts and made its text 'real'. This first communication between Cortés and the emperor offers an excellent example of 'multimedia' propaganda, enacted simultaneously through text, visual art and oral testimony. At its very beginning, the letter directly addressed the information about the recently discovered land (Yucatán) given to the emperor by the governor of Cuba and dismissed it as inaccurate. It then described the failure of two previous expeditions to explore the region, and continued by exposing Diego Velázquez's intrigues to obtain the rights to explore and conquer from the governors of Santo Domingo and the royal court, accusing him of cupidity, only being interested in plunder,

---

[52] Albrecht Dürer, *Diary of his Journey to the Netherlands, 1520–1521*, ed. J.-A. Goris and G. Marlier (London: Lund Humphries, 1971), p. 64: 'I saw the things which have been brought to the king from the new land of gold, a sun all of gold a whole fathom broad, and a moon all of silver of the same size, also two rooms full of the armour of the people there, and all manner of wondrous weapons of theirs, harness and darts, very strange clothing, beds, and all kinds of wonderful objects of human use, much better worth seeing than prodigies. These things were all so precious that they are valued at 100,000 florins. All the days of my life I have seen nothing that rejoiced my heart so much as these things, for I saw amongst them wonderful works of art, and I marvelled at the subtle ingenia of men in foreign lands.'

and claiming investments in ships and equipment which mostly belonged to the navigators. The letter then described Cortés's expedition, with its careful exploration of the coasts of Yucatán and Mexico before deciding to land at a place now called Vera Cruz. The self-image projected by Cortés was carefully composed to display him as a serious explorer who established fair relationships with indigenous people, who kept his word, avoided plundering and gathered information. He was also presented as a pious man wishing to spread Christ's message, a responsible captain who risked his expedition to save the lives of countrymen captured by Indians, a good subject who systematically imposed vassalage to his king, and a soldier who defeated resistance with military determination. In a word, he emerged as a man guided by service to the king, not self-interest.

The foundation of the new city of Vera Cruz was depicted as a collective act which the captain accepted. The letter stated that the *cabildo* (municipal council) read the powers and instructions given by Diego Velázquez and decided that they were no longer valid. Cortés saw his previous status revoked by the *cabildo* and was promptly reinvested as judge and captain to maintain peace and government in the king's name. Naturally, the letter explained why Cortés had been chosen: he had experience of service in the islands, and had exercised his responsibilities to general satisfaction; he had invested all his money in the expedition, but shown no interest in material gain, only in royal service. The *relación* then clarified his legal rupture from the governor of Cuba: 'we [the *cabildo*] received him in Your Royal name, into our council and chamber, as chief justice and captain of Your Royal armies, and so he is and shall remain until Your Majesties [Queen Juana and her son, King Charles] provide whatever is suitable to Your service'.[53] The letter then declared that they had decided to send all the first spoils from the land (not just the fifth part, which by law belonged to the crown) as a demonstration of their satisfaction in serving the king.

The last part of the letter addressed the issue of the concessions demanded by Velázquez, asking the king to deny or to revoke them

[53] *Letters from Mexico*, pp. 27–8.

because the greedy governor of Cuba would never have sent the king the objects they had 'acquired' and offered. They further accused him of the bad administration of justice in the islands and unfair division of the Indians, demanding an inspection (*residencia*) of his activities in order to remove him from his office. Claiming their status as settlers in a new land, the *cabildo* requested the king to provide 'a decree and letters-patent in favour of Fernando Cortés . . . so that he may govern us with justice until this land is conquered and pacified, and for as long as Your Majesties may see fit'.[54]

The second letter, dated 30 October 1520, was already signed by Cortés as 'Captain-General of New Spain'. The significant designation chosen for the land by the *conquistador* appeared here for the first time, in a clear projection of the Roman and medieval geographical concept of Iberia (Hispania). In this letter, written at Segura de la Frontera, the second town created by Spaniards in Mexico, Cortés addressed King Charles as 'most invincible Emperor' and immediately established a parallel between the size and richness of the lands he was conquering and the Holy Roman Empire: 'One might call oneself the Emperor of this kingdom with no less glory than that of Germany, which, by the Grace of God, Your Sacred Majesty already possesses.'[55] He justified his long silence by claiming that he had no news from the agents he had dispatched to the royal court, and that he had been occupied in conquering and pacifying the land. Obviously, communication between the New World and Castile was not yet well established.

The *relación* disclosed Cortés's project to conquer the territories ruled by Montezuma.[56] The *conquistadores* had established an alliance with the people of Cempoal, the native city dominating the region around Vera Cruz, who decided to join the Castilians and break their

[54] *Ibid.*, p. 39.   [55] *Ibid.*, p. 48.
[56] To deconstruct Cortés's *relaciones* as systematic political manipulation, see Inga Clendinnen, 'Cortés, signs, and the conquest of Mexico', in Anthony Grafton and Ann Blair (eds.), *The Transmission of Culture in Early Modern Europe* (Philadelphia: University of Pennsylvania Press, 1990), pp. 87–130. I do not share all the author's interpretations of Cortés's psychology or his (mis)understanding of local signs. Here I am simply trying to analyse the meaning of the narrative within a European intellectual and political framework.

ties with Montezuma. On 16 August 1519, Cortés began an expedition to Tenochtitlán; his main purposes were to destabilise the peripheries of the 'empire', as he had done at Cempoal, and build alliances to overthrow Montezuma. This explains why Cortés engaged in perpetual fights with local peoples in order to subjugate them and break their previous allegiance. His alliance with the people of Tlaxcala, after a series of battles in which he defeated the local army, proved crucial, because this was the only regional territory independent of Mexica rule. By now, Montezuma was aware of Cortés's presence and the disruption he was provoking in the territories of the Triple Alliance, and consequently sent an embassy with gifts. According to the *relación*, the ambassadors, greatly impressed by Tlaxcala's submission to Cortés, accepted vassalage to Charles V and offered tribute to avoid the entrance of Castilian troops into Tenochtitlán.

Resisting the pressure from the embassy, Cortés proceeded with his expedition to Tenochtitlán; Cholula, the holy city of the Triple Alliance, became his next target. It was taken only after thousands of men had been exterminated under the pretext of a plot to kill Cortés and his troops. Five thousand Indians from Tlaxcala and 400 from Cempoal fought alongside the Castilian troops, a clear indication of a coming attack on Tenochtitlán, where Cortés used Indians from every province he had conquered. Local conspiracies and the troops gathered around Cholula offered sufficient pretexts for accusing Montezuma of duplicity, threatening him with a devastating war and demanding that he clearly submit to Charles V. The letter depicted Montezuma's position as a defensive one from the very start, employing diplomatic rather than military skills to convince Cortés to abandon his plan, an approach maintained until he was in sight of Tenochtitlán at the beginning of November 1519.

The reception given to Cortés by Montezuma and the Mexica nobility outside Tenochtitlán formed an important part of this *relación*;[57] political ritual was used to express self-representation, define hierarchies and project perceptions of power. Cortés did not perform the native ceremonies of greeting, but merely stood and watched them

[57] *Letters from Mexico*, pp. 84–5.

as the main recipient. By that time, he must have been aware of most rituals; ignoring local habits and displaying distance in such a theatrical arena was a decisive political decision. Moreover, Cortés underlined his superior position by sitting on a horse. When Montezuma approached, Cortés dismounted and advanced to embrace him – a gesture which clearly placed him at the same level as the Mexica ruler ('Great Speaker King', *Uei Tlatoani*, in Nahuatl). The two lords next to Montezuma prevented Cortés from actually touching their leader. Then Montezuma, these two leading lords and the Mexica nobility greeted Cortés one by one, and kissed the earth. Montezuma's brother took the *conquistador* by the arm, while the ruler went ahead with the other lord. During the procession, Cortés managed to communicate with Montezuma by taking a necklace of pearls and cut glass he was wearing and placing it round the Mexica ruler's neck. Montezuma returned the gesture, ordering two necklaces to be brought and also placing them round Cortés's neck. If accurate, this description means that Montezuma accepted Cortés as a leader of approximately equivalent status. Probably, Cortés composed this description of the entry into Tenochtitlán[58] to show Charles V how respected he was and how well he represented the emperor.

The narrative of the meeting between Cortés and Montezuma at the palace prepared for the *conquistador* has become a hotly disputed piece of rhetoric. Cortés staged a speech in which Montezuma stated that his people were foreigners in that land, that the lord who had brought them there came back later, and asked them to return home. However, the lord's request had been rejected and his authority denied. Yet, his people knew that one day the descendents of that lord would return to conquer the land and make them vassals. He, Montezuma, believed that Cortés was the representative of their natural lord, whom he agreed to obey faithfully. He indicated that the main signs were the 'fact' that Cortés knew of their existence and that he came from the direction where the sun rose. Then Montezuma tried to convince Cortés of his

---

[58] The narrative in Bernal Diaz del Castillo, *Historia verdadera de la conquista de la Nueva España*, ed. Luis Sáinz de Medrano (Barcelona: Planeta, 1992), ch. 88, pp. 251–2, reveals the presence of Doña Marina (Malinche) as Cortés's translator and makes the greeting ceremony less personal.

good will, denying the rumours spread by his enemies that he believed he was a god and lived in a golden palace. Although it would have been difficult for Cortés to invent every piece of the narrative, it is undeniable that this legend became instrumental in his strategy to convince Charles V of his acceptance by the Mexica ruler, and also in his strategy to provoke discontent among natives against Montezuma, who supposedly confessed a doubtful legitimacy. As Anthony Pagden has pointed out, it is extremely unlikely that Montezuma ever raised his clothing and showed his body, grasping his arms and trunk and saying 'see that I am flesh and blood like you and all other men, and I am mortal and substantial'.[59]

In fact, Cortés acted as the new ruler. Exploiting old news about two Spaniards killed at Nautla (renamed Almería) by a local lord, he demanded that Montezuma arrest this vassal and those responsible for their deaths (already avenged by Castilian troops from Vera Cruz, who completely destroyed the city). Montezuma complied, sending troops to imprison local leaders and bring them back. As a guarantee, Cortés imposed the *Uei Tlatoani*'s detention in the palace which the Spaniards occupied. The local leaders (Qualpopoca, his son, and fifteen other people) were handed over to Cortés, who interrogated and then burned them in the main square, an act which astonished the natives. The fact that this occurred without public unrest expressed Cortés's total control. Under torture, the accused finally confessed Montezuma's involvement in the plot against the Spaniards, justifying Cortés's close control over the *Uei Tlatoani*, who became a prisoner and puppet of the *conquistador*.

Thus, a collective public execution became a founding moment defining a transfer of real power. Cortés had a strong sense of the impact of rituals and used them effectively. His next step, he reported to Charles V, was to announce 'publicly to all the natives, the chiefs as well as those who came to see me, that it was Your Majesty's wish that Mutezuma remain in power, acknowledging the sovereignty which Your Highness held over him, and that they could best serve Your Highness by obeying him and holding him for their lord, as they had

[59] *Letters from Mexico*, p. 86, and Pagden's comments, pp. 467–9.

done before I came to this land'.[60] Reinstating Montezuma's power through the will of (and dependency on) the foreign conquerors, in front of his own people, was the crowning piece in the process of deconsecrating and demoralising the ruler of Mexica. Afterwards, not only were the peripheries of the Mexica confederacy in open rebellion, but the centre itself had been disrupted.

This *relación* reflected a difficult and unsustainable coexistence between the two powers in Tenochtitlán. Formal power (and daily administration) remained with Montezuma, but Cortés acted as a representative of his suzerain. The letter demonstrates how Cortés tried to extend these boundaries back, demanding more and more from Montezuma, who strangely complied with all these requests: expeditions to the gold fields, including Spaniards who collected samples; mapping every river and cove along the coast, a task carried out by native cartographers; Spanish expeditions to explore different provinces, searching for places to establish cities; and suppressing a revolt (the first against both Cortés and Montezuma) in the province of Alcolhuacán. After imprisoning this rebellious lord, Montezuma summoned an assembly of every lord in the Aztec confederacy. This produced a second piece of contested rhetoric, in which he supposedly transferred power explicitly to Cortés by asking his vassals to obey him.[61] Immediately after this ceremony, Cortés demanded (still through Montezuma) that every lord pay a tribute to Charles V in gold, silver, jewellery, precious stones and featherwork. Spanish pressure extended to include religion when Cortés asked Montezuma to abolish idolatry and adopt the Christian faith. He received another fantastic answer: that Spaniards might well know best, having recently arrived from the original land, while they (the Mexica) were not natives and might have lost the purity of faith.[62] 'Idols' were then removed and sacrifices forbidden, introducing major disorder in local practices and beliefs.

[60] *Ibid.*, p. 91.
[61] *Ibid.*, pp. 98–9. Montezuma supposedly reproduced the same legend about the return of the first lord.
[62] *Ibid.*, p. 106.

This strange cohabitation lasted almost six months, from November 1519 to May 1520. It was disrupted only by the arrival of Panfilo de Narvaez's expedition to the coast, containing eighteen ships carrying over 800 well-armed men. Narvaez, representing the governor of Cuba, claimed to be the legitimate lieutenant-general and demanded that Cortés surrender as a rebel. In his letter to Charles V, Cortés explained the perils of this internal conflict between Spaniards in a country already subjugated to the emperor, with its ruler captured and its gold and jewels collected and awaiting shipment to Spain. He reported a first breakdown in this peace, claiming that rebellious Indians in coastal places such as Cempoal were taking Narvaez's side. With a typical manipulation of events, Cortés accused Narvaez of negotiating the detention of the Spaniards with Montezuma, so that he, Narvaez, could leave the land afterwards. After an unsuccessful exchange of emissaries, Cortés had to abandon Tenochtitlán and face his internal enemies. He started by contesting Narvaez's legitimacy, accusing him of lacking a royal decree to impose a transfer of power. Cortés further accused Narvaez of usurpation, treason and rebellion against the emperor, and commanded the newly arrived men to abandon such a commander. Finally, he managed to surprise Narvaez in his own camp and capture him, causing the troops to switch their allegiance.[63] This proved crucial, because the revolt had spread; although Cortés did not report the massacre of native noblemen perpetrated by Pedro de Alvarado in Tenochtitlán during the *Toxcatl* feast, which triggered it, the Spaniards in Tenochtitlán had been attacked and were now under siege. However, the entrance of Cortés and his men into the city did not solve the problem: it seemed as if the Mexica waited for his return to launch a major offensive and annihilate them all.

This time, Cortés's combination of resistance and diplomacy was ineffective, and his usual resource (Montezuma) received a blow to his head from a stone while trying to appease his people from the rooftop of a fortified palace. He died from the injury three days later. The event symbolised Montezuma's downfall and renewed political resistance from the Mexica. The Spaniards and their allies (3,000 Indians from

[63] *Ibid.*, pp. 115–27.

Tlaxcala) were now in a desperate situation, short of water and food, without their local intermediaries and facing determined resistance from a united people using new weapons, very long lances with flint heads. Eventually, the Spaniards withdrew, carrying the gold and jewels they had collected and believing that the captured provincial chiefs whom they had taken hostage would protect them. They tried to retreat as secretly as possible, leaving by night around the end of June 1520, but encountered fierce attacks from the alert Mexica, who harassed them relentlessly from inside the city to the borders of their state. Cortés and the majority of the Spaniards were lucky to survive, though all were wounded and exhausted. Their losses in the *noche triste* were severe: according to Cortés, who understated them to avoid suggesting they had suffered an irreversible defeat, 150 Spaniards, 2,000 Tlaxcala Indians, nearly all the hostages and 45 horses had been killed, while the Mexica had recovered almost all their treasure. Cortés noted also that many Spaniards had been killed in the provinces as a consequence of the revolt.

The final part of his second letter reported that the survivors found refuge at Tlaxcala, where they renewed their alliance with the natives, treated their wounds and restored their aggressive military will. Cortés understood the psychological aspect of war very well. He rejected a proposal to withdraw to Vera Cruz and rebuild their strength before launching another attack against the Mexica, foreseeing that further retreat would simply encourage the Mexica to launch another massive attack against the weakened Spaniards. Moreover, Cortés was also running out of time: Narvaez's expedition had been a major threat, and he could establish his position in the emperor's eyes only through a major conquest. Therefore Cortés returned to the offensive within two months of his defeat, in order to show that the Spaniards were not intimidated and to disrupt the fragile unity of the Mexica confederacy. Helped by native allies, he managed to subjugate the province of Tepeaca, near Tlaxcala, where he created a new town, Segura de la Frontera, and appointed all its officials. Then he accepted an alliance with Huaquechula (the future town of Puebla), which wanted to expel a garrison of 30,000 Mexica that had recently arrived to block the Spaniards' way. Victory there brought a new wave of native allies;

Cortés reported 120,000. By now, Cortés had received declarations of vassalage from several towns and provinces including Oaxaca, again tipping the balance of power in the Spaniards' favour.

Cortés adopted an intelligent strategy, securing his lines of communication to the coast and cutting any support to the Mexica from the eastern provinces. Meanwhile, he also sent several expeditions to Hispaniola (and even Cuba) to recruit men and buy equipment, integrating new reinforcements that arrived at the coast. His letter ended on a very optimistic note, guaranteeing the emperor that he would conquer Tenochtitlán and recover everything he had lost. Cortés even informed Charles V that he had begun building thirteen brigantines to fight Tenochtitlán from the lake. By April 1522 this letter was printed in Seville, with a postscript by the printer, Cromberger, stating that 'after this, there came on the first of . . . March past news from New Spain, of how the Spaniards had taken by storm the great city of Temixtitan [Tenochtitlán], in which more Indians died than Jews in Jerusalem during the destruction of that city by Vespasian'.[64]

The third letter was dated 15 May 1522, more than eighteen months after the previous *relación*. Cortés reported that smallpox had spread into the new continent before the Spaniards had started to besiege Tenochtitlán. This epidemic surely had a devastating effect on the native population, as sudden high mortality weakened their defence against the *conquistadores*. By Christmas 1520, the Spanish had assembled forty horsemen and 550 foot soldiers, including eighty crossbowmen and *harquebusiers*, at Tlaxcala, together with eight or nine field guns (cannons), but very little powder. Cortés made a speech recalling the causes of this war: the revolt by vassals of Emperor Charles V; subjugating a barbarian people in order to spread the faith; service to their king; protecting their own lives and the support they had received from the allied natives.[65]

Cortes's troops immediately entered the territory of the Nahua confederation, where they occupied Texcoco, the second most powerful city in the Triple Alliance, a place capable of billeting and supplying his troops. Avoiding an immediate attack on Tenochtitlán, Cortés

[64] *Ibid.*, p. 159.   [65] *Ibid.*, p. 166.

patiently devoted the next four months to encircling it by taking control of all the cities around the lake through battles or diplomacy. This tactic enabled him to know the region, impose alliances and gather information for an expected siege of Tenochtitlán. His thirteen brigantines were carried in disassembled form from Tlaxcala to Texcoco in a huge expedition several kilometres long, guarded by 200 Spaniards and 8,000 Tlaxcala Indians. As they were assembled, more reinforcements came from Vera Cruz in three ships loaded with men, horses, crossbows, harquebuses and powder.

Thousands of allied troops had assisted the Spaniards since the beginning of the campaign, but at the end of April 1521, Cortés sent messengers to all his allies asking them for full military support. The Tlaxcala Indians alone provided more than 50,000 men, divided between two companies of Spanish troops based at Tlacopán (later named Tacuba) and Coyouacán and commanded by Pedro de Alvarado and Cristóbal de Olid. A third company of Spaniards, commanded by Gonzalo de Sandoval and supported by 30,000 Indians from Chalco, Guaxocingo and Churultecal, would support the thirteen brigantines commanded by Cortés himself. The siege started at the end of May by cutting the fresh water supply from the aqueducts to the city. Warfare began with the arrival of the brigantines, launched via a new canal dug by the allies. The successful encirclement of the city and the victory of the brigantines against hundreds of Mexica canoes set a pattern for the following months: the Mexica entrenched themselves in the island-city of Tenochtitlán, barricaded all the land routes and defended them every day, breaking the causeways to prevent men and horses from advancing.

After two and a half months of constant fighting and killing, the siege ended on 13 August 1521. Expecting a quick surrender, the Spaniards and their allies had exerted permanent military pressure on the Mexica, entering the city every day along different paths, fighting to control the bridges and squeeze the defenders into ever-smaller territory. They razed houses to avoid attacks from the terraces, and restored the broken causeways to secure their safe return to the mainland. But they were facing a resilient people who had decided to die rather than surrender their autonomy. Cortés's *relación* included details of the daily fighting, not only to underline how difficult this enterprise was and praise the actions of his men and allies, but also to emphasise his vision as both military commander and diplomat – reacting to adversity, trying new tactics, fostering dissent among the enemy, and increasing the number of allies. For example, he boasted that D. Fernando, a young noble Mexica under Spanish control, who had been baptised and imposed as lord of Texcoco during the first military operations around the lake, had managed to send 50,000 men from the province of Alcolhuacán to assist the Spanish troops at the very beginning of the siege. This act raised the number of allied troops to the impressive total of some 130,000 men at the first stage of the siege. Even fighting against probably 250,000 people barricaded inside the city[66] (the *relaciones* indicated that many noble Mexica and warriors had abandoned some cities from the Triple Alliance to the Spaniards and concentrated on defending Tenochtitlán), its conquest clearly resulted from dissent among the natives, caused or manipulated by the Spaniards.

The number of people involved in the war fluctuated. When the Mexica managed to defeat the first serious attempt to capture the city's strategic marketplace, killing a significant number of Spaniards and allied troops, native support for the Spaniards dwindled and revolts broke out. Cortés had to renew his diplomatic and military efforts in the provinces, securing his rearguard before returning to the intense fight at Tenochtitlán.[67] In the last stage of the siege, the presence of allied troops intensified; natives from different provinces came to witness the fall of the Mexica rulers and participate in taking booty, developments that Cortés could not control. He even denounced the savage treatment of Tenochtitlán's defenders, accusing his allies of systematic cannibalism. He reported the killing of tens of thousands of Mexica in the final days of the siege, with the city's defenders

---

[66] Referring to previous estimates by Jean Delumeau and José Luis de Rojas, Serge Gruzinski calculates 300,000 people in Tenochtitlán before the conquest: *Histoire de Mexico* (Paris: Fayard, 1996), p. 189. This figure would place the city among the largest in the world, well ahead of Constantinople or Paris. The first wave of epidemics must have decreased this number, while warfare must have imposed contradictory movements, with some people fleeing to the countryside and others coming to the city to fight the enemy.

[67] *Letters from Mexico*, pp. 237–47.

completely exhausted by starvation and epidemics. Such events explain his dense description of the siege: Cortés wished to justify destroying the city and his ultimate inability to recover the royal treasure. He claimed to have tried repeatedly to negotiate an honourable surrender in order to preserve the city and avoid more deaths (a natural attitude of the image of a rational leader that he was trying to present to the emperor), but the *Tlatoani* never agreed to talk to him. This letter clearly demonstrates the view adopted by the Mexica political elite following Montezuma's submission to the Spaniards: honour required either victory or death.

This *relación* should have stopped with the city's conquest, but Cortés continued. First he reported receiving news about the 'Southern Sea' (later called the Pacific Ocean), and immediately sent missions to reconnoitre the south-western portions of the territories he had just conquered. One conquest opened new horizons, leading to further exploration projects and potential conquests. We will see that Cortés never abandoned such projects, launching several expeditions that would eventually produce Spanish colonisation of the Philippines forty years later, after they had mastered the system of winds and currents in the Pacific and established a permanent link between Mexico and the Far East, namely the famous annual galleon, laden with silver, that sailed from Acapulco to Manila. Cortés also informed Charles V of his decision to rebuild Tenochtitlán: 'as before it was capital and centre of all these provinces, so it shall be henceforth'.[68] Cortés's third *relación* also mentioned the military missions sent to pacify different provinces and impose Spanish rule. Cortés used precisely this issue, a recently conquered land at permanent risk of unrest and rebellion, to dismiss Cristóbal de Tapia, head of the mint in Hispaniola, who had arrived after the conquest at Vera Cruz to claim control of the government on behalf of Charles V. Facing opposition from the municipal councils (again manipulated by Cortés, who had recently created a new one in Medellín), Tapia was forced to return to Hispaniola, on the pretext that 'his arrival caused much upheaval and his presence would have caused great harm, if God had not remedied it'.[69]

---

[68] *Ibid.*, p. 270.   [69] *Ibid.*, pp. 272–5.

Cortés briefly recorded a plot against him, organised in Texcoco by Diego Velázquez's faction before the siege of Tenochtitlán, and how he executed its leader, Antonio de Villafaña, but spared the lives of the other conspirators. Since the king rarely delegated the right to condemn men to death, Cortés was in a particularly delicate position, but he had proceeded regardless, as if his was the only authority capable of maintaining order: 'without punishing those men, there is complete peace and tranquillity; but if I hear anything further, I will punish them as justice demands'.[70]

This letter concluded with his reflection on the status of the natives, who could not be enslaved like those in the islands, because 'the natives of these parts are of much greater intelligence . . .; indeed, they appeared to us to possess such understanding as is sufficient for an ordinary citizen to conduct himself in a civilised country'.[71] This reasoning allowed Cortés to justify (and request royal approval for) the system of *encomiendas* he created in Mexico immediately after the conquest. Dividing the natives among the Spanish settlers gave the *conquistadores* an immediate reward; but it also created endless problems of oppression and consequent unrest, which royal officials struggled to redress after a regular administration was established in Mexico. The way in which (to use Cortés's words) the *conquistadores* became settlers, justifying his new seigniorial institution by the need to control the Indians and to colonise the territory, seems particularly noteworthy.

The fourth letter was written on 15 October 1524, almost thirty months after the previous one. In the interval, Cortés had been finally invested as the official governor and captain-general of New Spain in a decree dated October 1522, which reached Mexico only in September

---

[70] *Ibid.*, p. 278.

[71] *Ibid.*, p. 279. Here the English translation is misleading; the term 'citizen' had a different meaning, and the expression 'civilised country' was unknown in those days: see Norbert Elias, *La civilisation des mœurs*, trans. Pierre Kamnitze (Paris: Calmann-Lévy, 1973) and Lucien Febvre, *Pour une histoire à part entière* (Paris: Ecole Pratique des Hautes Etudes, 1962), pp. 477–603. The original (Delgado Gomez (ed.), *Cartas*, p. 450) reads: 'los naturales destas partes eran de mucha más capacidad que no los de las otras islas; que nos parescían de tanto entendimiento y razón quanto a uno medianamente basta para ser capaz'.

1523. Whereas Cortés's first three letters to Spain justified his military actions and diplomatic manoeuvres to conquer territory in Mexico in order to persuade his sovereign to recognise his status, his last two recorded the *conquistador*'s efforts to maintain or extend his power against royal bureaucrats attempting to transform his charismatic leadership into a standard administration controlled from Europe. In fact, Cortés's appointment as governor had been accompanied by another decree appointing four officials (who arrived in Mexico in 1524) to assist him. In hindsight, Cortés's appointment was a brilliant way to appease this charismatic leader and his *conquistadores*, now seen as founding settlers and still controlling local power networks in the new colonial world. Yet it simultaneously ended Cortés's arbitrary and uncontrolled leadership, because all governmental actions were henceforth scrutinised by royal officials. As John Elliott suggested, this sudden and dramatic reduction in his autonomy may explain the bitterness of Cortés's last letters and his decision to lead an expedition to Honduras in person, or to travel to Spain to present his case to the emperor.

It is important here to analyse these last two letters, which historians have generally ignored. Cortés described new military missions to 'pacify' different provinces which had 'revolted' alongside Tenochtitlán and ensure loyalty to the new rulers, to found new settlements (Espíritu Santo, Zacatula) or transfer old ones like Segura de la Frontera and Medellín. Spanish military activity during these two years after the conquest of Tenochtitlán allowed them to expand well beyond the territories loosely controlled by the Triple Alliance. The struggle between Cortés and Bishop Fonseca, the counsellor responsible for affairs in the Indies, also became explicit in this letter. Cortés decided upon an open attack on Fonseca, under the pretext of letters seized by his men from the bishop's envoy, showing support for Cristóbal de Tapia. Those letters threatened Cortés and his *conquistadores*, and he claimed that they had provoked disturbances among both Spaniards and Indians. Cortés complained that the lack of recognition for his men's services made them wish to form a *comunidad* 'as had been done in Castile'; this reference to the *Comuneros* revolt of 1520–1 demonstrated how well Cortés was informed about political events in Spain. He also criticised the systematic persecution of his men at the *Casa de Contratación* in Seville on orders from Bishop Fonseca, causing money, reports and letters to be seized and blocking urgently needed reinforcements of soldiers, men and supplies.

Deciding to take personal command of an expedition to 'pacify' the province of Pánuco (targeted by the *adelantado* Francisco de Garay), the governor also founded the town of Santisteban del Puerto. This was a crucial move, because when a letter arrived from the emperor, commanding Garay not to interfere in that river or in any other places settled by Cortés, the *alcalde* of Santisteban played a major role in controlling the expedition's fate. Finding himself deserted by his soldiers and with badly maintained ships, Garay had to travel to Mexico to beg Cortés for assistance. He died in suspicious circumstances, vomiting all night after a dinner with the governor; but the latter's report claimed that news of his men's revolt in Pánuco province had major effects on the *adelantado*, who felt guilty and fell 'ill from his grief and from this sickness passed from this life within the space of three days'.[72] The letter continued by describing the pacification of the province, although Garay's remaining men were killed by 'rebellious' Indians. The complete failure of Garay's actions suited Cortés perfectly, because it provided an example that prevented further threats to his projects from developing in the region. Since the beginning, Cortés had understood that settlement was the key element in securing possession of the land and claiming political control. This explains why he sent out new expeditions commanded by Cristóbal de Olid and Pedro de Alvarado to explore the coast, although later in the same letter Cortés complained about Olid, who (encouraged by Diego Velázquez) had apparently rebelled in Honduras. In one of the rare cases when Cortés lost control of his emotions, he wrote: 'if this is so, then I am of a mind to send for the aforementioned Diego Velázquez and arrest him, and send him to Your Majesty'.[73]

The final part of the letter dealt with the reconstruction of Tenochtitlán (later called Mexico), specifically building a Spanish neighbourhood protected by a new solid fortress and canals,

[72] *Letters from Mexico*, p. 310.   [73] *Ibid.*, p. 332.

organising separate native neighbourhoods, and reviving markets and commerce. Cortés next informed Charles V about the discovery of copper, tin, saltpetre and sulphur in the provinces, which could now produce cannons and powder. He also reported on his projects to explore the coasts of America in both the northern and southern seas (Atlantic and Pacific), and to discover a better passage than that used by Magellan – and perhaps establish a connection between New Spain and the Spice Islands reported by Magellan's expedition. As a result of the presence of royal officials, the governor complained about spending all his own money on different military expeditions, plus borrowing from the royal treasury and indebting himself to merchants. Consequently, Cortés asked to be reimbursed with 50,000 *pesos de oro*. The governor also wrote extensively about the need for men of religion, Franciscans and Dominicans, openly declaring that he did not want bishops, accusing them of 'squandering the goods of the Church on pomp and ceremony, and other vices, and leaving entailed estates to their sons or kinsmen'. Cortés developed this delicate topic without mincing words: 'The evil here would be still greater, for the natives of these parts had in their time religious persons administering their rites and ceremonies who were so severe in the observance of both chastity and honesty that if any one of them was held by anyone to have transgressed, he was put to death.'[74] Cortés suggested that Charles V ask the pope for the privilege of collecting tithes, even estimating the amount of money involved. The letter concluded with more accusations against the officials of Hispaniola, who had forbidden the export of breeding animals to New Spain. He wanted their decision revoked, and emphasised the importance of sending breeding animals and plants for the 'colonisation' (he used the word several times) of New Spain.

His fifth letter, dated 3 September 1526, is the most tedious. Cortés reported extensively on his overland journey to Honduras from the Tabasco region through the swampy regions of Yucatán to Nito (nowadays in Guatemala), crossing over 800 kilometres under the worst possible conditions simply to defeat the rebel Cristóbal de Olid. When

[74] *Ibid.*, p. 333.

Cortés arrived on the coast of Honduras, he found two towns and heard of another one created by surviving Spaniards from previous expeditions. He went there to acquire information about Olid's rebellion and his struggle with Francisco de las Casas (sent previously by Cortés), which ended with Olid's execution. While there, he received news about feuds in Mexico between his followers and the royal officials, who, believing he was dead, had seized power, looted Cortés's properties and arrested the leaders of the governor's faction. The letter informed the emperor of various groups of rebellious Spaniards plundering the coast and enslaving the natives, provoking constant unrest and revolt. Cortés finally decided to sail back to New Spain and re-establish order in Tenochtitlán, stopping over in Havana and landing at Medellín.

Cortés recorded his reception and the journey to Tenochtitlán as a triumph, with all the Spaniards and natives crowding the roads and the towns, especially in the capital. It is plausible that this triumph had been organised by his followers, who had regained power in the capital as soon as they learned that the governor was alive and sailing back. But the sweet taste of his restored authority did not last long: soon he received a dispatch from Medellín, informing him that an investigative judge sent by Charles V had arrived with instructions to examine all of Cortés's official activities. The controls imported by the royal bureaucracy became annoyingly restrictive, and Cortés must have realised that he would never enjoy the same autonomy as before being appointed governor.

This judge, Ponce de León, was received by Cortés and the municipal council of Tenochtitlán, who accepted the emperor's letters and swore to implement them. Ponce de León announced the inquiry and suspended Cortés from his functions, but soon died. Cortés informed the emperor that the judge and thirty of his companions had died, suggesting an epidemic, but a rumour spread that Ponce de León had been poisoned. The judge had transferred his powers to Marcos de Aguilar, his *alcalde mayor*, who suspended the inquiry. Despite pressure from the municipal council, Cortés refused to resume power, awaiting further decisions from the emperor. Cortés devoted the rest of his letter to justifying his financial debts, claiming that if he had the 200 million that his enemies said he had taken from the provinces, he would offer them to the emperor in exchange for 20 million and a place at court to advise him on affairs in the Indies. In conclusion, he informed the emperor about his new projects of expansion, namely into Florida, and the launch of new expeditions to the Southern Sea (which he really did). This last point is very interesting, as he compared New Spain with the *Estado da Índia* in terms that became a topic of debate among historians:

I will undertake to discover a route to the Spice Islands and many others, if there be any between Maluco, Malaca and China, and so arrange matters that the spices shall no longer be obtained by trade, as the king of Portugal has them now, but as Your Majesty's rightful property; and the natives of those islands shall serve and recognise Your Highness as their rightful king and lord.[75]

Despite the bitterness of these last two letters, which revealed Cortés's disappointment at seeing power slip from his hands after finally obtaining Charles V's recognition, it is indisputable that this *conquistador* managed to achieve much more than his contemporaries – even Gonzalo Fernández de Córdoba, the *Gran Capitán*, who reconquered the kingdom of Naples for Fernando of Aragon, or Francisco Pizarro, who conquered the Inca Empire. When Cortés decided to present his case directly to the emperor, travelling to Castile in 1528, he was received with great pomp by Charles V, who elevated him to the status of marquis and recognised his vast domains in the finest lands of New Spain, including his patronage of dozens of thousands of native people. At the same time, a *Real Audiencia* (royal high court) was established in Mexico, which meant continuing the previous policy of simultaneously raising his status while withdrawing effective political power. Cortés never recovered his authority as governor after being suspended by the inquiry (*residencia*) in 1526.

In 1535, Charles V appointed Antonio de Mendoza as the first viceroy of Mexico and head of the *Real Audiencia*, concluding eleven years of brilliant political manoeuvring to transform a charismatic leadership into ordinary hierarchical administration. Cortés retained the titles of captain-general (recovered only by the second viceroy,

[75] *Ibid.*, p. 445.

appointed after the *conquistador*'s death) and *adelantado* of the Southern Sea, which reserved to him the right to explore the Pacific Ocean. He organised several voyages to identify the western coasts of America, tried to establish a regular link between America and Asia, and created the first shipyards in the New World.[76] However, as captain-general, Cortés remained subordinate to the viceroy and could take no initiative without permission from Antonio de Mendoza.[77]

Throughout the 1530s, Cortés sent a series of protests and memorials railing against what he considered to be insufficient recognition of his services. Even so, his voyage to Castile enabled him to enter the exclusive world of grandees, with one of the highest noble titles and certainly the best properties,[78] to remarry into that tiny exclusive group and definitively raise his status. Cortés offered one of the most impressive cases of social climbing through military service in Renaissance Europe, particularly from a man who began as an undistinguished local squire. He gained not only political legitimacy, but also the highest social recognition imaginable. Political power could not be held indefinitely, as he knew full well despite his protests. He was wise enough to avoid pushing these protests too far, never crossing the line of unbreakable loyalty that would have meant ruin, as later happened to Gonzalo Pizarro in Peru. In comparison, Afonso de Albuquerque, who came from a much higher social background, did not raise his status to the same extent. As we have seen, the descendants of his 'clan' of relatives benefited from Albuquerque's charisma and the memory of the man who founded the *Estado da Índia*; many of them were appointed captains, governors and viceroys, competing for most of the senior posts in India with the descendants of Vasco da Gama's 'clan'. Yet Afonso de Albuquerque never managed to establish

---

[76] Miguel León-Portilla, *Hernán Cortés y la Mar del Sur* (Madrid: Ediciones Cultura Hispanica, 1985).

[77] J. Ignacio Rubio Mañé, *El Virreinato*, vol. 1: *Orígenes y jurisdicciones, y dinamica social de los virreyes*, 2nd edition (Mexico: Fondo de Cultura Economica, 1983), pp. 19–26.

[78] Bernardo Garcia Martínez, *El Marquesado del Valle: tres siglos de régimen señorial en Nueva España* (Mexico: Centro de Estudios Históricos, 1969).

a new noble house, and, as he explicitly regretted in his last letters, he had failed to become a grandee.

COMPARISONS

An abyss separates the sets of letters from Cortés and Albuquerque: they differ in number, length, content, style and form. To begin with, Albuquerque's letters were printed only in the nineteenth century. Even if some chroniclers indicated he was 'literate' and understood Latin, he never intended to publish them. Portuguese publishing habits had been quite centralised since the beginning of printing. Many texts about Portuguese overseas expansion were published in Europe; but most of them were propaganda tools, either letters written by the Portuguese king or 'obedience speeches'[79] by Portuguese ambassadors to the pope. In 1507, Fracanzano da Montalboldo published *Paesi nouamente retrouati*,[80] a collection of travel accounts concerning the explorations of Ca' da Mosto, Pedro de Sintra, Columbus, Pinzón, Vasco da Gama, Pedro Álvares Cabral and Amerigo Vespucci, together with letters from Italian merchants, diplomats, and an interview in Rome with a Nestorian priest from Cranganore in India known as 'José Indiano'. Although Portuguese travel accounts circulated and were printed abroad, mainly in Italy, there are no known examples of such travellers publishing their own explorations and conquests.[81]

In Spain, a precedent existed for Cortés's publication of his actions: the letter written by Columbus to Luís de Santángel about his first voyage to the Caribbean islands, printed immediately in Barcelona in April 1493. This became widely diffused throughout Europe: the fifteenth century alone saw nine Latin editions in Barcelona, Antwerp,

---

[79] *Orações de obediência dos reis de Portugal aos Sumos Pontífices*, ed. Martim de Albuquerque, trans. Miguel Pinto de Meneses, 10 vols. (Lisbon: Inapa, 1988).

[80] See *Itinerarium Portugallensium*, ed. Luís de Matos (Lisbon: Fundação Calouste Gulbenkian, 1992) for a Latin version of the *Paesi nouamente retrouati*, which saw six editions in Italian, plus several Latin, German and French translations.

[81] Luís de Matos, *L'expansion portugaise dans la littérature latine de la Renaissance* (Lisbon: Fundação Calouste Gulbenkian, 1991); António Alberto Banha de Andrade, *Mundos novos do mundo: panorama da difusão pela Europa de notícias dos descobrimentos portugueses*, 2 vols. (Lisbon: Junta de Investigações do Ultramar, 1972).

Basel and Paris, plus four Italian editions in Rome and Florence, and one German edition in Strasbourg.[82] But as a modern example of propaganda and political persuasion, the context, scope and literary skills of Columbus's letter were very far removed from Cortés's *relaciones*.

The two conquerors had totally different political agendas. Albuquerque had been appointed captain and then governor by the king, while Cortés had cut his ties to his patron, the governor of Cuba, to engage in an autonomous project of conquest, for which he needed his sovereign's recognition. Since nobody knew him in Spain, the publication of Cortés's letters provided a way to make him visible, help build his reputation (again demonstrating the importance of public opinion), and put pressure on the royal court to recognise him as captain-general (and then governor) of the new Spanish dominions in Mexico. When the emperor finally brought the situation in New Spain under control, he forbade further printing of Cortés's letters. In contrast, Albuquerque had no interest in making public his disagreements with a king, with whom he always maintained a close relationship, although inevitably eroded over time by the dynamics of political interests. Albuquerque knew that the entire Portuguese power game was confined to a tiny but sharply divided and conflict-ridden royal court. While he struggled for political support, Cortés struggled for political legitimacy.

For such reasons, the style of these two sets of correspondence also differs greatly. Cortés developed a dual register, combining in-depth description of the geography, religion, politics, ethnography and economics of lands that were unknown in Europe with juridical arguments justifying his actions to Charles V. The contents of Albuquerque's letters were more diversified, often dealing with administrative and political matters. However, they shared some common aspects. In describing the Red Sea, then scarcely known in Europe, Albuquerque provided a very detailed description similar to Cortés's written images of Mexico. Likewise, when reporting on his diplomatic efforts or military actions, Albuquerque could become almost as detailed as Cortés.

---

[82] Christopher Columbus, *Textos y documentos completos*, ed. Consuelo Varela and Juan Gil, 2nd edition (Madrid: Alianza, 1992), pp. 219–26.

On the other hand, Albuquerque's style was generally much more concise than Cortés's, perhaps because he was writing dozens of letters every year. This enabled him to tackle separate issues in each letter, while Cortés preferred to concentrate all his information in long reports sent every year or eighteen months, whose timing was generally defined by his immediate situation.

They used different strategies of persuasion. Albuquerque was building on territory that had been discussed at the royal court for ten years, while Cortés had to convince the emperor to legitimise his conquests in a completely unknown land, about which he himself was providing all the information. Albuquerque tried to persuade his king through his actions, but also through his vision of the future Portuguese presence in the Indian Ocean, while Cortés never doubted that conquest was the only possible argument to establish his position. Albuquerque engaged in a debate on strategy; Cortés tried to persuade the emperor that he had personally won the trust of local allies, which was essential for the undertaking's success, so that there was no alternative to him. Albuquerque was engaged in a real exchange with the king, and their vivid correspondence covered a huge variety of subjects, while Cortés was producing long reports, making Charles V a recipient of unilateral information who was expected to approve the actions described.

The letters (and actions) of the founders of the two Iberian overseas dominions raised most of the political issues about European imperialism that (leaving aside Greek and Roman expansion) would be discussed for at least the next hundred years. For Cortés, the questions at stake in his policies of distributing *encomiendas* of natives (and the corresponding income) among the *conquistadores* and of separating Spanish and native municipal councils were how to recognise native political rights and native jurisdiction. The invasion of Mexico raised crucial issues about the respective rights of conquerors and conquered people, namely defining a legal basis for Europeans to override legitimate local powers, distribute land and assign native people to new overlords. This situation led to Bartolomé de las Casas's reaction: he condemned the invasion and held that the natives had a right to maintain their property, culture and political system. He influenced

Francisco de Vitoria and the Salamanca school (Domingo de Soto, Luís de Molina and Francisco Suárez) who supported recognition of native rights and refined the notion of a just war – two crucial issues for the development of *jus gentium*, a domain of juridical theory placed between natural law and human law, considering the whole world as a commonwealth.[83]

In contrast, Albuquerque created a state in India with a specific blend of Portuguese and local institutions which defined its political environment for the following centuries. During the sixteenth century, the *Estado da Índia* became a loose network of ports and small coastal territories, obtained through invasion, military threat and diplomatic negotiation, and which integrated some local institutions and even local rulers. This relatively hybrid result suited the highly complex urban and commercial societies encountered by the Portuguese, which defined a completely different set of possibilities and imposed constant compromise. Like Cortés, Albuquerque enjoyed wide autonomy that allowed both men to distribute jobs and rents among their soldiers; develop a policy of intermarriage (criticised by the king), in order to encourage settlers and produce a new mixed-race elite to provide the necessary manpower and access to local resources; and sustain a constant and intense diplomatic policy to extend their ruler's overseas presence. Unlike Cortés, from the very start Albuquerque enjoyed a formal and official link to his king, which simultaneously limited his autonomy. He knew that he might have to face an inquiry, and was acutely aware of the rule of replacement after a three-year term, although he did his best to keep the post as long as possible.

Since the start of Portuguese expansion in the Indian Ocean, governors tried to impose a policy of maritime monopoly, in which ships needed Portuguese authorisation for trade. Albuquerque managed to implement this policy, which remained relatively successful

---

[83] Bartolomé de Las Casas, *Obra indígenista*, ed. José Alcina Franch (Madrid: Alianza, 1985); *Brevíssima relación de la destrucción de las Indias*, ed. José Maria Reyes Cano (Barcelona: Planeta, 1994); Francisco de Vitoria, *Political Writings*, ed. Anthony Pagden and Jeremy Lawrance (Cambridge: Cambridge University Press, 1991). For a general approach, see Demetrio Ramos et al., *Francisco de Vitoria y la escuela de Salamanca: la etica en la conquista de America* (Madrid: CSIC, 1984).

until the 1570s. This practice raised difficulties in international law, since Spaniards and Portuguese alike claimed that oceans should be reserved for their exclusive navigation according to the papal division of the world between the two kingdoms, redefined by the Treaty of Tordesillas (1494).[84] Constant protests by the French kings (especially François I) against this shared monopoly influenced a first wave of juridical opinions about freedom of navigation, reflected in the Latin and French translations of Girolamo Benzoni's *Historia del Mondo Nuovo*.[85] The issue resurfaced after Dutch ships started sailing to India, when the shareholders of the *Verenigde Oost-Indisches Compagnie* wanted to know if the capture and booty of Portuguese ships was legally acceptable. Opposing the Portuguese version, young Hugo Grotius argued brilliantly in favour of *mare liberum* and the legitimacy of defensive and offensive action to reinforce the principle of free navigation.[86]

Albuquerque and Cortés shared the same political and military knowledge. They had obviously studied recent technological and tactical developments in the art of war at Granada (between Castilians and Muslims) and Naples (between Spaniards and French). Artillery proved very important not only in sieges of fortresses and cities, but also in naval warfare, particularly when used by Portuguese fleets in India. In Mexico, artillery had a major psychological impact, while in Asia the Portuguese faced Turkish competition around the same technological level, which quickly spread to other states. In Mexico, the Spaniards could exploit their cavalry superiority: horses were unknown to the native peoples, and their use proved crucial on the battlefield. The complementary deployment of military and diplomatic action, which had proved so important in stirring up dissidence and demoralisation during the war in Granada, became equally decisive in

---

[84] Julio Valdeón Baruque (ed.), *El Testamento de Adán*, exhibition catalogue (Lisbon and León: Sociedad V Centenario del Tratado de Tordesillas/CNCDP, 1994).

[85] Girolamo Benzoni, *La historia del Mondo Nuovo* (Venice: F. Rampazetto, 1565); *Novi Orbis Historia*, trans. Urbain Chauveton (Lyon: E. Vignon, 1578); *Histoire nouvelle du Nouveau Monde*, trans. Urbain Chauveton (Geneva: E. Vignon, 1579). This last version profoundly influenced the fourth part of *America*, with the engravings by Théodore de Bry (Frankfurt a.M.: J. Feirabend, 1594).

[86] Hugo Grotius, *The Free Sea*, trans. Richard Hakluyt with William Welwood's *Critique* and Grotius's *Reply*, ed. David Armitage (Indianapolis: Liberty Fund, 2004).

Mexico and in India. The capacity to cope with defeat and to rebuild military strength, exhibited in Naples by the *Gran Capitán*, Gonzalo Fernández de Córdoba,[87] became a source of inspiration for both Albuquerque and Cortés. The guerrilla tactics developed in Granada and the technological improvements from Naples also provided sources of inspiration when building brigantines in Mexico or using different types of ships in India. The spread of crossbows, harquebuses and pikes also explains European military technological superiority on the battlefield in Mexico – important from a psychological point of view, but less crucial than the capacity to create unrest and to mobilise native enemies of the Triple Alliance.

As we have seen, Cortés's political correspondence made explicit comparisons between the two Iberian empires. His contrast between Spanish territorial expansion and Portuguese naval expansion, between an empire built on conquest and an empire built through trade, developed into a stereotype still shared by most historians today. Curiously, this opposition defined the main lines of the European expansion in Asia until the eighteenth century. Even inside the Portuguese Empire, Albuquerque was accused of favouring expensive territorial conquest against Almeida's preference for trade monopolies and maritime dominion. The Dutch and English companies in Asia subsequently came to terms with this opposition, which reappeared in most of their expansion processes. Spanish ability to conquer and colonise, contrasted with Portuguese ability to trade and control ports, became a persistent topos of an essentialist approach that ignores such historical realities as Spanish failure to conquer either the Spice Islands or Indochina by the turn of the sixteenth to the seventeenth century, not to mention Portuguese control of most of Ceylon between 1590 and 1630 or especially the Portuguese colonisation of Brazil. This topos resulted from a Eurocentric point of view whereby any conquest or colonisation depended on the capacity (or 'nature') of the European power, regardless of local conditions and local capacities for resistance.

---

[87] *Crónicas del Gran Capitán*, ed. Antonio Rodriguez Villa (Madrid: Nueva Biblioteca de Autores Españoles, 1908); José Enrique Ruiz-Domènec, *El Gran Capitán: retrato de una época* (Barcelona: Península, 2002).

Albuquerque and Cortés also shared similarly 'realistic' perspectives in their letters. Both adopted a totally different approach from previous reports, in which a marvellous vision of the world still influenced descriptions of distant countries. The letters by Columbus and Vespucci about the western Atlantic, and Duarte Pacheco Pereira's long description of the coast of Africa,[88] all blended accurate observations with a mythological framework that shaped late medieval European visions of the world. Although Cortés was apparently touched by the messianic Franciscans' vision of the expansion, his letters to Charles V reveal no visionary framework. Equally, he was aware of local mythology but used it for political purposes. Moreover, he distorted the narrative of his reception outside Tenochtitlán and invented Montezuma's speeches to justify the legitimacy of his actions as a *conquistador*, arguing that Charles V's suzerainty had been recognised by the local ruler but broken by his subjects. 'Just politics', as would be said nowadays.

Albuquerque produced the first serious European description of the Red Sea and gave extremely accurate reports on the Asian powers in the Persian Gulf, South Asia and South-east Asia. His references to a possible conquest of Jeddah in order to destroy the Muslim centre of worship in Mecca, or to invade Sinai in order to conquer Jerusalem, have been mistakenly interpreted as signs of millenarianism, in line with the exclusively religious justification for Portuguese expansion developed from the 1930s to the 1960s by Portuguese historians influenced by a fascist regime.[89] I have also criticised the confusion between messianic vision, millenarianism and crusading spirit, which were all quite different cultural configurations. In Albuquerque's case, there are explicit references to a crusading spirit, with no trace of messianic vision or millenarianism. But even his 'crusading' rhetoric had clear

---

[88] Christopher Columbus, *Textos*; Amerigo Vespucci, *Il Mondo Nuovo*, ed. Mario Pozzi, 2nd edition (Alessandria: Edizioni dell'Orso, 1993); Duarte Pacheco Pereira, *Esmeraldo de situ orbis*, ed. Joaquim Barradas de Carvalho (Lisbon: Fundação Calouste Gulbenkian, 1991).

[89] For my refutation of this ideological interpretation, see Francisco Bethencourt, 'Le millénarisme: idéologie de l'impérialisme eurasiatique?', *Annales HSEE* (2002), pp. 189–94.

political purposes, as becomes obvious if his references are contextualised and his actions analysed; all of them seem extremely realistic and carefully prepared. Albuquerque targeted a small fraction of the Portuguese royal court open to the idea of a crusade, such as his friend Duarte Galvão; he wanted to exploit the pope's explicit support for Portuguese expansion and mobilise the religious argument to make his conquests in India seem unchallengeable at the royal court. In fact, after Albuquerque it became impossible to recycle the old enchanted vision of the world. The first accurate descriptions of the coasts of East Africa and Asia were made under Albuquerque's direct or indirect influence between 1513 and 1515 by Tomé Pires and Duarte Barbosa.[90]

The correspondence of both Albuquerque and Cortés reveals their ambition to be portrayed as heroes. Their letters include implicit references to classic examples of European conquerors like Alexander or Caesar, against whom they wished to be measured. Propaganda formed part of both men's strategy to obtain political support, but both captains also emphasised the exceptional nature of their completed actions to reinforce their fame and future reputation. Directly or indirectly, their correspondence influenced every chronicle and history of New Spain and Portuguese India. What is now contested as 'Prescott's paradigm'[91] is simply the narrative elaborated by Cortés, who enjoyed enormous fame during his lifetime: Pedro Mártir de Anglería followed his letters in the book *De Orbe Novo*, composing a flattering image of Cortés while reserving the name Caesar for Charles V.[92] This limit was obvious; Charles V had his own propaganda programme, mixing texts and images, also designed to portray

---

[90] *The Suma Oriental of Tomé Pires and the Book of Francisco Rodrigues*, ed. Armando Cortesão (London: Hakluyt Society, 1944); *The Book of Duarte Barbosa*, ed. Mansel Longworth Dames (London: Hakluyt Society, 1918–21); *O Livro de Duarte Barbosa*, ed. Maria Augusta da Veiga e Sousa, 2 vols. (Lisbon: Instituto de Investigação Científica Tropical, 1996–2000). Even though Duarte Barbosa was Albuquerque's adversary, they shared the same intellectual atmosphere.

[91] William H. Prescott, *History of the Conquest of Mexico and History of the Conquest of Peru* (New York: The Modern Library, 1936).

[92] Pedro Mártir de Anglería, *Decadas del Nuevo Mundo*, ed. Ramón Alba (Madrid: Polifemo, 1989).

him as a hero.[93] In contrast, Lucio Marineo Siculo exceeded the limit in his *Cosas memorables de España*, published in 1530,[94] by stating that Cortés deserved the title of king, comparing the *conquistador* to Hercules, Alexander, Jason and Caesar and asserting that he had brought more sheep to Christ than the Apostles. Needless to say, the book was prohibited. Gonzalo Fernández de Oviedo similarly accepted the essential aspects of Cortés's narrative, considering the conquest of Mexico more difficult than the conquests of Caesar.[95]

Besides influencing the main chroniclers during his lifetime, Cortés also commissioned his chaplain, Francisco López de Gómara, to write a biography.[96] Cortés's last years in Spain, between 1540 and 1547, when he participated in court life and the failed expedition to reconquer Algiers, were not simply a period of judicial unrest. Rather, he organised an intellectual circle including the papal nuncio, Cardinal Poggio; the Archbishop of Cagliari, Domenico Pastorelli; Bernardino Peralta; Antonio Peralta, Marquis of Falces (whose son became the third Viceroy of Mexico); and Pedro de Navarra.[97] Ninety years after Cortés's death, Baltasar Gracián attributed to him the qualities of a king and placed him among the highest heroes: 'the prodigious Marquis del Valle, don Fernando Cortés . . . made a triad with Alexander and Caesar, sharing between them the conquest of the world through different parts'.[98]

The impact of Cortés can also be measured outside Spain. Paolo Giovio included him among the gallery of portraits created in his palace at Como in 1539, later publishing the corresponding text in his

[93] Fernando Checa Cremades, *Carlos V y la imagen del heróe en el Renacimiento* (Madrid: Taurus, 1987).

[94] Lucio Marineo Siculo, *De las cosas memorables de Espana* (Alcalá de Henares, 1530), reproduced by Miguel León-Portilla in *Historia 16* (April 1985).

[95] Gonzalo Fernández de Oviedo, *História general y natural de las Indias*, ed. Amador de los Rios, vol. 3 (Madrid: Imprenta de la Real Academia de la Historia, 1853), p. 360 (bk. 33, ch. 20).

[96] Francisco López de Gómara, *La conquista de México*, ed. José Luiz de Rojas (Madrid: Historia 16, 1987).

[97] Salvador de Madariaga, *Hernán Cortés, Conqueror of Mexico*, 2nd edition (London: Hollis and Carter, 1954), p. 482.

[98] Baltasar Gracián, *El Heroe* (1st edition 1637) (Madrid: Espasa-Calpe, 1980), ch. IX (entitled *Del quilate rey*, meaning 'king's carat' or 'excellence'), p. 26.

book of eulogies that first focused on writers (1546) and later extended to military men (1551).[99] In one of his letters to Cosimo de' Medici from 1549, Giovio stated that he had collected portraits of famous men for thirty years. When he died in 1552, this seminal work (the first *Who's Who* combining portraits with texts) contained 146 eulogies of writers and 134 eulogies of kings and military men, but only three eulogies of artists, because Giovio had invited his friend Vasari to write the biographies of important artists. The only Portuguese in his gallery was Tristão da Cunha, an important captain in India but neither a governor nor a major conqueror; he had made his reputation in Europe as King Manuel's ambassador to the pope in 1514, staging an exotic entry into Rome replete with an elephant, wild animals and representatives of different people from all over the world.[100]

In 1584, the French royal cosmographer André Thevet published a volume of portraits of famous men, the only sixteenth-century work rivalling Giovio's. Thevet's book encompassed the world, because the author was a former traveller to America. His 232 biographies incorporated for the first time the lives of six native American rulers, including Montezuma and Atahualpa, whose states Thevet considered comparable to European societies. Hernán Cortés and Afonso de Albuquerque also appear as the founders of the two Iberian empires; their portraits and the descriptions of their actions were taken respectively from López de Gómara and Jerónimo Osório. While Cortés is portrayed with his coat of arms and a sword, making a gesture of command with his right hand, Albuquerque is portrayed with a sword and a compass, underlining his scientific knowledge.[101] Both *conquistadores*

[99] Paolo Giovio, *Gli elogi degli uomini illustri (letterati, artisti, uomini d'arme)*, ed. Renzo Meregazzi (Rome: Istituto Poligrafico dello Stato, 1972), pp. 467–71. Copies from Giovio's collection of portraits were commissioned by Marchioness Isabella Gonzaga d'Este, Duke Cosimo de' Medici (now at the Uffizi), Archduke Ferdinand of Habsburg and Cardinal Federico Borromeo.

[100] Paolo Giovio, *Elogi*, pp. 394–6. For several reports of this event by different ambassadors and humanists in Rome, see Banha de Andrade, *Mundos novos*, pp. 660–5.

[101] André Thevet, *Les vrais portraits et vies des homes illustres*, 2 vols. (Paris: N. Chesneau, 1584). See the English version, *Portraits from the Age of Exploration: Selections from André Thevet's 'Les vrais portraits et vies des homes illustres'*, ed. Roger Schlesinger, trans. by Edward Benson (Urbana: University of Illinois Press, 1993), pp. 36–61.

were known for their bold speech and blunt talk. Giovanni Botero recorded different stories and sayings, mainly by Albuquerque.[102] The reputation of their spontaneity inspired several authors through to the eighteenth century; for example, Voltaire's *Essai sur les mœurs* used a traditional story of a clash between Cortés and Charles V to elaborate on the ungratefulness of kings.[103]

Albuquerque's reputation was not truly established until the 1550s and 1560s, through the first chronicles of the Portuguese in Asia by João de Barros and Fernão Lopes de Castanheda,[104] the biography written by his son Brás de Albuquerque, and the chronicles of King Manuel by Damião de Góis and Osório,[105] who was the first to portray Albuquerque as a model of the virtues, the best general in war and the wisest politician in public administration, topics later developed by Pedro de Mariz. Luís de Camões's epic poem *The Lusiads*, published in 1572 to celebrate the Portuguese 'nation' and its expansion in Asia, focused mainly on the deeds of Vasco da Gama. Camões identified two captains, Duarte Pacheco Pereira (whom he compared to Achilles) and Afonso de Albuquerque, but criticised the latter for being too severe in punishing his soldiers.[106]

In 1591, the first statue of Albuquerque was erected in Goa, at the chapel where he had been buried, by order of Governor Matias de Albuquerque, a collateral descendant of his family. The first printed history of Portugal, published significantly in 1594 after the

---

[102] Giovanni Botero, *Detti memorabili di personaggi illustri* (Venice: Francesco Balzetta, 1610), fols. 23r, 54r, 68r, 74v–75r, 76v.

[103] Voltaire, *Essai sur les mœurs et l'esprit des nations et sur les principaux faits d'histoire depuis Charlemagne jusqu'à Louis XIII*, ed. René Pomeau, 2 vols. (Paris: Garnier, 1963), vol. 2, p. 353 (ch. 97): 'Enfin, malgré les titres dont Cortez fut décoré par sa patrie, il y fut peu considéré. A peine peut-il obtenir audience de Charles V: un jour il fendit la presse qui entourait le coche de l'empereur, et monta sur l'étrier de la portière. Charles demanda quel était cet homme. C'est, répondit Cortez, celui qui vous a donné plus d'Etats que vos pères ne vous ont laissé des villes.'

[104] Barros, *Ásia*, vol. 2; Lopes de Castanheda, *História do descobrimento*, vol. 1, bks. II–III.

[105] Brás de Albuquerque, *Commentaries*; Góis, *Chrónica*, pt. II, chs. 31–7, 43; pt. III, chs. 10–11, 16–22, 25–6, 28–30, 43–8, 80; Osório, *De rebus Emmanuelis*, bks. V–X.

[106] Luís de Camões, *The Lusiads*, trans. and ed. Landeg White (Oxford: Oxford University Press, 1997), canto X, verses 40–5.

unification of the Iberian crowns under Philip II, compared Albuquerque to Alexander and Nestor in terms of force and wisdom,
because 'he administrated the war as supreme emperor and governed
the republic as the most perfect magistrate'.[107] This signalled Albuquerque's final consecration, establishing his leading position in the
pantheon of Portuguese heroes, a position elevated still further during
the crucial period of nation-building in the nineteenth and twentieth
centuries.

[107] Pedro Mariz, *Diálogos de vária história* (Coimbra: António de Mariz, 1594),
dialogue IV, ch. 17.

CHAPTER 9

Spying in the Ottoman Empire: sixteenth-century encrypted correspondence

Dejanirah Couto

Sixteenth-century Europe, engaged in a long political, diplomatic and military struggle against the Ottoman Empire, also witnessed the consolidation of modern sovereign states in an institutionalised, centralised and bureaucratic form.[1] By offering symbolic settings for power, diplomacy ranked among the privileged instruments for reinforcing states, which in turn favoured its development. Nevertheless, neither could have assumed its modern form without an exponential increase in gathering information[2] and rational exploitation of this mass of news.[3] This increase was further nourished by the diffusion of new knowledge and techniques[4] and by geographical and economic novelties resulting from contacts with new lands and cultures.[5]

---

[1] Bertrand Badié, 'L'état moderne: le point de vue du politologue', in Noël Coulet and Jean-Philippe Genet (eds.), *L'état moderne: le droit, l'espace et les formes de l'état* (Paris: Editions du CNRS, 1990), pp. 211–27; Wolfgang Reinhard, 'Power elites: state servants, ruling classes, and the growth of state power', in Wolfgang Reinhard (ed.), *Power Elites and State Building* (Oxford: Clarendon Press, European Science Foundation, 1996) pp.1–18; R. Griffiths, 'Bureaucracy and the English state in the latter Middle Ages', and J. Nagle, 'Prosopographie et histoire de l'état: la France moderne xvie–xviie siècles', in Françoise Autran (ed.), *Prosopographie et genèse de l'état moderne* (Paris: CNRS, 1986), pp. 53–65, 77–90.

[2] Jerzy Senkowski, 'La chancellerie royale et son rôle dans l'administration de l'état polonais aux xve et xvie siècles', in Coulet and Genet (eds.), *L'état moderne*, pp. 170–3.

[3] Elisabeth Crouzet-Pavan, 'Les mots de Venise: sur le contrôle du langage dans une cité-état italienne', in *La circulation des nouvelles au Moyen Age* (Paris and Rome: Publications de la Sorbonne, Ecole Française de Rome, 1994), p. 215.

[4] Sometimes directly linked to Europe's wars: see Ann Katherine Isaacs and Maarten Prak, 'Cities, bourgeoisies, and states', in Reinhard (ed.), *Power Elites and State Building*, p. 223.

[5] Paolo Preto, *I servizi segreti di Venezia* (Milan: Il Saggiatore, 1994), pp. 87, 89; Vitorino Magalhães Godinho, *Mito e mercadoria, utopia e prática de navegar* (Lisbon: Difel,

Driven by this need for information, espionage and cryptography, its 'secret weapon', became major auxiliaries of diplomacy. At the beginning of the sixteenth century, diplomacy confronted both an escalation of traditional political rivalries and struggles for hegemony, together with a new extra-European dimension with economic and political implications. Under such conditions, acquiring information became more crucial than ever for political purposes; but it had to be organised and exploited, taking into consideration both the increasing complexity of its operational modes and the breadth of its network.[6]

Espionage organised and 'filtered' the information (usually from outside a state's borders) which diplomacy required in order to give a state advantages over its rivals and enemies. Its real force came from its relationship to state power, more precisely to its position at the heart of a state's political arsenal. Espionage was a double-edged weapon: besides operating abroad, it also assured a state's control over its dissident subjects by organising and orchestrating internal repression.

Although attempts to determine the priority of either form of espionage in European societies seem futile, we must however draw attention to the relationship between precocious networks of domestic spying and early structures of external espionage. Venice appears to offer the best-developed European example. Here one can discern a transition from a rudimentary fourteenth-century network, designed to preserve internal security, to the creation of an organised secret service

---

1990), pp. 497–531; *Os Descobrimentos e a economia mundial* (Lisbon: Presença, 1981), vol. 1, pp. 15–51; M. Mollat du Jourdin, *Les explorateurs du XIIIe au XVIe siècle: premiers regards sur des mondes nouveaux* (Paris, 1992); L. Filipe Barreto, *Descobrimentos e Renascimento: formas de ser e pensar nos séculos XV e XVI* (Lisbon: IN/CM, 1983); Jean Céard, 'Voyages et voyageurs à la Renaissance', in Jean Céard and Claude Margolin (eds.), *Voyager à la Renaissance. Actes du colloque de Tours, 1983* (Paris: Maisonneuve et Larose, 1987), pp. 596–610.

[6] Alain Hugon, 'L'information dans la politique étrangère de la Couronne d'Espagne', in *L'information à l'époque moderne* (Paris: Presses Universitaires de Paris-Sorbonne, 2001), pp. 30–4; René Ancel, 'Etude critique sur quelques recueils d'*avvisi*: Contribution à l'histoire du journalisme en Italie', *Mélanges d'archéologie et d' histoire de l'Ecole française de Rome* 28 (1908), 115–39.

for foreign policy two centuries later.[7] The permanent coexistence of
two forms of espionage with different methods and objectives did not
handicap either Venetian secret services or Venetian diplomacy; on the
contrary, it apparently contributed to their growth and consolidation.
Moreover, its effect on the growth of state inquisitions in the sixteenth
century – which have been called veritable 'political or state police'[8] –
seems obvious.

Sources of espionage: secrecy

Without claiming that an 'exacerbation' of secrecy occurred in the
fifteenth century, one observes an undeniable tendency towards an
increasing taste for secrecy. It was instrumentalised by the state, since
secrecy, as a sign and privilege of political power, helped to perpetuate
the symbolic order of social groups and catalyse relationships of force
by separating the sphere of government from the ordinary world of the
governed. It became part and parcel of the 'pragmatism' and principles
of rationality cherished by political theory when describing the art
of government.[9] A cerebral and sophisticated practice, combining
several mechanisms of dissimulation, secrecy fitted comfortably with
the pragmatism and rationality associated with 'Reason of State'.[10]
States – and particularly diplomacy – could not function without
secrecy, which helped to enable governments to foil the strategies of

---

[7] Preto, *Servizi segreti*, pp. 52–3; see, in general, Vladimir Lamansky, *Secrets d'état
de Venise: documents extraits, notices et études servant à éclaircir les rapports de la
Seigneurie avec les Grecs, les Slaves et la Porte ottomane à la fin du xve et au xvie
siècle* (St Petersburg: Imprimerie de l'Académie impériale des Sciences, 1884), vol. 1,
pp. 1–114 (reprint New York: Burt Franklin, 1968).

[8] Cited in Preto, *Servizi segreti*, p. 53 n. 2. On the Venetian Inquisition as a state
information network, see Alain Hugon's *Au service du Roi Catholique: 'honorables
ambassadeurs' et 'divins espions' face à la France. Représentation diplomatique et service
secret dans les relations hispano-françaises, 1598–1635* (Madrid: Casa de Velázquez,
2004); and Adriano Prosperi, *Tribunali della coscienza: inquisitori, confessori, missionari* (Turin: Giulio Einaudi, 1997), particularly pp. 196–206 and 219–57.

[9] Vittor Ivo Comparato, 'A case of modern individualism: politics and the uneasiness
of intellectuals in the in the Baroque age', in Janet Coleman (ed.), *The Individual
in Political Theory and Practice: The Origins of the Modern State in Europe* (Oxford:
Clarendon Press, European Science Foundation, 1996), p. 159.

[10] Michel Sennelart, *Machiavélisme et raison d'état, xiie–xviiie siècle* (Paris: PUF, 1989),
pp. 36–62; Comparato, 'Modern individualism', p. 158.

their enemies and overcome the passions disturbing their subjects. Such reasons led all European states, to greater or lesser degrees,[11] to forge myths of political secrecy and justify dissimulation. At the same time, governments struggled to overcome the inherent paradoxes resulting from the multiform manifestations and incomprehensible essence of secrecy, which was simultaneously visible and invisible; in Venice, the censorship of the Council of Ten over the mass of *avvisi* testifies to the difficulty of deciding what must remain secret and what could be revealed.[12]

Sixteenth-century religious and cultural developments made it impossible to confine secrecy to the purely political realm, whose frontiers were largely submerged. This development also coincided with the emerging cult of individualism; it joined the concepts of individual uniqueness and self-assertion, so characteristic of the Renaissance.[13] Secrecy remained intimate, an element of the autonomous subject; by authorising transgressions of social codes, it became an important right of individuals.[14] Unless it was extorted by violence, confession – secrecy's reverse image – discharged its transgressive burden.[15] Despite such characteristics (including a playful dimension to be discussed later), one should not forget that secrecy posed ethical problems, because it remained fundamentally a mechanism of dissimulation or even outright lying. A place where truth was manipulated, it was connected with treason; at the level of universal values, it engaged personal honour.

Secrecy and cryptography

Born in the shadows of secrecy, cryptography remains its quintessential representation and partly conditioned its material existence;

---

[11] On Venice as a paradigm, see Preto, *Servizi segreti*, pp. 55–6.

[12] *Ibid.*, pp. 89–90. On measures for controlling secrecy, see Gaetano Cozzi, *Repubblica di Venezia e stati italiani: politica e giustizia dal secolo XVI al secolo XVIII* (Turin: Einaudi, 1982), pp. 135–6.

[13] See Peter Burke, *The Italian Renaissance: Culture and Society in Italy*, 2nd edition (Cambridge: Polity Press, 1999), pp. 198–9.

[14] Dominique Rabaté, 'Le secret et la modernité', *Modernités* 14 (2001), 19.

[15] Even a coercive appeal on purely moral grounds could turn someone who revealed a secret into an informer: see Jean Delumeau, *L'aveu et le pardon: les difficultés de la confession XIIIe–XVIIIe siècle* (Paris: Fayard, 1992), especially pp. 11–19.

without cryptography, secrecy lacks material form or readability. However, this symbolic form of writing simultaneously guarantees and accentuates its hermeticism. Manipulation of the codes which create secret writing provided settings for deploying its mystery. Cryptography reveals the etymological sense of secrecy as a semantic category: it is put aside and 'sifted'.[16]

Such drama powerfully suggests a sphere of ritual. It presupposes a process of 'sacralisation' and legitimation, which provides considerable support for governments by reinforcing their clandestine operations and enlarging the gulf separating those who emit secret messages from those unable to decipher them. Cryptography, whether individual or collective, permits a constant unwinding of secrecy while controlling its immense plasticity.[17]

Unlike such steganographic procedures as invisible ink, cryptography does not attempt to conceal writing, but rather to make it unintelligible. It appears as a kind of game, an enigma in the form of a hermeneutically reducible equation requiring a 'closed' resolution. Individualistic and ludic motives contributed heavily to the increasing popularity of this type of enigma during the Renaissance, when coded writing invaded even private correspondence with no military or political secrets, creating a space for intimate and confidential exchanges outside collective social pressures.[18]

European cryptography before 1500

Such characteristics doubtless affected the changing status of western cryptography. Although coding and decoding had been practised in antiquity, linked to military information,[19] and Pope Sylvester II

---

[16] Latin *secretus* ('put aside') comes from *secerno* ('to sift'): A. Ernout and A. Meillet (eds.), *Dictionnaire étymologique de la langue latine* (Paris: Klincksieck, 2001), p. 115.

[17] Rabaté, 'Le secret et la modernité', p. 21.

[18] This chapter will not deal with steganographic procedures designed to preserve secrecy. On the development of epistolary arts since the Middle Ages, see Giles Constable, 'Letters and letter-collection', *Typologie des sources du Moyen-Age occidental*, fasc. 17–A II (Turnhout: Brepols, 1976), pp. 11–38 and 39–41; Peter Mason is studying the creation of codes in eighteenth-century private correspondence.

[19] Polybius, Plutarch, Herodotus and Aeneas the Tactician all mention coding and decoding. On espionage networks and information-gathering practices in the

(999–1003) left about fifteen coded letters, the practice remained rudimentary and confined to narrow circles for a very long period. During the Middle Ages, systems of secret writing were attributed to Rabanus Maur, Archbishop of Mainz. Roger Bacon (1214–94) described seven of them.[20] They were associated with various exotic magical practices: mathematics, the Jewish Kabbala, or occultism. In a predominantly illiterate world, where even alphabets remained mysterious for many people, manipulating figures and letters was necessarily associated with manifestations of invisible powers.

Signs of authentic cryptographic development accumulate in late medieval Europe. In Venice, crosses and dots replaced vowels in some words as early as 1226 and Greek or Hebrew letters began substituting for names in 'clear'[21] texts of some official Venetian registers by 1290. A qualitative and quantitative leap began in the fourteenth century through the convergence of humanistic intellectual curiosity with the dynamics of a few leading states, particularly Venice and the papacy.[22] By 1350, a Venetian embassy in Hungary used letters of the alphabet to identify sovereigns and other political figures.[23] The papacy evolved parallel systems; its chancery used a rudimentary code in 1326–7 and introduced blanks in 1338–40 and 1363–4. In 1379, Gabriel de Lavinde, secretary of the antipope Clement VII, left a *Liber Zifrarum* containing a system of keys used among two dozen of the pontiff's correspondents, combining a coded alphabet with a brief

---

Greco-Roman world, see Giovanni Brizzi, *I sistemi informativi dei Romani: principi e realtà nell'età delle conquiste oltremare, 218–168 a.C* (Wiesbaden: Franz Steiner Verlag, 1982), pp. 3–37, 244–58; Frank S. Russell, *Information Gathering in Classical Greece* (Ann Arbor: University of Michigan Press, 1999), pp. 190–212. Two cryptographic methods existed, the *scytale* and the 'shifted alphabet' of Julius Caesar: Rémi Cellier, *La cryptographie* (Paris: PUF, 1948), pp. 11, 23; James Westfall Thompson and Saul K. Padover, *Secret Diplomacy: Espionage and Cryptography, 1500–1815* (New York: Ungar, 1963), pp. 253–4.

[20] Edmond Lerville, *Les cahiers secrets de la cryptographie: le chiffre dans l'histoire des histoires du chiffre* (Paris: Editions du Rocher, 1972), p. 27.

[21] A 'clear' text changes from its original form to a comprehensible meaning: André Langue and E. A. Soudart, *Traité de cryptographie* (Paris: Librairie Félix Alcan, 1925), p. 6.

[22] David Kahn, *Codebreakers: The Story of Secret Writing* (New York: Macmillan, 1996), pp. 106–9.

[23] Thompson and Padover, *Secret Diplomacy*, p. 256; Preto, *Servizi segreti*, p. 268.

index of a dozen ordinary nouns and proper names translated into bigrams.[24]

Whether a parallel development or the result of western exchanges with the Islamic world, about the same time (1412) the *Subh al-a 'sha'* of Qalqashandī, an enormous fourteen-volume encyclopedia of all branches of knowledge, provided the first summary of possible combinations of numbered language outside Europe.[25] From a strictly technical viewpoint, the evolution of western cryptography was related to the development of other forms of writing and suffered from identical material constraints: the cost and scarcity of parchment in medieval Europe and the consequent need to economise the use of writing obviously affected it.[26]

Meanwhile, a secret Venetian chancery was reportedly created on 23 April 1402; its first complete code, dated 28 June 1411, can be found among the orders sent by Doge Michele Steno to the Venetian ambassador in Rome.[27] A secret agent, Andrea Dolceto, received a code from Andrea Barbarigo in 1431. Ten years later, an official dispatch to their ambassador at the papal court was totally coded.[28] Such Venetian precocity illustrated the irresistible growth and triumph of a coercive system founded on a highly efficient police and judicial network, where written or spoken words became instruments of internal and external state power, and where controlling information became crucial for maintaining it.[29] This development was probably also related to

---

[24] Kahn, *Codebreakers*, p. 107. See also n. 39.

[25] Kahn, *Codebreakers*, pp. 95–9; Preto, *Servizi segreti*, p. 262. The Ismaïlis used a code based on the movements of the knight in chess: Langue and Soudart, *Traité*, p. 27.

[26] Ideographic scripts, like Tyronian, had their hour of glory under the Carolingians, and the replacement of vowels by points was the basis of Rabanus Maur's system: see Thompson and Padover, *Secret Diplomacy*, p. 254.

[27] Christiane Villain-Gandossi, 'Les dépêches chiffrées de Vettore Bragadin, Baile de Constantinople (12 juillet 1564–15 juin 1566)', in *La Méditerranée aux XIIe–XVIe siècles* (London: Variorum Reprints, 1983) pp. 53–4 nn. 4–5.

[28] Preto, *Servizi segreti*, p. 268.

[29] Crouzet-Pavan, 'Mots de Venise', p. 206; also Pierre Sardella, *Nouvelles et spéculations à Venise au début du XVIe siècle* (Paris: Armand Colin, 1948), pp. 14–15. On Venetian political structures (and their faults) see Dennis Romano, '*Quod sibi fiat gratia*: adjustment of penalties and the exercise of influence in early Renaissance Venice', *Journal of Medieval and Renaissance Studies* 13 (1983), 251–68. Preto, *Servizi segreti*, p. 267.

applying the taste for rationality to everyday life, which arose from a fascination with numbers and methods of calculation noticeable in Italian cities since the thirteenth century.[30]

In 1466, Leon Battista Alberti's *De componendis cyfris* marked a new stage in the development of cryptographic language. Alberti introduced a new type of key based on the technique of poly-alphabetical substitution, adapted from another of his inventions, the numbered dial (later improved by Giambattista Della Porta). Alberti's research also included analyses of frequencies, including their reversal and suppression.[31] His most remarkable invention, well ahead of his time, was a mathematical supercode using all possible combinations of the numbers one through four, from 11 to 4444, in order to create a repertory of 336 groups whose cryptographic equivalents varied with the movements of his dial – a direct ancestor of today's coding machines.[32] Almost simultaneously (1465), Cicco Simonetta, secretary of the Sforza dukes of Milan, composed another cryptographic treatise, *Regulae extraendis litteras zifferatas sive exempio* (Pavia, 1474). It utilised a dozen rules for constructing and deciphering codes, recommending a system of substitution with multiple representations and adding symbols; Simonetta also studied the frequency of vowels.[33]

EARLY MODERN EUROPEAN CRYPTOGRAPHY

Major cryptograhic systems

The increasing complexity of contacts, the difficulties of mastering them, and the rise of long and recurrent international conflicts

---

[30] Burke, *Italian Renaissance*, p. 203.

[31] First published in Italian translation by Cosimo Bartoli in 1568, Alberti's treatise was recently reprinted: *Dello scrivere in cifra* (Turin: Galimberti, 1994).

[32] For its detailed workings, see Kahn, *Codebreakers*, pp. 125–30.

[33] Simonetta's text was republished by A. Meister in 1902: see Villain-Gandossi, 'Dépêches chiffrées', p. 7 n. 82; Preto, *Servizi segreti*, p. 257. His first six rules concern Italian and Latin. Simonetta drew attention to 'vulnerable' letters and made an inventory of the most common bigrams and trigrams: P. M. Perret, 'Les règles de Cicco Simonetta pour le déchiffrement des écritures secrètes', *Bibliothèque de l'Ecole des Chartes* 51 (1890), 516–25. On Simonetta, see also Lydia Ceroni, *La diplomazia sforzesca nella seconda metà del Quattrocento e i suoi cifrari segreti* (Rome: Fonti e Studi del *Corpus Membranarum Italicarum*, 7, 1970), 2 vols.

combined to promote a feeling of widespread insecurity bordering on paranoia. It persuaded European elites that state protection offered them a necessary 'supra-social' regulatory entity which guaranteed social cohesion. Meanwhile, by mythifying their enemies' nebulous threats, states exploited this sense of insecurity for their self-defence. Fernand Braudel saw the growth of secret information and deployment of its ever-increasing official means as 'psychological exorcism': a method for allaying social fears of external dangers, but also a strategy to remind its subjects of the need for vigilance and mobilisation by exaggerating them.[34]

By offering a solution to the problem of maintaining the confidentiality of correspondence in an age of uncertain transportation and possible interception,[35] cryptography provided a method of reassuring elites needing effective protection from the state. This process implied the multiplication and sophistication of encoding and decoding techniques, even if not all theoretical possibilities were actually used.[36]

Two major ciphering systems were employed in the fifteenth and sixteenth centuries: transposition (also called 'dispersed,' since letters kept their identity but lost their place, being shifted or mixed by prearranged rules) and substitution, where letters lost their identity but kept their place. This second system was also called the 'alphabetical system', because it replaced letters of the 'clear' alphabet with letters from one or more artificial alphabets known as substitution or numerical alphabets. Those using only one alphabet were called 'mono-alphabetical substitution'; systems mixing several coded alphabets became 'poly-alphabetical'.[37]

---

[34] On the insecurities provoked by rumours and eschatological fears, see Crouzet-Pavan, 'Mots de Venise', p. 213; on the spying psychosis, see Paolo Preto, 'Lo spionnagio turco a Venezia tra mito e realtà', in Giovanna Motta (ed.), *I turchi, il Mediterraneo e l'Europa* (Milan: Franco Angeli, 1998), pp. 123–32.

[35] On couriers, see Garrett Mattingly, *Renaissance Diplomacy* (Boston, MA: Houghton Mifflin, 1955), pp. 147–8, 247–8.

[36] Thompson and Padover, *Secret Diplomacy*, p. 259.

[37] Langue and Soudart (*Traité*, p. 94) divide artificial alphabets into random, reversed, reciprocal, inverted, complementary and parallel forms.

This mixture of two major methods made decoding more difficult. In the substitution method, every letter of the 'clear' alphabet might be replaced by one or several associated letters or numbers, to which conventional signs or symbols might be added, using a list drawn from the alphabet. Thus 'clear' letters had several alternative equivalents (called cryptographic units or homophones) taken from a single cryptographic alphabet, known as an alphabet of substitution with multiple equivalents (or simple substitution with frequencies either suppressed or reversed, replacing the most common letters by many different signs). At the beginning of the fifteenth century, homophones were used for vowels in alphabets of substitution, although they were applied to consonants only in the sixteenth century.[38]

Techniques of substitution thus offered several variants. Coding units might consist not just of one letter, but pairs of letters (bigrams), or more rarely of longer units called trigrams and polygrams (for syllables, words, or short phrases cut into units of equal length); these were called systems of literal and polygrammatical substitution. In a subcategory known as coded (as distinguished from literal) substitutions, the 'clear' text is cut into linguistic units of widely varied length, sometimes including entire sentences. Such methods required a panoply of instruments, the most important of which during the sixteenth century was the repertory, which might include letters, Arabic numerals, syllables, words, blanks (sometimes using symbols) or even entire phrases.[39]

Considered more complex and therefore safer than transposition, the method of substitution dominated the sixteenth century. Some of its modes had inconvenient features; for example, an exclusive use of Arabic numerals slowed both the coding and decoding of letters and dispatches, while also lengthening the format of the correspondence

---

[38] Kahn, *Codebreakers*, pp. 107–8.
[39] Langue and Soudart, *Traité*, pp. 189–90. This procedure, called 'nomenclature', originally comprised two separate lists. The first contained three categories: a ciphered alphabet (mono-alphabetical substitution); cryptographic units or homophones; a series of truncated or compounded words and entire expressions along with homophones, and sometimes with blanks (all together forming a deciphering table). The second list was composed of a list of equivalents. These two lists were ultimately fused together.

being sent.[40] In the second half of the sixteenth century, systems of substitution increasingly employed multiple representations for 'clear' letters corresponding to homophones, mixing Arabic numerals with letters from the Greek and Roman alphabets and sprinkling in some geometrical signs. The advantage of this system was that each word, syllable or alphabetical letter could be written in various ways, thus limiting repetitions, which were easy to spot and therefore dangerous if the document was intercepted. For increased security, the Arabic numerals, letters and geometrical signs were changed frequently; and if that seemed insufficient, additional keys were added to the ciphered contents.

Keys, indispensable tools for decoding

The key, which indicated the arrangement of letters in an alphabet of substitution or transposition, generally took the form of a sequence taken from a biblical phrase or a daily prayer; for example, 'in the name of the Father' was often employed as a key in sixteenth-century diplomatic correspondence. Keys were chosen very carefully, because they had magical connotations; they exorcised the secrecy of the message, put it under divine protection, and helped ensure it would reach its destination.

The numerical value of each letter of a key was added to the numerical value of every corresponding letter of the already coded text. Thus a key represented a series of figures (in an arithmetical sense of the term) which defined the mode of substitution or transposition to be employed.[41] Any courier, report or instruction became indecipherable to outsiders if the key (i.e. the value of each letter in a sequence) was known only to the correspondents.

Unwrapping a coded dispatch, letter or report thus depended ultimately on its key. This situation soon produced a specific problem,

---

[40] Barnard Allaire, 'Le décodage de la correspondance chiffrée des diplomates espagnols au XVIe siècle', *Correspondre, jadis et naguère. 120e Congrès national des sociétés historiques et scientifiques* (Aix-en-Provence: Comité des travaux historiques et scientifiques, 1995), p. 210.

[41] Kahn, *Codebreakers*, pp. xv, 103–4.

namely replacement. In order to prevent a key from being broken eventually by outsiders (a possibility which multiplied if the same key was used by several chanceries, ambassadors or agents of the same state), it must be changed frequently. In order to solve this problem, the Venetian Council of Ten created a dictionary with a common key for every ambassador in 1547, adding a separate number for each of its representatives.[42] Of course, this common key underwent more or less regular modifications, sometimes at very long intervals; one Venetian key remained unchanged for twenty-five years, probably because of the relatively rudimentary level of European chanceries and diplomatic services in this period.[43] Moreover, it was sometimes difficult to determine whether or not a code had been deciphered; for strategic reasons, enemies did not always react immediately after 'breaking' a code and reading a secret message.

Replacing keys caused further problems, because (at least in theory) they were confined to the memories of the interested parties; an entire textual 'arsenal' (prayers, biblical sequences – passages of the Psalms – Latin proverbs), known to all participants, was designed to reduce the burden of memorisation.[44] But it was a two-edged process: if it helped more people memorise it, it also made decoding easier. Moreover, choosing a key required careful thought for another reason; its length was as important as its content. If it was too long, it could not be memorised correctly. It required some formula which was easy to memorise, a mnemotechnical device providing a starting point for the biblical sequence and, therefore, the numerical key.

Nevertheless, the problems of having a limited number of keys in circulation were only solved by Giovanni Battista Bellaso, a gentleman from Brescia, in three treatises from 1553, 1555 and 1564. Bellaso created enormous flexibility by inventing literal and easily changeable keys, known to posterity as 'passwords' (*contrasegno*). The 'clear' text,

---

[42] Villain-Gandossi, 'Dépêches chiffrées', p. 71 n. 75. However, a unique key existed previously: *ibid.*, p. 78 n. 103.

[43] The same situation affected the recruitment of spies: see Dejanirah Couto, 'L'espionnage portugais dans l'empire ottoman', in *La découverte, le Portugal et l'Europe* (Paris: Fondation Calouste Gulbenkian, 1990), pp. 245–9.

[44] Cellier, *Cryptographie*, p. 17.

written underneath a password, might come from Italian, Latin or some other language. When aligned with each 'clear' letter, the letters of the password provided a precise key to the alphabet which would unscramble each coded letter.[45]

Innovations in cryptographic techniques

The sixteenth century brought several fundamental contributions to modern cryptography, both theoretical and practical. The former were developed primarily by Blaise de Vignière (1523–96), secretary to King Charles IX of France. In a 600-page book of 1585, *Traicté des chiffres ou secretes matières d'escrire*, he examined various methods of poly-alphabetical substitution, enumerating a large number of keys used by Italian states and elsewhere in Europe: words, dates, verses, phrases, etc.[46] A lawyer and mathematician, François Viète de la Bigotière, the coding expert for Henri IV of France, was a brilliant cryptanalyst,[47] as were Giovanni Battista and Matteo Argenti, papal coding secretaries from 1585 to 1591 and 1591 to 1605 respectively.[48]

The printing press contributed to a certain diffusion of cryptography beyond the inner circles of power. Abbot Johann of Heidelberg (1462–1516), better known as Trithemius, composed a *Polygraphiae libri sex* (1518), dedicated to Emperor Maximilian I, which showed the first square table representing cryptographical alphabets in a methodical system, creating a poly-alphabetical system which remained authoritative until the eighteenth century.[49] To increase the difficulties

---

[45] Kahn, *Codebreakers*, p. 137.

[46] On the importance and application of the 'Vignière' or 'square' method, see Kahn, *Codebreakers*, pp. 145–8; J. P. Devos, *Les chiffres de Philippe II (1555–1598) et du Despacho Universal durant le XVIIe siècle* (Brussels: J. Duculot, 1950), pp. 58–9. Vignière's *Traicté* was recently reprinted (Paris: G. Trédaniel, 1996).

[47] On Viète, see Devos, *Chiffres de Philippe II*, pp. 29–30.

[48] On Matteo's abridged code, which used Arabic numbers for only ten of the most common letters, see Villain-Gandossi, 'Dépêches chiffrées', p. 74, n. 9.

[49] Trithemius's treatise was reprinted in Frankfurt in 1550 and again in 1564, 1676 and 1721; five other editions are known between 1571 and 1637. It was translated into French by Gabriel de Collange, published as *Polygraphie et universelle escriture cabalistique* (Paris: J. Kerver, 1561), and was reprinted in 1625. Trithemius also composed a *Steganographia* which remained in manuscript until 1606.

of decoding, Trithemius advised using 'gates' (i.e. keys), modifying the order of letters or changing the letters which replaced them.

In his *De subtilitate* (Basel, 1547) and *De rerum varietate* (Lyon, 1556), the Milanese mathematician and physician Girolamo Cardano (1501–76) introduced the first autoclave system and the network of 'grills', simple methods of substitution using squares, circles or polygonal pieces of paper into which several 'windows' have been cut, each with a letter, and coded as the grill is turned.[50] Cardano's system was used by several European chanceries until the seventeenth century.

Giovanni Battista Della Porta, whose *De furtivis literarum notis vulgo de ziferis libri IV* (Naples, 1563) was often reprinted (Naples, 1602; Strasbourg, 1603, 1606, 1616),[51] was in Venetian service. Continuing Alberti's work, Della Porta also synthesised the work of his other predecessors and refined the method of probable words, which detected the most common terms through the position of various letters. His synthesis produced the modern form for the procedure of poly-alphabetical substitution, by offering multiple forms of automatically varying letters through changing transcriptions of one individual letter with another (thus using only twenty-six letters, designated automatically by a key); he also created the first bi-grammatical substitution, representing two characters by one symbol. Called the 'Porta system', this procedure exercised considerable influence across four centuries, despite its excessive complexity.[52] A few later contributions also deserve mention, including *Scotographia*, offered to the Venetian Republic in 1591 by Abraham Colorni and published two years later, or Agostino Amadi's *Della cifre* (1588), a work which, its author boasted, drew upon a real command of algebra.[53]

---

[50] On Cardano, see Kahn, *Codebreakers*, pp. 143–5; Preto, *Servizi segreti*, p. 264; Langue and Soudart, *Traité*, pp. 25–6. The 'window grill' was popularised by Pietro Partenio around 1600.

[51] J. P. Devos and H. Seligman, *L'art de deschiffrer: traité de déchiffrement du XVIIe siècle de la secrétairerie d'état et de guerre espagnole* (Louvain: Publications Universitaires, 1967), p. 8.

[52] On Della Porta's significance, see Kahn, *Codebreakers*, pp. 137–43 (with a table); Cellier, *Cryptographie*, p. 49. For criticisms, see Lange and Soudart, *Traité*, pp. 28–9.

[53] Preto, *Servizi segreti*, p. 265. Besides an exhaustive number of languages, Amadi's work included a 'diabolical' tongue: *ibid.*, p. 278 n. 152.

The chanceries of Europe's smaller principalities and religious orders gradually imitated Venice, the papacy and Christendom's major kingdoms. The Jesuits, for example, developed their own code, adopting secrecy because of opposition and criticism both inside and outside the church; if intercepted, internal documents risked being used as propaganda against them (as happened in 1614 with the *Monita Secreta Societatis Jesu*). Jesuit precautionary measures included abandoning the use of the order's official seal and introducing coded correspondence, especially for *segredo* letters to provincial Superiors and Visitors.[54] A 1588 letter from the society's general to Vasco Peres explained the necessity of writing in numbers in order to prevent the contents from being read by anyone except the recipient; the same reasoning reappears in a later instruction from 1640.[55]

The Jesuits sometimes employed a letter-for-letter substitution, sometimes multiple representations (Arabic numerals with or without letters and signs); in other words, they copied the encryption methods of the sixteenth-century Spanish chancery.[56] However, they often preferred mnemotechnical methods (to be discussed later), substituting words and expressions which they adapted and collated into the 'clear' text, so that an unwary reader would not recognise an apparently coherent text as actually coded.[57]

Training encoders

These new techniques required increased capabilities. Because coders needed a knowledge of mathematics and various languages (including Greek) which ordinary secretaries of royal or episcopal chanceries

---

[54] Nigel Griffin, *'Virtus versus Letters': The Society of Jesus 1550–1580 and the Export of an Idea*, EUI Working papers 95 (Florence: European University Institute, 1984), pp. 20–1. Numerous examples in Josef Wicki SJ, 'Die Chiffre in der Ordenskorrespondenz der Gesellschaft Jesu von Ignatius bis General Oliva (ca.1554–1676)', *Archivum Historicum Societatis Jesu* 32 (1963), 133–78.

[55] João Pedro Ferro, 'A epistolografia no quotidiano dos missionários jesuítas', *Lusitania Sacra* 5 (1993), 143–4 n. 27.

[56] Griffin, *'Virtus'*, p. 21.

[57] Simão Rodrigues used a particularly interesting mnemotechnic code in Jerusalem in 1554 (Wicki, 'Chiffre', 139).

rarely possessed, officials charged with coding documents became increasingly specialised. Once again, Venice led the way.[58] In 1531, Giovanni Tagliente, the chancery secretary, proposed to teach new employees several types of writing, including numerical codes. By 15 March 1541, the Most Serene Republic employed three official coders. Men like Giovanni Soro, one of the best Venetian encoders and author of a *Liber zifrarum* (Venice, 1539),[59] or Marco Rafaele trained a contingent of very fine cryptographers, including Pirrho Musefilli, Count of Sasseta, active in Florence from 1546 to 1557, or Triphon Bendo of Assisi, papal cryptographer in 1555.

Venetian ciphering secretaries were supervised by the Council of Ten. Government control over their activities intensified after the creation of *Inquisitori di stato* in 1539. Political conflicts, particularly with the Ottoman Empire, also favoured close governmental supervision over coding; as early as 1513, Marin Sanudo (Sanuto) noted the importance of 'letters from Constantinople translated from cipher'.[60] The sometimes urgent correspondence of Venetian ambassadors with the doge (especially their *dispacci*, preserved regularly after 1554) provides a rich harvest of coded documents, classified in the Venetian state archives as *Cifre (Code)*, *Busta* 1a.[61] Another source of considerable importance, the letters of Venetian *bailes* in Constantinople, received a special code.[62] However, it is unclear whether Venetian interpreters, especially those working in Turkish, became coding secretaries.

By 1569, the Most Serene Republic had assembled a vanguard of coding secretaries who, as Nuncio Antonio Facchinetti observed, 'decoded everything with great facility'. This was also the time when general regulations governing codes were put into operation. All coding secretaries were required to take oaths of obedience to the Council of Ten

---

[58] Preto, *Servizi segreti*, p. 274; Villain-Gandossi, 'Dépêches chiffrées', p. 53 n. 4.

[59] It was written by order of the Council of Ten, who eulogised its author in a document dated 1512: Villain-Gandossi, 'Dépêches chiffrées', p. 74 n. 86. On Soro's career, see Kahn, *Codebreakers*, p. 109.

[60] Marin Sanudo, *I diarii*, 58 vols. (Venice, 1879–1903).

[61] See Villain-Gandossi, 'Dépêches chiffrées', p. 54 and n. 6 (with a bibliography on Venetian codes).

[62] *Ibid.*, pp. 56–74, collected and partly published the letters of *baile* Vettore Bragadin.

and to register any entrance or exit of various codes, including those given to ambassadorial secretaries; codes were normally prohibited from leaving the ducal palace.[63] Decrees of 27 September 1577, 18 August 1578 and 27 August 1587 spelled out further measures taken by the republic to protect its coding system.[64] Coding (when the key was known) and decoding (when it was unknown) became the apanage of family dynasties which came to be authentic 'guardians of secrecy'.

Memorised codes

Coding and decoding systems never entirely replaced simpler forms of secret writing. In particular, European chanceries continued to use a very old memorisation method, known by the fifteenth century as *in parabula* or *sub enigma*. For example, the key (*ordo seu regula occulte scribendis*) used by the Navarrese Infante Don. Carlos during his trip to France in 1377 gave easily identifiable code-names to the kings of France and England, the pope and various cardinals.[65]

An elementary method of substitution, where one name was simply replaced by another, the *in parabula* method required neither competence in mathematics nor complicated manipulations. The ancestor of coded dictionaries containing thousands of words, this conventional language relied on techniques of memorisation, presented as glossaries or tables of synonyms built on figurative meanings, similarity of sounds or metaphors. Its greatest virtue, simplicity, was also its worst drawback: once its semantic field of reference was known, deciphering it through free association was as easy as memorising it. It seems obvious that, besides its simplicity, the weight of medieval tradition helped to preserve this method long after 1500.[66]

Nevertheless, one wonders why such primitive methods continued to be used even in Venice, which already possessed specialised personnel and excellent workable systems for coding and decoding.

[63] Preto, *Servizi segreti*, pp. 275, 272.
[64] Published from ASV, *Cifre*, *Busta* VI, by Villain-Gandossi, 'Dépêches chiffrées', pp. 105–6; see also pp. 78–9.
[65] Miguel Angel Ochoa Brun, *Historia de la diplomacia española* (Madrid: Ministerio de Asuntos Exteriores, 1991), vol. 3, pp. 351–2.
[66] For sixteenth-century examples, see Thompson and Padover, *Secret Diplomacy*, pp. 251–2.

Besides limiting the possibilities for error inherent in complex coding techniques,[67] it apparently seemed adequate for use by most spies and informers, who were usually uneducated people recruited from the waterfronts of major Mediterranean ports.[68]

Employing large numbers of such agents made managing information services more difficult and doubtless aggravated the problems involved with using codes. In addition, the increase in ciphered correspondence and the growing complexity of the systems employed led both secret agents and their employers to take dangerous risks by simplifying coding. Some dispatches even contained coded passages which contradicted the 'clear' parts of the same document;[69] some secret correspondence addressed to the sovereign (including some of Granvelle's letters to Philip II) was not coded, violating the general regulations of the Spanish monarchy.

Beyond their simplicity, messages employing memorisation codes offered the additional advantage of drawing less attention than ciphered messages. If intercepted, a letter written in Hebrew characters (which also virtually guaranteed the secrecy of its information) could be dangerous for its bearer, because it could easily be mistaken for cipher. However, cleverly constructed memorisation codes, like those used by Jesuits, could be mistaken for ordinary correspondence when intercepted.

The organisational shortcomings of sixteenth-century European chanceries also favoured the continuing popularity of this system. Despite a growing need to preserve the privacy of correspondence, their extreme specialisation made coding secretaries difficult to recruit, except for the papacy or major European governments like the duchy of Burgundy.[70] Even Venice, Europe's greatest information centre

---

[67] Noted by Fletcher Pratt, *Secret and Urgent: The Story of Codes and Ciphers* (Indianapolis: Bobbs-Merrill, 1939), p. 15.

[68] See Paolo Preto, *Persona per hora secreta: accusa e delazione nella Repubblica di Venezia* (Milan: Saggiatore, 2003), pp. 20, 42–9.

[69] See Enrique García Hernán, 'The price of spying at the battle of Lepanto', *Eurasian Studies: The Skilliter Centre–Istituto per l'Oriente Journal for Balkan, Eastern Mediterrenan, Anatolian, Middle Eastern, Iranian and Central Asian Studies* 2 (2003), 239.

[70] Christian de Borchgrave, 'Diplomates et diplomatie sous le duc de Bourgogne Jean sans peur', in Jean-Marie Cauchies (ed.), *A la cour de Bourgogne: le duc, son entourage, son train* (Turnhout: Brepols, 1998), pp. 67–83.

alongside Rome, employed only three coding secretaries in the first half of the sixteenth century. Limiting their number also had the advantage of reducing the danger of 'intoxication', strikingly revealed by a document from 1579: a certain Celio Malespina proposed his services to the Venetians as an expert forger who could produce imaginary codes for foreign couriers, along with bogus safe-conducts, passports, etc.[71]

Although we can establish no clear hierarchy between older and newer coding methods during the sixteenth century, the general tendency seems clear, despite numerous exceptions. Sophisticated methods of substitution were reserved primarily for diplomatic documents between governments, while memorisation techniques generally sufficed for instructing unofficial state agents. Moreover, one essential state institution long resisted employing any form of cryptography: army orders were often transmitted orally in the sixteenth century.

Venetian memorisation codes

Italy, and Venice in particular, seems to have been responsible for the wide diffusion of memorisation techniques known as 'jargon' or 'conventional language' (in parabula). It would be fastidious to sift through every example of this practice preserved at Venice.[72] A Venetian coder, Matteo Argenti, claimed the procedure was invented there; as early as 1496–1502, the future doge, Andrea Gritti, then a merchant at Istanbul, used commercial jargon to send secret information to Venice about Ottoman military movements. In 1505, another patrician, Leonardo Bembo, employed a similar mercantile lexicon.

The quantity and varieties of this type of code testify to its enormous diffusion throughout early modern southern Europe, from the Iberian peninsula to remote Levantine regions of the Ottoman Empire. Sometimes mixed with coding through substitution, this blend of a predominantly commercial language (where, for example, the word 'cargo' meant 'marriage' or 'merchandise' meant 'alliance')

---

[71] Printed by Lamansky, Secrets d'état, vol. 1, pp. 539–42.
[72] Numerous examples in Preto, Servizi segreti, pp. 269–70.

appears frequently in the correspondence of Charles V's chancery.[73] It seems linked to networks of Mediterranean merchants, often Jewish or 'New-Christian', who were frequently recruited as informers by the Venetians or the Habsburgs.[74]

One of the most successful examples of this form of code is undoubtedly the 'book' used by Hayyim Saruq, merchant and secret agent in Venetian service, during the Venetian–Turkish conflict over Cyprus in 1571. Saruq reportedly travelled disguised as an Albanian; his mission, plus support for his family in Venice for a year, cost 500 ducats.[75] The form of the nineteen-page code-glossary intended for him (10.5 × 25.5 cm, in easily readable script) offers many similarities with other codes used by agents of the Council of Ten on missions in Turkish territories;[76] structurally, it closely resembles the document reproduced as an appendix. We shall confine ourselves here to the peculiarities of its vocabulary.

The passage 'whatever cipher he will make' (*quella ʒifra che esso darà*) suggests that the council merely dictated a list of terms to be coded, with Saruq himself finding appropriate terminology. The glossary includes a mixture of various lexical groups; though probably designed to mislead, they may simply indicate Saruq's difficulty in creating new synonyms within the same lexical subfield.[77] In its vocabulary, terms of kinship and names of prominent leaders of the Venetian ghetto (rabbis Samuel Barocas, David Navara, David Jachia) alternated with words from Jewish social and religious life such as *esnoga*, *escama*, *tevet* or *tamus*. The code displayed some traces of humour; e.g. the term

---

[73] Franz Stix, 'Berichte und Studien zur Geschichte Karls V: die Geheimschriftenschlüssel der Kabinettskanzlei des Kaisers', *Nachrichten aus der Mittleren und Neueren Geschichte*, vol. 1 (1934–36) in *Nachrichten von der Gesellschaft der Wissenschaften ʒu Göttingen Philologisch-Historische Klasse*, Fachgruppe II, p. 208.

[74] See the case of Daniel Rodriga, 'Jewish consul' in Narenta and probably in Ragusa before becoming the consul of Ponentine Jews in Venice: Preto, *Serviʒi segreti*, p. 250.

[75] ASV, Consiglio dei Dieci, Secreti, Filza 15. See Benjamin Arbel, *Trading Nations: Jews and Venetians in the Early Modern Eastern Mediterranean* (Leiden: E. J. Brill, 1995), pp. 147–51, 210–15 (text). Saruq's glossary was placed alongside a code destined for an Albanian, which does not prove his disguise (see also *ibid.*, p. 150).

[76] Compare Preto, *Serviʒi segreti*, p. 269.

[77] Arbel, *Trading Nations*, p. 150, notes the correspondence between months of the Hebrew and Christian religious calendars.

'rabbi' (*raf* or *rab*) designated the pope, and 'alms for the poor' meant 'tribute'. Sprinkled throughout were commercial terms, with coded names substituted for ordinary Mediterranean merchandise.[78]

The Portuguese lag

Like much correspondence of Charles V, sixteenth-century Portugal also employed memorisation codes using merchant jargon. For example, a letter of November 1516 to King Manoel from his ambassador at Rome, Dom Miguel de Silva, Bishop of Evora,[79] mixed a code *in parabula* with a code of substitution. The main interest of this early Portuguese code lies in its lexicon. Although some words reappear in other European codes, it acquires a distinctive 'Lusitanian' flavour through a vocabulary based on the exotic products brought into European commerce by the Portuguese during their age of overseas discoveries – perhaps considering this specialised terminology safer because it was not yet widely known. In it, Prince João (the future King João III) was 'Brazil', Emperor Maximilian I became 'the pearl', the King of Castile was 'cardamon', the King of France, 'copper', and the Medicis 'mace' (*maças*). The future Emperor Charles V had the code name 'rhubarb'; royal marriages became 'sandalwood'; and Princess Eleanor was called '*malaguette*'.

However, the Portuguese chancery appears to lag behind its European peers, most notably Spain. While Charles V's chancery used this type of code with multiple substitutions, here and elsewhere the Portuguese chancery used only rudimentary substitutions: Bishop da Silva's letters merely replaced each 'clear' alphabetical letter by a single Arabic numeral, a single letter, or another conventional sign – a

---

[78] *Spetlarie, rubinetti, garofali, cremese, seda cremesina di Bursia, seda della Morea, seda lisin: ibid.*, pp. 151, 211–15 *passim*.

[79] Maria Augusta Lima Cruz and António Manuel Lázaro, 'A linguagem criptográfica na correspondência diplomática portuguesa de D. Miguel da Silva e de Pero Correia: origens e significado', in Roberto Carneiro and Artur Teodoro de Matos (eds.), *D. João III e o império* (Lisbon: Centro de História de Além-Mar, CEPCEP, 2004), p. 605 and annex 1. For Silva's biography, see Sylvie Deswarte, 'La Rome de D. Miguel da Silva (1515–1525)', in *O humanismo português 1500–1600* (Lisbon: Academia das Ciências, 1988), pp. 177–307.

system known as *ziffrete* and used regularly in Italy by spies and local informers.[80] Multiple codings for certain words (with a numbered word hiding a coded word)[81] added little to Portuguese sophistication.

Except for two numbered letters to King Manoel I in 1498,[82] Silva's 1516 letter is the oldest known coded letter in Portuguese.[83] As he complained when writing to King Manoel in his 'finest Portuguese' in March 1515, Bishop da Silva possessed no code whatsoever during eighteen months of his Roman embassy. Every other Roman ambassador, he informed his monarch in November 1515, had a code ('todo o embaxador as tem e usa'), adding that some cardinals and the pope himself professed astonishment that a power as great as Portugal did not possess one.[84] His complaints were heard. Dispatched on an embassy of congratulation to Charles V in Brussels early in 1517, Pedro Correia already coded some of his letters numerically. However, this process had apparently not yet been completely mastered in Portugal. Correia noted an error in coding his first letter; perhaps in order to avoid such mistakes, his second letter replaced numbering with a memorisation code.[85]

Unimportant during the 1530s, coded messages from the Portuguese court increased slightly after 1550 as Portugal became a more active player on Europe's diplomatic chessboard during the reign of King João III.[86] Besides some examples in cipher preserved in Portuguese

---

[80] Preto, *Servizi segreti*, p. 270.

[81] For example, Bishop da Silva's letter of 1516 used '7ff_m2' as a code for 'copper' to designate the King of France: Cruz and Lázaro, 'Linguagem criptográfica', p. 608.

[82] One of them fragmentary: see *ibid.*, p. 605 n. 19.

[83] The same ambassador sent another coded letter on 10 June 1523, recently printed fully in both coded and decoded versions: *ibid.*, pp. 610–14. We also possess the draft of a coded letter from King Manoel to ambassador da Silva dated 31 March 1521, published in Luís Augusto Rebello da Silva (ed.), *Corpo diplomático português* (Lisbon: Academia Real das Sciências, 1865), vol. 2, pp. 39–41, and two letters to King Manoel from his ambassador to the emperor, the first dated 23 October 1522: Cruz and Lázaro, 'Linguagem criptográfica', pp. 605–6.

[84] Quoted from *Corpo diplomatico português*, vol. 1, 1862, p. 324.

[85] Cruz and Lázaro, 'Linguagem criptográfica', p. 605.

[86] See Aude Viaud, *Correspondance d'un ambassadeur castillan au Portugal dans les années 1530 – Lope Hurtado de Mendoza* (Paris: Centre culturel Calouste Gulbenkian, 2001),

archives,[87] official instructions from 1552 show that state correspondence was being ciphered, probably by King João III's two principal secretaries, Antonio Carneiro and his son Pedro (employed from 1515 to 1568). Although these 1552 instructions emphasised the necessity of following a code for secret business scrupulously,[88] another document sent to the same agent merely underlines the passages to be ciphered.[89]

Spanish domination

Across the Iberian border, Spain had a long cryptographic tradition. The antiquarian Zurita mentions a ciphered letter of Alfonso V to the Duke of Milan in 1440.[90] In May 1452, Alfonso of Aragon, King of Naples and Sicily, composed his own cipher; his message to Emperor Frederick III contained a key to be used in their private correspondence.[91] In 1460, Juan II of Aragon used cryptography when

---

pp. 89–91, and Viaud's edition of *Lettres des souverains portugais à Charles V et à l'Impératrice, 1528–1532, conservées aux archives de Simancas* (Lisbon and Paris: Centre culturel Calouste Gulbenkian, 1994), pp. 38–47.

[87] See *Corpo Diplomático Português*, vol. 3, 1868, pp. 372–6, 406–12, 432–3; vol. 7, 1884, pp. 272–8, 305–11.

[88] See in Ernesto de Campos de Andrada (ed.), *Relações de Pero de Alcáçova Carneiro, Conde de Idanha, do tempo que ele e seu pai, António Carneiro serviram de secretários (1515 a 1568)* (Lisbon: Imprensa Nacional, 1937), p. 116: 'pella cifra que vos dara o secretario me escrevereis coisas que vos parecer que por cifra me deveis escrever'. Another document (AN/TT, *Colecção S. Vicente*, I, fol. 190v°) may also refer to this code: 'Item. Levaeys huua cifra pela qual me escrevereis aquellas cousas em que vos parecer que avera periguo. Não mas escreverdes senam por ela. Scrita em Almeirym a xvj dias do mes de fevereiro de 1552.'

[89] However, elsewhere the same document suggests it was sent entirely in cipher: 'esta foy escripta em cifra a Antonio de Saldanha que levou boroa (?) pela posta de Lisboa quarta-feira de trevas xiij dias do mes de abril de 1552': AN/TT, *Colecção de S. Vicente*, I, fols. 209–10.

[90] Ochoa Brun, *Historia de la Diplomacia*, p. 351 n. 196.

[91] Alan F. C. Ryder, *The Kingdom of Naples under Alfonso the Magnanimous: The Making of a Modern State* (Oxford: Clarendon Press, 1976), pp. 256–7 n. 276: 'Serenissime princeps, mitto vobis cifram sicut inter vos et me deliberatum fuit per quam poteritis michi scribere secreta. Tarditatis causa fuit quia mea propria manu eam scripsi, veniam date' (Archivo de la Corona de Aragón, reg. 2940, fol. 155).

corresponding with his ambassador in Lisbon. After 1470, the Catholic kings used codes regularly and ultimately possessed a glossary containing 600 coded words.[92] As a felicitous formula remarks, Spain's 'rise to power can be followed through the proliferation of its ciphering systems'.[93] Spain soon developed an effective system of simple substitution with multiple representations and some variants, demonstrating considerable progress since the cipher made by Miguel Perez Almazan around 1480. If Emperor Maximilian I was also using cipher by 1510, his grandson Charles V did so far more extensively. Twenty-four different ciphering codes from his reign are still preserved in Viennese archives, more or less elaborate according to the stature of his correspondents and the rank of their kingdoms.[94]

The golden age of Spanish cryptography corresponds to the reigns of Charles V and Philip II. The *Despacho Universal*, a branch of the *Secretaria de Estado*, managed coded diplomatic correspondence. Sometime around 1556, a *Nueva cifra general* was created, based on literal polygrammatical substitution and coded substitution. Supplemented by a *Cifra particular*, the *Nueva cifra general* offered a perfect nomenclature that produced dispatches in a format nearly identical to the 'clear' text, but very difficult to decode if intercepted.[95] Philip II organised his coding service pragmatically: the *Nueva cifra general* was reserved for correspondence of ambassadors with each other or the king, while the *Cifra particular* served for the sovereign's correspondence with his diplomats. The 'General Cipher' replaced twenty-two alphabetical letters with numbers from 1 to 37 (pointed or accented), accompanied by five symbols corresponding to five vowels. About 300 syllables were

[92] Cruz and Lázaro, 'Linguagem criptográfica', p. 608; Juan Carlos Galende Diaz, *Criptografía: historia de la escritura cifrada* (Madrid: Editorial Complutense, 1995), pp. 67–172.
[93] Kahn, *Codebreakers*, p. 114. Overview by Galende Diaz, *Criptografía*, pp. 91–5, 159–72.
[94] Stix, 'Geheimschriftenschlüssel', pp. 207–26 (with a repertory of all codes); see also his second volume (1936–9) [Fachgruppe II], pp. 61–70, especially 61.
[95] Allaire, 'Décodage', pp. 209–10, 212; see also Kahn, *Codebreakers*, pp. 114–16.

represented by homophones (pointed or accented), together with a dictionary of about 500 words represented by bigrams or trigrams.[96] The 'Particular Cipher' generally contained fewer words, replacing some by numbers from 38 to 150 and others by different bigrams and trigrams.[97]

However, numerous dispatches between the Council of the Low Countries and the major chanceries of Madrid and Vienna were only partially coded, thereby making the codes more fragile because 'clear' headings and ends of phrases betrayed the ciphered remainder of this correspondence.[98] Similar procedures were widespread: for example, a letter sent in March 1555 from Pietro Pacheco, Cardinal-Bishop of Siguenza, to Princess Juana mixed ciphered and 'clear' texts; it carries both interlinear and marginal translations.[99] Another ciphered document from 1543, now in the Viennese state archives, is accompanied by three numbered items, themselves followed by their respective transcriptions. The 'clear' title of the ciphered letter is transcribed in tiny letters above its Arabic numerals.[100] Such annotations to a coded text greatly compromised its security. Negligence of this sort was forbidden in Rome, where ciphers always appear as supplements to the 'clear' text (written on a separate sheet of paper), and where the papal chancery even added transposition onto substitution when corresponding with its agents in Venice.[101] Nevertheless, every secular European chancery, including the

---

[96] Devos, *Chiffres de Philippe II*, pp. 92–100, prints the 1556 code, followed by others from 1562, 1564, 1567, etc. Its key was the Latin phrase *Barbara pyramidum sileat miracula memphis.*

[97] Allaire, 'Décodage', p. 212; Devos (p. 60) lists 500 words represented by syllables of two or three letters.

[98] See, in general, Devos and Seligman, *L'art de deschiffrer.*

[99] AGS, Estado, Nápoles, Leg. 1048, fol. 110. Numerous examples in Giuseppe Coniglio, *Il viceregno di Napoli et la lotta tra Spagnoli e Turchi nel Mediterraneo,* vol. 1 (Naples: Giannini, 1987), pp. 83–5.

[100] *Haus-, Hof-, und Staatsarchiv,* Vienna, *Hungarica, XII* (1542), Konv. B, Fasc. 49, doc. 2, and 51–II, (1543), Konv. B, fasc. 50, doc. 43–8 (45, 46, 47), accompanied by the transcription: *Quod vero reginalis Magestas / 45; Quibus vero verbis nobiles juramentum mater se … / 46.; promitto fide et humanitate mea / 47;* signed on fol. 48 v° by *frater Georgius,* Sebernary, 14 February 1543.

[101] Devos, *Chiffres de Philippe II,* p. 64.

Venetian,[102] used such slipshod procedures, which disappeared only during the seventeenth century.

Of course, governments multiplied measures to prevent such malfunctions. Charles V's ambassadors sometimes received their codes from the emperor personally, or warned him secretly about the need to change codes, whereupon the old ciphers were returned.[103] But Philip II judged this sophisticated system insufficient and hastened to reform it by ordering new keys. Writing to his uncle Ferdinand on 24 May 1556, he declared that outdated codes had caused secret letters to be decrypted and that the people responsible for such blunders had been punished.[104] Probably inspired by the methods of the Roman Curia, where Matteo Argenti had introduced this practice, the *Cifra general* was henceforth to be renewed regularly every three or four years.[105]

Apart from subtle variations in the *Cifras particulares*, the Spanish code remained structurally unchanged until the end of the sixteenth century. By then it had incorporated a very large number of conventional signs; a code used by ambassador de Puebla in London contained around 2,400.[106] Vowels were represented by five different symbols and consonants by four. Each 'clear' letter could be decrypted from over fourteen signs, inevitably causing some mistakes. Nevertheless, the Spanish codes were still considered workable in the seventeenth century;[107] the code of the Count-Duke of Olivares generally resembled its sixteenth-century ciphers.[108]

---

[102] Bragadin's letters suffered from such negligence; see Villain-Gandossi, 'Dépêches chiffrées', pp. 75–6. Other examples in Viaud, *Correspondance diplomatique*, p. 63.

[103] See Diego Hurtado de Mendoza's correspondence in Angel Gonzáles Palencia and Eugenio Mele, *Vida y obras de D. Diego Hurtado de Mendoza* (Madrid: Instituto Valencia de D. Juan, 1941), vol. i, p. 104. On changes, see Allaire, 'Décodage', p. 211.

[104] Devos, *Chiffres de Philippe II*, pp. 61–2.

[105] See *ibid.*, pp. 300ff, for examples of changes in the 1580s.

[106] Thompson and Padover, *Secret Diplomacy*, p. 250.

[107] ASV, *Inquisitori di Stato*, Fasciculo 'Sozia 1609–1610' (unnumbered), *Busta* 516 (I wish to thank Giorgio Rota for sending me a photocopy of this document).

[108] Published by Jacques de Monts de Savasse, 'Les chiffres de la correspondance diplomatique des ambassadeurs d'Henri IV, en l'année 1590', in *Correspondre, jadis et naguère* (unpaginated annex).

CRYPTOGRAPHY, DIPLOMACY AND ANTI-OTTOMAN ESPIONAGE

Portuguese and Ottomans: coding primitivism

Rudimentary use of cryptography may not explain the failures of Portuguese policies in the Ottoman Empire, but Portugal's primitive methods certainly hampered negotiations with the Sublime Porte. Although King João III's instructions to his ambassador in Constantinople, drawn up in 1541, were not even encrypted, they were nevertheless highly important. Detailed examination of their contents reveals that King João III intended to prevent Ottoman incursions into Portugal's possessions on the Indian Ocean by reaching some general agreement with the Turks, even proposing a commercial treaty with reciprocal advantages which would have separated Portugal completely from imperial policy towards the Ottoman Empire.[109] Throughout the ensuing negotiations from 1541 to 1545, one finds no trace of coding among the surviving correspondence between the Portuguese court and its ambassadors at the Porte. On the contrary, King João III's 1542 instructions indicate that ambassador Diogo de Mesquita was expected to memorise the written clauses to be negotiated; if arrested before reaching Constantinople, he had to burn or destroy the papers that contain them.[110]

Such unciphered instructions may have been intended to allay Ottoman suspicions of European ambassadors who carried coded letters. In 1491, Bayazid II had declared a Venetian *baile* unacceptable

---

[109] Dejanirah Couto, 'Les Ottomans et l'Inde portugaise', in *Vasco da Gama e a India* (Lisbon and Paris: Fondation Calouste Gulbenkian, 1999), vol. 1, pp. 181–200; on the imperial policy, see other documents in Villain-Gandossi, 'Contribution à l'étude des relations diplomatiques et commerciales entre Venise et la Porte ottomane au XVIe siècle', in *La Méditerranée*, pp. 30–298 (articles 1–3), and Maria Pia Pedani, *In nome del Gran Signore: inviati Ottomani a Veneẓia dalla caduta di Constantinopoli alla guerra di Candia* (Venice: Deputazione, 1994), pp. 1–21.

[110] AN/TT, CCI, 71,28: the phrase 'e dereis de tomaar em vosa letra pera alguuas figuras a memorya da sustança de tudo' suggests he memorised his intructions by using a code.

because he used ciphered correspondence.[111] This attitude, and the Ottomans' occasional recourse to Europeans for decrypting intercepted correspondence,[112] rather than relying on their interpreters (*dragomans*) who translated official documents,[113] suggests that the Turks lacked specialised personnel for such purposes. Nevertheless, the Porte possessed its own 'code-breakers', even if it rarely used them. A ciphered letter of *baile* Bragadin to the Council of Ten, dated 13 March 1566 (six months before Suleiman's death), furnishes proof. In it, the *baile* worried that one of the codes entrusted to him had been decrypted by a certain 'Colombina'. Currently residing in the Seraglio, Colombina had been given some confiscated letters from the emperor to his ambassador along with some from the Council of Ten which had been intercepted by the *agha* of the Janissaries and handed to the 'Magnificent Pasha' (i.e. the grand vizier, Sokollu Mehmed Pacha).[114] Although Colombina had been unable to break the code, Bragadin thought him capable of breaking the Venetian code and therefore urged that it be changed immediately, because Colombina (who may have been a *dragoman* or a renegade) had previously lived in the *baile*'s residence and 'seen the secretaries write and translate codes, and perhaps even helped them do so'.[115] An analysis of Bragadin's

[111] Hans J. Kissling 'Venezia come centro di informazioni sui turchi', in H. G. Beck, M. Manoussacas and A. Pertusi (eds.), *Venezia centro di mediazione tra oriente e occidente (secoli XV–XVI): aspetti e problemi* (Florence: Leo Olschki, 1977), vol. 1, p. 101.

[112] *Lettres et mémoires d'Estat des rois, Princes, Ambassadeurs & autres Ministres, sous les regnes de François premier, Henry II & François II . . . par Messire Guillaume Ribier, Conseiller d'Estat*, vol. 2 (Paris: Frederic Leonard, imprimeur ordinaire du Roy . . . (1677), pp. 300–1: 'les autres qui estoient en chifre adressantes au dit Ambassadeur, me furent données à la Porte pour voir si je pourois les dechifrer'.

[113] On their activities, see J. Matuz, 'Die Pfortendolmetschter zur Herrschaftszeit Süleymâns des Prächtigen', *Südost Forschungen* 34 (1975), 26–56.

[114] Villain-Gandossi, 'Dépêches chiffrées', annex 1, published a facsimile of the intercepted letter, now in the Topkapi Palace archives (30 November 1565).

[115] *Ibid.*, p. 77 n. 101. On Ottoman codes, see M. J. A. Decourtemanche, 'Note sur quatre systèmes turcs de notation numérique secrète', *Journal Asiatique*, 9th series, 14 (1899), 258–71 (unfortunately based on a treatise which provides no dates for any of the codes it discusses).

dispatches shows that all four variants he employed were far less complex than the Spanish cipher.[116]

The in parabula *code of a Neapolitan spy*

Venice's state archives preserve an excellent but almost unknown example of an *in parabula* code, probably intercepted by Venetian espionage networks; published here for the first time, it not only complements Hayyim Saruq's 'book' but also offers interesting discursive arrangements.[117] It was dated 3 September 1535 and addressed to one 'Juan Camp(o)s', an Albanian living at Foggia (*Foxa*). It emanated from the kingdom of Naples, more precisely from Parco Castri (*Nova Neapolis*); its mixture of Spanish and Italian, style and form indicate a Spanish author.[118] We possess both a letter giving general instructions about the secret agent's mission and a coded glossary for him to use.

To summarise: the spy must proceed to Barletta and cross the Adriatic to Albania, where his nephew lived.[119] Once there, his first mission was to assess local Ottoman military forces and sound out Albanian authorities about a possible alliance with the emperor. His second mission was vastly more ambitious: he (or 'someone confidential whom you know personally') should travel on to Constantinople, and from there to the Ottoman camp on the Persian border. The information sought was primarily news about the Persian–Ottoman conflict, which was generating wild rumours in Europe. A second purpose was to get information about Turkish defence forces in Morea and about naval construction in the dockyards at Gallipoli. The Neapolitan employer also wanted to learn the date and circumstances of Suleiman's return to Constantinople. Finally, Campos should discover Turkish reactions to

---

[116] The *baile* was using a system of simple substitution with multiple variants, replacing some letters that were represented by points with other letters and others with Arabic numerals. Two of his codes resemble those used by Venetian ambassadors in Spain and England around 1550; the others, more recent, came from Giovanni Soranzo and Daniele Barbarigo.

[117] Barely mentioned by Preto, *Servizi segreti*, p. 121.

[118] The signature is difficult to read; it could be Antonio Pietro or Puente, the latter being the secretary of Don Pedro de Alarcon.

[119] Fol. 166r identifies his relative as a nephew.

the presence of a French ambassador to the sultan, and enquire about the impact of the recent imperial victory at Tunis.[120]

Contexts: the kingdom of Naples at war with the Ottomans

The type of information requested places this text within the classical genre of *avvisi de Constantinople*, a tiny fragment of a massive amount of seldom-reliable information concerning the Ottoman Empire now scattered across Mediterranean archives, especially Modena, Venice and Simancas,[121] with another rich supply in Vienna.[122] Collected from countless obscure missions, these *avvisi* were generally designed to reassure Christian nations and nourish continuing vigilance against the Turks.[123]

By 1535, such missions seemed more necessary than ever in the Mediterranean, and especially in the kingdom of Naples. On the imperial side, Charles V had suffered serious reverses; Andrea Doria's victory at Coron in 1532 or Charles V's expedition to Tunis in 1535 could not offset the loss of two key strongholds, Rhodes in 1522[124] and Algiers in 1529. Recent western naval shortcomings included the failure of the Knights of Rhodes at Modon in 1532, the Ottoman recapture of Coron in 1534, and especially the humiliating capture of both Tunis and Algiers in 1534 by the Grand Admiral and *beylerbey* Khayreddin Pacha, called 'Barbarossa'.[125]

---

[120] ASV, CCX. Lettere di Rettori e Altre Cariche, Busta 255 (Naples), fols. 165v°–166.

[121] Ancel, 'Etude critique', 117, 129–30, 136–7; Preto, *Servizi segreti*, pp. 90–1.

[122] For *avvisi* in the Viennese Haus-, Hof-, und Staatsarchiv, see section Türkei, k.1–2; on their reliability, see the contribution to this volume by Barbarics and Pieper.

[123] Giovanni K. Hassiotis, 'Venezia e i domini veneziani: tramite di informazioni sui turchi per gli spagnoli nel sec. XVI', in Beck, Manoussacas and Pertusi (eds.), *Venezia centro di mediazione*, vol. I, pp. 119–20.

[124] Nicola Vatin, 'La conquête de Rhodes', in *Les Ottomans et l'Occident (XVe–XVIe siècle)* (Istanbul: Editions Isis, 2001), pp. 31–51.

[125] For an Ottoman view of him, see Miguel A. de Bunes Ibarra and Emilio Sola (eds.), *La vida, y historia de Hayradin, llamado Barbarroja. Gazavât- Hayreddîn Pasa – La cronica del guerrero de la fé Hayreddîn Barbarroja (del manuscrito otomano de Seyyid Murâd)* (Granada: Universidad de Granada, 1997), pp. 17–18.

Moreover, there was reason to fear that Suleiman's 1529 and 1532 campaigns in Hungary presaged a stronger Ottoman thrust into Mediterranean Europe.[126] In 1531, the Tyrrhenian coast had been battered by raids from Barbary, and Turkish pirates, moving up from the region of Naples to the level of Rome, disembarked at several points between the island of Elba and the continent. In the years 1534–5 Khayreddin and other Ottoman pirates intensified their raids against the Spanish and Italian coasts; Calabria suffered such *razzias* as far as Gaeta and the Neapolitan coast as far as Fondi and Sperlonga. Inhabitants were captured and enslaved; the island of Capri was occupied.[127] In July 1536, Juan de Valdes reported pessimistically that 'the Viceroy has been told by a sure source in Pula that the Turkish Armada has already sailed'– an exasperating continuity with previous years.[128]

The need to fortify their most exposed outposts clashed with internal difficulties. Naples, considered a financial reservoir by Charles V, was crushed beneath fiscal demands; its strategic importance within the Spanish imperial network did not spare it from either budgetary or demographic deficits. Under these conditions, it was difficult for Naples to sustain its role as a frontier against Islam and withstand Ottoman attacks. On land, Don Fernando d'Alarcon, commanding the imperial troops at Naples, had been unable to overcome bureaucratic snafus and a shortage of personnel. The badly damaged network of fortresses had not been repaired, although efforts had been made to reinforce the most important among them, including Otranto,

---

[126] Jean Aubin, 'Une frontière face au péril ottoman: la terre d'Otrante (1529–1532)', in *Le latin et l'astrolabe: recherches sur le Portugal de la Renaissance, son expansion en Asie et les relations internationales* (Lisbon and Paris: Centre culturel Calouste Gulbenkian, 2000), p. 96. On the Ottoman navy, consult especially Palmira Brummet, 'The Ottomans as a world power: what we don't know about Ottoman seapower', in Kate Fleet (ed.), *The Ottomans and the Sea*, special issue of *Oriente Moderno* 20 (2001), 1–10.

[127] Giuseppe Coniglio, *Il viceregno di Napoli e la lotta tra spagnoli e turchi nel Mediterraneo* (Naples: Giannini, 1987), vol. I, pp. 8–9; Renata Pilati, *Officia principis: politica e amministrazione a Napoli nel Cinquecento* (Naples: Jovene, 1994), pp. 177–82. See also AGS, Estado, Nápoles, Legs. 1017, 1024 (1534).

[128] Carlos José Hernandez Sánchez, *Castilla y Nápoles en el siglo XVI: el Virrey Pedro de Toledo, linaje, estado y cultura (1532–1553)* (Salamanca: Junta de Castilla y León, 1994), p. 393.

Manfredonia, Taranto and a few others along the Straits of Messina.[129] It had been decided in 1532 to build a series of watchtowers along the northern coast of the *Terra di Lavoro* between Gaeta and Cape Miseno, and work was underway in Calabria and Apulia.[130]

At sea the situation was no better. Despite assistance from Andrea Doria, the kingdom of Naples possessed no genuine war fleet to oppose harassment from Turkish or Barbary pirates. Plans to create such a fleet, begun in 1530–1, had been quickly abandoned; and the attempt to substitute frigates, which were swifter and less costly to maintain than galleys, had not succeeded. Only after 1534, and especially after the Tunis expedition the following year, were four galleys built in anticipation of Turkish reprisals.[131]

Because of its location, the *Terra d'Otranto y Bari*, together with other provinces like *Capitanata* which bordered the Adriatic, was particularly exposed. So were some cities. Barletta was highly vulnerable. In 1532, Alarcon ordered Captain Sebastian Quiñones to repair its fortifications, but the work remained unfinished in 1541.[132] Brindisi was constantly attacked by pirates from their Albanian hideout at Valona (Avlona), only six hours away by sea; as late as 1560, a report to Philip II stressed its strategic importance and the need to fortify it.[133]

Such shortages of resources in the kingdom of Naples around 1535 meant that the Spanish authorities lacked any coherent policy for confronting the Turkish peril. Defence was organised haphazardly, governed by rumours and news that an offensive was imminent. If these rumours proved false, mobilisation was suspended immediately. In this climate of perpetual uncertainty, espionage, 'the most original

---

[129] See Aubin, 'Frontière', pp. 96–101, 111–15; José Maria del Moral, *El Virey de Nápoles D. Pedro de Toledo y la guerra contra el Turco* (Madrid: Consejo Superior de Investigaciones Científicas, 1966), pp. 36–7; Antonio Calabria, *The Cost of Empire: The Finances of the Kingdom of Naples in the Time of Spanish Rule* (Cambridge: Cambridge University Press, 1991), p. 130; Aurelio Musi, *L'Italia dei Viceré: integrazione e resistenza nel sistema imperiale spagnolo* (Salerno: Avagliano, 2001), pp. 28–9, 51.

[130] Hernandez Sánchez, *Castilla y Nápoles*, pp. 427–9.

[131] *Ibid.*, pp. 398–9; Aubin, 'Frontière', pp. 103–4.

[132] Hernandez Sánchez, *Castilla y Nápoles*, p. 428.

[133] Printed by Coniglio, *Viceregno*, pp. 222–32.

aspect of the kingdom's defence',[134] became vital – even more so when Charles V visited the kingdom of Naples in autumn 1535, partly in order to bestow symbolic honours upon local elites after the enterprise of Tunis. It was necessary to ensure his personal security, that of the grandees who accompanied him, and of the local patricians gathered to honour him at his *entrada* in November. Without establishing any direct causal link, the synchronism between the official confirmation of his visit, known at Naples on 4 August, and Campos's instructions on 3 September, seems significant.[135]

Rival information networks in the kingdom of Naples: Alarcon and Atripalda

In order to fulfil its role as a 'listening post', the kingdom of Naples had to rely primarily on indigenous sources, since information from such other centres as Rome or Genoa often had no precise connection to its local situation. The important mass of *avvisi* from Venice were reputedly contaminated by governmental manipulation; Charles V's Venetian ambassador, Rodrigo Niño, reported that Ottoman affairs were so secret in Venice that he could only learn whatever they allowed to filter through.[136] The situation seemed even more aggravating in 1535 because Venice was not only rumoured to be obstructing the anti-Ottoman coalition, but also accused of spreading disinformation, by exaggerating the Turkish danger in the Mediterranean in order to favour Jan Zapolya against the Habsburgs in Hungary.[137]

From 1539 to 1547, Spain's information services in Italy were co-ordinated by a humanist and man of letters, Don Diego Hurtado de Mendoza (1503–75), Charles V's ambassador to Venice after Rodrigo Niño and half-brother of Lope Hurtado de Mendoza, a member of the

---

[134] Quote from Aubin, 'Frontière', p. 126.
[135] Hernandez Sánchez, *Castilla y Nápoles*, pp. 285–90; in August, Charles V was still in Tunis.
[136] AGS, Estado, Nápoles, Leg. 1308, fol. 90 (Niño to emperor, 12.11.1530). In general, see Hassiotis, in 'Venezia e i domini', pp. 121–5.
[137] Aubin, 'Frontière', p. 120.

Imperial Council and Charles V's ambassador in Lisbon.[138] In Naples, the kingdom's secret services were divided between two separate networks, headed respectively by Don Fernando de Alarcon and by Don Afonso Granai Castriota, Marquis of Atripalda.

Less elaborate than its rival, the first network drew its information primarily from Ragusa and the Venetian *baile* at Corfu.[139] Around 1560, a letter from the Duke of Alcala, mentioning several *avisos* from Constantinople passed along by its Florentine agents (Lorenzo Miniati, his nephew Dimo Miniati, and Donato Antonio Lubelu) by way of Barletta, claimed that the route via Ragusa was 'the shortest and most secure of all'.[140] The relationship of this shadowy network to the kingdom's administrative elite, the *Secretario del Reino* and the Viceroy's different *Secretarios* (including the *Consiglio Collaterale* which managed the kingdom's postal services),[141] remains shrouded in deep secrecy, but its discreet operations had some impact on defence preparations. Through it, both real and bogus *nuevas de Levante* and *avvisi del Turco* inspired the fortification, beyond Apulia, of several places in Sicily.[142]

We rarely know the amounts of money paid to spies by either network during this period; the document concerning Juan Campos is one

---

[138] *Ibid.*, p. 126; Hassiotis, 'Venezia e i domini', p. 127; Enrique García Hernán, 'The price of spying, 228. On Lope Hurtado, see Viaud, *Correspondance d'un ambassadeur*, pp. 60–8.

[139] Aubin, 'Frontière', p. 126. Numerous *avisos* from Ragusa after 1550 are in AGS, Estado, Nápoles, Leg. 1077.

[140] AGS, Estado, Nápoles, Leg. 1056, fol. 84 (7.9.1567). These men figure on García Hernán's list of spies ('Price of spying', 267) but without any accurate mention of the document: Lorenzo was assassinated in 1566, Dimo and Donato paid irregularly in 1566 and 1567. See also Nicolaas H. Biegman, 'Ragusan spying for the Ottoman Empire: some 16th century documents from the State Archives at Dubrovnik', *Belleten* 27.106 (1963), 237–49, and his *The Turco-Ragusan Relationship according to the Firmans of Murad III (1575–1595) extant in the State Archives of Dubrovnik* (The Hague and Paris: Mouton, 1967).

[141] See Giuseppe Coniglio, *Il regno di Napoli al tempo di Carlo V: amministrazione e vita economico-sociale* (Naples: Edizioni scientifiche italiane, 1951), pp. 4–8.

[142] E.g. Syracuse, Augusta, Messina, Milazzo, Trapani and Crotone in Calabria: see Aubin, 'Frontière', p. 122.

of the few exceptions where we know the price (100 ducats). However, at a slightly later period (1561–74), Simancas provides some idea of Spanish rates from several sums paid to Spanish secret agents throughout the Mediterranean, including Constantinople.[143] Payments for agents by the kingdom of Naples provoked numerous complaints, since the information they provided was often considered inferior to that coming from Venice.[144] Cardinal Granvelle, the viceroy of Naples, complained vehemently in September 1574 that it seemed superfluous to pay Spanish spies who were often recruited among renegades and similar riffraff, gathered their information in taverns and predated their dispatches.[145]

Although certainly needing to be revised upwards, estimates of the number of agents paid by the Spanish embassy in Venice and by the kingdom of Naples (including Sicily) during the second half of the sixteenth century show how heavy this machinery had become. Omitting occasional help, around 1568–70 the Spanish crown employed more than 300 regular agents (half of them in Constantinople), costing around 5,000 ducats per year.[146] It is interesting to compare these figures with some from Venice. In 1581, Pietro Michiele, returning from a secret mission to Syria 'to have *avvisi* about Turkish matters and the war in Persia', acknowledged receipt of 300 *zecchini* from the Council of Ten for his expenses, but because he requested a further 54 ducats and 4 *lire*, Michiele attached a detailed expense account which enables us to separate his personal expenses (food, clothing, transportation,

---

[143] García Hernán, 'Price of spying', 235–8; his list of payments (printed on 237 with no source cited) comes from AGS, Estado, Nápoles, Leg.1056, fol. 89. For Portugal, see Couto, 'L'espionnage portugais', pp. 245–6. The lists of expenses published by Roberto Mantelli, *Il pubblico impiego nell'economia del regno di Napoli: retribuzioni, reclutamento e ricambio sociale nell'epoca spagnuola (sec. XVI–XVII)* (Naples: Nella sede dell'Istituto, 1986), apparently omit payments to spies.

[144] Hassiotis, 'Venezia e i domini', p. 124 n. 16, citing AGS, Estado, Nápoles, Leg. 1061, fol. 2.

[145] AGS, Estado, Nápoles, Leg. 1064, fol. 61.

[146] Hassiotis, 'Venezia e i domini', pp. 131–2, esp. nn. 43–50 on 132 (drawn from AGS, Estado, Nápoles, Legs. 1060, 1052, 1053); compare García Hernán, 'Price of spying', 235–8, for the period 1570–3.

lodging) from those concerning his mission (presents to authorities, bribes to middlemen, payments to couriers, etc.).[147]

The Atripalda network

In 1532, viceroy Don Pedro de Toledo brought a secretary and counsellor named Antonio de Puente to Naples; his salary was paid in the following years as his 'secretary responsible for ciphering' (*secretario de mandamiento que tiene las cifras*).[148] Since the signature on the instructions to Campos remains unidentified, we do not know if it came from de Puente and thus from the Alarcon network. Although both networks employed Albanians, Campos was probably the Albanian who was 'well-known, sure, and provides good information, who was chosen to go to Constantinople and wherever else seemed necessary to send Your Majesty useful information, and who has been well instructed; may God help him serve Your Majesty'.[149] The destination of his mission probably links this document to the Atripalda network.

Don Alfonso, Marquis of Atripalda, built a remarkable espionage network directed against the Ottoman Empire. Descended from the famous Skanderbeg,[150] the marquis, like his brother Don Fernando, Marquis of Santangelo, had fought alongside the *Gran Capitán* and received many privileges from King Ferdinand in regions populated by Greeks, Slavs and Albanians. Created Marquis of Atripalda by the Spanish crown, he was given the castle of Copertino and made

---

[147] ASV, Consiglio dei Dieci, Lettere dei rettori, Busta 225 (Aleppo), fols. 5, 6 (list dated 1584).

[148] Hernandez Sánchez, *Castilla y Nápoles*, pp. 195, 367 (on Puente); Coniglio, *Viceregno*, vol. I, pp. 168, 378 (payments in 1536 and 1539).

[149] 'conoscido y seguro y ombre de quien se tiene buena información el qual se a proferido de yr a Constantinopla y a todas las partes donde fuese necesario para avisar de todo lo que se ofresciere en servicio de V.M. el va bien instruido Dios le guíe pera que acierte a servir V.M.': Del Moral, *Virrey de Napoles*, p. 72, citing AGS, Estado, Nápoles, Leg. 1021, fol. 135, dated 18.8.1535; this was written a fortnight before Campos's official instructions were signed and dated.

[150] On him, see Athanase Gegaj, *L'Albanie et l'invasion turque au xve siècle* (Louvain: Bureaux de la Bibliothèque de l'Université, Paris: P. Geuthner, 1937), pp. 31–47.

governor of the *Terra d'Otranto y Bari* in 1519. Probably inspired by his glorious grandfather, he saw himself as the incarnation of Albanian resistance against the Turks[151] and maintained close connections to Albanian populations, whom he visited soon after Don Pedro became viceroy. In 1530 Atripalda asked the viceroy to promote a revolt by Greeks and Albanians in favour of the emperor, assuring him of their (perhaps imaginary) support for the Habsburgs.[152] A veiled echo of Atripalda's prejudices reappears in a phrase of Campos's instructions about the 'goodwill which Albanians have for Your Majesty's service'.[153]

Atripalda's handwritten notes from the outset of his governorship reveal a better-built network than that of Alarcon, relying on a cohort of agents easily recruited among his Greek and Albanian dependants, particularly by offering them positions in military service.[154] Greeks provided numerous informants for Spanish intelligence networks and even developed a 'specialty' in spying at Ottoman shipyards and naval arsenals at Gallipoli, the Sea of Marmora and Constantinople. Sometimes this information was sent through Venice, otherwise via Otranto or Lecce.[155] If Alarcon's agents got as far as Sofia in 1532, Atripalda's agents were sent frequently to Constantinople or even Cairo. Atripalda's experience and his criteria (he concentrated on military matters, while Hurtado de Mendoza basically sought diplomatic information) made him the hub of defensive preparations for the viceroy, with whom he maintained close military collaboration in exchange for privileges to his lineage.[156]

---

[151] See his letter to the emperor dated 14 July 1532: AGS, Estado, Nápoles, Leg. 1011, fol. 195 (published by Del Moral, *Virrey de Nápoles*, p. 229). On medieval Albania, see Alain Ducellier, *La façade maritime de l'Albanie au Moyen Age: Durazzo et Valona du XIe au XVe siècle* (Salonica: Institute for Balkan Studies, 1986).

[152] For his privileges, see Hernandez Sánchez, *Castilla y Nápoles*, p. 362 n. 36; also three letters to Charles V from 11 July to 3 December 1530: AGS, Estado, Nápoles, Leg. 1007, fols. 127–9.

[153] 'voluntad que los Albaneses tienen al servicio de su Magestad' (fol. 165).

[154] See M. Mendella, 'Arruolamento militare di Albanesi nel regno di Napoli durante il seicento', *Archivio Storico per le province napoletane* 90 (1972), 373–84.

[155] Hassiotis, 'Venezia e i domini', p. 129; García Hernán, 'Price of spying', 240–3.

[156] Hernandez Sánchez, *Castilla y Nápoles*, p. 362; Aubin, 'Frontière', p. 116. On his association with the 'Aragonese *partido*', see Carlos José Hernández Sánchez, *El*

In its detail, the second part of Campos's glossary bears the imprint of military intelligence. Like Saruq's glossary, its terminology rests on a series of synonyms split into semantic fields. As one would expect, Ottoman military hierarchies are recognisable beneath Latinised names (*sangacho, genisero, espay ogliani*), while ordinary types of Mediterranean boats (*galea, fusta*) are followed by their appropriate name, mingling maritime with terrestrial fauna.

A spy's glossary and its discursive arrangement

Pending further analysis of the most fruitful way to interrogate this document – its contribution to understanding sixteenth-century mental structures and how early modern espionage actually functioned as a social practice – we shall conclude by examining its categories and classifications. Its list of toponyms seems relatively orderly and separate from a previous list of long, complicated phrases which seem difficult to memorise, with correspondences indicated by passages expressed indirectly ('you will say that. . .').

On the other hand, Campos's glossary appears to lack order. But is it really disorderly? One could certainly argue that it constitutes a heterogenous 'catch-all', useful only for giving the spy a general outline of the conflict between Christendom and the Ottomans. Although the scribe surely did not enter these items randomly and pell-mell as they occurred to him, information about the mission's two main phases and geographical zones is completely jumbled together. It jumps from instructions about Albania and Morea to the distant war between the sultan and the *sophi*,[157] and from there back to information about military fortifications and Albanian demography. There are also some differences with his instructions; if one part desires information about

reino de Nápoles en el imperio de Carlos V: la consolidación de la conquista (Madrid: Sociedad Estatal para la Conmemoración de los Centenarios de Felipe II y Carlos V, 2001), pp. 232, 241, and Giuseppe Coniglio, 'Note sulla società napoletana ai tempi di Don Pietro di Toledo', in *Studi in onore di Riccardo Filangeri* (Naples: L'Arte Tipografica, 1959), vol. 2.

[157] Numerous *avvisi* on Levantine questions in AGS, particularly the series of *Estados pequeños de Italia*: e.g. Leg. 1456, 1465, 1466, 1468, etc. On relations with Safavid Persia, see AGS, Venezia, Legs. 1318, 1321, etc.

Venetian galleys and the possibility of an attack by Barbarossa, the other asks about a possible expedition by Shah Ta'masp against Amasia and Egypt. If the latter constituted a kind of vulgate of the Turco-Persian conflict, the other two are never mentioned in Campos's letter of instructions.

Studying the ciphered dispatches of *baile* Vittore Bragadin, Christiane Villain-Gandossi emphasised 'the code itself, rather than the coded message'; analysing a cryptographic system helps scholars appreciate 'the level of cultural preparation' of those who created and used it. However, cryptographic systems – of which Campos's glossary offers an excellent example – have an intrinsic worth as branches of knowledge, and especially as social and cultural practices revealing the interstitial and 'secret' products of a society. Understanding them enables us to grasp the organising concepts and modes of clandestine communication, those 'secret' parts of the conceptual universe in which information was processed and diffused.

CHAPTER 10

The correspondence of illiterate peasants in early modern Hungary

István György Tóth

This volume examines different aspects of the role of correspondence in early modern societies in Europe. But in one aspect, all these enquiries are alike: all the letters they analyse were obviously written by men and women who were literate, and similarly, they were intended for people who could read. However, in early modern Europe, and particularly in early modern central Europe, most of the population were peasants, the great majority of whom could neither read nor write. Nevertheless, these illiterate people corresponded rather frequently, and this chapter examines this very special type of communication – letters written by those who could not write and sent to those who could not read them.

In a period without any of the technological communication devices of the twenty-first century, from telephones to radios, people had to find other ways to communicate effectively with each other, even if they were illiterate. Nowadays, it is extremely simple for any literate person to write a letter and read a notice or brochure. For illiterates in early modern times, though, this caused grave difficulties and required the assistance of others. Before the widespread use of the telephone, most people practised their writing ability mainly through sending letters to relatives. Among the peasantry, however, the single most important subjective criterion of letter writing – compositor's skill – was missing. Among the material prerequisites, only quills were easily available; ink and paper were rare and expensive, while writing-sand was as scarce as a well-lit, quiet nook in which to go about the slow and laborious work of tracing letters. Nevertheless, many people tried to maintain contact with distant kinsfolk through correspondence.[1]

Because of the general illiteracy of Hungarian society, its networks of oral communication were extensive. In particular, oral messages were frequently sent through trusted intermediaries, as many lawsuits and depositions show. Moreover, wandering artisans and students, mobile elements in an otherwise rather stable society, were frequently asked to enquire about the well-being of distant relatives.[2] Quite often, however, an oral message could not replace correspondence, the exchange of written letters.[3] This was particularly true wherever the distance between the sender of the message and its recipient became too great, as often happened in times of war. The sons and husbands of Hungarian and Transylvanian peasants in the imperial army were sent to distant provinces to fight the French or the Turks. Despite the distances involved, some peasant women tried to keep in contact with their soldiers through letter writing.

Peasants were also required to correspond with various authorities – landlords and their officials, the priest, the county clerk – through written rather than verbal means.[4] Where such letters were required, even if their contents were meant to be confidential, peasants typically employed a third party to write the letter on their behalf. In such cases, a written correspondence via delegated handwriting served the purposes of illiterate peasants. Similarly, when a letter arrived, its recipient often had to ask someone to read it aloud for him. This chapter will examine

---

[1] Roger Chartier, 'Du livre au livre', in Roger Chartier (ed.), *Pratiques de la lecture* (Marseille: Rivages, 1985), pp. 61–81; Harvey J. Graff, *The Legacies of Literacy* (Bloomington: Indiana University Press, 1987), pp. 218–27.

[2] Marie-Elizabeth Ducreux, 'Lire à en mourir', in Roger Chartier (ed.), *Les usages de l'imprimé* (Paris: Fayard, 1987), pp. 281–2; David Vincent, *The Rise of Mass Literacy: Reading and Writing in Modern Europe* (Cambridge: Polity Press, 2000), pp. 150–68, with a good overview of the recent literature on uses of literacy.

[3] Egil Johansson, 'The history of literacy in Sweden', in Harvey J. Graff (ed.), *Literacy and Social Development in the West* (Cambridge: Cambridge University Press, 1981), pp. 151–82; Rab A. Houston, *Literacy in Early Modern Europe*, 2nd edition (London: Longman, 2002), with a good bibliography of the recent literature on pp. 285–7.

[4] Emmanuel Le Roy Ladurie, *Les paysans de Languedoc* (Paris: EHESS, 1966), pp. 345–6; David Cressy, *Literacy and the Social Order: Reading and Writing in Tudor and Stuart England* (Cambridge: Cambridge University Press, 1980), pp. 60–1.

the problems and implications of this 'correspondence of illiterates' among early modern Hungarian peasants.

Using letters concerning the purchase or sale of land by Hungarian peasants, we can confirm that literacy, i.e. the capacity to write and to sign a document, remained an exceptional phenomenon for the peasantry of western Hungary in the sixteenth and seventeenth centuries. Only some 2–3 per cent of peasants could sign such documents in the eighteenth century; despite this clear increase in the number able to write, peasant literacy still remained extremely low. While there must have been several who possessed a passive knowledge of the letters (i.e. they could decipher them, although with difficulty), we can safely affirm that the overwhelming majority of this peasantry remained illiterate.[5]

The percentage of those able to read in the region can only be approximated, yet an estimate should be attempted.[6] My research on the history of elementary village schools established that by the second half of the eighteenth century, one-fifth to one-sixth of all children living in villages attended them. These children, therefore, had at least learned to read and interpret written words, even when attending school only in the winter and intermittently. Nevertheless, many other children could have learned to read outside school, taught informally by literate relatives, friends or artisans; such cases are often mentioned in court records. Therefore it seems probable that in the second half of the eighteenth century, one-third to one-fifth of peasants in these villages could read. In all probability, the proportion of boys who learned to read was significantly higher than that of girls.[7]

Even if this proportion remains only an estimate, we also have supplementary data from this region about semi-literates who could read

---

[5] István György Tóth, 'Une société aux lisières de l'alphabète: la paysannerie hongroise aux XVIIe et XVIIIe siècles', *Annales ESC* 56 (2001), 863–80, with further lliterature.

[6] István György Tóth, 'Hungarian culture in the early modern age', in László Kósa (ed.), *A Cultural History of Hungary: From the Beginnings to the Eighteenth Century* (Budapest: Corvina-Osiris, 1999), vol. 1, pp. 154–228.

[7] István György Tóth, 'How many Hungarian noblemen could read in the eighteenth century?', in Andrea Petö (ed.), *Central European University History Department Yearbook* (Budapest: Central European Univesity, 1994), pp. 67–81.

books, but were unable to reproduce the letters by hand. A carpenter, residing in the village of Kisunyom, died in 1786. His personal effects, which were put up for auction, included 'one large book and a small one' – his entire library. Unfortunately, the records reveal nothing about the content of either. However, they do demonstrate that although the deceased artisan had always put a cross on the papers he had to sign (making scholars count him as illiterate), he still kept two books at home; i.e. he could read. Another peasant, a widow, was also semi-literate, buying books although she could not write. In 1796, she attended an auction in Szombathely where the chattels of a county warden were put up for sale. The widow purchased his prayerbook (apparently the only book offered for sale) for three forints. She concluded the purchase by putting a large cross on the account, in place of the signature. So did a Lutheran woman from Körmend on her last will and testament, even though her itemised personal effects, abounding in dresses and utensils, also listed a book of hymns.[8]

In the villages, it was usually the local notary or schoolmaster who drew up letters and documents for illiterate peasants. Estate archives of the seventeenth and eighteenth centuries preserve hundreds of petitions from peasants, all put on paper by a notary or teacher. For the sixteenth century, such petitions were still very few and far between. However, after the mid sixteenth century, we find the letters of peasants from western Hungary, especially from the estate of a very cultivated aristocrat, the Palatine Tamás Nádasdy, who employed an unusually high level of written correspondence in the administration of his domains. Most of these peasant letters were written to their landlords, complaining about their situation and duties or about abuses committed by the landlord's bailiffs.

Thus in 1551, the peasants of the village of Csicso wrote a letter to Count Nádasdy. They had hoped to approach their landlord personally and tell him their complaints orally, but because the count was too far away, they had to write him a letter. They complained that the bailiffs of Nádasdy had introduced 'new and unheard-of' duties in these villages, especially concerning the vineyards. Some years later, the peasants of

---

[8] Archives of Vas County, Szombathely, Orphanalia IV/1/f, fasc. 4, no. 21, 45.

another village, Somodor, wrote to Nádasdy's wife, Orsolya Kanizsai: they had performed all the tasks demanded of them, the peasants wrote, but the soldiers of the neighbouring villages' landlords were continuously pestering them.[9]

The peasants living in the villages around the castle of Kanizsa wrote similar letters to Orsolya Kanizsai: they lived not far from the Turkish frontier, and were troubled not only by the Turkish soldiers of the bey Kasin, but also by the bailiffs of the Nádasdys, who demanded new duties from them, especially at ploughing and harvesting times. The peasants of Gelse village complained by letter about the bailiff who had taken away the lands of serfs and converted them into domain lands. Most of these letters contain only complaints against the bailiffs, since the peasants hoped for protection from the aristocrats themselves. However, in 1559 the peasants of Mártély wrote a letter to Count Tamás Nádasdy because they wished to praise the captain of the neighbouring castle, Benedek Bornemissza, who had defended them against the Turkish bey Dzafer. They wrote that Bornemissza 'loves us as if he were our father and mother and because of him, we live as peacefully in our land as we had during the reign of that King Mathias' – thereby revealing their great collective nostalgia for the then-distant reign of Matthias Corvinus (1458–90).[10]

In these letters, we find not even a single allusion to the actual writer. None have a signature or cross at the end. Instead, all of them were written in the name of 'all the faithful peasants of the village'. Because peasant literacy was virtually non-existent in the sixteenth century, it was not important to mention who actually wrote these letters, as would become necessary by the second half of the eighteenth century. All the early letters were written by clerks who set down the words of the peasants gathered at his house. Because of the general illiteracy, nobody supposed that a piece of correspondence should be corroborated with crosses in lieu of signatures; rather, it was supposed that the collective memory of those peasants present could testify about who had dictated the letter's contents. Thus even when the 'author' of

---

[9] Hungarian National Archives (hereafter HNA), Archivum camerae, Archivum familiae Nádasdy, E 185, 1561.

[10] *Ibid.*, 1559.

the letter was certainly unable to write this piece of correspondence himself, nobody thought it necessary to excuse himself because of this detail.

In 1717, a peasant woman from the Transylvanian village of Szentmárton complained in a long letter about her debts and asked her landlord for three forints in order to redeem her cow. If she could not reclaim this cow in three days, another serf would sell it to a butcher who would skin it. The landlord, Count Sándor Teleki, wrote back to this woman and ordered three forints be given her from the price of the wine sold in the village in order to redeem the pawned cow. This correspondence contains not the slightest allusion to the fact that somebody had to write the letter in her name and somebody had to read Count Teleki's answer to her. Everyone involved understood that such writing and reading were delegated to a scribe, so this fact was not mentioned in this case, although there is not the slightest doubt that this particular Transylvanian peasant woman could not possibly read or write these pieces of correspondence – as she stated herself, she was not only old and poor, but blind as well.[11]

The lower levels of administration on the landlords' estates were filled by officials drawn from the peasantry. However, the often difficult correspondence of these officials reveals a high level of illiteracy even among these so-called 'clerks' of domains, who obviously preferred oral communication to written correspondence. The Prince of Transylvania, George Rákoczi I (1630–48) was a very careful manager of his domains in Transylvania as well as in his latifundia in Habsburg-ruled Upper Hungary. Rákoczi wanted as many written reports as possible about agricultural production on his lands. However, the low level of literacy among his officials often made this impossible. In the correspondence between the prince and the bailiff of the domain at Szekelyhida, we often find complaints about the lack of written documents. He could not send a letter about the harvest, wrote the bailiff in 1647, 'as literate people are quite few here'. The herdsmen were all illiterate, the groom could write but only very badly, in an almost

---

[11] HNA, Archivum familiae Teleki, Missiles no. 4170; Éva H. Balázs (ed.), *Jobbágylevelek* [Serfs' letters] (Budapest: Közoktatás, 1951), pp. 136–7.

illegible way, and 'I could not find a literate man to make this letter be written.' Thus it was difficult for the bailiff to maintain a correspondence about the domain; but, he wrote to the prince with great indignation, he was prepared to take an oath about it. According to his view, the landlord should trust not the written correspondence but rather the oral testimony of a honest man.[12]

The general illiteracy of peasants often made even the correspondence of their landlords difficult. Count Miklós Bethlen was one of the most cultivated men in seventeenth-century Hungary; he was the chancellor of the Transylvanian principality, and his autobiography written in prison ranks among the masterpieces of seventeenth-century Hungarian literature. However, his bailiff was illiterate and this caused the count great trouble. Bethlen once received a fat packet of correspondence, but realised too late that these letters were not written to him, but to his nephew with a similar name, Farkas Bethlen. The illiterate servant of another aristocrat, Count Mihály Teleki, 'gave this correspondence to my bailiff, who was himself illiterate as well', wrote Miklós Bethlen in his autobiography. Because of these letters mistakenly read by him, great animosity arose between him and his nephew, which lasted for the rest of their lives.[13]

In the western Hungarian domains of Count Ádám Batthyány, during the first half of the seventeenth century, the correspondence of the landlord with his servants was no less difficult due to the peasants' general inability to read and write. The bailiff of Ujvár wrote to the count in 1635: 'Here in Ujvár, we are very few, there is not one literate official here, and the only one of the servants who could read and write died of plague last week.' Therefore he urged his landlord, Count Batthyány, to send him someone from a neighbouring domain who could read and write. Two years later, the bailiff on another estate

[12] László Makkai (ed.), *I. Rákóczi György birtokainak gazdasági iratai* [Documents concerning agriculture from the domains of Prince George Rákóczi I] (Budapest: Akadémiai, 1954), pp. 543–50.

[13] V. Windisch Éva (ed.), *Bethlen Miklós önéletírása* [The autobiography of Miklós Bethlen] (Budapest: Szépirodalmi, 1980), pp. 714–15. Cf. István György Tóth, *Politique et religion en Hongrie au XVIIe siècle: lettres des missionnaires de la Propaganda Fide* (Paris: Champion-Slatkine, 2004), pp. 50–6.

of Count Batthyány voiced a similar complaint: 'This young clerk can neither read, nor write, nor count, and as we have a lot of wine kept here, we really need a much more learned person for these tasks.' Due to the lack of literate officials in his domains, the landlord's correspondence with these officials was only possible through the mediation of third parties: 'When I received the letter of Your Lordship, I went immediately to the merchant in the neighbouring village who read it for me without any delay', another servant assured the same landlord. On the estate of Dobra in 1654, a new person was recommended to Count Batthyány for service at the castle: he would be good not only as a deputy, but even as a chief castellan, since he can even write, whereas the actual chief castellan can neither read nor write and must dictate the letters he sends to the landlord.[14]

Hungarian aristocrats administered their domains with the help of written correspondence, although it was often conducted only with great difficulty because of the scarcity of people in their villages who could write and read these letters. On the other hand, the petty nobility directed their few peasants without written correspondence; because they relied primarily on oral instructions, we know much less about the life of their peasants. However, Pál Weöres, a petty nobleman from western Hungary who was often ill and remained much of the time in his sick-bed, had to direct his miniature domain by letters. Like the great aristocrats a century and a half earlier, this petty nobleman also discovered that the widespread illiteracy of his peasants presented a serious obstacle to official correspondence. 'Have my letters read to you quite often', Weöres wrote to one of his servants in 1787. In other letters, he urged his servants to send to him not only messengers with oral reports but written letters as well, and enumerated the literate persons in the different villages to whom the servants could dictate them.[15]

Hungarian peasants carried on correspondence not only with their landlords, but even between themselves. When illiterate peasants

[14] HNA, Archivum familiae Batthyány, P 1314, Missiles nos. 13878, 7609, 15971, 54750, 33636. HNA, Archivum familiae Batthyány, P 1322 Instructiones no. 42.
[15] Archives of Vas County, Szombathely, Archivum familiae Weöres, Instructiones, XII. 43.

exchanged letters, they necessarily shared their innermost thoughts with anyone who offered to commit these to paper. In 1568, Count György Thurzo, a Hungarian aristocrat, described for his (illiterate) wife a love letter written by one of his men. 'János Trombitás wrote a letter to his wife in the Slovak language, it was taken down as he dictated, couched in fine Slovak words. I have sent it to you, but do not pass it on to his wife until you have it read out to yourself; at least you will have something to laugh at.' So illiterate János Trombitás had to profess his ardent love for his wife in front of another man.[16]

More than two centuries later, in 1780, at Keszthely, a market town near Lake Balaton belonging to the counts of Festetich, a woman was charged with incest in the manorial court. The woman, who faced the death penalty, admitted during her trial that she had received love letters from her lover, who was none other than her sister's husband. The defendant told the judges that her brother-in-law 'hath sent me a letter from the village of Hahot, which must have been noted down there by the local publican, I think'. Her brother-in-law and lover was a German master carpenter, forty-eight years old, who was also a resident of this market town of Keszthely. This carpenter originally came from the Bavarian town of Regensburg, i.e. from a more developed region than western Hungary. Even so, this man obviously could not write. The testimony of this Keszthely woman demonstrates clearly that she knew that her lover could not have written a letter by himself, even if its contents revealed an illicit relationship between two relatives that should obviously have been kept secret.[17]

In 1713, a judge in the small market town of Jászó in Upper Hungary accused his wife of becoming the lover of a German military drummer known to us only by his nickname: *Manó* ('Goblin'). *Manó* wrote 'scandalous' letters to his lover, an apparently literate woman. At her trial, some male witnesses could describe the 'horrendous' contents of these letters. The female witnesses, like fifty-five-year-old Anna Komlosi, however, had seen them, but not read them; she told the

---

[16] Miklós Kubinyi (ed.), *Bethlenfalvi gróf Thurzó György levelei nejéhez* [Letters of Count György Thurzó of Bethlenfalva to his wife] (Budapest: Athenaeum, 1876), vol. 1, p. 261.

[17] HNA, Archivum familiae Festetich, Acta juris gladii P 235, 136, no. 154.

judges that she saw these letters but knew nothing about their contents. Similarly, the eighteen-year-old wife of a peasant testified only that she was present as others read these letters; it would probably have been a waste of time for *Manó* to send love letters to her.[18]

Thus, peasants corresponded through delegated writing, even when the contents of their letters was extremely confidential.[19] Not only the love letters of illegitimate lovers, but even letters about the consequences of such illegitimate relations had to be dictated by peasants. In 1763, an eighteen-year-old servant-maid had an extraordinary (and vitally important) letter written for her in the village of Báhony, near the former Hungarian capital of Pozsony (Bratislava). Unwed, she had borne an illegitimate child which the father did not want to know about. The desperate mother decided to leave the unwanted baby at the neighbouring market town of Nagyszombat (Trnava). She had left her infant child on the steps leading to the entrance of the Nagyszombat Catholic Seminary, hoping that her baby would be found by the priests and given out to be raised. She left an amulet around its neck, containing a short, desperate letter addressed to whoever happened to find the child. She could not have prepared the letter herself, however. Since she was completely illiterate, she had to avail herself of the services of a servant of the parish priest of Pozsony, a guest at the house where she herself served. But she was not the only unwed mother to leave her child with a dictated letter at the Nagyszombat seminary. Anna Klukán, another eighteen-year-old illiterate servant-maid, also from Pozsony county, also wanted to leave her newborn baby in the hands of the Catholic priests of Nagyszombat. However, she could not write this most delicate letter herself, nor could she write to the father of her baby. He did not want to hear about the child or about a marriage with her, stubbornly refusing to acknowledge paternity or propose to her. This illiterate maid had to dictate her letter about a

---

[18] Slovak National Archives, Bratislava, Archivum abbatiae Jaszoviensis, Elenchus III, fasc. K, no. 13.

[19] On dictated letters of immigrants in the seventeenth century see also David Cressy, *Coming over: Migration and Communication between England and New England in the Seventeenth Century* (Cambridge: Cambridge University Press, 1987), passim.

most intimate matter, and asked the parish priest of Istvánfalva to pen a letter to her ex-lover on her behalf.[20]

In this largely illiterate world, oral messages often replaced written letters. They were sent by itinerant merchants and wandering craftsmen as well as by peasants going to fairs or on pilgrimage. However, in many cases, because of the great distances, this type of oral message could not substitute written letters, even if the 'writer' was not able to write, nor the 'reader' able to read. Peasants recruited for soldiers and sent to distant battlefields tried their best to let their beloved know they were alive, begging them to wait for them. Such letters were usually taken down by the clerk of the regiment or the army chaplain. A further difficulty was for the women to whom such messages were addressed to read these. One fifty-year-old woman, living in the market town of Hodmezövásárhely, in the domains of Count Károlyi, told the judges of the manorial court of the Károlyi domains that she had frequently received letters from her son, who served as a soldier in the imperial army on the Rhine, fighting against the French army in Germany. However, as she told the court in her deposition, each time she had to find someone in the neighbourhood to read her son's letter aloud to her.[21]

The number of illiterate people who needed to have letters or petitions written for them must have been high. As in some of the least-developed countries today, volunteer scribes were available for a fee in the main squares of Hungarian market towns. They were usually schoolmasters or students trying to earn a few *denarii* from such activities. And having no way of knowing, such scribes sometimes unwittingly collaborated in frauds. In the sizable town of Pozsony in 1770, the wife of a knife-grinder from a neighbouring village had a petition drawn up for her by a schoolmaster whom she found during the fair on the church square; when questioned afterwards, she said that 'I myself

---

[20] Slovak National Archives, Bratislava, Archivum familiae Pálffy, Almarium II, Ladula 9, fasc. I, no. 12; Archives of Abauj County, Kosice, Criminalia, 90, fasc. 12, no. 15; *ibid.*, Processus criminales, 385, fasc. 4, no. 13; Archives of Pozsony County, Bratislava, Criminales processus, A XII, nos. 653, 295, 298.

[21] Archives of Csongrád County, Szentes, Processus criminales b/21; *ibid.*, Archivum familiae Károlyi, Acta sedis dominalis, a/26.

dictated to him what to put down.' The letter provoked an official inquiry because its contents were far from truthful. In 1786, a forged letter was written in the name of a chief magistrate for use by the mother of the steward of Szikszo. However, the forged letter was supplied with the wrong name. She therefore tried to correct it, but was unable to do so. As the woman confessed at the tribunal, 'I requested a student lodged at the house of the Franciscan friars at Kassa (Košice) . . . who hath adjusted the characters.' Thus even a steward's mother needed the services of a student in a neighbouring town to amend a bogus letter.

Other scribes were probably complicit in composing written frauds. In the town of Eger in 1766, a discharged soldier was caught. After serving in the imperial army, he decided to begin a new life, leaving not only the army, but his wife as well. However, the bigamist was caught and the authorities initiated an inquiry to learn how he could marry again while his wife was still alive. They discovered that the word 'married' had been scratched from the discharge letter he had received from the regiment's clerk, and the alteration which replaced it enabled him to marry again. 'Who hath inscribed in it a different word . . . since thou knowest no writing?', the judges asked the bigamist soldier, upon which he confessed that it was a student from the town of Pápa who had made the necessary changes.[22]

Few peasants could read and write; even fewer could write well enough to meet the standards of official documents. This fact induced those peasants who possessed such exceptional capacities to forge pieces of the correspondence of landlords' bailiffs for their own benefit as much as for that of others. In 1762, a peasant living in the village of Nádalja named György Spaics (nicknamed 'the deaf clerk') submitted various papers to the steward. The surveyors' suspicion was merely aroused while consulting two pieces of correspondence dated 1605 and 1657, noting that the allegedly 100- to 150-year-old letters may have been drawn up much later; however, on seeing another supposedly prepared twenty-seven years earlier, they had no doubt that it was

[22] Archives of Heves County, Archivum criminale episcopi, XII- 3-b-10. fasc. O, no. 14-c; Archives of Abauj-Torna County, Kosice, Criminalia 90, fasc. 12, no. 15; Archives of Abauj County, Kosice, Processus criminales, 385, fasc. 4, no. 13.

spurious. In this instance, oral testimony defeated falsified writing. The village mayor and those councillors old enough to remember professed no knowledge whatsoever of any letter drawn up then on their behalf and addressed to the landlords. Spaics, a former clerk of the landlords' administration who had to resign his post owing to his deafness and returned to tilling the land, faced no serious difficulties when employing his skills: he merely had to imitate the crosses the magistrates would have put on this letter.[23]

General illiteracy may have encouraged a schoolmaster to commit a quite extraordinary kind of forgery in 1738. Upon his lover's request, he stole paper from the archives of St Gotthard Abbey and drew up a letter supposedly written by the abbey's bailiff, stating that his lover's husband had died. This letter thus must have looked very official; needless to say, the man was alive. To what use the lovers put such paper is unknown – it may have been just an insipid prank. It is true though that another woman from Felsöbár remarried with the help of a similar forged letter. In 1778, Magdolna Groff abandoned her syphilitic husband and married a titled nobleman. When the bigamist was brought to court, it turned out that 'last year she had sought out a clever student for the purpose of commissioning him to draw up a letter for her about her husband's death'. A letter sent by the county official, stating that 'one man clad in a blue pelisse lined with black fur' had been interred, served as the model for this forgery. Magdolna needed it reworded to fit the description of her husband. However, the local notary refused to oblige her and write this letter, so Magdolna approached a student from the high school of Magyarovár.[24] He too turned down her request, and the person who eventually prepared the forged document is unknown. It emerges from the court records that the two peasant women chiefly involved could not even read these pieces of official correspondence, let alone copy them; they were illiterate, and could only understand what was in them when a student read it out for them. Yet their illiteracy did not prevent them from

[23] HNA, Archivum familiae Batthyány, Acta sedis dominalis, fasc. 5. no. 69–4; fasc. 11, no. 96; *ibid.*, Majoratus Ladula 8/a, no. 114.

[24] Archives of Vas County, Szombathely, Archivum abbatiae Sancti Gotthardi, Acta sedis dominalis 'B', 1738.

commissioning a forgery and participating in this curious correspondence between peasants and authorities.

Mátyás Kocsis, a peasant from Korlát, was one of the few rich peasants who could write fluently. However, in his correspondence he had similarly resorted to forgery in an attempt to conceal his adultery. Having lived in matrimony for twenty-two years, he impregnated his servant-maid. He bought some supposedly abortifacient concoction at the Gönc fair, but the container broke and its expensive contents were lost. Kocsis then sent the pregnant woman away to procure an abortion far from her village. For this purpose, he drew up a forged letter for her addressed to the local authorities in his own hand and sealed with the village seal, yet on behalf of another village elder. He gave this letter to his servant-maid, warning her to present his letter anywhere except one village, where his handwriting was likely to be recognised. It can be inferred that the peasant dared to commit forgery on this occasion because literate men were few and far between in his village, and he may have indeed been the only one able to fabricate such a letter.[25]

Not all peasants were aware of what kind of letters they possessed. In 1733, one peasant woman presented 'a certain useless letter' received from the landlord's bailiffs in court in Körmend, concerning a plot of land she held, which she said concerned a mortgage of eight forints, 'albeit the letter does not say the sum'. In the same year, in Lövö, a peasant named Pál Radics submitted official letters which he believed irrefutably justified his claim to own certain clearings. The estate office-holders, however, informed him that 'in these same letters presented, no mention is made as to the mode of possession Radics has over the lands'. Pál Radics probably lacked the ability to read, like Dániel Kis of Nemeskér, who nevertheless claimed he could not present the letters given to him by the landlord concerning a piece of land for 'he could not find it amongst the numerous letters he possessed'. In 1762, at Berkifalu, a serf tried to justify his claim to have purchased the piece of land under dispute in perpetuity by presenting a letter. However, he could hardly have known its contents, because it concerned a plot

---

[25] Archives of Abauj County, Kosice, Acta criminalia, fasc. II, no. 30 (1715).

in another village.[26] Peasants who presented the wrong documents in support of their claims were obviously unable to read these carefully preserved writings.

The correspondence between illiterate peasants concerning the paternity of an illegitimate child or an incestuous love affair was obviously not only extremely confidential but also potentially dangerous. However, letters sent by the peasants of one village to peasants in other villages, inciting them to join a peasant rebellion, seem even more dangerous, because they risked collective rather than individual punishment. Nevertheless, illiterate peasants needed to resort to written correspondence in these cases too. From Cromwell's time to Robespierre's, written documents played a crucial role in mobilising the masses in the great revolutions of early modern Europe. However, the general illiteracy of the local peasantry made the organisation of the peasant uprising in 1765 in western Hungary quite difficult.

In 1764 Queen Maria Theresa of Hungary raised peasant expectations of agrarian reform and rumours flew around the countryside about the imminent reform of peasant duties and forced labour. But when the queen failed to introduce agrarian legislation at the Hungarian diet in Pozsony that year, a peasant rebellion broke out in western Hungary. Although this revolt remained generally bloodless and non-violent, it encouraged Maria Theresa to introduce agrarian reform by decree patent, without the consent of the diet, two years later. During the peasant revolt, letters were frequently sent from one village to another, containing news of the latest events. The bailiff of Szentkut, György Löréncz, heard from many peasants that such letters circulated in the villages; as he told the magistrates who subsequently conducted an inquiry into this revolt, 'he has seen and read the many letters sent by a serf named János Kramer'.[27]

János Kramer was one of the main leaders of this peasant movement, and he had indeed sent a great number of such 'impertinent' letters

---

[26] HNA, Archivum familiae Batthyány, Majoratus, Dominium Körmend, Conscriptiones, P 1322, nos. 10, 44.

[27] Dezső Szabó (ed.), *A magyarországi urbérrendezés története Mária Terézia korában* [The regulation of serfdom in the age of Maria Theresa in Hungary] (Budapest: Athenaeum, 1933), pp. 407–9, 480–2 (publication of documents).

stating that Queen Maria Theresa had received peasant delegations favourably. According to these letters, which circulated from village to village, it was only the Hungarian landlords who were impeding the abolition of serfdom, which had already been decided upon by the Habsburg queen. These rumours were false, although their circulation was not discouraged by the Viennese court. However, János Kramer did not write these letters himself, but instead dictated them to local schoolmasters. When Kramer returned from Vienna, where he had been received by high-ranking officials of the Habsburg court, one such schoolmaster testified that Kramer came directly to his house, saying: 'My friend! Dear Master! You should write something important for me, but you should keep it secret!', and then began to dictate his letter to the other villages.[28]

However, not only the writing, but also the reading of these 'indecent' letters caused the peasants who received them major difficulties. One serf of the Batthyány counts, the judge of the village of Nagymedves, received such a letter, containing secret details on the organisation of the peasant revolt then in preparation, but he could not do anything with it immediately. 'The letter came to the hand of the witness', he later told the members of the committee of inquiry sent out by the county, 'because he was the judge of the village, but he had to go with it to the neighbouring vineyard where a literate person could be found. There he had it read for him and understood its content.' After having heard this letter's content, the judge then followed the demand of the peasant revolt's organisers and set out for the peasant rebels' gathering in the name of his village.

The messengers themselves could not always read the letters they brought in such great secrecy to other villages. A serf living in Istvand admitted to the judges that the other peasants of the village had entrusted him to carry a letter that they had dictated to the local schoolmaster, but claimed that 'he did not know at all what was written in it'. The judges did not question him further, as it was highly probable that this serf, like his illiterate fellow-villagers, had no idea of the contents of the letter he was carrying.[29]

[28] *Ibid.*   [29] *Ibid.*

In other cases, however, the messenger was informed about the precise contents of the letter he took to another village. As the messenger who carried the letter as well as the peasants who received it most probably could not decipher its contents, the messenger was additionally charged to tell the peasants in his own words everything that the letter contained. As one peasant from the village of Lipoc explained, 'one man took a letter to them from the village of Strém, and this messenger told them that the content of this letter in question was that two peasants in the name of the whole village should come to the gathering of the rebellious peasants at Dobrafalva'. Here we find an interesting and revealing example of the combination of written correspondence and oral communication. As the messenger was in all likelihood just as illiterate as the peasants to whom he handed over the letter, the written document in this correspondence was neither read silently nor aloud; instead, the messenger simply told the peasants of this village the contents of the letter. However, even in a case like this, the presence of a written letter was of crucial significance: a written document, even if unread, proved the authenticity of the message transmitted orally.[30]

Similarly, in 1692 the inhabitants of the village of Veresmart wrote a letter to their landlord, the abbot of Pécsvárad. In it, they complained bitterly about the atrocities committed by German soldiers and proposed that the abbot send them an official who could speak fluent German. The peasants evidently hoped that a German-speaking official could negotiate more satisfactorily with marauding German soldiers. Nevertheless, the peasants wrote no further details about their problems to the abbot, but simply stated that 'this man who carries our letter would tell more about all these facts to Your Lordship'. In this case also, a written letter existed primarily as proof for the more authentic oral message.[31]

In the western counties of Hungary, the peasants rose up against their landlords in 1765 in the hope that Queen Maria Theresa would introduce agrarian reforms. In other parts of Hungary, where the peasants enjoyed better conditions, this same royal decree, reforming and

[30] *Ibid.*   [31] Balázs, *Jobbágylevelek* [Serfs' letters], p. 116.

simultaneously standardising peasant obligations, induced the serfs
to revolt. Thus in the Great Hungarian Plain, at the market town of
Vásárhely, the rebellious population protested vehemently against the
introduction of the same new agrarian order for which the peasants
in western Hungary had previously rebelled. However, the low level
of literacy similarly proved an obstacle to peasant correspondence in
this better-off part of Hungary. As the peasants emerged from the
church, witnesses recorded later, the rebels came to them with a letter
of protest they had written and planned to send to the landlord. However, their leader, a peasant named Dajka, was unable to read the letter
aloud and therefore asked another inhabitant of the market town of
Vásárhely named János Lázy to take the letter and read it from the pul-
pit which the notary used to read official letters arriving at the market
town.[32]

In this period of Counter-Reformation and tensions between
Protestants and Catholics, peasant movements also broke out to defend
their confessional churches.[33] Thus, in 1763 the Catholic parish priest
of Gönc initiated a procession to the statue of St John Nepomuk in
order to pray for a good harvest with the local peasants. However,
after many previous unpleasant experiences, the neighbouring Protestants believed this procession was a covert attempt to forcibly occupy
the Reformed church in the next village. Thus the Protestant peasants
guarded this church with pitchforks and scythes, while their Protestant
pastor wrote a letter to the peasants of the neighbouring villages asking
them for help. The judge of the next market town received this letter,
'but as he himself could not read', he asked his deputy to read it.[34] As
this deposition was made during an inquisition into the rebellion at
the county tribunal, one might suppose that this man only pretended
to be illiterate in order to diminish his role in the 'rebellion' and thus

---

[32] Archives of Csongrád County, Szentes, Processus criminales b/21, and for a similar
case: Archives of Bars County, Sala, Criminales processus, XII, fasc. 8, no. 46.

[33] István György Tóth, 'Old and new faith in Hungary, Turkish Hungary and Transylvania', in Ronnie Po Chia Hsia (ed.), *A Companion to the Reformation World* (Oxford:
Blackwell, 2003), pp. 205–20.

[34] Archives of Abauj County, Kosice, Sedria, Acta criminalia, fasc. VIII, no. 6.

avoid severe punishment. However, he never denied that he had led the armed peasants to the Protestant church, a much graver offence in the eyes of this tribunal. Therefore we can believe that despite his important office, this judge was truly unable to read.

Many peasants read prayer-books, the use of which is well documented among the Hungarian peasantry. At first sight this seems a great contradiction: much testimony survives about peasants reading prayer-books, while much also survives depicting peasants unable to read their own correspondence. This is a contradiction, however, only if illiteracy is considered in black-and-white terms, that is in terms of a peasantry either fully literate or completely illiterate. The majority of the peasantry, however, belonged to one of the many categories of semi-literate people. Such peasants knew how to read their own prayer-books. First, these were printed books rather than handwritten texts, and their owners knew the contents almost by heart. Semi-literates could most easily do justice to a prayer-book, which serves as the classic example of intensive reading: the reader repeatedly peruses a few, or even a single, highly appreciated text, which he probably knows by heart, as opposed to scanning large quantities of constantly changing texts, in the way one reads a newspaper today. Even those with scant reading abilities must have been able to negotiate the prayers they knew half or fully by heart, less engaging in reading the text than in glancing at it from time to time in order to refresh their memory – much like reciting a poem. However, the same peasants were completely unable to decipher a handwritten letter of unknown content, seen for the first time.[35]

Their correspondence was therefore necessarily a correspondence of delegated writing and delegated reading, but even so, their illiteracy did not impede a lively correspondence whenever and wherever they felt it necessary to communicate by writing. However, the intimacy that characterises nineteenth-century private correspondence was completely lacking from these letters. Unwed but pregnant

[35] István György Tóth (ed.), *Mil ans de l'histoire hongroise* (Budapest: Osiris-Corvina, 2003), pp. 318–21 (sixteenth–eighteenth centuries), and pp. 410–11 (nineteenth century).

women, wives of soldiers serving in remote regions, desperate illegitimate lovers, indebted peasants and rebellious serfs – they all had to dictate their letters and they generally even asked somebody else to read the answer aloud. These letters, pieces of an *indirect* correspondence, preserve in written form the voices of the otherwise mute majority of early modern peasants.

Bibliography

Ágoston, G. and Oborni, T., *A tizenhetedik század története* [History of the seventeenth century] (Budapest, 2000).

Alberti, L. B., *De componendis cyfris* (1466; reprinted as *Dello scrivere in cifra*, Turin, 1994).

Alberti, L. B., *On Painting*, trans. C. Grayson (Harmondsworth, 1991).

Albuquerque, B. de, *Commentaries of the Great Afonso de Albuquerque*, translated by W. de Gary Birch, 4 vols. (London, 1875–80).

Allaire, B., 'Le décodage de la correspondance chiffrée des diplomates espagnols au XVIe siècle', in *Correspondre, jadis et naguère. 120e Congrès national des sociétés historiques et scientifiques* (Aix-en-Provence, 1995), pp. 207–18.

Alpers, S., *The Art of Describing: Dutch Art in the Seventeenth Century* (London, 1983).

Ambrosini Massari, A. M., 'La solitudine dei capolavori', in R. Morselli (ed.), *Gonzaga. La Celeste Galeria. L'esercizio del collezionismo*, exhibition catalogue, Palazzo Tè – Palazzo Ducale, Mantova (Milan, 2002), vol. 2, pp. 1–38.

Anagnostou, S., *Jesuiten in Spanisch-Amerika als Uebermittler von heilkundlichem Wissen* (Stuttgart, 2000).

Ancel, R., 'Etude critique sur quelques recueils d'*Avvisi*: contribution à l'histoire du journalisme en Italie', *Mélanges d'Archéologie et d' Histoire de l'Ecole Française de Rome* 28 (1908), 115–39.

Andrade, A. A. Banha de, *Mundos novos do mundo: panorama da difusão pela Europa de notícias dos descobrimentos portugueses*, 2 vols. (Lisbon, 1972).

Arbel, B., *Trading Nations: Jews and Venetians in the Early Modern Eastern Mediterranean* (Leiden, 1995).

Aretino, P., *Dialogo Ragionamento* (Milan, 1984).

Aretino, P., *Lettere*, ed. P. Procaccioli, 6 vols. (Rome, 1997–2002).

Aubin, J., 'Une frontière face au péril ottoman: la terre d'Otrante (1529–1532)', in *Le latin et l'astrolabe: recherches sur le Portugal de la Renaissance, son expansion en Asie et les relations internationales* (Lisbon and Paris, 2000), pp. 93–127.

Bachrach, A. G. H., *Sir Constantine Huygens and Britain, 1596–1687: A Pattern of Cultural Exchange* (Leiden, 1962).

Badié, B., 'L'état moderne: le point de vue du politologue', in N. Coulet and J. P. Genet (eds.), *L'ètat moderne: le droit, l'espace et les formes de l'etat* (Paris, 1990), pp. 211–27.

Balázs, E. H. (ed.), *Jobbágylevelek* [Serfs' letters] (Budapest, 1951).

Baldriga, I., *L'occhio della lince: i primi lincei tra arte, scienza e collezionismo (1603–1630)* (Rome, 2002).

Balducci Pegolotti, F., *La pratica della mercatura*, ed. A. Evans (Cambridge, MA, 1936).

Balducci, R., 'Dei, Benedetto', *Dizionario Biografico degli Italiani* (Rome, 1961–), vol. 36, pp. 252–3.

Barbarics, Z., 'Tinte und Politik in der frühen Neuzeit: handschriftliche Zeitungen als überregionale Nachrichtenquellen für die Machthaber', unpublished PhD thesis (Graz, 2006).

Barbaro, Z., *Dispacci: 1 novembre 1471–7 settembre 1473*, ed. G. Corazzol (Rome, 1994).

Barona, J. L. and Gómez i Font, X. (eds.), *La correspondencia de Carolus Clusius con los científicos españoles* (Valencia, 1998).

Barreto, L. F., *Descobrimentos e Renascimento: formas de ser e pensar nos séculos XV e XVI* (Lisbon, 1983).

Barros, J. de, *Ásia*, ed. A. Baião and L. F. Cintra Lindley, 2 vols. (Lisbon, 1932–74).

Baskin Barron, J., 'The development of corporate financial markets in Britain and the United States, 1600–1914: overcoming asymmetric information', *Business History Review* 62 (1988), 199–237.

Bassani Pacht, P. and Crépin-Leblond, T. (eds.), *Marie de Médicis: un gouvernement par les arts*, exhibition catalogue (Paris, 2003).

Basso, J., *Le genre épistolaire en langue italienne (1538–1662): répertoire chronologique et analytique*, 2 vols. (Nancy, 1990).

Bataillon, M., 'Hernán Cortés, autor proibido', in *Libro Jubilar de Alfonso Reyes* (Mexico, 1963), pp. 77–82.

Bätschmann, O., *Nicolas Poussin: Dialectics of Painting* (London, 1990).

Baulant-Duchaillut, M. (ed.), *Lettres de négociants marseillais: les frères Hermite (1570–1612)* (Paris, 1953).

Bayle, P., *Dictionnaire historique et critique*, 3rd edition, corrected by the author (Rotterdam, 1720).

Bazzano, N., '"A Vostra Eccelenza di buon cuore mi offero e raccomando": il linguaggio della politica attraverso il carteggio di Marco Antonio Colonna (1556–77)', in M. A. Visceglia (ed.), *La nobiltà romana in età moderna: profili instituzionali e pratiche sociali* (Rome, 2001), pp. 133–64.

Bellamy, A., *The Politics of Court Scandal in Early Modern England: News Culture and the Overbury Affair, 1603–1660* (Cambridge, 2002).

Bellocchi, U., *Storia del giornalismo italiano* (Bologna, 1974).

Benedict, P., *Christ's Churches Purely Reformed: A Social History of Calvinism* (New Haven, 2002).

Benzoni, G., *La historia del mondo nuovo* (Venice, 1565); Latin translation *Nuovi Novi Orbis Historia* by U. Chauveton (Lyon, 1578), and French translation *Histoire nouvelle du Nouveau Monde* by U. Chauveton (Geneva, 1579).

Berendts, A., 'Carolus Clusius (1526–1609) and Bernardus Paludanus (1550–1633): their contacts and correspondence', *Lias* 5 (1978), 49–64.

Berengo, M. (ed.), *I giornali veneziani del '700* (Milan, 1962).

Berkvens-Stevelinck, C., Bots, H. and Häseler, J. (eds.), *Les grands intermédiaires culturels de la République des Lettres: études de réseaux de correspondence du xvie au xviiie siècles* (Paris, forthcoming).

Bethencourt, F., 'A expulsão dos judeus', in D. Curto (ed.), *O tempo de Vasco da Gama* (Lisbon, 1998), pp. 271–80.

Bethencourt, F., 'O Estado da Índia', in F. Bethencourt and K. Chaudhuri (eds.), *História da expansão portuguesa*, vol. 2 (Lisbon, 1998), pp. 284–314.

Bethencourt, F., 'Le millénarisme: idéologie de l'impérialisme eurasiatique?', *Annales HSS* 1 (2002), 189–94.

Biagioli, M., 'Etiquette, interdependence, and sociability in seventeenth-century science', *Critical Inquiry* 22 (1996), 193–238.

Biegman, N. H., 'Ragusan spying for the Ottoman Empire: some 16th century documents from the State Archives at Dubrovnik', in *Belleten* 27, 106 (1963), 237–49.

Biegman, N. H., *The Turco-Ragusan Relationship according to the Firmans of Murad III (1575–1595) extant in the State Archives of Dubrovnik* (The Hague and Paris, 1967).

Blindow, U., *Berliner geschriebene Zeitungen des 18. Jahrhunderts* (Berlin and Würzburg, 1939).

Blunt, A., *Poussin* (London, 1995).

Boccalini, T., *Ragguagli di Parnaso* (Venice, 1612).

Bongi, S., 'Le prime gazzette in Italia', *Nuova Antologia* 11 (1869), pp. 311–46.

Book of Duarte Barbosa, The, ed. M. Longworth Dames, 2 vols. (London, 1918–21).

Borchgrave, C. de, 'Diplomates et diplomatie sous le duc de Bourgogne Jean sans peur', in J. M. Cauchies (ed.), *A la cour de Bourgogne: le duc, son entourage, son train* (Turnhout, 1998), pp. 67–83.

Borea, E., 'Stampa figurativa e pubblica dall'origine all'affermazione nel Cinquecento', in *Storia dell'arte italiana*, part 1, vol. 2: *L'artista e il pubblico* (Turin, 1979), pp. 389–90.

Borges, C. J., SJ, 'Native Goan participation in the Estado da Índia and the inter-Asiatic trade', in A. T. de Matos, and L. F. Reis Thomaz (eds.), *A*

Carreira da Índia e as rotas dos estreitos: Actas do VIII *seminário internacional de história indo-portuguesa* (Braga, 1998), pp. 667–86.

Borlandi, A., *Il manuale di mercatura di Saminiato de' Ricci* (Genoa, 1963).

Borlandi, F., *El libro di mercantie et usanze de' paesi* (Turin, 1936).

Botero, G., *Detti memorabili di personaggi illustri* (Venice, 1610).

Bots, H. (ed.), *Correspondance de Jacques Dupuy et Nicolas Heinsius (1646–1656)* (The Hague, 1971).

Bots, H. and Waquet, F., *La République des Lettres* (Paris, 1997).

Bottari, G. G., *Raccolta di lettere sulla pittura, scultura ed architettura scritte da' più celebri personaggi dei secoli* XV, XVI, *e* XVII / *pubblicata da Gio: Bottari e continuata fino ai nostri giorni da Stefano Ticozzi* (Milan, 1822).

Bouchon, G., *Albuquerque: le lion des mers d'Asie* (Paris, 1992).

Boureau, A., 'La norme épistolaire, une invention médiévale', in R. Chartier (ed.), *La correspondance: les usages de la lettre au* XIXe *siècle* (Paris, 1991), pp. 127–57.

Bouza, F., *Comunicación, conocimiento y memoria en la España de los siglos* XVI *y* XVII (Salamanca, 1999).

Bouza, F., *Corre manuscrito: una historia cultural del Siglo de Oro* (Madrid, 2001).

Bouza, F., *Palabra e imagen en la corte: cultura oral y visual de la nobleza en el Siglo de Oro* (Madrid, 2003).

Boxer, C. R., *The Portuguese Seaborne Empire 1415–1825* (London, 1969).

Bracciolini, P., *Lettere*, ed. H. Harth, 3 vols. (Florence, 1984–7).

Braudel, F., *Civilisation matérielle, économie et capitalisme*, 3 vols. (Paris, 1979); English edition: *Civilization and Capitalism, 15th–18th Century*, 3 vols. (New York, 1981–4).

Braudel, F., *La méditerranée et le monde méditerranéen à l'époque de Philippe II*, 2 vols., 2nd edition (Paris, 1966); English edition: *The Mediterranean and the Mediterranean World in the Age of Philip II*, 2 vols. (New York, 1972–3).

Bresson, A., *Les correspondants de Peiresc*, electronic paper, www.peiresc.org (1992).

Brizzi, G., *I sistemi informativi dei Romani: principi e realtà nell'età delle conquiste oltremare, 218–168 a.C* (Wiesbaden, 1982).

Browne, J., *Charles Darwin: The Power of Place*, volume 2 of a biography (London, 2002).

Brummet, P., 'The Ottomans as a world power: what we don't know about Ottoman seapower', in K. Fleet (ed.), *The Ottomans and the Sea* (Rome, 2001), pp. 1–10.

Bunes Ibarra, M. A. de and Sola, E. (eds.), *La Vida, y Historia de Hayradin, llamado Barbarroja Gazavât- i Hayreddín Pasa – La Cronica del guerrero de la fé Hayreddín Barbarroja (del Manuscrito Otomano de Seyyid Murâd)* (Granada, 1997).

Burke, P., *The Italian Renaissance: Culture and Society in Italy*, 2nd edition (Cambridge, 1999).

Burke, P., 'Early modern Venice as a center of information and communication', in J. Martin and D. Romano (eds.), *Venice Reconsidered: The History and Civilisation of an Italian City-State, 1297–1997* (Baltimore, 2000), pp. 389–419.

Burke, P., 'Rome as a center of information and communication for the Catholic world, 1550–1650', in P. M. Jones and T. Worcester (eds.), *From Rome to Eternity: Catholicism and the Arts in Italy, c.1550–1650* (Leiden, 2002), pp. 253–69.

Burkhardt, J., *Vornehmsten Korrespondenten der deutschen Fürsten im 15. und 16. Jahrhundert* (Leipzig, 1928).

Burkhardt, J., *Das Nachrichtenwesen der deutschen Fürsten im 16. und 17. Jahrhundert* (Leipzig, 1930).

Burkhardt, J., *Zeitungsgeschichtliche Schätze in Stettiner Bibliotheken* (Leipzig, 1933).

Burkhardt, J., *Das Reformationsjahrhundert: deutsche Geschichte zwischen Medienrevolution und Institutionenbildung 1517–1617* (Stuttgart, 2002).

Burlingham, C., 'Portraiture as propaganda: printmaking during the reign of Henry IV', in K. Jacobson (ed.), *The French Renaissance Prints from the Bibliothèque Nationale de France* (Los Angeles, 1994), pp. 139–51.

Caizzi, B., *Dalla posta del re alla posta di tutti: territorio e comunicazioni in Italia dal XVI secolo all'Unità* (Milan, 1993).

Calabria, A., *The Cost of Empire: The Finances of the Kingdom of Naples in the Time of Spanish Rule* (Cambridge, 1991).

Camões, L. de, *The Lusiads*, translated with introduction and notes by L. White (Oxford, 1997).

Campbell, L., *Renaissance Portraits: European Portrait-painting in the 14th, 15th and 16th Centuries* (New Haven and London, 1990).

Campos de Andrada, E. de, *Relações de Pero de Alcáçova Carneiro, Conde de Idanha, do tempo que éle e seu pai, António Carneiro serviram de secretários (1515 a 1568)* (Lisbon, 1937).

Caracciolo Aricò, A. (ed.), *L'impatto della scoperta dell'America nella cultura veneziana* (Rome, 1990).

Cardano, G., *De subtilitate* (Basel, 1547).

Cardano, G., *De rerum varietate* (Lyon, 1556).

Care, H., *The Female Secretary* (London, 1671).

Carrera, R., 'Pierre Jaquet-Droz: l'uomo a orologeria', *Art. FMR. Secolo xviii* 1 (Milan, 1990), 237–56.

Carrier, D., 'Blindness and the representation of desire in Poussin's paintings', *Res* 19–20 (1991), 31–52.

Carrière, C., *Négociants marseillais au* XVIIIe *siècle: contribution à l'étude des économies maritimes* (Marseille, 1973).

Carrière, C., Gutsatz, M., Courdurié, M. and Squarzoni, R., *Banque et capitalisme commercial: la lettre de change au* XVIIIe *siècle* (Marseille, 1976).

Cartas de Affonso de Albuquerque, seguidas de documentos que as elucidam, ed. successively by B. Pato and H. Lopes de Mendonça, 7 vols. (Lisbon, 1884–1935).

Casas, B. de las, *Obra indígenista*, ed. J. Alcina Franch (Madrid, 1985).

Casas, B. de las, *Brevissima relación de la destrucción de las Indias*, ed. J. M. Reyes Cano (Barcelona, 1994).

Castanheda, F. Lopes de, *História do descobrimento e conquista da Índia pelos portugueses*, ed. M. Lopes de Almeida, 2 vols. (Porto, 1979).

Castronovo, V., Ricuperati, G. and Capra, C., *La stampa italiana dal Cinquecento all'Ottocento* (Bari, 1976).

Céard, J. and Margolin, J. C., *Voyager à la Renaissance. Actes du colloque de Tours 1983* (Paris, 1987).

Cecchi, E., *Le lettere di Francesco Datini alla moglie Margherita (1385–1410)* (Prato, 1992).

Cecchi, G. M., *Poesie pubblicate per la prima volta da Michele dello Russo* (Naples, 1866).

Cellier, R., *La cryptographie* (Paris, 1948).

Ceroni, L., *La diplomazia sforzesca nella seconda metà del Quattrocento e i suoi cifrari segreti*, Fonti e studi del *Corpus membranarum italicarum* 7, 2 vols. (Rome, 1970).

Chappuys, G., *Le secrétaire* (Lyon, 1588).

Chapuis, A. and Gélis, E., *Le monde des automates: étude historique et technique* (Paris, 1928).

Chartier, R., 'Du livre au livre', in R. Chartier (ed.), *Pratiques de la lecture* (Marseille, 1985), pp. 61–81.

Chartier, R., 'Des "secrétaires" pour le peuple?', in R. Chartier (ed.), *La correspondance: les usages de la lettre au* XIXe *siècle* (Paris, 1991), pp. 159–87.

Chartier, R., '*Secrétaires* for the people? Model letters of the ancient régime: between court literature and popular chapbooks', in R. Chartier, A. Boureau and C. Dauphin (eds.), *Correspondence: Models of Letter-Writing from the Middle Ages to the Nineteenth Century* (Princeton, NJ, 1997), pp. 59–111.

Chartier, R. (ed.), *The Culture of Print: Power and the Uses of Print in Early Modern Europe* (Princeton, 1989).

Checa Cremades, F., *Carlos V y la imagen del heróe en el Renacimiento* (Madrid, 1987).

Clément, P. (ed.), *Lettres, instructions et mémoires de Colbert*, vol. 5 (Paris, 1868).

Clendinnen, I., 'Cortés, Signs, and the conquest of Mexico', in A. Grafton and A. Blair (eds), *The Transmission of Culture in Early Modern Europe* (Philadelphia, 1990), pp. 87–130.

Columbus, C., *Textos y documentos completos*, ed. C. Varela and J. Gil, 2nd edition (Madrid, 1992).

Comparato, V. I., 'A case of modern individualism: politics and the uneasiness of intellectuals in the Baroque age', in J. Coleman (ed.), *The Individual in Political Theory and Practice: The Origins of the Modern State in Europe* (Oxford, 1996), pp. 149–70.

Coniglio, G., *Il regno di Napoli al tempo di Carlo V: amministrazione e vita economico-sociale* (Naples, 1951).

Coniglio, G., 'Note sulla società napoletana ai tempi di Don Pietro di Toledo', in *Studi in onore di Riccardo Filangeri*, vol. 2 (Naples, 1959), pp. 345–65.

Coniglio, G., *Il Viceregno di Napoli e la lotta tra spagnoli e turchi nel Mediterraneo*, vol. 1 (Naples, 1987).

Conlon, F. F., *A Caste in a Changing World: The Chitrapur Saraswat Brahmans, 1700–1935* (Berkeley, Los Angeles and London, 1977).

Constable, G., *Letters and Letter-collection* (Turnhout, 1976).

Coronelli, V., *Biblioteca universale sacro-profana antico-moderna* (Venice, 1701–9).

Corpo Diplomático Português, ed. L. A. Rebello da Silva, C. Leal, A. Ferrão and L. Coelho, vols. 1–2 (Lisbon, 1862–5).

Corpo Diplomático Português, ed. J. da Silva Mendes Leal, vol. 7 (Lisbon, 1884).

Correia, G., *Lendas da Índia*, ed. M. Lopes de Almeida, 4 vols. (Porto, 1975).

Correspondances, Les. Leur importance pour l'historien des Sciences et de la Philosophie. Problèmes de leur édition (*Revue de Synthèse*, série générale 97, 3rd series, 81–2) (Paris, 1976).

Cortés, H., *Cartas y documentos*, ed. M. Hernández Sanchez Barba (Mexico, 1963).

Cortés, H., *Letters from Mexico*, trans., ed. and presented by A. Pagden, introduction by J. H. Elliott, 2nd edition (New Haven, CT, 1986).

Cortés, H., *Cartas de Relación*, ed. A. Delgado Gomez (Madrid, 1993).

Costo, T., *Lettere* (Venice, 1602).

Cotta, I., *Lettere italiane/Pietro Paolo Rubens* (Rome, 1987).

Couto, D. do, *Décadas da Ásia* (Lisbon, 1736).

Couto, D., 'L'espionnage portugais dans l'Empire ottoman', in *La découverte, le Portugal et l'Europe* (Paris, 1990), pp. 243–67.

Couto, D., 'Les Ottomans et l'Inde portugaise', in *Vasco da Gama e a India* (Lisbon, 1999), vol. 1, pp. 181–200.

Cozzi, G., *Repubblica di Venezia e stati italiani: politica e giustizia dal secolo* XVI *al secolo* XVIII (Turin, 1982).

Cressy, D., *Literacy and the Social Order: Reading and Writing in Tudor and Stuart England* (Cambridge, 1980).

Cressy, D., *Coming over: Migration and Communication between England and New England in the Seventeenth Century* (Cambridge, 1987).

Crónicas del Gran Capitán, ed. A. Rodriguez Villa (Madrid, 1908).

Cropper, E. and Dempsey, C., *Nicolas Poussin: Friendship and the Love of Painting* (Princeton, NJ, 1996).

Crouzet-Pavan, E., 'Les mots de Venise: sur le contrôle du langage dans une cité-état italienne', in *La circulation des nouvelles au Moyen Age*, (Société des Historiens Médiévistes de l'Enseignement Supérieur Public) (Paris and Rome, 1994), pp. 205–18.

Curtin, P. D., *Cross-Cultural Trade in World History* (Cambridge, 1984).

Danesi Squarzina, S. (ed.), *Caravaggio e i Giustiniani. Toccar con mano una collezione del Seicento*, exhibition catalogue, Palazzo Giustiniani (Rome, 2001).

Davis, N. Z., *The Gift in Sixteenth-Century France* (Oxford, 2000).

Day, A., *The English Secretary*, ed. with an introduction by R. O. Evans (Gainsville, FL, 1967; 1st edition 1586).

Decourtemanche, M. J. A., 'Note sur quatre systèmes turcs de notation numérique secrète', *Journal Asiatique*, 9th series, 14 (1899), 258–71.

Della Porta, G., *Le commedie*, ed. V. Spampanato (Bari, 1910–11).

Della Porta, G., *De furtivis literarum notis vulgo de ziferis libri IV* (Naples, 1563).

Delumeau, J., *Vie économique et sociale de Rome dans la seconde moitié du* XVIe *siècle* (Paris, 1957).

Delumeau, J., *L'aveu et le pardon: les difficultés de la confession.* XIIIe–XVIIIe *siècle* (Paris, 1992).

Derrida, Jacques, *La vérité en peinture* (Paris, 1978).

Description de la ville de Lisbonne . . . (Amsterdam, 1730).

Deswarte, S., 'La Rome de D. Miguel da Silva (1515–1525)', in *O Humanismo Português 1500–1600*, Academia das Ciências de Lisboa (Lisbon, 1988), pp. 177–307.

Deswarte, S., *Il 'perfetto cortegiano' D. Miguel de Silva* (Rome, 1989).

Devos, J. P., *Les chiffres de Philippe II (1555–1598) et du Despacho Universal durant le* XVIIe *siècle* (Brussels, 1950).

Devos, J. P. and Seligman, H., *L'art de déchiffrer: traité de déchiffrement du* XVIIe *siècle de la Sécretairie d'Etat et de Guerre espagnole*, Recueil des travaux d'histoire et de philologie de l' Université de Louvain, 4th series, 36 (Louvain, 1967).

Diaz del Castillo, B., *Historia verdadera de la conquista de la Nueva España*, introduction and notes by L. Sáinz de Medrano (Barcelona, 1992).

Dibon, P. 'Les échanges épistolaires dans l'Europe savante du XVIIe siècle', *Revue de synthèse*, 3rd series, 81–2 (1976), 31–50.

Didi-Huberman, G., *Devant l'image* (Paris, 1990).

Dilg, P., 'Apotheker als Sammler', in A. Grote (ed.), *Macrocosmos in Microcosmo. Die Welt in der Stube. Zur Geschichte des Sammelns 1450 bis 1800* (Opladen, 1994), pp. 453–74.

Dini, B., 'L'archivio Datini', in S. Cavaciocchi (ed.), *L'impresa, industria, commercio, banca secc. XIII–XVIII* (Florence, 1991), pp. 45–58.

Dooley, B. and Baron, S. (eds.), *The Politics of Information in Early Modern Europe* (London and New York, 2001).

Doria, G., 'Conoscenza del mercato e sistema informativo: il know-how dei mercanti-finanzieri genovesi nei secoli XVI e XVII', in A. De Maddalena and H. Kellenbenz (eds.), *La repubblica internazionale del denaro tra XV e XVII secolo* (Bologna, 1986), pp. 57–121.

Dowley, F. H, 'Thoughts on Poussin, time, and narrative: The Israelites gathering manna in the desert', *Simiolus* 25 (1997), 329–48.

Ducellier, A., *La façade maritime de l'Albanie au Moyen Age: Durazzo et Valona du XIe au XV e siècle* (Salonica, 1986).

Ducreux, M. E., 'Lire à en mourir', in R. Chartier (ed.), *Les usages de l'imprimé* (Paris, 1987), pp. 281–2.

Durante, S., 'The Medici cycle', in *Peter Paul Rubens: A Touch of Brilliance*, exhibition catalogue (Munich, New York and London, 2003), pp. 86–8.

Dürer, A., *Diary of his Journey to the Netherlands, 1520–1521*, ed. J. A. Goris and G. Marlier (London, 1971).

Durling, R. J., 'Konrad Gessner's Briefwechsel', in R. Schmitz and F. Krafft (eds.), *Humanismus und Naturwissenschaften*, Beiträge zur Humanismusforschung 6 (Boppard, 1980), pp. 101–12.

Edelmayer, F. (ed.), *Die Korrespondenz der Kaiser mit ihren Gesandten in Spanien*, vol. 1: *Der Briefwechsel zwischen Ferdinand I., Maximilian II., und Adam von Dietrichstein 1563–1565* (Munich, 1997).

Egmond, F. and Mason, P., *The Mammoth and the Mouse: Microhistory and Morphology* (Baltimore and London, 1997).

Egmond, F. and Mason, P., 'A horse called Belisarius', *History Workshop Journal* 47 (1999), 240–52.

Eisenstein, E., *The Printing Press as an Agent of Change: Communication and Cultural Transformations in Early Modern Europe* (Cambridge, 1979).

Elias, N. *La civilisation des mœurs*, trans. Pierre Kamnitze (Paris, 1973).

Elias, N., *The Court Society*, trans. from the German by E. Jephcott (Oxford, 1983).

Erasmus, *De conscribendarum epistolarum ratio* (Lyon, 1531).

Erasmus, *Opus epistolarum*, ed. P. S. Allen et al., 12 vols. (Oxford, 1906–58; reprint 1992).

Erasmus, *The Correspondence of Erasmus*, ed. P. S. Allen et al. and trans. into English by R. A. B. Mynors and D. F. S. Thomson, annotated by W. K. Ferguson, 12 vols. so far (Toronto, 1974–2003).

Ernout, A. and A. Meillet (eds.), *Dictionnaire étymologique de la langue latine* (Paris, 2001).

Febvre, L., *Pour une histoire à part entiére* (Paris, 1962).

Fedele, C. and Gallenga, M., *'Per servi̧zio di Nostro signore': strade, corrieri e poste dei papi dal medioevo al 1870* (Prato, 1988).

Fernández de Oviedo, G., *Historia general y natural de las Indias*, ed. A. de los Rios, 4 vols. (Madrid, 1851–55).

Ferrari, G. B., *De florum cultura* (Rome, 1633).

Ferrari, O., *Origines linguae italicae* (Padua, 1676).

Ferro, J. P., 'A epistolografia no quotidiano dos missionários jesuítas', *Lusitania Sacra* 5 (1993), 137–58.

Fieiliilg, N., 'The transatlantic Republic of Letters: a note on the circulation of learned periodicals to early eighteenth century America', *The William and Mary Quarterly*, 3rd series, 33.4 (1976), 642–60.

Findlen, P., *Possessing Nature: Museums, Collecting and Scientific Culture in Early Modern Italy* (Berkeley, 1994).

Findlen, P., 'The formation of a scientific community: natural history in sixteenth-century Italy', in A. Grafton and N. Siraisi (eds.), *Natural Particulars* (Cambridge, MA, 1999), pp. 369–400.

Findlen, P., 'Un incontro con Kircher a Roma', in E. Lo Sardo (ed.), *Athanasius Kircher: Il Museo del Mondo*, exhibition catalogue (Rome, 2001), pp. 39–47.

Finnegan, R., *Literacy and Orality: Studies in the Technology of Communication* (Oxford, 1988).

Fisher, S. H. E., *The Portugal Trade: A Study of Anglo-Portuguese Commerce 1700–1770* (London, 1971).

Fitzler, M. H., *Die Entstehung der sogenannten Fuggerḁeitungen in der Wiener Nationalbibliothek* (Banden bei Wien, 1937).

Florio, J., *A Worlde of Wordes* (London, 1598).

Florio, J., *Queen Anna's New World of Words or Dictionarie of the Italian and English Tongues* (London, 1611).

Fortunati, M., *Scrittura e prova: i libri di commercio nel diritto medievale e moderno* (Rome, 1996).

Franchini, D. A., Margonari, R., Olmi, G., Signorini, R., Zanca, A. and Tellini Perina, C., *La scieņza a corte: collȩzionismo eclettico, natura e immagine a Mantova fra Rinascimento e Manierismo* (Rome, 1979).

Franzesi, M., 'Capitolo sopra le nuove a M. Benedetto Busini', in F. Berni, *Il secondo libro delle opere burlesche* (Florence, 1555), pp. 58–9.

Freedberg, D., *The Eye of the Lynx: Galileo, his Friends, and the Beginnings of Modern Natural History* (Chicago and London, 2002).

Fumaroli, M., 'A l'origine d'un art français: la correspondance familière', in *La diplomacie de l'esprit: de Montaigne à La Fontaine* (Paris, 1998), pp. 163–81.

Fumaroli, M., 'La conversation savante', in H. Bots and F. Waquet (eds.), *Commercium litterarium, 1600–1750* (Amsterdam, 1994), pp. 67–80.

Fumaroli, M., *Nicolas-Claude Fabri de Peiresc: Prince de la République des Lettres*, electronic paper, www.peiresc.org (1992).

Fumaroli, M., *Nicolas Poussin. Sainte Françoise Romaine* (Paris, 2001).

Furber, H., *Rival Empires of Trade in the Orient 1600–1800* (Minneapolis, 1976).

Furlotti, B., *Le collezioni Gonzaga: il carteggio tra Bologna, Parma, Piacenza e Mantova (1563–1634)* (Cinisello Balsamo, 2000).

Furlotti, B., *Le collezioni Gonzaga il carteggio tra Roma e Mantova (1587–1612)* (Cinisello Balsamo, 2003).

Gaeta, G., *Storia del giornalismo* (Milan, 1966).

Galende Diaz, J. C., *Criptografía: historia de la escritura cifrada* (Madrid, 1995).

García Hernán, E., 'The price of spying at the battle of Lepanto', *Eurasian Studies: The Skilliter Centre–Istituto per l'Oriente Journal for Balkan, Eastern Mediterranean, Anatolian, Middle Eastern, Iranian and Central Asian Studies* 2 (2003), 227–50.

García Martínez, B., *El Marquesado del Valle: tres siglos de régimen señorial en Nueva España* (Mexico, 1969).

Gassendi, P., *Vie de l'illustre Nicolas-Claude Fabri de Peiresc, conseiller au parlement d'Aix*, trans. from the Latin by R. Lassalle and preface by J. Emelina (Paris, 1992).

Gazette des estats & de ce temps. Du Seigneur servitour de Piera Grosa gio: traduite d'Italien en François le premier janvier 1614 (s.n.t.).

Gegaj, A., *L'Albanie et l'invasion turque au XVe siècle* (Louvain and Paris, 1937).

Germer, S. (ed.), *Bellori, Félibien, Passeri, Sandrart, Vies de Poussin* (Paris, 1994).

Giesecke, M., *Der Buchdruck in der frühen Neuzeit: eine historische Fallstudie über die Durchsetzung neuer Informations- und Kommunikationstechnologien* (Frankfurt am Main, 1998).

Ginori Conti, P., *Lettere inedite di Charles de l'Escluse (Carolus Clusius) a Matteo Caccini, floricultore fiorentino: contributo alla storia della botanica* (Florence, 1939).

Ginzburg Carignani, S., 'Domenichino e Giovanni Battista Agucchi', in C. Strinati and A. Tantillo (eds.), *Domenichino, 1581–1641*, exhibition catalogue (Milan, 1996), pp. 121–37.

Ginzburg, C., 'Le peintre et le bouffon: le *Portrait de Gonella* de Jean Fouquet', *Revue de l'Art* 111 (1996), 25–39.

Giovio, P., *Gli elogi degli uomini illustri (letterati, artisti, uomini d'arme)*, ed. R. Meregazzi (Rome, 1972).

Gluckman, M., *The Judicial Process among the Barotse of Northern Rhodesia (Zambia)* (Manchester, 1955).

Góis, D. de, *Chronica do felicissimo rei Dom Emanuel*, 4 vols. (Lisbon, 1566–7).

Goitein, S. D., 'Letters and documents on the India trade in medieval times', in *Studies in Islamic History and Institutions* (Leiden, 1966), pp. 329–50.

Goitein, S. D., *A Mediterranean Society: The Jewish Communities of the Arab World as Portrayed in the Documents of the Cairo Geniza*, 6 vols. (Berkeley and Los Angeles, 1967–93).

Goitein, S. D., *Letters of Medieval Jewish Traders Translated from the Arabic with Introductions and Notes* (Princeton, 1973).

Goldgar, A., *Impolite Learning: Conduct and Community in the Republic of Letters, 1680–1750* (New Haven and London, 1995).

Gonzáles Palencia, A. and Mele, E., *Vida y obras de D. Diego Hurtado de Mendoza* (Madrid, 1941).

Goodman, D., *The Republic of Letters: A Cultural History of the French Enlightenment* (Ithaca, NY, and London, 1994).

Gouw, J. L. van der, 'Marie de Brimeu: een Nederlandse prinses uit de eerste helft van de tachtigjarige oorlog', *De Nederlandsche Leeuw* 64 (1947), 5–49.

Gozzi, G., 'Lettera capitata allo stampatore signor Marcuzzi', *Gazzetta veneta* I (6 February 1760).

Gracián, B., *El Heroe* (Madrid, 1980; 1st edition, 1637).

Graff, H. G., *The Legacies of Literacy* (Bloomington, 1987), pp. 218–27.

Grasshoff, R., *Die briefliche Zeitung des XVI. Jahrhunderts* (Leipzig, 1877).

Greif, A., 'Reputation and coalition in medieval trade: evidence on the Maghribi traders', *Journal of Economic History* 49 (1989), 857–82.

Greif, A., 'Contract enforceability and economic institutions in early trade: the Maghribi traders' coalition', *American Economic Review* 133 (1992), 525–48.

Greif, A., 'Cultural beliefs and the organization of society: a historical and theoretical reflection on collectivist and individualist societies', *Journal of Political Economy* 102 (1994), 912–50.

Gremigni, E., *Periodici e almanacchi livornesi secoli XVII–XVIII* (Livorno, 1996).

Griffin, N., *Virtus versus Letters: The Society of Jesus 1550–1580 and the Export of an Idea*, EUI Working Papers 95 (Florence, 1984).

Griffiths, R., 'Bureaucracy and the English State in the latter Middle Ages', in F. Autran (ed.), *Prosopographie et genèse de l'état moderne* (Paris, 1986), pp. 53–65.

Groth, O., *Die Geschichte der deutschen Zeitungswissenschaft: Probleme und Methoden* (Munich, 1948).

Grotius, H., *Briefwisseling*, 17 vols. (The Hague, 1928–2001).

Grotius, H., *The Free Sea*, trans. R. Hakluyt, with W. Welwood's Critique and Grotius' Reply, ed. with an introduction by D. Armitage (Indianapolis, 2004).

Gruzinski, S., *Histoire de Mexico* (Paris, 1996).

Guarini, B., *Il segretario* (Venice, 1594).

Guenée, B., *L'opinion publique à la fin du moyen Age, d'après la 'Chronique de Charles VI' du Religieux de Saint Denis* (Paris, 2002).

Guerreiro, I. and Rodrigues, V. L. Gaspar, 'O "grupo de Cochim" e a oposição a Afonso de Albuquerque', *Studia* 51 (1992), 119–44.

Guilmartin, J. F., *Gunpower and Galleys: Changing Technology and Mediterranean Warfare at Sea in the Sixteenth Century* (Cambridge, 1980).

Habermas, J., *The Structural Transformation of the Public Sphere: An Inquiry into a Category of Bourgeois Society* (Cambridge, MA, 1989; 1st German edition, 1962).

Haffemayer, S., 'La géographie de l'information dans la Gazette de Renaudot de 1647 à 1663', in H. Duranton and P. Rétat (eds.), *Gazettes et information politique sous l'Ancien Régime* (Saint-Étienne, 1999), pp. 21–31.

Hancock, D., *Citizens of the World: London Merchants and the Integration of the British Atlantic Community, 1735–1785* (Cambridge, 1995)

Hancock, D., '"A revolution in the trade": wine distribution and the development of the infrastructure of the Atlantic market economy, 1703–1807', in J. J. McCusker and K. Morgan (eds.), *The Early Modern Atlantic Economy* (Cambridge, 2000), pp. 105–53.

Harkness, D. E., '"Strange" ideas and "English" knowledge: natural science exchange in Elizabethan London', in P. H. Smith and P. Findlen (eds.), *Merchants and Marvels: Commerce, Science and Art in Early Modern Europe* (New York and London, 2002), pp. 137–60.

Harms, W., 'Das illustrierte Flugblatt in Verständigungsprozessen innerhalb der frühneuzeitlichen Kultur', in W. Harms and A. Messerli (eds.), *Wahrnehmungsgeschichte und Wissensdiskurs im illustrierten Flugblatt der Frühen Neuzeit (1450–1770)* (Basel, 2002), pp. 11–21.

Harris, S. M. (ed.), *American Women Writers to 1800* (Oxford, 1996).

Härting, U. (ed.), *Gärten und Höfe der Rubenszeit: im Spiegel der Malerfamilie Brueghel und der Künstler um Peter Paul Rubens*, exhibition catalogue, Gustav-Lübcke-Museum, Hamm, and Landesmuseum, Mainz (Munich, 2000).

Haskell, F., *Painters and Patrons: A Study in the Relations between Italian Art and Society in the Age of the Baroque* (New Haven and London, 1980).

Haskell, F. and Penny, N., *Taste and the Antique* (New Haven and London, 1981).

Hassiotis, G. K., 'Venezia e i domini veneziani: tramite di informazioni sui turchi per gli spagnoli nel sec. XVI', in H. G. Beck, M. Manoussacas and H. Pertusi, *Venezia centro di mediazione tra oriente e occidente (secoli XV–XVI): aspetti e problemi*, vol. 1 (Florence, 1977), pp. 117–36.

Hauser, H., 'Le "Parfait Négociant" de Jacques Savary', *Revue d'histoire économique et sociale* 13 (1925), 1–28.

Healey, F., 'Drawings after the Antique and the "Rubens Cantoor"', in K. Lohse Belkin and F. Healy (eds.), *A House of Art: Rubens as Collector*, exhibition catalogue (Antwerp, 2004), pp. 298–9.

Herklotz, I., *Cassiano dal Pozzo und die Archäologie des 17. Jahrhunderts* (Munich, 1999).

Hernandez Sánchez, C. J., *Castilla y Nápoles en el siglo XVI: el Virrey Pedro de Toledo, Linaje, Estado y Cultura (1532–1553)* (Salamanca, 1994).

Hernandez Sánchez, C. J., *El reino de Nápoles en el imperio de Carlos V: la consolidación de la conquista* (Madrid, 2001).

Hervey, M. F. S., *The Life, Correspondence & Collections of Thomas Howard, Earl of Arundel* (Cambridge, 1921).

Hespanha, A. M., 'La economia de la gracia', in *La gracia del derecho: economía de la cultura en la edad moderna* (Madrid, 1993), pp. 151–76.

Hess, A. C., 'The battle of Lepanto and its place in Mediterranean history', *Past and Present* 57 (1972), 53–73.

Hoock, J., Jeannin, P. and Kaiser, W. (eds.), *Ars Mercatoria: eine analytische Bibliographie*, 3 vols. (Paderborn, 1991–2001).

Houston, R. A., *Literacy in Early Modern Europe: Culture and Education 1500–1800* (London, 1988; 2nd edition London, 2002).

Howarth, D., *Lord Arundel and his Circle* (New Haven and London, 1985).

Huch, R., 'Die Wick'sche Sammlung von Flugblättern und Zeitungsnachrichten in der Stadtbibliothek Zürich', *Neujahrsblatt* (1895), 1–26.

Hugon, A., 'L'information dans la politique étrangère de la Couronne d'Espagne', in *L'information à l'époque moderne*, Association des Historiens Modernistes des Universités (Paris, 2001), pp. 25–53.

Hugon, A., *Au service du Roi Catholique: 'honorables ambassadeurs' et 'divins espions' face à la France. Représentation diplomatique et service secret dans les relations hispano-françaises, 1598–1635* (Madrid, 2004).

Huizenga, E., *Tussen autoriteit en empirie: de Middelnederlandse chirurgieën in de veertiende en vijftiende eeuw en hun maatschappelijke context* (Hilversum, 2003).

Hunger, F. W. T., *Charles de l'Escluse (Carolus Clusius) Nederlandsch Kruidkundige, 1526–1609*, 2 vols. (The Hague, 1927 and 1942).

Huygens, C, *De briefwisseling*, ed. J. A. Worp, 6 vols. (The Hague, 1911–17).

Infelise, M., 'Le marché des informations à Venise au XVIIe siècle', in H. Duranton and P. Rétat (eds.), *Gazettes et information politique sous l'Ancien Régime* (Saint-Etienne, 1999), pp. 117–28.

Infelise, M., 'The war, the news and the curious: military gazettes in Italy', in B. Dooley and S. Baron (eds.), *The Politics of Information in Early Modern Europe* (London and New York, 2001), pp. 216–36.

Infelise, M., *Prima dei giornali: alle origini della pubblica informazione (secoli XVI–XVII)* (Bari and Rome, 2002).

Infelise, M., 'Roman *avvisi*: information and politics in the seventeenth century', in G. Signorotto and M. A. Visceglia (eds.), *Court and Politics in Papal Rome 1492–1700* (Cambridge, 2002), pp. 212–28.

Isaacs, A. K. and Prak, M., 'Cities, bourgeoisies, and states', in W. Reinhard (ed.), *Power Elites and State Building* (Oxford, 1996), pp. 207–34.

Israel, J., *Diasporas within a Diaspora: Jews, Crypto-Jews and the World Maritime Empires, 1540–1740* (Leiden, Boston and Cologne, 2002).

Itinerarium Portugallensium, ed. L. de Matos (Lisbon, 1992).

Jaffé, D., 'Peiresc, Rubens and the Portland Vase', *The Burlington Magazine* 131 (1989), 554–9.

Jeannin, P., 'La diffusion de l'information', in S. Cavaciocchi (ed.), *Fiere e mercati nella integrazione delle economie europee secc. XIII–XVIII* (Florence, 2001), pp. 231–62.

Johansson, E., 'The history of literacy in Sweden', in H. J. Graff (ed.), *Literacy and Social Development in the West* (Cambridge, 1981), pp. 151–82.

Jones, W., *William Turner: Tudor Naturalist, Physician, Divine* (London, 1988).

Jordan, A., *Retrato de corte em Portugal: o legado de António Moro (1552–1572)* (Lisbon, 1994).

Jouhaud, C., *Mazarinades: la fronde des mots* (Paris, 1985).

Kahn, D., *Codebreakers: The Story of Secret Writing* (New York, 1996).

Kamen, H., *Philip of Spain* (New Haven and London, 1997).

Kissling, H. J., 'Venezia come centro di informazioni sui Turchi per gli Spagnoli nel sec. XVI', in H. G. Beck, M. Manoussacas and H. Pertusi, *Venezia centro di mediazione tra oriente e occidente (secoli XV–XVI): aspetti e problemi*, vol. I (Florence, 1977), pp. 97–109.

Kleinpaul, J., *Die Fuggerzeitungen 1568–1605* (Leipzig, 1921).

Kleinpaul, J., *Die vornehmsten Korrespondenten der deutschen Fürsten im 15. und 16. Jahrhundert* (Leipzig, 1928).

Kleinpaul, J., *Das Nachrichtenwesen der deutschen Fürsten im 16. und 17. Jahrhundert* (Leipzig, 1930).

Kubinyi, M. (ed.), *Bethlenfalvi gróf Thurzó György levelei nejéhez* [Letters of Count György Thurzó of Bethlenfalva to his wife] (Budapest, 1876).

Ladurie, E. Le Roy, *Les paysans de Languedoc* (Paris, 1966).

Lafayette, Madame de, *La Princesse de Clèves*, ed. by J. Mesnard (Paris, 1980; reprinted 1996).

Lamansky, V., *Secrets d'Etat de Venise: documents extraits, notices et études servant à éclaircir les rapports de la Seigneurie avec les Grecs, les Slaves et la Porte ottomane à la fin du xve et au xvie siècle*, 2 vols. (New York, 1968; 1st edition, St Petersburg, 1884).

Lancellotti, S., *L'hoggidi, overo gl'ingegni non inferiori a' passati* (Venice, 1681; 1st edition 1623).

Lane, F. C., *Andrea Barbarigo, Merchant of Venice (1418–1449)* (Baltimore, 1944).

Lang, H., 'Die neue Zeitung des 15. und 17. Jahrhunderts. Entwicklungsgeschichte und Typologie', in E. Blühm and H. Gebhardt (eds.), *Presse und Geschichte II. Neue Beiträge zur historischen Kommunikationsforschung* (Munich, 1987), pp. 57–60.

Langue, A. and Soudart, E. A., *Traité de cryptographie* (Paris, 1925).

Lapeyre, H., *Une famille de marchands: les Ruiz* (Paris, 1955).

Larsen, A. R. and Winn, C. H. (eds.), *Renaissance Women Writers: French Texts/American Context* (Detroit, 1994).

Lee, R. W., *Ut pictura poesis: humanisme et théorie de la peinture xve–xviiie siècles* (Paris, 1991).

León-Portilla, M., *Hernán Cortés y la Mar del Sur* (Madrid, 1985).

Lerville, E., *Les cahiers secrets de la cryptographie: le chiffre dans l'histoire des histoires du chiffre* (Paris, 1972).

Lettere di artisti italiani ad Antonio Perrenot di Granvella: Tiziano, Giovan Battista Mantovano, Primaticcio, Giovanni Paolo Poggino ed altri (Madrid, 1977).

Lettere e carte Magliabechi: regesto, ed. M. Doni Garfagnini, 2 vols. (Rome 1981).

Letters of Medieval Women, ed. A. Crawford (Stroud, 2002).

Lettres et mémoires d'Estat des rois, Princes, Ambassadeurs & autres Ministres, sous les regnes de François premier, Henry II & François II . . . par Messire Guillaume Ribier, Conseiller d'Estat, vol. 2 (Paris, 1677).

Levi, G., 'I commerci della Casa Daniele Bonfil e figlio con Marsiglia e Costantinopoli (1773–1794)', in S. Gasparri, G. Levi and P. Moro (eds.), *Venezia: itinerari per la storia della città* (Bologna, 1997), pp. 223–43.

Lightbown, R. W., 'Charles I and the tradition of European princely collecting', in A. MacGregor (ed.), *The Late King's Goods: Collections, Possessions and Patronage of Charles I in the Light of the Commonwealth Sale Inventories* (London and Oxford, 1989), pp. 53–72.

Lima Cruz, M. A. and Lázaro, A. M., 'A linguagem criptográfica na correspondência diplomática portuguesa de D. Miguel da Silva e de Pero Correia: origens e significado', in R. Carneiro and A. T. de Matos (eds.), *D. João III e o Império* (Lisbon, 2004), pp. 601–20.

Lipsius, J., *Epistolæ*, ed. A. Gerlo et al., 13 vols. (Brussels, 1978–2000).

Lipsius, J., *Epistolario de Justo Lipsio y los españoles (1577–1606)*, ed. A. Ramirez (Madrid, 1966).

Lipsius, J., *Principles of Letter-writing: A Bilingual Text of Justi Lipsii Epistolica institutio*, ed. and trans. R. V. Young and M. Thomas Hester (Carbondale, IL, 1996).

Livro de Duarte Barbosa, O, ed. M. A. Veiga Sousa, 2 vols. (Lisbon, 1996–2000).

Logan, A. M. S., *The Cabinet of the Brothers Gerard and Jan Reynst* (Amsterdam, 1979).

Logan, A. M. S. (ed.), *Peter Paul Rubens: The Drawings*, exhibition catalogue, Metropolitan Museum of Art (New York, 2005).

Lohse Belkin, K. and Healy, F. (eds.), *A House of Art: Rubens as Collector*, exhibition catalogue, Rubenshuis (Antwerp, 2004).

Longeon, C. and Sabot, A. (comments and trans.), *Conrad Gesner: vingt lettres à Jean Bauhin fils (1563–1565)* (Saint-Etienne, 1976).

López de Gómara, F., *La conquista de México*, ed. J. L de Rojas (Madrid, 1987).

Lopez, R. S., *The Commercial Revolution of the Middle Ages, 950–1350* (Englewood Cliffs, NJ, 1971).

Lopez, R. S. and Raymond, I. W., *Medieval Trade in the Mediterranean World: Illustrative Documents Translated with Introductions and Notes* (New York, 1955).

Loviot, L. (ed.), *La Gazette de 1609* (Paris, 1914).

Lowood, H., 'The New World and the European catalog of nature', in K. Ordahl Kupperman (ed.), *America in European Consciousness, 1493–1750* (Chapel Hill and London, 1995), pp. 295–323.

Lucchetta, G., 'L'Oriente mediterraneo nella cultura di Venezia tra Quattro e Cinquecento', in *Storia della cultura veneta* (Vicenza, 1976–86), vol. 3, pp. 375–432.

MacCarthy, B. G., *The Female Pen: Women Writers and Novelists, 1621–1818* (Cork, 1994).

Madariaga, S. de, *Hernán Cortés, Conqueror of Mexico*, 2nd edition (London, 1954).

Maffei, S., 'Introduzione', *Giornale de' letterati d'Italia*, vol. 1 (1710), pp. 13–16.

Magalhães Godinho, V., *Os descobrimentos e a economia mundial*, vol. 1 (Lisbon, 1981), pp. 15–51.

Magalhães Godinho, V., *Les finances de l'Etat Portugais des Indes Orientales (1517–1635)* (Paris, 1982).

Magalhães Godinho, V., *Mito e mercadoria, utopia e prática de navegar* (Lisbon, 1990).

Makkai, L. (ed.), *I. Rákóczi György birtokainak gazdasági iratai* [Documents concerning agriculture from the domains of Prince George Rákóczi I] (Budapest, 1954), pp. 543–50.

Malynes, G., *Consuetudo, vel, Lex mercatoria, or, The Ancient Law-Merchant . . .* (London, 1622).

Mančal, J., 'Zu Augsburger Zeitungen vom Ende des 17. bis zur Mitte des 19. Jahrhunderts: Abendzeitung, Postzeitung und Intelligenzzettel', in H. Gier and J. Janota (eds.), *Augsburger Buchdruck und Verlagswesen: von den Anfängen bis zur Gegenwart* (Wiesbaden, 1997), pp. 683–733.

Mandrou, R., *Histoire de la pensée européenne*, vol. 3: *Des humanistes aux hommes de science (XVIe et XVIIe siècle)* (Paris, 1973).

Mantelli, R., *Il pubblico impiego nell'economia del regno di Napoli: retribuzioni, reclutamento e ricambio sociale nell'epoca spagnola (sec. XVI–XVII)* (Naples, 1986).

Marin, L., *Détruire la peinture* (Paris, 1977).

Marin, L., *Sublime Poussin* (Paris, 1995).

Marineo Siculo, L., *De las cosas memorables de Espana* (Alcalá de Henares, 1530; reproduced by M. León-Portilla, in *Historia 16*, April 1985).

Marino, C., *La galeria* (Venice, 1618).

Mariz, P., *Diálogos de vária história* (Coimbra, 1594).

Martínez, J. L., *Hernán Cortés* (Mexico, 1990).

Mártir de Anglería, P., *Epistolario*, Spanish translation of the *Opus epistolarium*, ed. J. López de Toro, 4 vols. (Madrid, 1953–7).

Mártir de Anglería, P., *Opus epistolarium* (Alcalá de Henares, 1530).

Mártir de Anglería, P., *Decadas del Nuevo Mundo*, ed. R. Alba (Madrid, 1989).

Marzi, C., 'Degli antecessori dei giornali', *Rivista delle biblioteche e degli archivi* 24 (1913), 181–5.

Mascardi, A., *Dell'arte istorica* (Florence, 1859; 1st edition Rome, 1636).

Mason, P., 'Lecciones superficiales: transparencia y opacidad en las Américas, siglo XVI', *Aisthesis: Revista Chilena de Investigaciones Estéticas* 31 (1998), 76–88.

Mason, P., 'Pretty vacant: Columbus, conviviality and New World faces', in J. Overing and A. Passes (eds.), *The Anthropology of Love and Anger* (London, 2000), pp. 189–205.

Mason, P., 'Troca e deslocamento nas pinturas de Albert Eckhout de sujeitos brasileiros', *Estudos de Sociologia. Revista do programa de pós-Graduação em sociologia da UFPE* 7. 1 and 2 (2001), 231–49.

Mason, P., 'Reading New World bodies', in F. Egmond and R. Zwijnenberg (eds.), *Bodily Extremities* (Aldershot, 2003), pp. 148–67.

Mathias, P., 'Risk, credit and kinship in early modern enterprise', in J. J. McCusker and K. Morgan (eds.), *The Early Modern Atlantic Economy* (Cambridge, 2000), pp. 15–35.

Matilla Tascón, A. (ed.), *Testamentos de 43 personajes del Madrid de los Austrias* (Madrid, 1983).

Matos, L. de, *L'expansion portugaise dans la littérature latine de la Renaissance* (Lisbon, 1991).

Matthews, L. G., *The Royal Apothecaries* (London, 1967).

Mattingly, G., *Renaissance Diplomacy* (Boston, 1955).

Matuz, J., 'Die Pfortendolmetschter zur Herrschaftszeit Süleymâns des Prächtigen', *Südost Forschungen* 34 (1975), 26–56.

Mauss, M., *The Gift: The Form and Reason for Exchange in Archaic Societies* (London, 1990; originally 'Essai sur le don: forme et raison de l'échange dans les sociétés archaïques', *L'Année Sociologique*, 2nd series, 1, 1923–4).

Mazauriac, S., 'La diffusion du savoir en dehors des circuits savants: le bureau d'adresse de Théophraste Renaudot', in H. Bots and F. Waquet (eds.), *Commercium litterarium, 1600–1750* (Amsterdam, 1994), pp. 15–172.

Mazzei, R., *Itinera mercatorum: circolazione di uomini e di merci nell'Europa centro-orientale, 1550 1650* (Pisa, 1999).

McCusker, J. J., 'The Italian business press in early modern Europe', in S. Cavaciocchi (ed.), *Produzione e commercio della carta e del libro secc. XIII–XVIII* (Florence, 1992), pp. 797–841.

McCusker, J. J., 'The demise of distance: the business press and the origins of the information revolution in the early modern Atlantic world', *American Historical Review* 90 (2005), 295–321.

McCusker, J. J. and Gravesteijn, C., *The Beginning of Commercial and Financial Journalism: The Commodity Price Currents, Exchange Rate Currents, and Money Currents of Early Modern Europe* (Amsterdam, 1991).

McGrath, E., *Rubens Subjects from History. Corpus Rubenianum Ludwig Burchard XIII (I)*, vol. 2: *Catalogue and Indexes* (London, 1997).

Méchoulan, H., *Etre Juif à Amsterdam au temps de Spinoza* (Paris, 1991).

Melis, F., *Aspetti della vita economica medievale (Studi nell'Archivio Datini di Prato)*, 2 vols. (Siena, 1962).

Melis, F., *Documenti per la storia economica dei secoli XIII–XVI* (Florence, 1972).

Melis, F., 'L'intensità e regolarità nella diffusione dell'informazione economica generale nel Mediterraneo e in Occidente alla fine del Medioevo', in *Mélanges en l'honneur de Fernand Braudel*, vol. 1: *Histoire économique du monde méditerranéen, 1450–1650* (Toulouse, 1973), pp. 389–424.

Menagio, E., *Le origini della lingua italiana* (Geneva, 1685).

Menard, R. R., 'Transport costs and long-range trade, 1300–1800: was there a European "transport revolution" in the early modern era?', in J. D. Tracy (ed.), *The Political Economy of Merchant Empires* (Cambridge, 1991), pp. 228–75.

Mendella, M., 'Arruolamento militare di Albanesi nel regno di Napoli durante il seicento', *Archivio storico per le province napoletane* 90 (1972), 373–84.

Menkis, R., 'The Gradis Family of Eighteenth Century Bordeaux: A Social and Economic Study', unpublished PhD thesis, Brandeis University (1988).

Mentz, S., 'English private trade on the Coromandel coast, 1660–1690: diamonds and country trade', *Indian Economic and Social History Review* 33 (1996), 155–73.

Merle Du Bourg, A., 'De Florence à Cologne, Marie de Médicis et Pierre Paul Rubens (1600–1642)', in P. Bassani Pacht and T. Crépin-Leblond (eds.), *Marie de Médicis, un gouvernement par les arts*, exhibition catalogue (Paris, 2003), pp. 94–109.

Meulen, M. van der, *Petrus Paulus Rubens Antiquarius: Collector and Copyist of Antique Gems* (Alphen aan de Rijn, 1975).

Meyboom, P. G. P., *The Nile Mosaic of Palestrina: Early Evidence of Egyptian Religion in Italy* (Leiden, 1995).

Michael, I., 'O primeiro Conde de Gondomar (1567–1626): home e imaxe', *Mar por medio. V Xornadas de cultura galega: unha visión de Galicia dende o Reino Unido* (Lugo, 2000), pp. 81–96.

Miller, P. N., *Peiresc's Europe: Learning and Virtue in the Seventeenth Century* (New Haven, CT, 2000).

Molho, A. (ed.), *Social and Economic Foundations of the Italian Renaissance* (New York, 1969).

Mollat du Jourdin, M., *Les explorateurs du XIIIe au XVIe siècle: premiers regards sur des mondes nouveaux* (Paris, 1992).

Monts de Savasse, J. de, 'Les chiffres de la correspondance diplomatique des ambassadeurs d'Henri IV, en l'année 1590', in *Correspondre, jadis et naguère. 120e Congrès national des sociétés historiques et scientifiques* (Aix-en-Provence, 1995), pp. 219–22, unpaginated annex.

Moral, J. M. del, *El Virey de Napoles D. Pedro de Toledo y la guerra contra el Turco* (Madrid, 1966).

Morán Turina, M. and Portús Pérez, J., *El arte de mirar: la pintura y su público en la España de Velázquez* (Madrid, 1997).

Moreau, F., *De bonne main: la communication manuscrite au XVIIIe siècle* (Paris, 1993).

Morford, M., *Stoics and Neostoics: Rubens and the Circle of Lipsius* (Princeton, NJ, 1991).

Morineau, M., *Incroyables gazettes et fabuleux métaux: les retours des trésors américains d'après les gazettes hollandaises (XVIe–XVIIIe siècles)* (London, New York and Paris, 1985).

Morselli, R. (ed.), *Gonzaga. La Celeste Galeria. L'esercizio del collezionismo*, exhibition catalogue Palazzo Tè – Palazzo Ducale, Mantova (Milan, 2002).

Muldrew, C., *The Economy of Obligation: The Culture of Credit and Social Relations in Early Modern England* (New York, 1999).

Muller, J. M., *Rubens: The Artist as a Collector* (Princeton, NJ, 1989).

Müller, L., *The Merchant Houses of Stockholm, c.1640–1800: A Comparative Study of Early-Modern Entrepreneurial Behaviour* (Uppsala, 1998).

Murphy, J. J., *Rhetorics in the Middle Ages: A History of Rhetoric Theory from St Augustine to the Renaissance* (Berkeley, 1974).

Musi, A., *L'Italia dei Viceré: integrazione e resistenza nel sistema imperiale spagnolo* (Salerno, 2001).

Nagle, J., 'Prosopographie et histoire de l'état: la France moderne XVI–XVIIe siècles', in F. Autran (ed.), *Prosopographie et genèse de l'état moderne* (Paris, 1986), pp. 77–90.

Neddermeyer, U., *Von der Handschrift zum gedruckten Buch: Schriftlichkeit und Leseinteresse im Mittelalter und in der frühen Neuzeit. Quantitative und qualitative Aspekte* (Wiesbaden, 1998).

Norden, L. van, 'Peiresc and the English scholars', *The Huntington Library Quarterly* 12 (1949), 369–89.

Ochoa Brun, M. A., *Historia de la diplomacia Española*, 3 vols. (Madrid, 1991).

Olmi, G., *Ulisse Aldrovandi: scienza e natura nel secondo cinquecento* (Trento, 1976).

Olmi, G., '"Molti amici in vari luoghi": studio della natura e rapporti epistolari nel secolo XVI', *Nuncius: Annali di Storia della Scienza* 6 (1991), 3–31.

Olmi, G., *L'Inventario del mondo: catalogazione della natura e luoghi del sapere nella prima età moderna* (Bologna, 1992).

Orações de obediência dos reis de Portugal aos Sumos Pontífices, ed., introduction and notes by M. de Albuquerque, Portuguese translation by M. Pinto de Meneses, 10 vols. (Lisbon, 1988).

Ortiz, L., *Memoria, entendimiento y voluntad: empresas que enseñan y persuaden su buen uso en lo moral y en lo político* (Seville, 1677).

Orvieto, P., 'Un esperto orientalista del '400: Benedetto Dei', *Rinascimento* 20 (1969), 205–75.

Osório, J., *De rebus Emmanuelis regis Lusitaniae invictissimi virtute et auspicio gestis* (Lisbon, 1571).

Otte, E., *Letters and People of the Spanish Indies: The Sixteenth Century* (Cambridge, 1976).

Pantin, I., *Les Fréart de Chantelou: une famille d'amateurs au XVIIe siècle entre Le Mans, Paris et Rome* (Le Mans, 1999).

Papadopoli Aldobrandini, N., *Le monete di Veneẓia* (Venice, 1893–1919).

Pardo Tomás, J. (with Lopez Pinero, J. M.), *La influencia de Francisco Hernándeẓ (1515–1587) en la constitución de la botánica y de la materia médica modernas* (Valencia, 1996).

Pearson, M. N., 'Banyas and Brahmins: their role in the Portuguese Indian economy', in *Coastal Western India: Studies from the Portuguese Records* (New Delhi, 1981), pp. 93–115.

Pedani, M. P., *In nome del Gran Signore: inviati ottomani a Veneẓia dalla caduta di Constantinopoli alla Guerra di Candia* (Venice, 1994).

Peiresc, N. C. Fabri de, *Lettre de M. de Peiresc écrite d'Aix à son frère alors à Paris, dans laquelle il lui donne des détails sur une visite qu'il lui avait fait le cardinal Barberini, neveu du Pape Urbain VIII, légat en France, le 27 octobre 1625* (Aix-en-Provence, 1816).

Peiresc, N. C. Fabri de, *Lettres inédites de M. de Peiresc*, ed. F. de Saint Vincent (Aix-en-Provence, 1816).

Peiresc, N. C. Fabri de, *Lettres à Cassiano dal Pozzo (1625–1635)*, ed. and anno tated by J. F. Lhote and D. Joyal, preface by J. Guillerme (Clermont-Ferrand, 1989).

Pelling, M. and Webster, C., 'Medical practitioners', in C. Webster (ed.), *Health, Medicine and Mortality in the Sixteenth Century* (Cambridge, 1979), pp. 165–235.

Pereira, D. Pacheco, *Esmeraldo de situ orbis*, ed. J. Barradas de Carvalho (Lisbon, 1991).

Peri, G. D., *Il negoẓiante . . .* (Venice, 1662; 1st edition 1638).

Perini, G., 'Le lettere degli artisti da strumento di comunicazione, a documento, a cimelio', in E. Cropper, G. Perini and F. Solinas (eds.), *Documentary Culture: Florence and Rome from Grand-Duke Ferdinand I to Pope Alexander VII* (Bologna, 1992), pp. 165–83.

Perret, P. M., 'Les règles de Cicco Simonetta pour le déchiffrement des écritures secrètes', *Bibliothèque de l'Ecole des Chartes* 51 (1890), 516–25.

Petit, C., '*Mercatura* y *ius mercatorum*: materiales para una antropología del comerciante premoderno', in C. Petit (ed.), *Del ius mercatorum al derecho mercantil: III Seminario de Historia del Derecho Privado (Sitges, 28–30 de mayo de 1992)* (Madrid, 1997), pp. 15–70.

Piazza, A., 'Parole di chi scrive questo foglio a chi legge', *Gaẓẓetta urbana veneta* 1 (2 June 1787).

Piccinelli, R. *Le colleẓioni Gonẓaga: il carteggio tra Firenẓe e Mantova (1554–1626)* (Cinisello Balsamo, 2000).

Piccinelli, R. *Le colleẓioni Gonẓaga: il carteggio tra Milano e Mantova (1563–1634)* (Cinisello Balsamo, 2003).

Pieper, R., *Die Vermittlung einer neuen Welt: Amerika im Nachrichtennetz des Habsburgischen Imperiums 1493–1598* (Mainz, 2000).

Pigaillem, H., *La bataille de Lépante (1571)* (Paris, 2003).

Pilati, R., *Officia principis: politica e amministrazione a Napoli nel cinquecento* (Naples, 1994).

Pinto, C., *Trade and Finance in Portuguese India: A Study of the Portuguese Country Trade, 1770–1840* (New Delhi, 1994).

Pissurlencar, P. S. S., *The Portuguese and the Marathas* (Bombay, 1975).

Pizzamiglio, G. (ed.), *Foglio in cui certamente qualche cosa è stampata* (Venice, 2002).

Portús, J., 'Soy tu hechura: un ensayo sobre las fronteras del retrato cortesano en España', in F. Checa (ed.), *Carlos V: retratos de familia* (Madrid, 2000), pp. 181–219.

Portús, J., 'España y Francia: dos maneras de convivir con la pintura', in F. Checa Cremades (ed.), *Cortes del Barroco: de Bernini y Velázquez a Luca Giordano*, exhibition catalogue, Palacio Real de Madrid and Palacio Real de Aranjuez (Madrid, 2003), pp. 99–112.

Poussin, N., *Correspondance de Nicolas Poussin*, ed. C. Jouanny, Archives de l'art français, nouvelle période, vol. 5 (Paris, 1911).

Poussin, N., *Nicolas Poussin: lettres et propos sur l'art*, ed. A. Blunt (Paris, 1989).

Pratt, Fletcher, *Secret and Urgent: The Story of Codes and Ciphers* (Indianapolis, 1939)

Prescott, W. H., *History of the Conquest of Mexico and History of the Conquest of Peru* (New York, 1936).

Preto, P., *I servizi segreti di Venezia* (Milan, 1994).

Preto, P., 'Lo spionnagio turco a Venezia tra mito e realtà', in G. Motta (ed.), *I turchi, il Mediterraneo e l'Europa* (Milan, 1998), pp. 123–32.

Preto, P., *Persona per hora secreta: accusa e delazione nella Repubblica di Venezia* (Milan, 2003).

Price, J. M. (ed.), *Joshua Johnson's Letterbook 1771–1774: Letters from a Merchant in London to his Partners in Maryland* (London, 1979).

Prinz, W., *Galleria. Storia e tipologia di uno spazio architettonico*, ed. C. Cieri Via (Modena, 1988).

Priuli, G., *I diarii*, 4 vols. (Città di Castello and Bologna, 1912–39).

Prose fiorentine (Florence, 1745).

Prosperi, A., *Tribunali della coscienza: inquisitori, confessori, missionari* (Turin, 1997).

Prosperi, A., 'L'Europa cristiana e il mondo: alle origini dell'idea di missione', in *America e Apocalisse e altri saggi* (Pisa and Rome, 1999), pp. 89–112.

Prosperi, A., *Dare l'anima: storia di un infanticidio* (Turin, 2005).

Quaderni Puteani 4: The Paper Museum of Cassiano dal Pozzo (Milan, 1993).

Rabaté, D., 'Le secret et la modernité', *Modernités* 14 (2001), 9–32.

Ramos, D. et al., *Francisco de Vitoria y la escuela de Salamanca: la etica en la conquista de America* (Madrid, 1984).

Raposo, J. do Nascimento, 'Don Gabriel de Silva: a Portuguese-Jewish banker in eighteenth century Bordeaux', unpublished PhD thesis, University of York, Ontario (1989).

Rath, G., 'Die Briefe Conrad Gessners aus der Trewschen Sammlung', *Gesnerus* 7 (1950), 140–70, and *Gesnerus* 8 (1951), 195–215.

Rebuffat, F., *Répertoire numérique des Archives*, vol. 2: *Fonds annexes de la Chambre* (Marseille, 1965).

Reeds, K., *Botany in Medieval and Renaissance Universities* (New York and London, 1991).

Reinhard, W., 'Power elites: state servants, ruling classes, and the growth of state power', in W. Reinhard (ed.), *Power Elites and State Building* (Oxford, 1996), pp. 1–18.

Renouard, Y., 'Information et transmission des nouvelles', in C. Samaran (ed.), *L'histoire et ses méthodes* (Paris, 1961), pp. 95–142.

Ricard, S., *Traité général du commerce . . .*, 5th edition (Amsterdam, 1732).

Ricci, G., *Il principe e la morte: corpo, cuore, effigie nel Rinascimento* (Bologna, 1998).

Roberts, R. S., 'The early history of the import of drugs into England', in F. N. L. Poynter (ed.), *The Evolution of Pharmacy in Britain* (London, 1965), pp. 165–86.

Romanin, S., *Storia documentata di Venezia*, 3rd edition (Venice, 1972–5).

Romano, D., '*Quod sibi fiat gratia*: adjustment of penalties and the exercise of influence in early Renaissance Venice', *Journal of Medieval and Renaissance Studies* 13 (1983), 251–68.

Roover, R. de, 'The organization of trade', in M. M. Postan, E. E. Rich and E. Miller (eds.), *The Cambridge Economic History of Europe*, vol. 3: *Economic Organization and Policies in the Middle Ages* (Cambridge, 1965), pp. 42–118.

Rosenberg, P. (ed.), *Nicolas Poussin 1594–1665*, exhibition catalogue, Galeries nationales du Grand Palais (Paris, 1994).

Rosenberg, P. and Prat, L. A. (eds.), *Nicolas Poussin: la collection du musée Condé à Chantilly*, exhibition catalogue, Musée Condé, Château de Chantilly (Paris, 1994).

Roulez J., 'N. De Stoop', in *Biographie nationale publiée par l'Académie Royale des sciences, des lettres et des beaux-arts de Belgique* (Brussels, 1866–1986), vol. 5, p. 810.

Rubens, P. P., *The Letters of Peter Paul Rubens*, ed. R. Saunders Magurn (Evanston, IL, 1991).

Rubio Mañé, J. I., *El Virreinato*, vol. 1: *Orígenes y jurisdicciones, y dinamica social de los virreyes*, 2nd edition (Mexico, 1983).

Rühl, E., 'Die nachgelassenen Zeitungssammlungen und Gelehrtenkorrespondenz Hugo Blotius' des ersten Bibliothekars der Wiener Hofbibliothek', unpublished PhD thesis, University of Vienna (1958).

Ruíz Martin, F., *Lettres marchandes échangées entre Florence et Medina del Campo* (Paris, 1965).

Ruiz-Domènec, J. E., *El Gran Capitán: retrato de una época* (Barcelona, 2002).

Russell, F. S., *Information Gathering in Classical Greece* (Ann Arbor, 1999).

Ryder, A. F. C., *The Kingdom of Naples under Alfonso the Magnanimous: The Making of a Modern State* (Oxford, 1976).

Samuel, E., 'Diamonds and pieces of eight: how Stuart England won the rough-diamond trade', *Jewish Historical Studies* 38 (2004), 23–40.

Sansovino, F., *Del secretario* (Venice, 1564).

Sanudo, M., *I diarii*, 58 vols. (Venice, 1879–1903).

Sapori, A., *Le marchand italien au Moyen Age* (Paris, 1952).

Sardella, P., *Nouvelles et spéculations à Venise au début du XVIe siècle* (Paris, 1949).

Sarpi, P., *Lettere italiane . . . al signor dell'Isola Groslot* (Verona, 1673).

Savary, J., *Le parfait négociant ou Instruction générale pour ce qui regarde le commerce des marchandises de France et des pays étrangers* (Paris, 1675).

Schepelern, H. D., 'Natural philosophers and princely collectors: Worm, Paludanus and the Gottorp and Copenhagen collections', in O. Impey and A. MacGregor, (eds.), *The Origins of Museums: The Cabinets of Curiosities in Sixteenth and Seventeenth-century Europe* (Oxford, 1985), pp. 121–7.

Schierbeek, A., *Van Aristoteles tot Pasteur: leven en werken der groote biologen* (Amsterdam, 1923).

Schnapper, A., 'The king of France as collector in the seventeenth century', in R. I. Rotberg and T. K. Rabb (eds.), *Art and History: Images and their Meaning* (Cambridge, 1986), pp. 185–202.

Schnapper, A., *Curieux du grand siècle: collections et collectionneurs dans la France du XVIIe siècle* (Paris, 1994).

Schottenloher, K., *Flugblatt und Zeitung: ein Wegweiser durch das gedruckte Tagesschrifttum* (Berlin, 1922).

Schrenck von Notzing, J., *Augustissimorum imperatorum, serenissimorum regum, atque archiducum, illustrissimorum principum, necnon comitum, baronum, aliorumque clarissimorum virorum qui . . . verissimae imagines & rerum ab ipsis domi, forisque gestarunt succintae descriptiones . . . a Serenissimo Principe Ferdinando, Archiduce Austriae . . . opus* (Oeniponti, 1601).

Schröder, Th., *Die ersten Zeitungen: Textgestaltung und Nachrichtenauswahl* (Tübingen, 1995).

Secord, J. A., 'The crisis of nature', in N. Jardine, J. A. Secord and E. C. Spary (eds.), *Cultures of Natural History* (Cambridge, 1996), pp. 447–59.

Seguin, J. P., *L'information en France de Louis XII à Henri II* (Geneva, 1961).

Seguin, J. P., *L'information en France avant le périodique: 517 canards imprimés entre 1529 et 1631* (Paris, 1964).

Seneca, *Epistles*, trans. R. M. Gummere, 3 vols., Loeb Classical Library (Cambridge, MA, 1917).

Senkowski, J., 'La chancellerie royale et son rôle dans l'administration de l'état polonais aux xve et xvie siècles', in N. Coulet and J. P. Genet (eds.), *L'état moderne: le droit, l'espace et les formes de l'état* (Paris, 1990), pp. 167–73.

Sennelart, M., *Machiavélisme et raison d'état, xiie–xviiie siècle* (Paris, 1989).

Sermidi, M., *Le collezioni Gonzaga: il carteggio tra Venezia e Mantova (1588–1612)* (Cinisello Balsamo, 2003).

Setton, K. M., *The Papacy and the Levant (1204–1571)*, 3 vols. (Philadelphia, 1984).

Shils, E., *Center and Periphery: Essays in Macrosociology* (Chicago, 1975).

Silva, J. G. da, *Marchandises et finances: lettres de Lisbonne 1563–1578*, 3 vols. (Paris, 1959).

Simmel, G., 'Exchange', in *On Individuality and Social Forms*, ed. with an introduction by D. N. Levine (Chicago, 1971), pp. 43–69.

Simonetta, C., *Regulae extruendis litteras zifferatas sive exempio* (Pavia, 1474; republished by A. Meister, 1902).

Smith, P. H. and Findlen, P. (eds.), *Merchants and Marvels: Commerce, Science and Art in Early Modern Europe* (New York and London, 2002).

Sogliani, D. *Le collezioni Gonzaga: il carteggio tra Venezia e Mantova (1563–1587)* (Cinisello Balsamo, 2002).

Solinas, F. (ed.), *I segreti di un collezionista: le straordinarie raccolte di Cassiano dal Pozzo 1588–1657*, exhibition catalogue, Galleria Nazionale d'Arte Antica, Palazzo Barberini (Rome, 2000).

Solinas, F. (ed.), *I segreti di un collezionista: le straordinarie raccolte di Cassiano dal Pozzo 1588–1657*, exhibition catalogue, Museo del Territorio Biellese (Biella, 2002).

Solinas, F., *L'Uccelliera: un libro di arte e di scienza della Roma dei primi Lincei* (Florence, 2000).

Solinas, F., 'La pêche du corail de Pierre de Cortone retrouvée à Tsarskoïe Selo', *Gazette des Beaux-Arts* 138 (2001), 233–49.

Soro, G., *Liber zifrarum* (Venice, 1539).

Souza, T. R. de, 'Mhamai house records: indigenous sources for Indo-Portuguese historiography', in *II Seminário Internacional de História Indo-Portuguesa: Actas* (Lisbon, 1985), pp. 933–41.

Souza, T. R. de, 'French slave-trading in Portuguese Goa (1773–1791)', in T. R. de Souza (ed.), *Essays in Goan History* (New Delhi, 1989), pp. 119–31.

Sparti, D. L., *Le collezioni dal Pozzo: storia di una famiglia e del suo museo nella Roma seicentesca* (Modena, 1992).

Spicer, J., 'Roelandt Savery and the discovery of the Alpine waterfall', in E. Fučíková et al. (eds.), *Rudolf II and Prague: The Imperial Court and Residential City as the Cultural Heart of Central Europe* (Prague, London and Milan, 1997), pp. 146–56.

Spooner, F. C., *L'économie mondiale et les frappes monétaires en France: 1493–1680* (Paris, 1956).

Stanić, M. (ed.), *Chantelou, Journal de voyage du Cavalier Bernin en France* (Paris, 2001).

Stix, F., 'Berichte und Studien zur Geschichte Karls V. Die Geheimschriften-schlüssel der Kabinettskanzlei des Kaisers', in *Nachrichten von der Gesellschaft der Wissenschaften zu Göttingen Philologisch-Historische Klasse*, Neue Folge, Fachgruppe II, vol. 1: *Nachrichten aus der mittleren und neueren Geschichte* (Göttingen, 1936), pp. 207–68.

Strinati, C. and Tantillo, A. (eds.), *Domenichino, 1581–1641*, exhibition catalogue (Milan, 1996).

Strong, R., *The Renaissance Garden in England* (London, 1979).

Stumpo, E. (ed.), *La gazzetta de l'anno 1588* (Florence, 1988).

Suma Oriental of Tomé Pires and the Book of Francisco Rodrigues, The, ed. A. Cortesão (London, 1944).

Sutton, P. C. (ed.), *The Age of Rubens*, exhibition catalogue, Museum of Fine Arts Boston (Ghent, 1993).

Szabó, D. (ed.), *A magyarországi urbérrendezés története Mária Terézia korában* [The regulation of serfdom in the age of Maria Theresa in Hungary] (Budapest, 1933).

Talamo, A. M., 'I Gonzaga e le incisioni', in R. Morselli (ed.), *Gonzaga. La Celeste Galeria. L'esercizio del collezionismo*, exhibition catalogue (Milan, 2002), vol. 2, pp. 139–49.

Tamizey de Larroque, P. (ed.), *Lettres de Peiresc aux frères Dupuy: janvier 1629–décembre 1633*, Collection de documents inédits sur l'histoire de France, 2nd series (Paris, 1890).

Thevet, A., *Les vrais portraits et vies des homes illustres*, 2 vols. (Paris, 1584).

Thevet, A., *Portraits from the Age of Exploration: Selections from André Thevet's 'Les vrais portraits et vies des homes illustres'*, ed. R. Schlesinger, trans. E. Benson (Urbana, 1993).

Thompson, J. W. and Padover, S. K., *Secret Diplomacy: Espionage and Cryptography, 1500–1815* (New York, 1963).

Thuillier, J., *Nicolas Poussin* (Paris, 1988).

Toni, G. B. de, *Il carteggio degli italiani col botanico Carlo Clusius nella biblioteca Leidense* (Modena, 1911).

Tóth, I. G., 'How many Hungarian noblemen could read in the eighteenth century?', in A. Petö (ed.), *Central European University History Department Yearbook* (Budapest, 1994), pp. 67–81.

Tóth, I. G., 'Hungarian culture in the early modern age', in L. Kósa (ed.), *A Cultural History of Hungary: From the Beginnings to the Eighteenth Century*, vol. 1 (Budapest, 1999), pp. 154–228.

Tóth, I. G., 'Une société aux lisières de l'alphabète: la paysannerie hongroise aux xviie et xviiie siècles', *Annales ESC* 56 (2001), 863–80.

Tóth, I. G., 'Old and New Faith in Hungary, Turkish Hungary and Transylvania', in R. P. C. Hsia (ed.), *A Companion to the Reformation World* (Oxford, 2003), pp. 205–20.

Tóth, I. G., *Politique et religion en Hongrie au xviie siècle: lettres des missionnaires de la Propaganda Fide* (Paris, 2004).

Tóth, I. G. (ed.), *Mil ans de l'histoire hongroise* (Budapest, 2003).

Trenard, L., 'La presse française des origines a 1788', in C. Bellanger, J. Godechot, P. Guiral and F. Terrou (eds.), *Histoire générale de la presse française* (Paris, 1969–72), vol. 1, pp. 27–402.

Trithemius (Abbot Johann of Heidelberg), *Polygraphiae libri sex* (s.l., 1518).

Trivellato, F., 'Juifs de Livourne, Italiens de Lisbonne et Hindous de Goa: réseaux marchands et échanges interculturels à l'époque moderne', *Annales HSS* 58 (2003), 581–603.

Tucci, U., *Lettres d'un marchand vénitien: Andrea Berengo (1553–1556)* (Paris, 1957).

Turner, N., 'Some of the copyists after the antique employed by Cassiano', *Quaderni Puteani 4: The Paper Museum of Cassiano dal Pozzo* (Milan, 1993), pp. 27–37.

Two Renaissance Book Hunters: The Letters of Poggius Bracciolini to Nicolaus de Niccolis, translated from the Latin and annotated by P. W. Goodhart Gordan (New York, 1974).

Ubrizsy Savoia, A., 'Environmental approach in the botany of the 16th century', in Z. Mirek and A. Zemanek (eds.), *Studies in Renaissance Botany*, Polish Botanical Studies, Guidebook Series 20 (Crakow, 1998), pp. 73–86.

Udovitch, A. L., 'Formalism and informalism in the social and economic institutions of the medieval Islamic world', in A. Banani and S. Vryonis Jr (eds.), *Individualism and Conformity in Classical Islam* (Wiesbaden, 1977), pp. 61–81.

Valdeón Baruque, J., *El testamento de Adán*, exhibition catalogue (Lisbon and León, 1994).

Várkonyi, A. R., 'A tájékoztatás hatalma' (The power of informing), in T. Petercsák and M. Berecz (eds.), *Információáramlás a magyar és a török végvári rendszerben* (Eger, 1999), pp. 9–31.

Vatin, N., 'La conquête de Rhodes', in *Les Ottomans et l'Occident (XVe-XVIe siècle)* (Istanbul, 2001), pp. 31–51.

Vázquez de Prada, V., *Lettres marchandes d'Anvers*, 4 vols. (Paris, 1960).

Venturini, E., *Le collezioni Gonzaga: il carteggio tra la Corte Cesarea e Mantova (1559–1636)* (Cinisello Balsamo, 2002).

Vera y Figueroa, J. A. de, *Le parfait ambassadeur* (Paris, 1642).

Verdi, R. (ed.), *Cézanne and Poussin: The Classical Vision of Landscape*, exhibition catalogue, National Gallery of Scotland, Edinburgh (Edinburgh, 1990).

Versluys, M. J., *Aegyptiaca Romana: Nilotic Scenes and the Roman Views of Egypt* (Leiden, 2002).

Vespucci, A., *Il Mondo Nuovo*, ed. M. Pozzi, 2nd edition (Alessandria, 1993).

Viaud, A. (ed.), *Lettres des souverains portugais à Charles V et à l'Impératrice, 1528–1532, conservés aux archives de Simancas* (Lisbon and Paris, 1994).

Viaud, A., *Correspondance d'un ambassadeur castillan au Portugal dans les années 1530 – Lope Hurtado de Mendoza* (Paris, 2001).

Vignière, B. de, *Traicté des chiffres ou secretes matières d'escrire* (1585; reprinted, Paris, 1996).

Villain-Gandossi, C., 'Contribution à l'étude des relations diplomatiques et commerciales entre Venise et la Porte ottomane au XVIe siècle', in *La Méditerranée aux XIIe–XVIe siècles* (London, 1983), three previously published articles with their original pagination: pp. 22–45, pp. 13–47 and pp. 290–8.

Villain-Gandossi, C., 'Les dépêches chiffrées de Vittore Bragadin, Baile de Constantinople (12 juillet 1564–15 juin 1566)', in *La Méditerranée aux XIIe–XVIe siècles* (London, 1983), pp. 52–106.

Vincent, D., *The Rise of Mass Literacy: Reading and Writing in Modern Europe* (Cambridge, 2000).

Vitoria, F. de, *Political Writings*, ed. A. Pagden and J. Lawrance (Cambridge, 1991).

Vocelka, K., *Die politische Propaganda Kaiser Rudolfs II.* (Vienna, 1981).

Voltaire, F. M. A. de, *Essai sur les mœurs et l'esprit des nations et sur les principaux faits d'histoire depuis Charlemagne jusqu'à Louis XIII*, ed. R. Pomeau, 2 vols. (Paris, 1963).

Wagle, N. K., 'The history and social organization of the Gauda Sāraswata Brāhmanas of the west coast of India', *Journal of Indian History* 48 (1970), 7–25 and 295–333.

Walker, K., *Women Writers of the English Renaissance* (New York, 1996).

Waquet, F., 'L'espace de la république des lettres', in H. Bots and F. Waquet (eds.), *Commercium litterarium, 1600–1750* (Amsterdam, 1994), pp. 175–89.

Warburg, A., *The Renewal of Pagan Antiquity* (Los Angeles, 1999).

Weber, M., *General Economic History* (New Brunswick and London, 1981; 1st German edition, 1923).

Weisz, L., *Der Zürcher Nachrichtenverkehr vor 1780* (Zurich, 1954).

Wellisch, H., 'Conrad Gessner: a bio-bibliography', *Journal of the Society for the Bibliography of Natural History* 7 (1975), 151–247.

Wenzel, H., 'Luthers Briefe im Medienwechsel von der Manuskriptkultur zum Buchdruck', in T. A. Brady (ed.), *Die deutsche Reformation zwischen Spätmittelalter und Früher Neuzeit* (Munich, 2001), pp. 203–29.

Werner, Th. G., 'Das kaufmännische Nachrichtenwesen im späten Mittelalter und in der Frühen Neuzeit und sein Einfluß auf die Entstehung der handschriftlichen Zeitung', *Scripta Mercatorae* 2 (1975), 3–51.

Whitaker, L., 'L'accoglienza della collezione Gonzaga in Inghilterra', in R. Morselli (ed.), *Gonzaga. La Celeste Galeria. L'esercizio del collezionismo*, exhibition catalogue (Milan, 2002), vol. 2, pp. 233–49.

White, C., 'Rubens and Antiquity', in P. C. Sutton (ed.), *The Age of Rubens*, exhibition catalogue, Museum of Fine Arts, Boston (Ghent, 1993), pp. 146–57.

Wicki, J., 'Die Chiffre in der Ordenskorrespondenz der Gesellschaft Jesu von Ignatius bis General Oliva (c.1554–1676)', *Archivum Historicum Societatis Jesu* 32 (1963), 133–78.

Wilke, J., *Grundzüge der Medien- und Kommunikationsgeschichte: von den Anfängen bis ins 20. Jahrhundert* (Cologne, 2000).

Wilson, K. M. and Warnke, F. J. (eds.), *Women Writers of the Seventeenth Century* (Athens, OH, and London, 1989).

Windisch Éva, V. (ed.), *Bethlen Miklós Önéletírása* [The autobiography of Miklós Bethlen] (Budapest, 1980).

Woodall, J., 'Patronage and portrayal: Antoine Perrenot de Granvelle's relationship with Antonis Mor', in K. de Jonge and G. Janssens (eds.), *Les Granvelle et les anciens Pays-Bas: Liber doctori Mauricio Van Durme dedicatus* (Louvain, 2000), pp. 245–77.

Xavier, F., *Epistolae S. Francisci Xaverii aliaque eius scripta (1535–1552)*, ed. G. Schurhammer and J. Wicki, 2 vols. (Rome, 1944–5).

Yates, F. A., *John Florio: The Life of an Italian in Shakespeare's England* (Cambridge, 1934).

Yogev, G., *Diamonds and Coral: Anglo-Dutch Jews and Eighteenth-Century Trade* (Leicester, 1978).

Zemanek, A., 'Renaissance botany and modern science', in Z. Mirek and A. Zemanek (eds.), *Studies in Renaissance Botany*, Polish Botanical Studies, Guidebook Series 20 (Cracow, 1998), pp. 9–47.

Zimmermann, H., 'Zur Ikonographie des Hauses Habsburg. II. Angebliche und wirkliche Bildnisse des Don Carlos', *Jahrbuch der Kunsthistorischen Sammlungen des Allerhöchsten Kaiserhauses* 28 (1909–10), 153–70.

Index